D1526995

WORKERS, STRIKES, AND POGROMS

WORKERS, STRIKES, AND POGROMS

THE DONBASS–DNEPR BEND IN LATE IMPERIAL RUSSIA, 1870–1905

Charters Wynn

PRINCETON UNIVERSITY PRESS PRINCETON, NEW JERSEY

Published by Princeton University Press, 41 William Street,
Princeton, New Jersey 08540
In the United Kingdom: Princeton University Press, Oxford

Library of Congress Cataloging-in-Publication Data

Wynn, Charters, 1953–
Workers, strikes, and pogroms : the Donbass-Dnepr Bend
in late imperial Russia, 1870–1905 / Charters Wynn.
p. cm.
Includes bibliographical references and index.
ISBN 0-691-03152-5
1. Labor movements—Donets Basin (Ukraine and R.S.F.S.R.)—History.
2. Working class—Donets Basin (Ukraine and R.S.F.S.R.)—History.
3. Radicalism—Donets Basin (Ukraine and R.S.F.S.R.)—History.
4. Donets Basin (Ukraine and R.S.F.S.R.)—Industries—History.
5. Donets Basin (Ukraine and R.S.F.S.R.)—Ethnic relations.
6. Soviet Union—History—Revolution of 1905.
I. Title.
HD8529.D66W96 1992
322′.2′0947716—dc20 91-30496

This book has been composed in Linotron Galliard

Princeton University Press books are printed
on acid-free paper, and meet the guidelines
for permanence and durability of the Committee
on Production Guidelines for Book Longevity
of the Council on Library Resources

Printed in the United States of America

10 9 8 7 6 5 4 3 2 1

To Joan

Contents

Illustrations

Maps:

Following page 130:

Tables

Acknowledgments

I WANT to express my gratitude to all those who made this book possible, indirectly or directly, beginning with my parents and friends, colleagues and teachers—especially Terence Emmons, my dissertation adviser at Stanford. Reginald Zelnik helpfully commented on my first formulation of this topic. More recently, the manuscript benefited from a close reading by Gerald Surh, who offered useful suggestions and criticisms. My thanks, too, to Princeton University Press's readers and editors for their valuable advice and corrections. My brother, Christopher Wynn, generously somehow found the time to make the maps while meeting the demands of the commercial art world.

It is also a pleasure to record my indebtedness to the International Research and Exchanges Board for giving me the opportunity to spend a year in Soviet archives and libraries. This study would not have been possible without that support and without the cooperation of the archivists and librarians of the Central State Archive of the October Revolution in Moscow, the Central State Historical Archives in Leningrad and Kiev, the Lenin Library in Moscow, and the library of the Academy of Sciences in Leningrad. Back home, the rich collection of the library of the Hoover Institution was also especially valuable. I am indebted to the librarians there, as well as to those at the Stanford University Library, the New York Public Library, and the Bund Archive of the Jewish Labor Movement. This work also benefited from the libraries and interlibrary-loan staffs of Lafayette College, the University of Houston at Clear Lake, Rice University, and the University of Texas at Austin.

Above all I want to thank my wife and colleague, Joan Neuberger, to whom this book is dedicated, for helping me through moments of discouragement and for taking time away from her own work to offer truly innumerable stylistic and substantive suggestions on successive drafts of this work, from the dissertation to the final manuscript. Whatever virtues this book has owe much to her.

Abbreviations

The following abbreviations have been used in the footnotes for archival citations:

TsGAOR	Tsentral'nyi gosudarstvennyi arkhiv Oktiabr'skoi revoliutsii (Central State Archive of the October Revolution)
TsGIA	Tsentral'nyi gosudarstvennyi istoricheskii arkhiv (Central State Historical Archive)
TsGIA USSR	Tsentral'nyi gosudarstvennyi istoricheskii arkhiv Ukrainskoi SSR (Central State Historical Archive of the Ukrainian SSR)

f.	fond (collection or category)
op.	opis' (inventory or list)
d.	delo (dossier or file)
ch.	chast' (part)
DP OO	Departament politsii, Osobyi otdel (Department of Police, Special Section)
M. Iu.	Ministerstvo iustitsii (Ministry of Justice)

References to *listy* use *p.* and *pp.* instead of *l.* and *ll.*, and *vol.* is used for the Russian *tom.*

WORKERS, STRIKES, AND POGROMS

Introduction

NOWHERE in late imperial Russia did the working class grow more dramatically than in the Donbass–Dnepr Bend industrial region. Because local Ukrainians proved reluctant to enter the labor force, what began as a trickle in the 1870s became a flood in the 1890s as tens of thousands of peasant migrants from the villages of European Russia, along with thousands of Jews from the towns of the northwestern Pale of Settlement, annually poured into this booming corner of the Russian empire. Seeking the relatively high wages offered in the Donbass–Dnepr Bend, they came south to work in the mines, steel mills, and artisanal workshops just opening there. They entered a rough world. The industrial boomtowns offered few amenities and quickly developed a well-deserved reputation as bleak and violent frontier towns. The predominantly young, male population was renowned for drinking and fighting.

Workers in the Donbass–Dnepr Bend also became known for their exceptionally militant and violent labor movement. To understand how these workers collectively expressed their discontent is the chief concern of this study. It is my hope that an analysis of the labor movement in what was fast becoming Russia's industrial heartland will contribute to a more realistic conception of the dynamics of Russian labor unrest.

This history of the Donbass–Dnepr Bend working class and labor movement addresses fundamental historiographic questions about Russian workers' "consciousness" and the role of workers in the 1905 Revolution. It examines whether the mass of workers shared the aspirations of the radicals intent on organizing them, and whether the revolutionary movement could overcome the tensions within the working class that were rooted in differences in workers' regional origins and, more important, in ethnic differences between industrial workers and artisans. It approaches from a new perspective the problem Laura Engelstein raised in her study of the 1905 Revolution in Moscow: "The working class was not a passive element in the revolutionary upheaval. It is clear that educated political leaders were not free to manipulate the masses in whatever direction they desired. It is difficult, however, to determine the degree to which socialist ideology corresponded to the workers' actual motives and desires."[1] As in Moscow, revolutionary leaders in the Donbass–Dnepr Bend faced serious problems trying to channel working-class discontent. But in the Donbass–Dnepr

[1] Laura Engelstein, *Moscow, 1905: Working-Class Organization and Political Conflict* (Stanford, 1982), p. 2.

Bend, at least, it was not just workers' commitment to socialist or any other political ideology, but workers' class consciousness—their sense of solidarity with other workers—that would be at issue.

Labor historians commonly speak of Russian workers' "mixed consciousness." To a far greater extent than their Western European counterparts during the comparable stage of industrialization, Russian workers did not sever their peasant ties. Because of their failure to conform to conventional Marxist notions of proletarianization, their consciousness is thought to have retained both peasant and proletarian characteristics.[2] In the Donbass–Dnepr Bend, in addition to the worker-peasant mixed consciousness, to which historians have devoted considerable attention, worker participation in both revolutionary and reactionary mass actions reveals that another sort of mixed consciousness existed in the Russian working class—one that historians have overlooked.

Workers in the Donbass–Dnepr Bend proved to be among the most militant in Russia. During the 1905 Revolution, the "dress rehearsal" for 1917, Russian workers were instrumental in forcing Tsar Nicholas II to grant the people a constitution, civil rights, and a parliament, bringing to an end almost three hundred years of unlimited autocratic rule. During 1905, Donbass–Dnepr Bend workers repeatedly responded en masse to revolutionary appeals to strike and demonstrate, which often led to bloody confrontations with soldiers and Cossacks. In these mass actions, workers displayed a unity cutting across the ethnic and other lines that ordinarily divided workers in the Donbass–Dnepr Bend. At the same time, however, industrial workers in this region also participated en masse in some of the most devastating pogroms in prerevolutionary Russia. In many cases, workers who participated in radical strike activity with the support and praise of radical party *intelligenty* also engaged in the brutal, destructive violence of pogroms. Radical activists' attempts to constrain workers' ethnic violence repeatedly proved futile. Thus, although a politically active, radical working-class movement had developed in the Donbass–Dnepr Bend by 1905, the upsurge in the revolutionary movement did not displace reactionary elements in the working class. Just as movement from the village to the Donbass–Dnepr Bend was not a one-way trip—workers continually moved back and forth between village and factory or mine—the radicalization of workers in the late nineteenth and early twentieth centuries was not a linear process.

With the Bolshevik Revolution of 1917 in view, labor historians have been preoccupied with explaining the radicalization of the Russian labor

[2] On the peasant character of the Russian working class, see Robert Eugene Johnson, *Peasant and Proletarian: The Working Class of Moscow in the Late Nineteenth Century* (New Brunswick, N.J., 1979); and Theodore Von Laue, "Russian Labor between Field and Factory," *California Slavic Studies* 3 (1964): 33–66.

movement. When examining labor unrest, Russian labor historiography in both the Soviet Union and the West has concentrated on the role of the labor elite and their intelligentsia organizers to explain the labor movement's emergence and progress from what are viewed as primitive forms of protest—isolated, peasantlike outbursts of violence—to more coordinated, political mass actions. Three pathbreaking studies by Richard Pipes, Allan Wildman, and Reginald Zelnik have explored the radicalization and complex mentality of Russian workers at the turn of the twentieth century, primarily through the experiences of the worker-*intelligent* and through the relations between such extraordinary workers and the intelligentsia revolutionary leadership.[3] During the boom in labor historiography in the last decade or so, there has been a growing recognition, building upon work by Leopold Haimson, of the need to explore the subgroups that constituted the Russian working class and to refute Soviet attempts to explain workers' militance as the result of a linear proletarianization and maturing of the working class.[4] Even so, Western labor historians continue to concentrate primarily on the most politically "conscious" (*soznatel'nye*) and active stratum of the working class.

There is no denying the importance of such workers. A core of workers

[3] Richard Pipes, *Social Democracy and the St. Petersburg Labor Movement, 1885–1897* (Cambridge, Mass., 1963); Allan K. Wildman, *The Making of a Workers' Revolution: Russian Social Democracy, 1891–1903* (Chicago, 1967); Reginald E. Zelnik, "Russian Bebels: An Introduction to the Memoirs of Semen Kanatchikov and Matvei Fisher," parts 1, 2, *Russian Review* 35, nos. 3, 4 (1976): 249–289, 417–447.

[4] Leopold Haimson, "The Problem of Social Stability in Urban Russia, 1905–1917," parts 1, 2 *Slavic Review* 23, no. 4 (1964): 619–642; 24, no. 1 (1965): 1–22. Although the authors of recent valuable studies on the 1905 and 1917 revolutions "from below" have concentrated on the skilled workers in the metal and machine trades and textile industry, they also examine issues connected to the stratification of the labor force. See Gerald Dennis Surh, *1905 in St. Petersburg: Labor, Society, and Revolution* (Stanford, 1989); Engelstein, *Moscow, 1905*; Diane Koenker, *Moscow Workers and the 1917 Revolution* (Princeton, 1981); David Mandel, *The Petrograd Workers and the Fall of the Old Regime* (London, 1983) and *The Petrograd Workers and the Soviet Seizure of Power* (London, 1984); and S. A. Smith, *Red Petrograd: Revolution in the Factories, 1917–1918* (Cambridge, England, 1983). See also Heather Hogan, "Industrial Rationalization and the Roots of Labor Militance in the St. Petersburg Metalworking Industry, 1901–1914," *Russian Review* 42, no. 2 (1983): 163–190; and Tim McDaniel, *Autocracy, Capitalism, and Revolution in Russia* (Berkeley, 1988). In *Roots of Rebellion: Workers' Politics and Organizations in St. Petersburg and Moscow, 1900–1914* (Berkeley, 1983), Victoria Bonnell shows that along with the more educated, skilled workers in metal industries, the skilled artisans in small workshops were among the most active and radical workers in St. Petersburg and Moscow. Henry Reichman highlighted the radicalizing role of the skilled metalworkers in the railroad workshops in his study *Railwaymen and Revolution: Russia, 1905* (Berkeley, 1987). On railroad workers, see also William G. Rosenberg, "The Democratization of Russia's Railroads in 1917," *American Historical Review* 86, no. 5 (1981): 983–1008. On women workers, see Rose L. Glickman, *Russian Factory Women: Workplace and Society, 1880–1914* (Berkeley, 1984).

from among the skilled elite in Donbass–Dnepr Bend steel mills and railroad and artisanal workshops played a leading role in the radicalization of the labor movement in the Donbass–Dnepr Bend, just as they did in the capitals. Many Donbass–Dnepr Bend workers selflessly sacrificed much in the struggle to improve working-class conditions and overthrow the autocracy. Yet the focus on the labor elite that was active in radical party politics and willing to risk imprisonment to bring about social and economic change has led historians to neglect the large number of workers who did not live up to the heroic image that has gained prominence in the literature on Russian labor.

As was generally the case throughout industrial Russia, in the Donbass–Dnepr Bend's giant steel mills, which supplied a large percentage of the region's radical working-class activists, politically "conscious" workers were surrounded by a sea of what skilled workers and radical organizers referred to as "benighted" (*temnye*) or "backward" (*otstalye*) workers. The miners in the region were almost uniformly so described. Most skilled workers felt condescension toward this mass of their fellow workers, especially toward those illiterates fresh from the countryside. In their daily lives, most skilled workers joined their employers and foremen in continually subjecting unskilled workers to ridicule. Even those skilled workers who espoused socialist ideas and recognized that radical change was impossible without class solidarity shared these attitudes, though less openly. It was not just the day laborers doing the most menial, manual jobs whom skilled workers viewed with scorn; they lumped the semiskilled together with the mass of the unskilled. Skilled workers quite accurately did not locate semiskilled workers halfway between the most and least skilled workers. A vast gulf separated those workers whose skills had been acquired in a few weeks or months from those who had undergone years of apprenticeship. For their part, unskilled workers both envied the privileges and prestige skilled workers enjoyed and resented their contempt.

Concentration on the tiny percentage of workers active in revolutionary politics and working-class organizations has meant that our understanding of the Russian revolutionary process still lacks an appreciation of the role played by the mass of unskilled laborers and semiskilled workers in that process. Everyone who has studied the Russian working class agrees that individuals from the mass of workers rarely entered the ranks of the revolutionary parties or represented their enterprise or industry in the soviets that emerged in October 1905. Yet while unskilled workers are less important as individual leaders, and less accessible to the historian, there is no denying their importance to the revolutionary movement. Their support in general strikes is what gave the revolutionary movement its power during 1905.

It is not enough, however, to study the economic, social, and political forces that could unite the working class in collective action. Shared workplace pressures, a torrent of revolutionary propaganda, and the sense of power that mass actions produced could bridge the differences separating workers. But at the same time, other concerns—as well as the frustrations mass actions produced—could blow these fragile bridges asunder. Workers' intolerance and their proclivity for violence coexisted with hopes for economic improvement and social leveling. This should not be surprising. Not unlike their class enemies, Donbass–Dnepr Bend workers exhibited a mix of class and ethnic or regional identities.[5] The rapid industrialization of the Donbass–Dnepr Bend brought together traditionally antagonistic groups, creating intraclass stresses that ran along regional and ethnic lines. These regional differences within the industrial labor force in the Donbass–Dnepr Bend—and, more important, ethnic differences between industrial workers and artisans—proved to be a source of violent intraclass conflict.

By examining the role of young, unskilled workers in pogroms, this study presents a long-needed portrait of the "low consciousness" and ethnic rivalries that existed within the Russian working class alongside support for revolutionary mass actions.[6] During the 1905 Revolution, in the Donbass–Dnepr Bend, any semblances of class consciousness or solidarity repeatedly disappeared in the face of regional and ethnic animosities. Aggravated by its frustration with the outcome of mass actions, the predominantly Great Russian and Ukrainian industrial work force again and again engaged in reactionary as well as radical mass actions. As my research into Donbass–Dnepr Bend working-class conditions and radicalism progressed, it became increasingly clear that worker anti-Semitism played a major role in the evolution of the labor movement in the Donbass–Dnepr Bend and that a thorough examination of this issue is crucial to a proper understanding of the Russian labor movement and the 1905 Revolution.

[5] It is interesting to note that in the recently reemergent labor movement in the Soviet Union, workers have expressed a strong sense of industry identity. During the general strike in the Donets Basin in the summer of 1989, a reporter for the *New York Times* stated that "a major anxiety for the Kremlin during the coal strike was the possibility that with living conditions such a source of general dissatisfaction, the miners' strike might easily spread to related industries . . . [but] amid the general enthusiasm for change, the mill workers strongly indicated that they do not equate themselves with the coal miners, contrary perhaps, to some outsiders' notion of worker solidarity" (*New York Times*, July 27, 1989, p. 6).

[6] A start in this direction was made by Daniel R. Brower in "Labor Violence in Russia in the Late Nineteenth Century," *Slavic Review* 41, no. 3 (1982): 417–453. See also William G. Rosenberg and Diane P. Koenker, "The Limits of Formal Protest: Worker Activism and Social Polarization in Petrograd and Moscow, March to October, 1917," *American Historical Review* 92, no. 2 (1987): 296–326; Haimson, "Social Stability"; and Joan Neuberger, "Crime and Culture: Hooliganism in St. Petersburg, 1900–1914" (Ph.D. diss., Stanford University, 1985), chap. 2.

What might be called the ruffian element in the Russian labor movement—the mass of especially violent, less ideologically oriented workers—was willing to go to the streets in organized mass actions against its economic enemies. These workers were also willing to unleash humanity's lowest passions in ferocious violence against those they considered their ethnic enemies, primarily Jews.[7] In doing so, they showed a distinct lack of respect for the authority of the revolutionary parties trying to lead the working-class movement.

The emphasis here on the link that existed between revolutionary and reactionary forms of mass action is not intended to suggest a return to the mob theories of violence in revolution. Such interpretations failed to subject the working class to close study and instead focused on political elites and their manipulation of the supposedly mindless crowd. This book follows the lead of studies of the crowd in early industrial Europe or America in recognizing that a rioting mass of workers, even when drunk and in a fit of passion, cannot be dismissed as an irrational mob blinded by drink and rage. Such workers chose to lash out in violence in a selective manner and as a means for pursuing particular ends, however abhorrent or wrongheaded we may think they were. The social histories of Russian labor published beginning in the 1960s have provided an important corrective to mob theories by demonstrating the workers' sense of separateness and oppression. This study will show the way in which those qualities were turned to violence and destruction in the service of revolutionary *and* reactionary ends.[8]

[7] The traditional historical treatment of pogroms shared the view of many contemporaries that the tsarist government conspired with right-wing political groups to organize pogroms to divert popular discontent away from the government. See, for example, Simon Dubnov, *The History of the Jews in Russia and Poland*, trans. I. Friedlaender (Philadelphia, 1916–1920), vol. 4. Recently, scholars have reexamined pogroms and concluded that while the authorities' anti-Semitic policies indirectly encouraged pogroms, there is no evidence to substantiate the theory of a government plot (Shlomo Lambroza, "The Pogrom Movement in Tsarist Russia, 1903–1906" [Ph.D. diss., Rutgers University, 1981]; Hans Rogger, *Jewish Policies and Right-Wing Politics in Imperial Russia* [Berkeley, 1986]; I. Michael Aronson, "Geographical and Socioeconomic Factors in the 1881 Anti-Jewish Pogroms in Russia," *Russian Review* 39, no. 1 [1980]: 18–31). The conspiracy theory was fueled by the willingness of police and troops to stand aside during pogroms, or by the fact that individuals from their ranks sometimes did join the pogromists. But even though the authorities often did little to stop pogroms, government officials were far too concerned with suppressing political discontent to run the risks of unleashing any form of mass unrest. The government opposed all mass violence, including pogroms. For an examination of the workers' role in the October 1905 pogrom in Odessa, see Robert Weinberg, "Workers, Pogroms, and the 1905 Revolution in Odessa," *Russian Review* 46, no. 1 (1987).

[8] As will become clear, the political consciousness of the mass of workers was neither revolutionary nor reactionary in any well-developed sense. But the significance of that distinction is dubious, since workers repeatedly engaged in revolutionary and reactionary mass actions. The emphasis on reactionary working-class actions in this study is not meant to deemphasize

The regional focus of this study helps redress another critical imbalance in Russian labor historiography. Studies of the Russian labor and revolutionary movements have been overwhelmingly oriented toward the two capitals, St. Petersburg and Moscow.[9] We have had few non-Soviet regional labor histories.[10] The concentration on the capitals is understandable, given the centralization of the Russian empire and the superiority of sources for the capitals; but regional studies are long overdue. The ethnic diversity of the empire and the uneven development of Russia's labor force and revolutionary movement demand regional studies so that historical syntheses can accurately portray regional differences.

The Donbass–Dnepr Bend is an excellent place to examine the Russian labor movement outside the capitals. Not only were industrial development and urbanization extremely rapid, intensifying problems found in other regions, but the Donbass–Dnepr Bend region is located almost entirely within the Pale of Settlement, the part of the Russian empire to which Jews were legally confined. Because its workers and the environment in which they lived and worked were ethnically and regionally mixed, the Donbass–Dnepr Bend provides insight into the crucial importance of ethnic tensions within the working class. It seems likely that the sort of mixed consciousness displayed by the mass of workers in the Donbass–Dnepr Bend, and the problems it posed for revolutionary leaders, existed elsewhere in the empire (if usually in more muted forms) but has been overlooked. In addition, the common assumption that the provincial industrial centers merely followed the lead of the capitals in the 1905 Revolution, reproducing on a smaller and less militant scale events in St. Petersburg and Moscow, needs to be revised. This study demonstrates that one of the most combative workers' movements in Russia was concentrated in the

---

radical actions; that it seems to is a reflection of the size of the historiographic gap this study is trying to fill.

[9] In addition to the works cited above, see Reginald E. Zelnik, *Labor and Society in Tsarist Russia: The Factory Workers of St. Petersburg, 1855–1870* (Stanford, 1971).

[10] Theodore H. Friedgut's *Iuzovka and Revolution*, vol. 1, *Life and Work in Russia's Donbass, 1869–1924* (Princeton, 1989) was published as I was completing the final draft of this book, a revision of my 1987 Stanford University Ph.D. dissertation, "Russian Labor in Revolution and Reaction: The Donbass Working Class, 1870–1905." See also Susan Purves McCaffray, "The New Work and the Old Regime: Workers, Managers, and the State in the Coal and Steel Industry of Ekaterinoslav Province, 1905–1914" (Ph.D. diss., Duke University, 1983); Robert Weinberg, "Worker Organizations and Politics in the Revolution of 1905 in Odessa" (Ph.D. diss., University of California, Berkeley, 1985) and "Social Democracy and Workers in Odessa: Ethnic and Political Considerations," *Carl Beck Papers in Russian and East European Studies*, no. 504 (1986); and selections in Michael F. Hamm, ed., *The City in Late Imperial Russia* (Bloomington, Ind., 1986). The regional studies of 1917 include Donald J. Raleigh, *Revolution on the Volga: 1917 in Saratov* (Ithaca, N.Y., 1986); and Ronald Grigor Suny, *The Baku Commune, 1917–1918: Class and Nationality in the Russian Revolution* (Princeton, 1972).

Donbass–Dnepr Bend and was the product of a combination of conditions—some nationwide, some unique to the region.

The major primary sources for this study of the Donbass–Dnepr Bend working class and the motivations of the largely anonymous individuals who participated in the mass movement were government documents, the revolutionary press and local legal press, reports of the local industrialists' association, health investigations, and memoirs of radical activists. Government documents that proved useful include a wide variety of official reports, such as police investigations of labor unrest and of revolutionary activity, communiqués sent by various local authorities to the central government describing working-class conditions and events, reports of the factory inspectorate, and lengthy indictments from the trials of those arrested in the major labor disturbances, as well as the intercepted personal letters preserved in the police archives.[11] Also especially useful were correspondent reports written by members of the numerous radical parties in the Donbass–Dnepr Bend that were published in these parties' national and regional organs. While many of these reports present exaggerated or contradictory accounts, they nonetheless provide a wealth of detail. Most important, the correspondents' occasional frankness about their views of Donbass–Dnepr Bend workers and their hopes and fears concerning the region's revolutionary movement were invaluable. Still another perspective was provided by the reports from the annual congresses of the Association of Southern Coal and Steel Producers and by reports in the Association's newspaper, which present the views of management. Local legal newspapers, particularly *Pridneprovskii krai* (*The Dnepr Territory*) and *Vestnik Iuga* (*The Southern Herald*), supplemented and balanced the government, party, and industry accounts of the working-class and mass actions by providing accounts somewhat less partisan than those in the other sources. A large number of memoirs by Social Democratic veterans of the revolutionary movements in the Donbass–Dnepr Bend were published during the early 1920s and are relatively free of the ideological straitjacket that makes later memoirs of little value. These early memoirs often have an immediacy lacking in the other sources. In addition to these primary sources, the most useful secondary sources also come from the early 1920s, in the form of early histories of the Donbass–Dnepr Bend labor movement. Many of

[11] While the tsarist government's determination to uproot seditious activities—a determination so fully documented in the archives—has obvious advantages for the historian, official reports must be read with a close eye for police self-interest and possible malfeasance, as revelations concerning Ekaterinoslav's police chief, Rittmeister Krementskii, dramatically illustrate. Krementskii had greatly impressed his superiors in the capital with his vigilance and efficiency by uncovering three or four underground presses in Ekaterinoslav annually. Krementskii's reputation and rise up the career ladder, as well as the perception of the strength of the revolutionary movement, suffered a sudden reversal, however, when it was learned that Krementskii had set up the presses himself (Abraham Ascher, *The Revolution of 1905: Russia in Disarray* [Stanford, 1988], pp. 13–14).

these histories were, significantly, written by former party activists. Later Soviet studies of the Donbass–Dnepr Bend labor movement completely ignore the movement's reactionary side.

This study is divided into two parts. The first three chapters provide the background necessary to understand the discontent of the newly created labor force. The history of the Donbass–Dnepr Bend region's economic development is treated in chapter 1, the composition of the working class in chapter 2, and workers' daily life in chapter 3. Knowledge of the working-class milieu, including sources of conflict as well as sources of solidarity, is essential for understanding the mentality and actions of Donbass–Dnepr Bend workers. How workers acted on ordinary days provides insight into why workers acted as they did on days of mass ferment. The remaining five chapters examine the history of the Donbass–Dnepr Bend labor and revolutionary movements from the 1870s to December 1905. Chapter 4 is devoted to the late nineteenth century and examines the first mass actions to appear in the region and the first examples of Donbass–Dnepr Bend workers' mixed consciousness. Revolutionary agitation was an important factor in explaining workers' roles in revolution and reaction and is examined in chapter 5. Chapters 6 and 7 treat the revolutionary upsurge from 1903 through October 1905. Chapter 6 discusses radical working-class activity and establishes the extraordinary militance of the region's workers. Chapter 7 looks at reactionary and pogromist mass actions during the same period and demonstrates the remarkable complexity of the labor movement. Revolution and reaction came together again in the aftermath of October 1905, leading up to and significantly shaping the December insurrection examined in Chapter 8.

One final introductory note is necessary. I chose to call the region this study focuses on the *Donbass–Dnepr Bend*, even though convention and a desire for conciseness have permitted historians and contemporaries to use *Donbass* as a substitute for the more accurate, but I hope not impossibly cumbersome, term I use here. The Donbass, short for the Donets Basin, includes only the lower valley of the Donets River, where the region's coalfield is located. The Donbass–Dnepr Bend encompasses the entire region that participated in the industrial boom that transformed the iron- and coal-mining areas of the eastern Ukraine into an economic entity that transcended administrative boundaries. The Donbass–Dnepr Bend labor movement—which involved the coal miners of the Donets Basin, the iron-ore miners of the Krivoi Rog, and the steelworkers, railroad workers, and artisans of the large and small steel towns scattered along the region's railroad lines and rivers—extended beyond Ekaterinoslav province into part of the Don Cossack Territory.

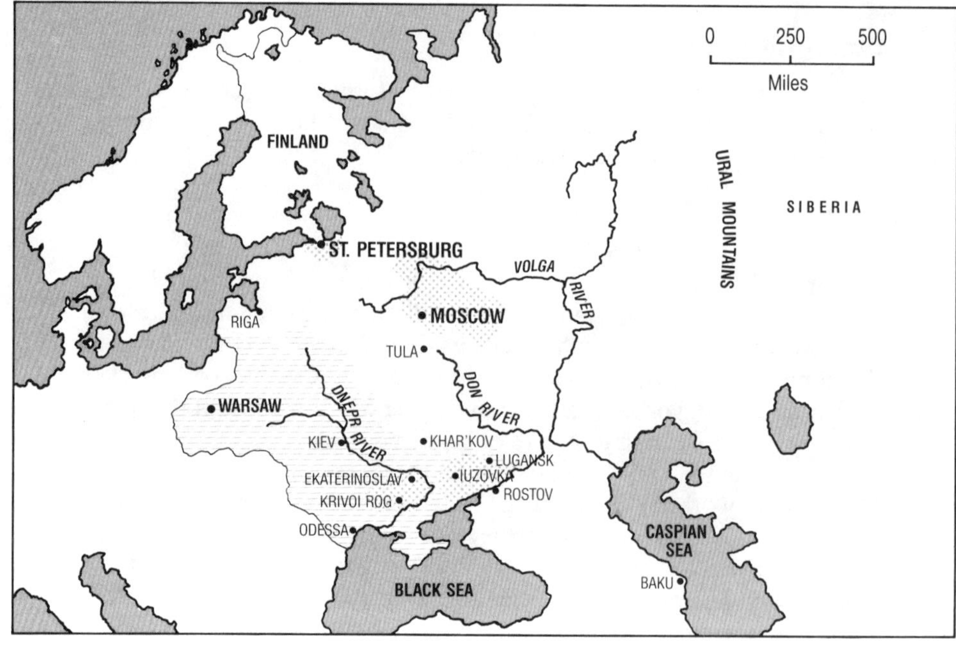

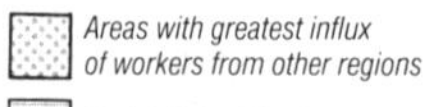

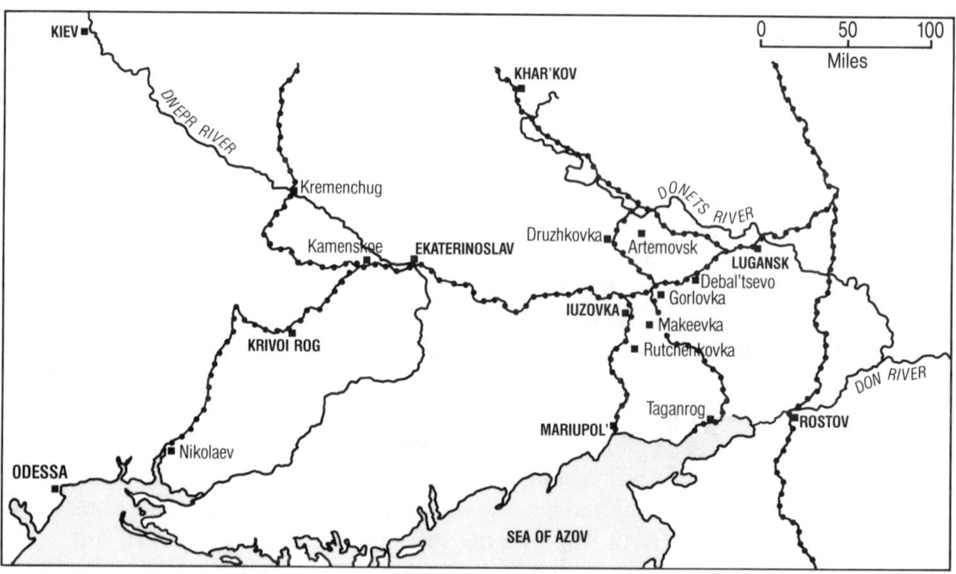

The Donbass–Dnepr Bend Industrial Region

Part One

THE WORKING-CLASS MILIEU

1

The Industrial Boom: 1870–1900

> I worked at a factory owned by Germans, at coal pits owned by a Frenchman, and at a chemical plant owned by Belgians. There [in the Donbass–Dnepr Bend] I discovered something about capitalists. They are all alike, whatever their nationality. All they wanted from me was the most work for the least money. . . . So I became a Communist.
> (*Nikita Khrushchev*)

THE RAPID industrialization of the Donbass–Dnepr Bend occurred in what had been an economically undeveloped region, even by Russian standards. Before the last decades of the nineteenth century, the future home of Russia's most important mining and metallurgical region was of such little consequence economically that the sparsely populated agrarian area was still known by the epithet "*dikoe pole*," or "wild field." By the turn of the century, the Donbass–Dnepr Bend had one of the greatest regional concentrations of workers and large enterprises in all of Russia.[1]

The Donbass–Dnepr Bend was neither ideally suited for nor prepared to handle an economic boom in the late nineteenth century. Until relatively late in Russian history, when Catherine the Great colonized the region in the late eighteenth century, its vulnerability to invaders had kept it an untamed frontier. The Donbass–Dnepr Bend is located on the seemingly endless southern steppe, and unlike the steppe to its north, it lacked even the protection offered by forests.[2] Easily penetrable from all directions and the headquarters of the Cossacks, the Donbass–Dnepr Bend steppe had long attracted only fugitive serfs fleeing the worsening plight of the Russian peasantry. It is not surprising, then, that the abundant raw materials

[1] On the eve of the 1905 Revolution, the southern industrial region possessed the third-largest number of workers in Russia, behind only the Moscow and St. Petersburg regions. The Donbass–Dnepr Bend ranked fourth if the Russian empire's Polish provinces are included.

[2] The only topographic feature of any prominence in the region is the Donets ridge, which proved to be of great economic significance as a coal repository.

with which the Donbass–Dnepr Bend was blessed were left untouched when Russia first attempted to industrialize.

Russia's first metallurgical boom occurred long before the boom in the Donbass–Dnepr Bend. Russia developed into the world's largest producer and exporter of iron in the late eighteenth century. It was the employment of cheap serf labor in the Urals, not advanced technology, that allowed Russia to attain and hold this position of international supremacy in metallurgy until the beginning of the nineteenth century. But the rapidly widening technological gap between Russia and the West, as well as the absence of coal in the Ural Mountains, took its toll. As John McKay summarized Russia's early industrial development: "A hearty newcomer under Peter and a lusty youngster under Catherine, eighteenth-century Russian metallurgy . . . failed to come of age and adopt the methods of the industrial revolution."[3] The Russian iron manufactories in the Urals failed to introduce the technological breakthroughs that revolutionized the industry in Western Europe and the United States: coke smelting, puddling and rolling, the hot blast, and later the converter and the open-hearth furnace. From its position as world leader, the Russian iron industry fell so precipitously that in the mid-nineteenth century it accounted for only 4 percent of world production.[4] For an industrial renaissance to occur in Russia, resources outside the Urals, both natural and entrepreneurial, needed to be uncovered and exploited.

It was military humiliation in the Crimean War (1853–56) that finally pushed the tsarist state to start implementing policies designed to promote rapid industrial development. Russia had been unable to sustain a war with the more industrialized European powers; the defeat exposed the extent to which military success was coming to depend on industrial development. Many of the most powerful figures in this still premodern, autocratic state grudgingly realized that unless Russia took the politically risky steps necessary to facilitate the country's industrialization, the Russian empire's international position would continue to deteriorate. A succession of finance ministers adopted measures that in combination represented an unprecedented government attempt to stimulate industrialization. Some of these measures—emancipation of the serfs, fiscal reforms and protectionist tariffs, large-scale railroad construction, and the encouragement of foreign investment—were new to Russia, while other aspects of the government's financial policy, notably increased taxation of the peasantry, were all too familiar. In the short term, the government effort appeared to be a great

[3] John P. McKay, *Pioneers for Profit: Foreign Entrepreneurship and Russian Industrialization, 1885–1913* (Chicago, 1970), pp. 112–113.

[4] Clive Trebilcock, *The Industrialization of the Continental Powers, 1780–1914* (London, 1981), p. 207.

success.[5] As the Donbass–Dnepr Bend enjoyed "an influx of capital and initiative beyond anything experienced in Russia since the time of Peter the Great," the region grew quickly and emerged as an internationally prominent industrial heartland.[6]

Over a dozen new iron and steel plants, which were for the most part as technologically sophisticated as any in the world, produced a growth rate with few parallels in the Western world. Donbass–Dnepr Bend industry grew with "American speed" to become the main Russian producer of iron and steel. Output statistics graphically demonstrate how suddenly heavy industry rose and flourished.[7] After providing 0.3 percent of Russia's pig iron in 1867, the Donbass–Dnepr Bend in 1885 produced 2 million puds[8] of pig iron, still only 6.2 percent of the empire's total production. In 1900, just fifteen years later, workers poured 91.8 million puds of metal out of Donbass–Dnepr Bend furnaces, over half (51.3 percent) of the Russian total. Russian output of pig iron increased 178 percent from 1885 to 1900, an increase due largely to the plants in the Donbass–Dnepr Bend; and Russia rose from eighth to fifth place among the largest producers in the world.[9] By 1900, Donbass–Dnepr Bend workers on average were almost six times more productive than workers in the technologically backward factories in the Urals.[10]

[5] In the 1890s, the annual rate of growth for the empire as a whole was 8 percent, impressive by international standards (William L. Blackwell, *The Industrialization of Russia* [New York, 1970], p. 42). Russian industry grew at an annual rate of almost 16 percent between 1893 and 1897 (Teodor Shanin, *Russia as a 'Developing Society'*, vol. 1, *The Roots of Otherness: Russia's Turn of Century* [Houndmills, Basingstoke, Hampshire, 1985], p. 104).

[6] Abraham C. Burstein, "Iron and Steel in Russia, 1861–1913" (Ph.D. diss., New School for Social Research, 1963), p. 157.

[7] These output statistics demonstrating the growth of the Donbass–Dnepr Bend mining and metallurgical industries come from V. V. Morachevskii, "Promysly i zaniatiia naseleniia," in *Rossiia: Polnoe geograficheskoe opisanie nashego otechestva*, ed. V. P. Semenov-Tian-Shanskii (St. Petersburg, 1910), 14:370; Blackwell, *Industrialization of Russia*, p. 78; G. D. Bakulev, *Razvitie ugol'noi promyshlennosti Donetskogo basseina* (Moscow, 1955), p. 651; E. E. Kruze, *Polozhenie rabochego klassa Rossii v 1900–1914 gg.* (Leningrad, 1976), pp. 78–79; and M. Balabanov, "Promyshlennost' Rossii v nachale XX veka," in *Obshchestvennoe dvizhenie v Rossii v nachale XX-go veka*, ed. L. Martov, P. Maslov, and A. Potresov (St. Petersburg, 1909), 1:51.

[8] A pud is a Russian unit of weight equal to 36.11 pounds.

[9] Production in the Donbass–Dnepr Bend was far more concentrated in large plants than production elsewhere in Russia. In 1900, plants with a capacity of over 80,000 tons accounted for 66.5 percent of all the pig iron produced in the Donbass–Dnepr Bend, while in the rest of the empire almost the reverse was true—54.6 percent of the pig iron came from plants with a capacity below 16,000 tons (Konstantyn Kononenko, *Ukraine and Russia: A History of the Economic Relations between Ukraine and Russia, 1654–1917* [Milwaukee, 1958], p. 143). By the end of the century, the five largest Donbass–Dnepr Bend steel factories accounted for almost half of all the pig iron smelted in Russia. Each one of these five steel factories produced more than the combined output of all forty-six of the smelters operating in Russia's central industrial region, which was even more technologically backward than the Urals region (Burstein, "Iron and Steel," pp. 170, 172, 194, 198).

[10] S. I. Potolov, *Rabochie Donbassa v XIX veke* (Moscow-Leningrad, 1963), p. 99.

Mining also achieved a remarkable growth rate during the late nineteenth century. Coal mining began earlier than the metallurgical industry in the Donbass–Dnepr Bend, but it is only in comparison with metallurgy that the coal industry's growth could be considered anything less than meteoric. The mining of the Donets coalfield's rich veins, which began in the late eighteenth century, progressed slowly until the region's late-nineteenth-century takeoff. Table 1 illustrates how rapidly coal mining grew in the Donbass–Dnepr Bend, especially between 1895 and 1900. With coal mines in the Donets Basin extracting 68 percent of the Russian total in 1900, the region's share of national output became even more dominant in coal mining than in metallurgy.

Similarly spectacular growth occurred in the Krivoi Rog iron fields, located in the western part of the Donbass–Dnepr Bend. The Krivoi Rog held Russia's largest and richest iron deposits, although for all practical purposes no iron mining took place there before 1885. Just how little was known of the Krivoi Rog's rich deposits prior to the late nineteenth century is conveyed by a German traveler, who could write in 1841 that "in all of the South of Russia there is not one place where one could find any metal. This huge area of Europe is deprived of metals; not enough iron can be found to make a single nail."[11] By 1900, Krivoi Rog iron-mine production accounted for over 56 percent of the Russian total.

TABLE 1
Coal Production in the Donets Basin, 1870–1900

	Donets Basin (in million puds)	*Russian Total (in million puds)*	*Donets Basin's Percentage of Total*
1870	15.6	42.4	36.8
1875	51.4	104.3	49.3
1880	86.3	200.8	43.0
1885	114.9	260.6	44.1
1890	183.2	367.2	50.0
1895	298.3	555.5	53.7
1900	671.7	986.3	68.1

Source: O. A. Parasun'ko, *Polozhenie i bor'ba rabochego klassa Ukrainy, 1860–90-e gody XIX v.* (Kiev, 1963), p. 60.

[11] Quoted in Kononenko, *Ukraine and Russia*, p. 141. Iron mining in the Krivoi Rog, and by extension the development of the Donbass–Dnepr Bend metallurgical industry, owes much to the perseverance of an eccentric nobleman, Aleksandr Pol'. After rediscovering the existence of iron ore in the Krivoi Rog in 1872, Pol' poured his considerable wealth into years of surveying and fruitless attempts to solicit governmental and private capital to mine this buried treasure. Nearly bankrupt, Pol' hocked his family silverware and with the borrowed money traveled to Paris, where he was welcomed. Pol' became a millionaire in 1880

TABLE 2
Iron Production in the Krivoi Rog, 1885–1900

	Krivoi Rog (in million puds)	*Russian Total (in million puds)*	*Krivoi Rog's Percentage of Total*
1885	118.5	1,067.6	11.1
1890	376.7	1,802.4	20.9
1895	968.3	2,823.0	34.3
1900	3,440.9	6,111.7	56.3

Source: "Krivorozhskii zhelezorudnyi bassein," *Bol'shaia sovetskaia entsiklopediia*, 1937, 35:66.

The economic boom in the Donbass–Dnepr Bend was the greatest success story in Russia's late-nineteenth-century industrialization drive. The government deserves a large part of the credit. Construction of the Ekaterinin railroad line brought together the necessary ingredients for a modern metallurgical industry. Although the roughly two hundred miles separating the coal of the Donets Basin and the iron ore of the Krivoi Rog is not a great distance, the cost of transporting these bulky raw materials by oxcart or horse and wagon on dirt or, often, mud roads had been prohibitive. Construction of the Ekaterinin railroad began in 1879 and was completed in 1886. During the 1890s, railroad construction expanded so rapidly in the Donbass–Dnepr Bend that the region became interconnected by a railroad network denser than anywhere else in the empire.[12]

Providing a cheap transportation link between the region's iron and coal deposits and between the Donbass–Dnepr Bend and other regions of Russia, while crucial, was not the only way government-sponsored railroad construction stimulated industrial investment in the Donbass–Dnepr Bend. Russia's railroad-building boom during the late nineteenth century created an enormous demand for coal, iron, and steel. This demand, coupled with guaranteed government contracts (at generously inflated prices) for the large quantities of rails and for the steel needed to manufacture locomotives and railroad cars—as well as concessions, low-cost state loans, direct subsidies, protectionist tariffs for coal, iron, and steel, and a government campaign to publicize the high profits being made—attracted a flood of foreign investment into the Donbass–Dnepr Bend.[13]

---

following the founding of the French Company of Krivoi Rog Ores (Burstein, "Iron and Steel," pp. 159–160).

[12] The distance covered by railroads in the Donets Basin increased from only 118 kilometers in 1891 to 1,691 in 1893, 2,272 in 1896, and 2,865 in 1898 (Burstein, "Iron and Steel," p. 164; Kononenko, *Ukraine and Russia*, p. 205).

[13] Most of the large foreign-owned steelworks earned only modest profits even during the boom in the second half of the 1890s, although investors in a few firms did indeed strike it

Foreigners played the central role in the Donbass–Dnepr Bend's rapid industrial development; industrial workers employed there were far more likely to work for foreign bosses than not. A few Russian joint-stock companies operated in the Donbass–Dnepr Bend, but French and Belgian corporations built almost all the modern steel mills and the bulk of the large mines in the southern industrial region.[14] Western European capital and technology also helped build the railways.

The foreign contribution to the industrial development of the Donbass–Dnepr Bend began even before the opening of the Ekaterinin railway. A single foreign industrialist, the celebrated Welshman John Hughes, showed the way by building a modern ironworks in the Donbass–Dnepr Bend in the early 1870s. With the backing of financial circles in England and leading governmental figures in St. Petersburg, Hughes put into operation in Iuzovka (Hughes-ovka) the first of the Donbass–Dnepr Bend's large, modern ironworks, and he opened coal mines just outside the city. The factory and mines together employed almost thirteen thousand workers by the late 1890s. The Russian government had encouraged Hughes to invest by granting him free rights to the coal and iron on the rich crown lands there, a thirty-seven-year loan of half a million rubles, and a premium on the pig iron and rails he produced. Even with all this support, the difficulties of manufacturing on the steppe proved enormous. Despite producing more pig iron than any other company in Russia, Hughes's firm, the New Russia Coal, Iron, and Railmaking Company, "almost closed for good" in 1885, according to one contemporary study.[15] The potential profitability of Hughes's venture was realized only after the completion of the Ekaterinin railway and the introduction of additional protectionist measures in the following year. The New Russia Company's profits began to soar, and foreign investment poured into Donbass–Dnepr Bend industry.

Russians and Ukrainians displayed little interest in investing in Donbass–Dnepr Bend industry.[16] Following the opening in 1887 of the sole

---

rich. Between 1895 and 1900, the earnings of some of the mills—namely, the few integrated mills that possessed their own iron ore and coal mines—soared to around 40 percent annually over the cost of production. They distributed annual dividends of over 20 percent on the principal investment (Burstein, "Iron and Steel," pp. 56–61; Peter Gatrell, *The Tsarist Economy, 1850–1917* [New York, 1986], p. 211).

[14] V. V. Modestov, *Rabochee i profsoiuznoe dvizhenie v Donbasse do velikoi oktiabr'skoi sotsialisticheskoi revoliutsii* (Moscow, 1957), p. 6. From 1888 to 1902, foreigners invested 316 million rubles in 112 enterprises in the Donets Basin (I. Berkhin, *Luganskaia bol'shevistskaia organizatsiia v periode pervoi russkoi revoliutsii* [Leningrad, 1947], p. 6).

[15] Paul Chapuy, "Journal de voyage, 1887: Russie, Bassin du Donets," student senior thesis, Ecole supérieure des Mines (Paris, 1887), cited in McKay, *Pioneers for Profit*, p. 96.

[16] To be fair, native entrepreneurs failed to invest in the Donbass–Dnepr Bend at least partly because they were not in a financial position to do so. Even with the state's considerable assistance, to build a modern steel mill required enormous capital, technical expertise, and a

Russian-built metallurgical factory—the enormous Briansk Ironworks in Ekaterinoslav, which employed more than seven thousand workers during the 1890s—fifteen large foreign-owned steel mills opened in rapid succession in southern Russia. By the first years of the twentieth century, foreign-controlled companies produced about 90 percent of the iron and steel in the Donbass–Dnepr Bend.[17] In some respects, the economy there was tied more closely to Europe than to central Russia. In addition to the capital invested in Donbass–Dnepr Bend industry, almost all the technology and know-how—including, initially, the most highly skilled laborers, foremen, technicians, engineers, and directors—were European in origin. Their particular nationality depended on the origins of a firm's capital. At the New Russia Company's ironworks in Iuzovka, for example, Englishmen initially filled almost every responsible position, from director down to highly skilled worker.[18] By the end of the century, however, plants reduced somewhat their reliance on foreign administrators and skilled workers, supplementing them with personnel educated and trained in Russia.[19]

The Donbass–Dnepr Bend's modern steel mills exemplified what Alexander Gerschenkron meant when he attributed Russia's rapid economic growth to the advantages of industrializing late.[20] Foreign investors thought the positive aspects of the Donbass–Dnepr Bend's clean slate outweighed the negative aspects of investing in an economically backward and undeveloped region. Foreign steel producers in already-developed countries considered the Donbass–Dnepr Bend a perfect place to implement recent scientific discoveries and technological innovations in metallurgy. The costliness of reequipping outdated steel factories in developed Western regions was a disincentive that did not exist in the Donbass–Dnepr

---

willingness to invest in long-term projects. The modern stock corporation is best suited for such ventures, and in Russia the capitalist form of ownership was still mostly personal and familial (Burstein, "Iron and Steel," p. 167).

[17] A. I. Fenin, *Vospominaniia inzhenera: K istorii obshchestvennogo i khoziaistvennogo razvitiia Rossii, 1883–1906* (Prague, 1938), p. 8; Ralph Carter Elwood, *Russian Social Democracy in the Underground: A Study of the RSDRP in the Ukraine, 1907–1914* (Assen, the Netherlands, 1974), p. 7; John P. McKay, "Foreign Businessmen, the Tsarist Government, and the Briansk Company," *Journal of European Economic History* 2, no. 2 (1973): 274–280 and "Elites in Conflict in Tsarist Russia: The Briansk Company," in *The Rich, the Well Born, and the Powerful*, ed. Frederic Cople Jaher (Urbana, Ill., 1973), pp. 179–202; V. V. Morachevskii, "Ekaterinoslav i raskhodiashchiiasia ot nego puti," in Semenov-Tian-Shanskii, *Polnoe geograficheskoe opisanie*, 14:567.

[18] F. Zaitsev, "Bol'sheviki Iuzovki do 1918 g.," *Literaturnyi Donbass*, no. 10–12 (1933): 154.

[19] *Istoriia ekaterinoslavskoi sotsial-demokraticheskoi organizatsii, 1889–1903*, ed. M. A. Rubach (Ekaterinoslav, 1923), p. xxxii.

[20] Alexander Gerschenkron, *Economic Backwardness in Historical Perspective* (Cambridge, Mass., 1962).

Bend.[21] In the late nineteenth century, the annual output of an average blast furnace in the Donbass–Dnepr Bend exceeded that of one in Great Britain, Germany, France, or Belgium. Only the furnaces in the United States produced more.[22]

Russian operations functioned alongside foreign-owned enterprises to a greater extent in the coal industry than in metallurgy. But even in mining, domestic ownership dramatically declined in the late nineteenth century. In the first half of the nineteenth century, the Donbass–Dnepr Bend coal industry consisted almost entirely of extremely small, Russian-owned mines. These simple operations were referred to as peasant mines, and they could extract coal only from seams close to the surface. "Whether on gentry or communal lands, they were actually little more than small vertical holes a few meters deep. A hand-operated windlass raising and lowering a bucket of coal, just as in a well, was the most sophisticated device."[23] It is not surprising, then, that by 1890 peasant mines were responsible for only around 3 percent of the Donbass–Dnepr Bend coal industry's production.[24] While there was more than enough shallow coal to keep such peasant operations busy, most Donbass–Dnepr Bend coal was located in seams over one hundred meters below the surface. The construction of deep shaft mines required capital and expertise far beyond peasant capabilities.

Members of the local nobility opened most of the first large coal mines in the Donets Basin. A few of these landowners, such as the Rutchenko family, invested thousands of rubles in the mines constructed on their land. Generally, though, local industrialists were reluctant to invest in laborsaving machinery and equipment. Noble mines were often just larger versions of the peasants' primitive operations. Even when blessed with rich coal deposits on their land, noblemen in the Donets Basin were no more motivated to become serious businessmen than were the majority of their peers elsewhere in Russia. For most, coal mining was merely a sideline, a supplement to their agricultural earnings. The emancipation of the serfs deprived these coal operators of their cheap labor force, and during the

[21] French and Belgian corporations built steel plants in the Donbass–Dnepr Bend that were even more sophisticated than most plants in their home countries. In McKay's words: "Major foreign newcomers after 1885 did not evolve gradually from modest beginnings through long-term reinvestment of profits, as most enterprises in western Europe or northern Russia had done, but rather sprang fully grown into existence" (*Pioneers for Profit*, p. 159). The Nikopol'-Mariupol' Metallurgical Company, located just outside the Donbass–Dnepr Bend, bought an entire functioning pipe plant in America and then reassembled it beside its "ultramodern American-style blast furnaces" (ibid., p. 184).

[22] Ibid., p. 123.

[23] Ibid., p. 144. Hitting solid rock or water brought this type of mining to a stop. Commonly, such mines also temporarily ceased operating whenever farming called (Iulii Gessen, *Istoriia gornorabochikh SSSR*, vol. 2, *Vtoraia polovina 19-go veka* [Moscow, 1929], p. 106).

[24] Potolov, *Rabochie Donbassa*, p. 83.

course of the Donbass–Dnepr Bend's industrialization drive, the role of such local industrialists rapidly decreased until it was negligible.[25]

With the winnowing out of the smaller, domestic coal operators, it was not just the steelworkers who worked in large, foreign-owned enterprises. Miners employed at the sixteen largest mines extracted over 73 percent of the Donbass–Dnepr Bend's total coal output in 1900, while miners at just the seven largest extracted 44 percent.[26] But even in the large, relatively modern mines that foreign firms built, mechanization was limited to bringing coal above ground. Down in the dark shaft, a miner cut the coal "sitting, kneeling, lying on his side, his back, or his belly," usually equipped with nothing more sophisticated than a pick, hammer, and shovel.[27] The foreign-owned coal industry in the Donets Basin chose not to invest in drills, preferring to rely on Russia's cheap labor despite the difficulties in recruiting a stable, hardworking labor force.

The growth of the mining and steel industries also stimulated the growth of metalworking, machine building, chemicals, engineering, and other support industries, which employed large numbers of workers in the Donbass–Dnepr Bend. Fourteen finishing steel plants, fifteen machine-construction and mechanical factories, and seventeen other factories were constructed in the Donbass–Dnepr Bend between 1887 and 1897 to manufacture tools and some of the machines needed in the steelworks and mines.[28]

As important as the metallurgical, mining, and auxiliary industries were, however, other sections of the Donbass–Dnepr Bend economy showed little vitality and remained technologically backward. The boom was extremely uneven and narrow in its scope, as mechanization did not reach beyond heavy industry. The government offered subsidies and guaranteed

[25] Nine of the 86 delegates at the first meeting of the Association of Southern Coal and Steel Producers in 1882 identified themselves as landowners; in 1914, only 2 of 489 did so (Susan P. McCaffray, "The Association of Southern Coal and Steel Producers and the Problems of Industrial Progress in Tsarist Russia," *Slavic Review* 47, no. 2 [1988]: 466).

[26] O. A. Parasun'ko, *Polozhenie i bor'ba rabochego klassa Ukrainy, 1860–90-e gody XIX v.* (Kiev, 1963), p. 58; V. I. Bovykin, "Kontsentratsiia promyshlennogo proizvodstva v Rossii v kontse XIX–nachale XX v.," *Istoricheskie zapiski* 110 (1984): 186–187. Just over one hundred coal mines were in operation in 1900. This number does not include peasant mines, which were so small they accounted for a negligible share of the total amount of coal extracted. The domination of the Donbass–Dnepr Bend coal industry by large mines had been advanced by the crisis in 1881–82, when overproduction caused prices to drop and forced many smaller mines to close.

[27] V. N. Rubin, "Rabochii vopros na s"ezdakh gornopromyshlennikov Iuga Rossii," in *Nekotorye problemy klassovoi bor'by v periode kapitalizma* (Moscow, 1966), pp. 4–5. See also McCaffray, "New Work," pp. 57, 114–115; Morachevskii, "Ekaterinoslav," p. 841; Potolov, *Rabochie Donbassa*, pp. 83–84; and McKay, *Pioneers for Profit*, p. 382.

[28] Alfred J. Rieber, *Merchants and Entrepreneurs in Imperial Russia* (Chapel Hill, N.C., 1982), p. 238.

contracts only to heavy industry, and foreign corporations showed no interest in investing in other sectors of the Donbass–Dnepr Bend economy.[29] A sea of agrarian backwardness surrounded the islands of industry. The development of the Donbass–Dnepr Bend metallurgical industry did not even bring metal plows to the local peasantry; within sight of the mills, peasants could be seen plowing with dull, timeworn wooden plows. Poverty in the Ukraine and throughout Russia also essentially precluded the production of metal for consumer goods; one historian graphically described the peasants' situation: "The Ukrainian population was supplied with iron and its products on a starvation level; 98% of the peasants' homes were straw-thatched, all utensils were earthenware, not only in the villages, but also to a large extent in the cities, carts had wooden axles, gates and doors were hung on wooden hinges."[30] While the undeveloped character of the Donbass–Dnepr Bend economy obviously did not deter foreign investors, the British, French, Belgian, and German capitalists underestimated the problems new industrial enterprises would face on the "naked" steppe—namely, the lack of even an elementary infrastructure (other than the railroad) and the absence of a sufficient pool of workers, experienced or otherwise.

The workers Donbass–Dnepr Bend industrialists managed to recruit lived and worked in three distinct industrial environments: the older cities suddenly transformed by the economic boom, such as Ekaterinoslav and Lugansk; new industrial towns, exemplified by Iuzovka; and mining settlements that grew from scratch or from tiny villages, such as Rutchenkovka.

Ekaterinoslav was the only truly large industrial city to rise on the Donbass–Dnepr Bend steppe (prior to Stalin's industrialization drive in the 1930s). In addition to its much greater size, Ekaterinoslav's older and more diversified character distinguished it from the other two types of industrial centers that emerged in the Donbass–Dnepr Bend.

No Donbass–Dnepr Bend city ever challenged Ekaterinoslav's position as the premier city in the region. Of course, with respect to the period before the late nineteenth century, that is saying very little. Ekaterinoslav itself exhibited no vitality whatsoever before the mid-1880s, when smoke began belching out of the tall smokestacks of the city's new Briansk steel

[29] The narrow scope of the government's intervention in the economy and the ways in which the government's demand for credit hindered capital formation in the private sector have led economic historians such as Peter Gatrell to argue recently that the tsarist state's role in promoting industrialization has been overstated (Gatrell, *The Tsarist Economy*, p. 232).

[30] Kononenko, *Ukraine and Russia*, pp. 153–154.

plant. Until then, Ekaterinoslav was just a small provincial capital, where the rhythms of daily life were ever so slow.

Ekaterinoslav's history illustrates how suddenly industrialization and the concomitant urbanization occurred in the Donbass–Dnepr Bend. Catherine the Great founded the city of Ekaterinoslav at the site of a Cossack village in the late eighteenth century to commemorate and preside over the domestication and planned economic development of New Russia, as the whole steppe between the Black and Azov seas was called.[31] She and her favorite, Prince Grigorii Potemkin, the city's first governor-general and the de facto viceroy of southern Russia, had big plans for Ekaterinoslav. Potemkin envisioned Ekaterinoslav as the "Athens of southern Russia" and as Russia's third capital—"the center of the administrative, economic, and cultural life of southern Russia."[32] The autocracy spent enormous sums of public money on the city. The city center was carefully planned along lines much more imperial than those normally imposed on imperial Russia's provincial administrative centers. Long, wide streets were laid out, with huge squares and spacious parks.

That the city would not come close to fulfilling the grandiose hopes of its founders became quickly apparent. "In 1795, the only inhabitants . . . were a few officials, a few soldiers and a few peasants. All that remained of the original dream were the imposing palace and the expensive orangeries of Potemkin on which millions had been wasted."[33] Ekaterinoslav became a sleepy provincial center of the sort that abounded in pre-emancipation tsarist Russia. In the middle of the nineteenth century, the city fathers were the first to admit that Ekaterinoslav stayed alive "thanks solely to its importance as the major administrative point in the province."[34] Tallow melting was the city's leading industry.[35] Ekaterinoslav's lack of population growth reflected its economic stagnation. The census takers counted a paltry 8,476 city residents in 1844, a decrease of 107 residents since 1811.

The veneer of urbanity that existed in mid-nineteenth-century Ekateri-

[31] Catherine's armies had just acquired this part of the Ukraine from the Turks. In 1926 the Soviet government changed the city's name to Dnepropetrovsk.

[32] "Ekaterinoslavskaia guberniia," in *Ekonomicheskoe sostoianie gorodskikh poselenii Evropeiskoi Rossii v 1861–62 g.* (St. Petersburg, 1862), 1:4–6, quoted in Daniel Brower, "Urbanization and Autocracy: Russian Urban Development in the First Half of the Nineteenth Century," *Russian Review* 42, no. 4 (1983): 383.

[33] R. N. Bain, *Slavonic Europe: 1447–1796* (Cambridge, England, 1908), p. 415. Ekaterinoslav's failure to grow had more to do with the city's isolation than its layout. Ekaterinoslav arose on what was still largely an empty steppe, an isolated frontier cut off from the rest of Russia and devoid of entrepreneurial talent (Xavier Hommaire de Hell, *Travels in the Steppes of the Caspian Sea, the Crimea, the Caucasus, &c.* [London, n.d.], p. 69).

[34] "Ekaterinoslavskaia guberniia," 1:4–6, quoted in Brower, "Urbanization and Autocracy," p. 383.

[35] W. H. Parker, *An Historical Geography of Russia* (Chicago, 1968), p. 248.

noslav was extremely thin, even compared to other Russian provincial capitals. Judging by the lack of regulation of traffic on the city's main boulevards, Ekaterinoslav made little attempt to impress the occasional visitor. In a letter written during a visit to the city, the critic V. G. Belinsky observed that "pigs with their sucklings along with disoriented horses wander" on the city's wide streets.[36] Another commentator, A. M. Fadeev, noted that Ekaterinoslav residents did not seem to feel any compunction about letting their cattle loose to graze on downtown streets.[37] This was the provincial backwater that would shortly become one of the most important industrial cities in the entire Russian empire.

Industrialization catapulted Ekaterinoslav into the ranks of Russia's ten largest cities. Its strategic location explains the city's metamorphosis. The "capital" of Russia's southern industrial strip became both a railroad junction and a port. The Ekaterinin railroad line, connecting the iron mines of the Krivoi Rog with the coalfields of the Donets Basin, crossed the Dnepr River and joined the Moscow and Odessa lines in Ekaterinoslav. Although distant from both the iron and coal mines, Ekaterinoslav was the crucial Donbass–Dnepr Bend junction and a city with some available housing, and it therefore became a desirable location for a steel plant. Within a year of the completion of the Ekaterinin line in 1884, the Briansk Ironworks Company began construction of its giant steel mill in Ekaterinoslav.

By the turn of the century, the view from the Dnepr River of Ekaterinoslav's old city center was obscured by smoke from the numerous new factories. Ekaterinoslav had become a classic example of a new industrial city, so rare in Russia. I. Kh. Lalaiants, an experienced Social Democratic activist from St. Petersburg, went south around the turn of the century to help organize the new working class in Ekaterinoslav. He later recalled his first impressions of the city: "Ekaterinoslav struck us as a seething, unusually rapidly expanding city. It was not a great provincial cultural or intellectual center in the usual sense, such as Kiev for instance. But in Ekaterinoslav, life was bubbling over—the life of big industry. . . . Soon after you became acquainted with the city, you were no longer drawn to Kiev, or Khar'kov, or other similar centers."[38] In a similar vein, Luigi Villari, a foreign commentator, noted in 1905 that

> Ekaterinoslav produces a very different impression to that of most other Russian towns, even including the industrial centers. As a rule industrialism appears rather incongruous in Russia. . . . But at Ekaterinoslav one feels oneself at once

[36] *Dnepropetrovsku 200 let, 1776–1976: Sbornik dokumentov i materialov*, ed. I. V. Vasil'ev (Kiev, 1976), p. 41.

[37] Ibid., p. 48.

[38] I. Lalaiants, "O moikh vstrechakh s V. I. Leninym za vremia 1893–1900 gg.," *Proletarskaia revoliutsiia*, no. 84 (1929): 58–59.

in a really go-ahead industrial city. . . . There is no beauty and no picturesqueness in Ekaterinoslav, but there is an air of genuine activity and business which . . . may already stand comparison with some of the great industrial centers of Germany or England; it is a business town existing solely for business. We are in the real "New Russia," the Russia that will some day occupy an assured place among the modern and industrial countries of Europe.[39]

A massive influx of people into Ekaterinoslav followed the opening of the Briansk steel mill in 1887. No other factory in Ekaterinoslav ever equaled the Briansk mill in size, but soon dozens of other new industrial enterprises—mills, foundries, forges, engineering plants, and machine shops—were built on the fringes of the booming city. After the Briansk factory, the railroad was the largest employer in the city, for Ekaterinoslav's railroad yard and maintenance and repair workshop were among the largest in the empire.[40] Ekaterinoslav, in contrast to the Donbass–Dnepr Bend's other industrial cities and towns, also offered a large number of nonindustrial jobs in which a worker's family members might work. With over two thousand stores and workshops, the city became an important retail and artisanal center for the region.[41]

Between 1887, when the Briansk mill opened, and 1904, Ekaterinoslav's population more than tripled, from 47,000 to 156,611. In the larger time frame between 1863 and 1914, Ekaterinoslav grew twelvefold.[42] By the turn of the century, 40,000 laborers worked in Ekaterinoslav and its industrial suburbs. About 30,000 worked in heavy industry; the remaining 10,000 were mostly artisans and service personnel, employed in the city's workshops, offices, and shops.[43]

While artisans lived near the center of town, most of Ekaterinoslav's industrial workers lived either in Chechelevka, the working-class district on the outskirts of the city, or outside the city limits in Ekaterinoslav's largest suburbs, Amur and Nizhnedneprovsk. These working-class suburbs were located just across the Dnepr River, on the left bank. In the 1890s, a number of factories were built in or near Amur and Nizhnedneprovsk, so most

[39] Luigi Villari, *Russia under the Great Shadow* (London, 1905), pp. 103–104.

[40] Reichman, *Railwaymen and Revolution*, p. 18.

[41] By the early twentieth century, over eighteen hundred stores did forty million rubles' worth of business annually; and nearly two hundred handicraft workshops produced consumer goods in Ekaterinoslav (David Lane, *The Roots of Russian Communism* [Assen, the Netherlands, 1969], p. 159).

[42] The smaller city of Tsaritsyn was the only sizable city in the entire empire to grow at a faster clip than Ekaterinoslav during this period (A. G. Rashin, *Naselenie Rossii za 100 let: 1811–1913 gg.* [Moscow, 1956], pp. 89–91).

[43] *Otchet komissii po ustroistvu narodnykh chtenii v g. Ekaterinoslave za 1899 god* (Ekaterinoslav, 1900), p. 36.

of the working-class residents there no longer needed to commute.[44] As a result of this industrial development, Amur, which was just a dot on the map after its founding in 1875, began to grow rapidly in the 1890s.[45] By the end of the century, urban and industrial growth had made Ekaterinoslav the fifth-largest manufacturing center in Russia. After its industrial and population explosion, Ekaterinoslav resembled Pittsburgh or Manchester more than the Athens of Potemkin's dreams.

More typical, though, were the numerous new industrial towns the boom created. They represented "the closest approximation of tsarist Russian industrialization with that of the English Midlands."[46] Here and there along the railroad lines crisscrossing the Donbass–Dnepr Bend, factory chimneys sprouted, alone and in groups, surrounded by worker huts and barracks, on what only recently had been open steppe with a scattering of villages. The pit chimneys and spoil heaps of mining settlements also quickly came to dot the Donbass–Dnepr Bend countryside. The factory town of Alchevsk, not far from Lugansk, had been little more than a railroad station before the construction in 1895 of the Donets-Iur'evsk steel plant, which immediately employed four thousand workers.[47] In the decade from 1887 to 1897, a number of other industrial towns grew rapidly in the Donbass–Dnepr Bend. Druzhkovka grew from a railroad station with a few dozen employees to a town of 6,000, Krivoi Rog grew from 6,000 to 17,000, and Kamenskoe grew from 2,000 to 18,000. By 1903 Kamenskoe had doubled again, to 35,000.[48] The population of Iuzovka, which was founded on what had been completely empty steppe in 1869, exceeded 40,000 in 1905.[49] Regardless of their size, all these towns and cities grew up around new industrial enterprises and had little identity beyond that of factory or mining towns.

The new Donbass–Dnepr Bend industrial towns were typically single-industry, single-company towns. They lacked the diversity of older indus-

[44] *Iuzhnaia zaria*, August 20, 1906, p. 3.

[45] In the decade between 1895 and 1905, Amur's population increased from 3,000 to 11,000 (Morachevskii, "Ekaterinoslav," p. 556). The combined population of the two working-class suburbs exceeded 20,000 in 1905 (*Ves' Ekaterinoslav* [Ekaterinoslav, 1912], pp. 105–113).

[46] William L. Blackwell, "Modernization and Urbanization in Russia: A Comparative View," in *The City in Russian History*, ed. Michael F. Hamm (Lexington, Ky., 1976), p. 308.

[47] Patricia Herlihy, "Ukrainian Cities in the Nineteenth Century," in *Rethinking Ukrainian History*, ed. Ivan L. Rudnytsky (Edmonton, 1981), pp. 149–150.

[48] Tsentral'nyi statisticheskii komitet Ministerstva vnutrennikh del, *Goroda Rossii v 1904 godu* (St. Petersburg, 1906); McKay, *Pioneers for Profit*, p. 244; TsGAOR, DP OO, f. 102, 1898, op. 1, d. 4, ch. 18 (*Gubernator Keller—Zapiska po rabochemu voprosu v Ekaterinoslavskoi gubernii*), p. 12.

[49] M. S. Semenov, "Rostov-na-Donu i vostochnaia chast' Novorossii," in Semenov-Tian-Shanskii, *Polnoe geograficheskoe opisanie*, 14:841.

trial centers elsewhere in Russia. Alfred Rieber, arguing that Donbass–Dnepr Bend cities were more industrialized in the early twentieth century than the cities in any other Russian region, stated that 80 percent of the commercial-industrial population in Donbass–Dnepr Bend cities engaged in industrial activity. That was roughly double the proportion in Moscow and the Baltic provinces, where only 43 and 35 percent of the commercial-industrial population worked in industry.[50] To a greater extent than even other Russian industrial centers, Donbass–Dnepr Bend industrial towns lacked a sizable middle class to serve as a buffer between the industrial elite and the mass of workers.

Squalor went hand in hand with the development of industry. Especially during the early years, Donbass–Dnepr Bend industrial towns and enterprises proved woefully unequal to meeting the enormous challenges of rapid industrial and population growth—namely, the challenges of creating a reasonably safe and pleasant environment. Donbass–Dnepr Bend industrial towns offered opportunity to young engineers, radical activists, and those in need of work, but journalists and writers described these factory towns and mining settlements in the same outraged tone their counterparts in Europe and the United States used in discussing the misery in their own industrial slums. Much was written about how the factories and mines fouled the air with their smoke and fumes. The writer Konstantin Paustovsky's first impressions of prerevolutionary Iuzovka were of filthy air: "The smoke came not only out of the factory chimneys, but out of all its buildings. The smoke was as yellow as fox fur, and it stank like burned milk. An improbable crimson flame danced over the open hearths. Greasy soot dripped from the sky. Everything that was supposed to be white took on a dirty gray color, with yellow designs in it."[51]

Iuzovka was the classic example of a rapidly growing Donbass–Dnepr Bend company town. But even Iuzovka and a few others of the new, large industrial towns had the semblance of a planned center in the classic style—which is not to say that the centers in these instant cities could compare with the city centers in the older provincial or even district capitals. Residents of Iuzovka considered its few paved streets a source of civic pride.[52]

[50] Rieber, *Merchants and Entrepreneurs*, pp. 220–221; V. Semenov-Tian-Shanskii, "Gorod i derevnia v Evropeiskoi Rossii," *ZIRTO* 10, no. 2 (1910): 178–179.

[51] Konstantin Paustovsky, *The Story of a Life*, trans. Joseph Barnes (New York, 1982), p. 429.

[52] Iuzovka certainly had nothing comparable to the centerpiece of downtown Ekaterinoslav—Ekaterininskii Prospekt, a long, wide avenue with a tree-shaded promenade running down the middle, flanked by tram lines and lined by exclusive shops, government offices, an impressive gold-domed cathedral, a museum, churches, theaters, and hotels, all built of stone (TsGIA, f. 23, op. 30, d. 47, p. 122; Villari, *Russia*, pp. 103–111; Karl Baedeker, *Russia* [Leipzig, 1914], p. 401; V. D. Mashukov, *Vospominaniia o gorode Ekaterinoslave (1887–1910 gg.)* [Ekaterinoslav, 1910], p. 3).

Iuzovka's late-nineteenth-century pride in its three paved streets was not altogether unwarranted, since in smaller industrial towns even the main avenue and the central square were unpaved. Outside the center of town, however, all of Iuzovka's other streets were not only unpaved but without sidewalks or streetlights. In many ways, most of Iuzovka resembled more an overgrown village than a modern industrial center. Unpaved streets became rivers of mud during much of the year, and even a team of four horses would have difficulty moving. The strong, hot, dry winds of summer turned the dirt streets into whirling clouds of dust, soot, and chicken feathers.[53]

Iuzovka displayed the squalid, unplanned, bustling look that came to typify new Donbass–Dnepr Bend industrial towns. For the most part, urban growth in the Donbass–Dnepr Bend occurred in what appeared to be a haphazard fashion. John Hughes's desire to be considered a model employer and to reduce labor turnover led the New Russia Company to construct orderly rows of new housing for skilled members of the factory work force, but much of the town continued to consist of dense rows of flimsily built wooden hovels and clay huts covered with soot. Paustovsky remarked that "different neighborhoods were called by words like 'dog' and 'filthy,' and the gloomy humor of the names is the best proof of just how wretched and miserable they were."[54] The proper name of the working-class district known as "Dogpatch" (Sobachevka) was "The Happy Homestead" (Veselyi khutor), which obviously invited this derision.[55] In such districts, all but the most highly paid workers lived crammed together either in factory barracks or in a variety of different forms of private housing, often just mud huts workers built themselves. Miners employed in the New Russia Company's mines on the outskirts of town commonly resided in the most deplorable housing in Sobachevka and other neighborhoods scattered along the banks of the Kalmius River in Iuzovka. Pictures and descriptions of worker housing typically depict walls far from level and roofs that sink to one side or another. Visitors to Iuzovka were struck by the disparity between the large, modern steel factory and the slipshod buildings surrounding it.[56] Indeed, the contrast between the awesome factory John Hughes built and the squat clay shacks around it could seem surreal. At

[53] M. Tatarskii, "Otchet ob epidemii kholery v Iuzovke i prilegaiushchikh shakhtakh i zavode Novorossiiskogo Obshchestva Bakhmutskogo uezda Ekaterinoslavskoi gubernii v 1910 godu," *Vrachebno-sanitarnaia khronika Ekaterinoslavskoi gubernii*, no. 2–3 (February–March 1911): 382; Zaitsev, "Bol'sheviki Iuzovki," pp. 152–153.

[54] *Story of a Life*, p. 429.

[55] N. M. Cheremukhin, "Kak zhivut i pitaiutsia rabochie Rykovskikh kopei v poselke Iuzovke," *Vrachebno-sanitarnaia khronika Ekaterinoslavskoi gubernii*, no. 1 (January 1910): 1.

[56] Villari, *Russia*, p. 103; TsGAOR, DP OO, 4-e d-vo, f. 102, 1907, op. 116, d. 18, ch. 9 (*Po Ekaterinoslavskoi gub. obshchestvennoe nastroenie*), p. 15.

night the bright lights of the factory emitted the only street lighting in the working-class district. With the pouring of steel after dark, orange and other fiery colors flashed across the night sky.[57]

The most isolated workers in the Donbass–Dnepr Bend—socially and politically, as well as geographically—were the miners. Although a few mines, such as those owned by the New Russia Company, were located just outside the steel towns, most coal miners lived in relatively small, remote pit villages. The isolation of the typical mining settlement is easily explained. The location of accessible raw materials dictated where coal or iron companies could dig their mines and build their settlements, even in the absence of such basic amenities as roads.

Just as smoke-shrouded Iuzovka can be considered the classic Donbass–Dnepr Bend factory boomtown in character and history, Rutchenkovka provides a classic example of a Donbass–Dnepr Bend mining settlement. In the 1860s, Rutchenkovka was still a tiny village in Ekaterinoslav province, consisting of thirteen households with a total of 114 residents. Even then, though, the local peasants extracted coal from the extraordinarily rich seam lying just below their feet. Their landlord, Nikolai Rutchenko, built the first of a number of extremely shallow, primitive pits in 1860. When word spread of the profits made at Hughes's nearby mines, the Rutchenkovka coalfield attracted the attention of a number of foreign firms. In 1873 the French Mining Company reached an agreement with the Rutchenko family in which the company leased from the family approximately one thousand hectares for thirty-six years, at twenty thousand rubles a year.[58] By the turn of the century, thousands of miners worked the French Mining Company's seven large mines in Rutchenkovka.[59]

In a recent social history of British coal miners, John Benson wrote that "there is a tendency to think of the traditional nineteenth-century mining community as being synonymous with all that is dreary and depressing. We think of a remote village or small town, built on a grid-iron pattern, with endless rows of insanitary, colliery-owned terrace houses, a few tawdry shops, lots of pubs, a chapel and perhaps a school, all dependent on one, or at most a handful of nearby pits."[60] Benson disputes this bleak

[57] *Vestnik Iuga*, September 10, 1905, p. 3; P. Smidovich, "Rabochie massy v 90-x godakh," *Proletarskaia revoliutsiia*, no. 36 (1925): 163.

[58] TsGIA, f. 23, op. 14, d. 52 (*Otchety i balansy Rutchenkovskikh kamennougol'nykh kopei*), p. 9.

[59] In 1903, 2,700 miners extracted 42 million puds of high-quality coal from the Rutchenkovka mines, which was worth 2,484,286 rubles. By 1910 the mines employed as many as 4,000 workers during peak times (I. I. Boikov, "Otchet o kholernoi epidemii na rudnikakh Rutchenkovskogo gornopromyshlennogo o-va Bakhmutskogo u. VI–X 1910 goda," *Vrachebno-sanitarnaia khronika Ekaterinoslavskoi gubernii*, no. 1 [January 1911]: 405).

[60] John Benson, *British Coal Miners in the Nineteenth Century: A Social History* (New York, 1980), p. 81.

stereotype of British mining settlements, but even such a portrait is rosy compared with actual conditions in the mining villages of the Donbass–Dnepr Bend. Only the most favored workers could hope for a residence as nice as a row house.

Observers in the Donets Basin invariably reported mining settlements, such as Rutchenkovka, to be monotonously ugly. The typical mining settlement was little more than a collection of squat huts and company housing. The main street was "a long, dingy lane flanked by time-worn shacks and raw-new barracks. A pall of coal dust enveloped everything."[61] Worker barracks gave many Donbass–Dnepr Bend mining and factory towns "the appearance of an army camp."[62] Typically, no greenery whatsoever could be seen around the mine or the nearly adjacent workers' barracks, although some of the largest mining firms planted some sort of public park.[63]

A severe housing shortage initially confronted the workers employed at almost every Donbass–Dnepr Bend industrial enterprise. Before the mining and metallurgical firms began to devote considerable amounts of capital to the construction of worker housing, the Donbass–Dnepr Bend had a well-deserved reputation for the worst working-class housing conditions in Russia. As one contemporary publicist noted, "no speculator appeared in those solitary areas to construct houses to let for high rents."[64] Donbass–Dnepr Bend enterprises had responded to the housing crisis by building housing for their clerical and technical staffs first.[65] Before the end of the 1890s, all but the most highly skilled, highly paid workers lived crowded together in a variety of improvised living quarters unfit for human habitation. Peasants mercilessly exploited the housing shortage in the villages near mines. One zemstvo doctor reported that many peasants charged miners considerable rent for spots in their chicken coops.[66]

According to the Soviet historian A. A. Nesterenko, before the 1890s "the absolute majority of Donbass workers lived in *zemlianki*."[67] Miners

[61] Victor Kravchenko, *I Chose Freedom: The Personal and Political Life of a Soviet Official* (New York, 1946), p. 35. That stark depiction was of a mining settlement in the Alchevsk district during the early 1920s, but its author could just as easily have been describing Donbass–Dnepr Bend settlements one, two, three, or four decades earlier.

[62] Olga Crisp, "Labour and Industrialization in Russia," in *The Cambridge Economic History of Europe*, ed. Peter Mathias and M. M. Postnan (Cambridge, England, 1978), vol. 7, pt. 2:370.

[63] The South Russian Coal Company provided a spectacular exception to the rule. The company set aside one hundred acres in Gorlovka for a public park, in which it planted over a million trees (McKay, *Pioneers for Profit*, p. 246).

[64] Marcel Lauwick, *L'industrie dans la Russie méridionale, sa situation, son avenir* (Brussels, 1907), p. 140, quoted in McKay, *Pioneers for Profit*, p. 246.

[65] Crisp, "Labour and Industrialization," p. 369.

[66] A. S. Kirzner, *Gornorabochie Donbassa i Krivorozh'ia v pervoi rossiiskoi revoliutsii* (Khar'kov, 1926), p. 7.

[67] A. A. Nesterenko, *Ocherki istorii promyshlennosti i polozheniia proletariata Ukrainy v kontse XIX i nachale XX v.* (Moscow, 1954), p. 88.

themselves constructed these primitive, often quite large, earthen-floor dugouts from wood and clay supplied by the mines. Built with speed and economy foremost in mind, *zemlianki* quickly became terribly dilapidated. Workers slept on the earthen floors as well as on plank beds, and most *zemlianki* lacked even small windows. Privacy was an unknown luxury for the mass of Donbass–Dnepr Bend workers. At the Rutchenkovka mines, the average *zemlianka* provided shelter for fifteen workers. The number of workers reported to have lived crammed together in some *zemlianki* defies belief. To cite an extreme example—unbelievable even if it was during the summer and the miners worked different shifts—sixty Gorlovka miners reportedly shared a *zemlianka* seventy feet by sixty-three feet.[68] Accounts of hygienic conditions in *zemlianki* present a gloomy picture. Cattle were said to live in better conditions.[69] Zemstvo statisticians reported that just a couple of minutes in the stinking, stuffy air of a *zemlianka* was enough to drive them outside.[70] Unfortunately, such conditions were often what migrant workers from the Russian countryside were accustomed to.

Dismal conditions were not restricted to mining settlements, although miners generally did live much worse than steelworkers. When Ekaterinoslav's governor reported to the ministry of internal affairs on the causes of an 1899 strike at the Providence steel mill, he emphasized the dehumanizing effects of housing conditions for steelworkers there: "While barracks and small houses provide housing for approximately 4,000 people, for the remaining 3,757 people accommodations consist of huts constructed of thin boards. . . . These huts serve as residences in winter as well as summer. Heavy rains turn their floors to mud, lowering conditions to an animal level. Men and women share common plank beds, which are infested with bugs."[71] *Zemlianki* existed even in Ekaterinoslav, where they arose first on a stretch of city land on the outskirts of town. Ekaterinoslav residents had been able for decades to lease small parcels of this land from the city for family gardens and plots. During the first years of Ekaterinoslav's industrialization, workers, along with some other members of the city's new poor, simply seized parcels of this land. In place of vegetable gardens, a jagged line of huts appeared. This worker housing consisted largely of mud shanties whose flat clay roofs had been plastered in a slapdash manner with tar. The city government lacked either the will or the means to evict the squatters. Later, many of these mud houses were replaced by more substantial shelters, some of which were even built of stone. It was in this way that Chechelevka, the main working-class district in Ekaterinoslav, gradually

[68] Ibid.

[69] A. A. Auerbakh, "Vospominaniia o nachale razvitiia kamennougol'noi promyshlennosti v Rossii," *Russkaia starina*, 1909 (December): 557.

[70] Potolov, *Rabochie Donbassa*, pp. 170–171.

[71] TsGIA, f. 574, 1902, d. 205, p. 33.

arose in an area almost adjoining the older, established districts of the city.[72]

During the economic boom of the 1890s, Donbass–Dnepr Bend enterprises embarked on a series of more ambitious housing and welfare improvements. Many firms began to build company housing on a large scale. The bigger Donbass–Dnepr Bend enterprises began to spend on average 10 to 15 percent of their budgets on housing and such other indirect labor costs as medical aid, worker insurance, and schools. This percentage far exceeded the national average in Russia and was much higher than the percentage the Western European corporations that owned most Donbass–Dnepr Bend mines and factories allowed for similar expenses in the West.[73] By 1905 over 90 percent of coal and iron miners lived in company housing. Although most of these workers now lived in barracks, at some mines as much as half of the work force continued to be housed in company *zemlianki*. Donbass–Dnepr Bend steel companies in 1905 still provided housing for only 28 percent of their workers—partly because the better-paid steelworkers demanded higher-quality, more spacious housing than miners, but more because companies in the established cities of Ekaterinoslav and Lugansk never built housing. Even in Iuzovka, a considerable number of the more settled, highly paid factory workers rented quarters of better quality than company housing, or even managed to buy a small house.[74]

Even though company barracks were a major improvement over *zemlianki*, they were nonetheless still quite makeshift. Typically, barracks walls were constructed of brick or stone, but approximately one-third had earthen rather than cement floors. Almost all had plank beds. Small in comparison with worker barracks built elsewhere in Russia, the usually one-room structures in the Donbass–Dnepr Bend housed twenty-five to thirty workers and included a kitchen. The barracks residents commonly were divided into separate groups known as *artels*—work gangs consisting of as many as twenty members.[75]

Worker barracks generally received no sanitary supervision from the company and in almost every instance soon became filthy, even though artels customarily hired a woman to serve as cook and housekeeper.[76] Gov-

[72] Mashukov, *Vospominaniia*, pp. 8, 82; Ivan Knyshev et al., *Zarevo nad Brianskoi* (Dnepropetrovsk, 1970), p. 12; L. Stal', "Ot narodnichestva k marksizmu," *Istoriia ekaterinoslavskoi*, p. 7.

[73] Crisp, "Labour and Industrialization," p. 405.

[74] TsGIA, f. 37, op. 58, d. 299 (*Dnevnik komissii A. A. Shtofa*), pp. 82, 90, 96; Iu. I. Kir'ianov, *Zhiznennyi uroven' rabochikh Rossii: Konets XIX–nachalo XX v.* (Moscow, 1979), pp. 235, 263; Parasun'ko, *Polozhenie i bor'ba*, p. 165.

[75] P. I. Pal'chinskii, "Zhilishcha dlia rabochikh na rudnikakh Donetskogo basseina," *Gornyi zhurnal*, no. 9 (September 1906): 441.

[76] A. E. Vartminskii, "K voprosu o zhilishchnykh usloviiakh gornorabochikh Donetskogo raiona," *Vrachebno-sanitarnaia khronika Ekaterinoslavskoi gubernii*, no. 7–9 (July–September

ernment investigations of company housing in the Donbass–Dnepr Bend reported that these quarters "quite often appear to be breeding grounds for contagious diseases. The city administration does not turn its attention to these dormitories, viewing them as private apartments and therefore not subject to regular sanitary inspection, which would be highly desirable."[77] One Russian mine administrator graphically related just how bug-infested the barracks were upon his arrival in the Donbass–Dnepr Bend: "After visiting three or four barracks, I was already tortured by bites and discovered with horror that the top of my boot was so covered with bugs it seemed to be alive."[78] Miners' lack of personal hygiene compounded sanitation problems. Even at mines with bathing facilities, miners lived coated with coal dust. U. S. Chursin later recalled that few of the seventy other miners he lived with in a company barracks "ever took the time to go to the bath [*bania*], even on Saturday, because of the line."[79]

If the view was pleasing anywhere in a mining settlement such as Rutchenkovka, it was at the "colony," as the more or less comfortable compound for the administrative staffs of the largest mines and factories was called. The colonies ensured that the management, the technical personnel, the "salaried employees" (or clerks), and often even the most highly skilled workers would not need to rub elbows with, or even see, the mass of workers after the whistle signaling the end of their workday. The contrast between the living conditions of the mass of Donbass–Dnepr Bend workers and those of their enterprises' administration could not have been more stark.

If the colonies did not always have a private park or apple and plum orchards—or even a man-made lake for boating and fishing, as in Iuzovka—they almost always included at least a tree-lined promenade. Those privileged workers granted an apartment in the colony could expect their residence to include a small yard. The grounds surrounding the residences of the directors of most of the large firms were full of greenery. To compensate for working in such a hardship post, Donbass–Dnepr Bend industrialists commonly tried to live as sumptuously as was possible on the steppe. In Iuzovka, where the New Russia Company owned large mines as well as its steel mill, the director had two mansions: one downtown with beautiful gardens; and the other outside town, a new estate that was built

1910): 502–504. The cook bought and cooked the artel's food and washed clothes. The artel often hired the wife of one of the artel members to be the cook, but it was almost as common for the cook's status and attachments to be far less clear. Artel "cooks" commonly also acted as a shared wife. Disputes over this "*tsaritsa*," or "madam," were often the cause of drunken fights in artel households (P. Algasov and S. Pakentreiger, *Brianskie razboiniki* [Moscow, 1929], pp. 14–15; *Pridneprovskii krai*, January 16, 1900, p. 2).

[77] TsGAOR, f. 7952, op. 6, d. 86 (*Izdatel'stvo "Istorii fabrik i zavodov"*), p. 104.

[78] Fenin, *Vospominaniia*, p. 56.

[79] A. B. Zaks, "Trud i byt rabochikh Donbassa," in *Istoriko-bytovye ekspeditsii, 1951–1953*, ed. A. M. Pankratova (Moscow, 1955), p. 93.

on a large tract of wooded land. Aleksandr I. Fenin recalled that when he became director of the Russian-Belgian Company's mine, he was "provided with an old landowner's house—quite a mansion—Aposhnianovka, with a big garden, a brook, a horse stable, and horses. We started living like true landlords . . . far removed from the noisy industrial invasion. Our life was almost idyllic."[80] Similarly, the administration of the Hartmann factory in Lugansk lived on what previously had been a large noble estate. Surrounded by a wall and police, to some hostile eyes it conjured up a miniature Kremlin.[81]

In addition to family residences, the larger company colonies included a social center, usually named the English Club or the Engineers' Club. At the colony of the South Russia Dnepr Metallurgical Company in Kamenskoe, the club included a ballroom, "[a] richly decorated hall from whose ornate ceiling hung brilliant chandeliers that cast a glitter on the glossy parquet floors. The strains of music often came from the Upper Colony, signaling that a ball was being held for the management and the technical elite of the mill. Sometimes, perching on the wall, children of steelworkers watched as the masters played tennis or croquet."[82] Such factory clubs usually explicitly prohibited membership to "persons employed . . . in the capacity of workers."[83]

Rapid industrialization and urbanization created especially harsh conditions in the Donbass–Dnepr Bend, even by Russian standards. These conditions laid the foundation for working-class discontent and created a potential for mass unrest. To understand how that potential took the shape it did in the Donbass–Dnepr Bend, we turn now to the formation and composition of the region's working class and to the daily lives of the workers.

[80] Aleksandr I. Fenin, *Coal and Politics in Late Imperial Russia: Memoirs of a Russian Mining Engineer*, trans. Alexandre Fediaevsky, ed. Susan P. McCaffray (De Kalb, Ill., 1990), p. 71.

[81] I. Nikolaenko, *Revoliutsionnoe dvizhenie v Luganske* (Khar'kov, 1926), p. 53; Boikov, "Otchet o kholernoi epidemii," p. 410; K. E. Voroshilov, *Rasskazy o zhizni (Vospominaniia)* (Moscow, 1971), p. 154. To give an example of how much Donbass–Dnepr Bend managers earned, in 1903 the annual income of the top seven members of the Hartmann factory administration ranged from 15,307 to 30,020 rubles—and this despite continual charges from all sides of mismanagement.

[82] This plausible depiction appeared in the Soviet Academy of Sciences' hagiographic biography of Leonid Brezhnev (the Academy of Sciences of the USSR, *Leonid I. Brezhnev: Pages from His Life* [New York, 1978], p. 18).

[83] Quoted in A. I. Priimenko, *Legal'nye organizatsii rabochikh Iuga Rossii v period imperializma (1895 g.–fevral' 1917 g.)* (Kiev-Donetsk, 1977), p. 124.

2

The Labor Force

> Life at the mines has the appearance of forced labor, which impels workers to flee at the first opportunity.
>
> (*Governor of Ekaterinoslav*)

> If the Russian people suffer more than other peoples, if the Russian proletariat is more exploited than any other proletariat, there exists yet another class of workers who are still more oppressed, exploited, and ill-treated than all the others; this pariah among pariahs is the Jewish proletariat.
>
> (*Karl Kautsky*)

THE PECULIAR formation and composition of the Donbass–Dnepr Bend mining and metallurgical labor force, as well as the concentration of Jewish artisans and merchants in the area, help account for the differences between the labor movement in the Donbass–Dnepr Bend and movements elsewhere in Russia. Jews constituted a significant portion of the population—20 to 35 percent—in the larger Donbass–Dnepr Bend industrial towns. The mining and metallurgical labor force contained an unusually high proportion of migrants from distant provinces and was characterized by an unusually high rate of transience throughout the period this study covers. Most industrial workers in the region were "nomads alternating between industry and agriculture," as the French consul observed in 1893, which accounts for the extraordinary degree to which workers in the Donbass–Dnepr Bend exhibited a mixed mentality as "peasant-workers."[1]

[1] Quoted in McKay, *Pioneers for Profit*, p. 247. Most Western historians have argued that even after years in industry, the mass of workers throughout Russia, to a far greater extent than their Western European counterparts, avoided becoming proletarianized. This view has long been hotly contested, ever since the Marxist-Populist debates of the nineteenth century. Unlike Soviet historians, who have followed Lenin's thesis that workers' peasant ties were fast disappearing by the late nineteenth century and that proletarianization was at the root of labor unrest, Western labor historians have generally adopted, in a refined form, the Populist argument that except for an elite of skilled workers, Russian workers do not fit a Marxist or Western European model. For examples of Soviet attempts to buttress Lenin's anti-Populist

The mass of Donbass–Dnepr Bend workers maintained especially strong ties to their native peasant communities. These ties account, to a large extent, for the transience and volatility of the Donbass–Dnepr Bend working class—two factors that contributed to the exceptional combativeness the region's labor movement displayed. But while peasant ties, labor turnover, and ethnic diversity were all exceptionally pronounced, it should be noted that differences between the Donbass–Dnepr Bend and other regions were a matter of degree. Those conditions existed elsewhere in modified forms, so that while provincial labor movements often did follow the lead of revolutionaries in the capitals, conditions indigenous to the Donbass–Dnepr Bend also set the pattern for labor movements elsewhere.

The Donbass–Dnepr Bend labor force was composed primarily of three distinct groups: skilled factory and railroad workers; miners and semiskilled or unskilled factory workers; and Jewish artisans. Workers in the first group, whose jobs entailed such skilled tasks as overseeing the "cooking" and pouring of molten pig iron, rolling steel ingots into rails, pipes, and beams, repairing or servicing locomotives and rolling stock, and cutting metal patterns for bearings and pipe ends, were similar to skilled workers elsewhere in Russia. As in the capitals, the labor aristocracy of skilled steelworkers, and metal craftsmen and machinists in the railroad workshops and machine construction factories, were better paid; more literate, stable, and respected; and more likely to be attracted to revolutionary activities than their less skilled and experienced fellow workers. Because labor historians have devoted considerable attention to this elite group, there is no need to dwell on it in this chapter.

Semiskilled and unskilled workers, whose living and working conditions contrasted sharply with those of skilled workers, are emphasized here both because they remain little studied and because of their pivotal role linking pogroms and strikes in the Donbass–Dnepr Bend. Most data on the region's semiskilled and unskilled workers concerns the miners, with whom contemporaries were particularly intrigued, but what is said about miners generally can be applied to the mass of factory, railroad, and construction workers. In fact, the unskilled workers often moved from job to job during their stays in the Donbass–Dnepr Bend. When the opportunity presented itself, coal miners exchanged their pit tools for the wheelbarrows and shovels of a factory yard gang. Regardless of which industry they worked in, unskilled workers typically had little or no education, lived in deplorable conditions, and carried out dirty, grueling, and hazardous tasks. They lacked a long-term commitment to their jobs and responded to political

argument, see Kruze, *Polozhenie rabochego klassa*; and Iu. I. Seryi, *Rabochie Iuga Rossii v period imperializma (1900–1913)* (Rostov-on-Don, 1971). The most systematic Western treatment of the peasant elements in Russian workers' consciousness is Robert Eugene Johnson's *Peasant and Proletarian*.

events in a similar manner. The political history then being made in the Donbass–Dnepr Bend was a secondary concern for most of these workers, who generally were peasant migrants more interested in earning higher wages to improve their lot in the countryside.

Later in this chapter, some attention will be devoted to the third component of the labor force, which consisted of tailors, shoemakers, seamstresses, other artisans, and sales and clerical workers. The artisans and clerks working long hours in the Donbass–Dnepr Bend were mostly Jewish, which separated them from the skilled and unskilled industrial workers—who were almost exclusively Slavs, primarily Russians. But artisans were like skilled industrial workers in that in addition to having acquired (or being in the process of acquiring) a specialized skill, they were more literate, stable, and urbanized than the mass of workers. During reactionary backlashes to the revolutionary movement, skilled workers commonly chose to align themselves with Jewish artisans and clerks in opposition to the mass of unskilled and semiskilled workers and miners. Although artisans and clerks were dispersed in numerous small shops, their relatively settled lives and ability to read—as well as the anti-Jewish atmosphere and policies of the Russian empire—help account for why a disproportionate percentage of them developed a revolutionary consciousness and became politically active.

Recruiting workers and establishing stability in the work force proved to be insurmountable problems for Donbass–Dnepr Bend metallurgical and mining enterprises.[2] The recruiting problems were not the same in metallurgy and mining, however. Here, as throughout this study, it is important to differentiate between the two industries. Donbass–Dnepr Bend industry needed two distinct labor pools—skilled or trainable workers, and those with little to offer beyond their muscles and a willingness to do heavy, sweaty, dangerous work. Both were in short supply, though for different reasons. For Donbass–Dnepr Bend mine operators, simply recruiting enough workers, regardless of skill, was a never-ending, losing battle. The problem in the steel industry was the shortage of skilled and experienced workers, or applicants with the minimum of schooling thought to be necessary to make them suitable for training. Positions went begging at the coal mines, but there generally was no shortage of unskilled job seekers trying to find work at the modern, technologically sophisti-

[2] Donbass–Dnepr Bend industrialists at the annual conventions of the Association of Southern Coal and Steel Producers complained about the labor shortages and high turnover more than about anything else. Their problems elicited little sympathy because of the high profits many of the large mining and metallurgical firms earned despite these labor conditions.

cated iron and steel plants as manual laborers (*chernorabochie*) or day laborers (*podenshchiki*). Migrants flocked to the steel towns hoping to land one of the relatively well paid semiskilled jobs, such as helping to tend the intensely hot and deafeningly loud furnaces or tearing down spent furnaces. The large number of less well paid jobs, which required the most simple manual labor—such as cleaning up and removing spilled metal or slag, or loading and wheelbarrowing coal—were often parceled out only on a daily basis and also could be hard to come by. At the Briansk mill in the 1890s, "the job seekers gathered at the factory gates in the early morning and at lunch time, waiting for the factory administrators, whom they would ask for jobs. The seekers almost always exceeded the number of jobs. . . . The bosses, feeling in command of the situation, would speak to no one, or worse—when the applicants gathered at the gates in crowds of a hundred or more, the bosses, for their own amusement, would order the watchman to pour water on them."[3]

No pool of experienced industrial workers existed locally from which Donbass–Dnepr Bend industrialists could draw. The number of skilled workers that these firms induced to leave other industrial regions in Russia fell far short of what was needed, even though native Russian skilled steelworkers could earn twelve hundred rubles a year in the Donbass–Dnepr Bend in the 1890s—far above the national average for working-class wages and far above what bookkeepers, policemen, or teachers earned.[4] The Donbass–Dnepr Bend became a magnet for skilled workers from western and eastern Europe, as managers of the large, modern steel plants felt they had no choice but to "damn the expense" and recruit foreign workers to be foremen and to fill the most skilled jobs until their Russian apprentices could be trained.[5] They paid imported foreign workers salaries triple and quadruple those of their Russian counterparts.

The shortage of skilled workers was more serious in the metallurgical industry, but this is not to say that skill was not a desired commodity in the mines, too. A mine operator certainly valued highly any applicant experienced in dynamiting, masonry, carpentry, or mechanics, as well as mining. But most skills in the mines could be taught comparatively easily, and mine operators faced with a chronic shortage of workers could hardly af-

[3] K. Norinskii, "Moi vospominaniia," in *Ot Gruppy Blagoeva k "Soiuz Bor'by" (1886–1894)*, p. 24, quoted in Glickman, *Russian Factory Women*, p. 5. The hiring bosses could not be as heavy handed during the hot summer months when it became more difficult to find applicants eager to work near the torrid furnaces.

[4] In 1900, when the average industrial worker in Russia earned 204 rubles yearly, the average Donbass–Dnepr Bend miner earned 425 rubles (Akademiia nauk Ukrainskoi SSR, *Istoriia rabochikh Donbassa* [Kiev, 1981], 1:42; K. M. Norinskii, "Na svoikh khlebakh," *Istoriia ekaterinoslavskoi*, p. 39).

[5] Lane, *Roots*, p. 159.

ford to be discriminating when hiring. Generally, they were happy to hire anyone possessing strength and endurance. Some Donbass–Dnepr Bend mines operationally capable of extracting millions of puds of coking coal a year never extracted even half their capacity, simply because they lacked enough workers. The problem was so severe that on rare occasions the whole extracting process at a mine could grind to a halt.[6]

One obvious reason Donbass–Dnepr Bend heavy industry suffered severe labor shortages was the speed with which the demand for labor grew as new industrial enterprises began production one after another during the 1880s and 1890s.[7] Despite their success in recruiting increasing numbers of workers to the Donbass–Dnepr Bend, supply rarely met the demand.

Other than through the very expensive option of importing workers from abroad, where could the necessary number of applicants be found? In Russia's old and economically more stable cities, former artisans and handicraftsmen, along with their children and the children of industrial workers, could make some contribution, albeit small, to the formation and replenishment of the working class during Russia's late-nineteenth-century industrialization drive. No similar resource existed in the Donbass–Dnepr Bend. As we have seen, urbanization there essentially coincided with industrialization. The number of local city-born or city-bred recruits in the Donbass–Dnepr Bend working class could only be minuscule.

If labor was to be found locally, recruits from among the peasantry had to be the main source. It soon became clear, however, that most of these peasant recruits would have to come from distant villages. The relatively sparse population on the Donbass–Dnepr Bend steppe was only one reason for the minimal contribution of the local peasantry to the mining and metallurgical work force.[8] Donbass–Dnepr Bend industrialists were forced to look elsewhere for workers primarily because the native peasant population displayed an especially deep aversion to industrial labor. This was particularly true when it came to working underground in mines, and for that reason this chapter will be devoted primarily to the formation and composition of the mining labor force.

[6] *Pridneprovskii krai*, January 4, 1900, p. 1.

[7] Although the labor supply failed to meet the demand, from the 1860s to 1900 the industrial labor force in the two Donbass–Dnepr Bend provinces, Ekaterinoslav and the Don Territory, grew 1,240 and 2,300 percent respectively. This was a rate of increase far in excess of that in any other region of Russia. In just the last two decades of the nineteenth century, the Donbass–Dnepr Bend working class increased 1,000 percent (A. G. Rashin, *Formirovanie rabochego klassa Rossii* [Moscow, 1958], p. 193).

[8] Before the industrial boom, the population density of such central Russian provinces as Kursk and Tula, which proved to be fertile recruiting ground, was over six and one-half times that of the Don Territory and almost two and one-half times that of Ekaterinoslav province (Rubin, "Rabochii vopros," p. 15).

Local peasants sought work in mines only under extreme duress. Of course, as will become increasingly clear, Donets Basin mining had little (if any) intrinsic appeal for anyone, despite the opportunity to earn relatively good wages. There is no shortage of impressionistic and quantitative evidence testifying to the backbreaking and dangerous nature of mine work in the Donbass–Dnepr Bend. In the view of the regional factory inspector V. Sviatlovskii, even if the misery of French miners' lives described by Emile Zola in his novel *Germinal* were raised to the third power, that still "would not be a true representation of the heavy working and living conditions of our workers."[9] Underground explosions, such as the one killing fifty-six miners and badly burning sixty-three at the Rykov mine in January 1891, provided tragic reminders that mining could be lethal as well as backbreaking.[10] But the rigors and dangers of the work do not explain why peasants in the Donbass–Dnepr Bend were in a better position than central Russian peasants to shun mining.

Most of the Ukrainian peasants on the fertile Donbass–Dnepr Bend steppe farmed large amounts of land by Russian standards. Despite their own "land hunger" (the emancipatory legislation reduced by over one third the size of peasant land allotments in the region), which between 1905 and 1907 erupted in large-scale looting and destruction of gentry estates, Donbass–Dnepr Bend peasants enjoyed a relatively strong financial position and did not feel as strong a need to look for off-farm jobs to supplement their household income as did their fellow peasants to the north.[11] In addition, few were willing to enter the labor force of the local mines

[9] *Voenno-meditsinskii zhurnal* 160, no. 12 (1887): 489, quoted in Parasun'ko, *Polozhenie i bor'ba*, p. 221.

[10] Donbass–Dnepr Bend miners lacked the skills and work habits necessary in such a dangerous industry, increasing the risk of injury; but the mine operators and government deserve the bulk of the blame for the large number of accident victims. Operators not only failed to make working conditions safer, they ignored the regulations the tsarist government promulgated. In his sanitary inspection, the *uezd* doctor Bergun found forty-three of forty-nine Krivoi Rog mine operators in violation of the laws. Even at the turn of the century, around one-third of the workers of the average Donbass–Dnepr Bend mine suffered some sort of injury annually (*Vestnik finansov promyshlennosti i torgovli*, no. 1 [1908]: 11–12, cited in Theodore H. Friedgut, "Labor Violence and Regime Brutality in Tsarist Russia," *Slavic Review* 46, no. 2 [1987]: 246; Parasun'ko, *Polozhenie i bor'ba*, pp. 179–186). The mining engineers and factory inspectors charged with the job of rectifying miners' and steelworkers' just grievances were grossly overtaxed. In the 1880s, for example, a single assistant aided the factory inspector responsible for the nearly 150,000 square miles and thousands of enterprises in the Khar'kov factory district, of which the Donbass–Dnepr Bend was only a small part. This district, which extended from Tula to Baku, encompassed an area larger than Great Britain (Frederick C. Griffin, "The Formative Years of the Russian Factory Inspectorate, 1882–1885," *Slavic Review* 25, no. 4 [1966]: 644).

[11] Unlike peasants in central and northern Russia, peasants in the Donbass–Dnepr Bend traditionally had eschewed even cottage work (*kustar* and artisanal crafts) (Potolov, *Rabochie Donbassa*, p. 117; Pal'chinskii, "Zhilishcha," p. 422).

because mine work and miners had long been held in contempt. Local peasants looked upon work in underground mines as convicts' labor, a view grounded in historical fact. Convicts exiled to work in the Donbass–Dnepr Bend provided the region with many of its first miners; and even as late as the end of the nineteenth century, some Donets Basin mines still sought to employ convict labor.[12]

In examining Donbass–Dnepr Bend labor unrest, it is important to keep in mind that mine operators were so desperate for workers during the late-nineteenth-century boom that they remained far from selective about whom they hired. Even without convicts, Donbass–Dnepr Bend mines had more than their share of unsavory types. In the 1870s and 1880s especially, mines hired job seekers who would have been hard-pressed to find honest work elsewhere. One of the leading figures in the southern mining industry, A. A. Auerbakh, later recalled that when he first arrived at Kurakhovka and Rutchenkovka in the 1870s, "the worker contingent consisted almost exclusively of passportless vagabonds, the majority of whom were from the central provinces."[13] Later—especially during bumper-crop years, when recruiting workers proved to be extra difficult—Donbass–Dnepr Bend employers continued to turn a blind eye to the passport system.[14] For the mine operator, hiring workers who had no passports or whose papers had expired had obvious advantages beyond just filling positions. Illegal workers were in no position to go to governmental authorities to complain about illegal mine practices.[15]

The attraction and hiring of those outside the law and of unsavory characters of all types contributed to the disdain the local population felt to-

[12] The major mine in the Donbass–Dnepr Bend in the first years of the nineteenth century, the Lisichansk mine near Lugansk, employed convicts alongside compulsory serf labor. Later, at the annual conventions of the Association of Southern Coal and Steel Producers in 1892 and 1900, some industrialists sought to revive the practice of using convicts as a source of workers, with proposals to send a petition to the government requesting the transfer of convicts to Donbass–Dnepr Bend mines. These proposals failed. Opponents of the proposals reminded their fellow industrialists that to inject convicts into the body of workers was hardly a sound way to cure other aspects of the labor problem in Donbass–Dnepr Bend mines, since "the compulsory labor of convicts will always be less productive than that of free workers" (S. An-skii, "Ocherk kamennougol'noi promyshlennosti," *Russkoe bogatstvo*, no. 2 [1892]: 13–14; see also Rubin, "Rabochii vopros," pp. 19–20).

[13] Gessen, *Istoriia gornorabochikh*, p. 88.

[14] Potolov, *Rabochie Donbassa*, p. 103. Tsarist law required migrants to have a passport issued at their place of origin, as well as a residence permit from the police, to legally seek work and reside in a city. The Donbass–Dnepr Bend's reputation as a region in Russia beyond the law was not out of character historically. To the disenfranchised and alienated peasants north of the Donbass–Dnepr Bend, the southern border had long been a place of relative opportunity and refuge (as was noted in chapter 1).

[15] Gessen, *Istoriia gornorabochikh*, pp. 89, 130; V. Kolpenskii, "Kholernyi bunt' v 1892 godu," *Arkhiv truda v Rossii*, no. 3 (1922): 112.

ward miners and to the low status of mining in their eyes. According to a priest in Iuzovka in 1905, the local peasants, who thought miners "capable of any vileness[,] . . . remained so estranged from the mine workers that mothers, wishing to discipline their children, threaten them with the bogey-man of the miners."[16]

Local Ukrainian peasants in need of wages favored agricultural labor on the large southern estates or in the region's older, small industrial enterprises such as the distilleries, even though mining and metallurgy paid much better. When peasants overtaken by extraordinarily dire circumstances (and perhaps fit for no other work) sought employment in coal mining, they often preferred to work for local kulaks in the so-called peasant mines.[17] These coal mines offered much lower wages than the larger enterprises, but the locals considered these shallow mines to be more appealing. The peasant mines did not require long days underground breathing air polluted with coal dust in dank, dark, cramped pits, in which fires, cave-ins, the release of poisonous gas, drownings, and other accidents left miners disabled or dead at such an appalling rate.[18] The local peasants also considered peasant mines to be more attractive because they were owned and worked solely by fellow peasants.[19] Those local peasants who did go work among the migrants in the large, usually foreign-owned mines typically accepted only one of the many low-paid jobs above ground.[20] Peasants in the Donets Basin willing to mine also often chose to leave the basin to work in the Krivoi Rog iron mines. Iron mining was preferred to coal mining because it generally did not require going underground. In contrast to coal mines, iron mines were open pits.[21]

The Donbass–Dnepr Bend miners who constituted the so-called local contingent in any particlar mine were rarely peasants from neighboring villages. The local miners were typically drawn from villages eighty or more

[16] Quoted in Friedgut, *Iuzovka and Revolution*, 1:207.

[17] Potolov, *Rabochie Donbassa*, p. 118.

[18] Working in a large mine possessed one appealing feature that other forms of industrial labor lacked. Once they descended into the pit, the small crews of miners working in the numerous dark tunnels and chambers enjoyed freedom from close supervision by management. Under these conditions, the operators ensured production by tying wages to the amount of coal the work crews extracted.

[19] N. S. Avdakov, "O merakh k obezpecheniiu gornykh promyslov rabochimi rukami i ob ucherulirovanii prodazhi vodki v raione gornykh promyslov," *Doklad komissii XVIII sovet s"ezda* (Khar'kov, 1894), p. 334.

[20] As many as one-third of the workers in the Donbass–Dnepr Bend coal industry worked above ground, primarily sorting coal or tending the coke ovens (L. M. Ivanov, "Pod"em massovogo dvizheniia gornozavodskikh rabochikh Donbassa letom 1906," in *Iz istorii rabochego klassa i revoliutsionnogo dvizheniia*, ed. V. V. Al'man [Moscow, 1958], p. 355).

[21] E. Taskin, *K voprosu o privlechenii i uderzhanii rabochikh na kamennougol'nykh kopiakh Donetskogo basseina* (Khar'kov, 1899), p. 14.

versts away.[22] Peasants who lived near large mines, by that very fact, often were those least in need of such work, since the local population often profited from the opening of a mine. Renting and selling commune land, or only the right to mine it, put money in the peasants' pockets, permitting them to manage without help from mine wages.[23]

The Donbass–Dnepr Bend labor force was extremely migratory, even by Russian standards. The typical Donbass–Dnepr Bend miner or steelworker—80 percent of such workers, according to some sources—was a migrant drawn from a distant village.[24] In the Imperial Russian Census of 1897, Ekaterinoslav province ranked second only to St. Petersburg in the percentage of its workers who were migrants. The Don Territory, which encompassed a part of the Donbass–Dnepr Bend that fell outside Ekaterinoslav province, had the third-highest percentage of migrants.[25]

During the late nineteenth century, the rapidly expanding demand for workers and the relatively high wages paid in Donbass–Dnepr Bend mines and factories became increasingly well known in remote central Russian villages, provoking mass migrations.[26] Central Russian villagers suffered most from the "agrarian crisis" afflicting the Russian peasantry.[27] Rapid growth in the peasant population without commensurate growth in available land led to tiny subdivisions of holdings. Combined with the failure of most peasants to abandon the primitive agricultural techniques of their

[22] Fenin, *Vospominaniia*, p. 18.

[23] Pal'chinskii, "Zhilishcha," p. 422.

[24] *Trudy XVIII s"ezda gornopromyshlennikov Iuga Rossii, byvshego v g. Khar'kove s 1 po 14 dekabria 1893 goda* (Khar'kov, 1894), p. 334. The percentage of Donbass–Dnepr Bend workers classified as migrants varied from year to year but usually presented roughly the same picture. As late as 1907–8, according to data provided by the Association of Southern Coal and Steel Producers, 80 percent of the 180,000 miners in the Donbass–Dnepr Bend were migrants, mostly from the black-soil villages of central Russia (A. L. Smidovich, "Ob organizatsii nochlezhno-prodovol'stvennykh punktov dlia gornorabochikh," *Vrachebno-sanitarnaia khronika Ekaterinoslavskoi gubernii*, no. 11–12 [November–December 1910], p. 750).

[25] According to the 1897 census, 72.6 percent of the industrial workers in Ekaterinoslav province were natives of some other province or country. Migrants accounted for 70.6 percent of the workers in the Don Territory (Rashin, *Formirovanie*, pp. 358–359). The native workers employed in industry in Ekaterinoslav province and the Don Territory worked primarily in very small enterprises; when only workers employed at industrial enterprises with over five employees are counted, the percentage of migrant workers in Ekaterinoslav province exceeded St. Petersburg's percentage to become the highest of any Russian province—82.8 percent according to a 1902 census (A. V. Pogozhev, *Uchet chislennosti i sostava rabochikh v Rossii* [St. Petersburg], cited by Rashin, *Formirovanie*, p. 362).

[26] According to the 1897 census, 74 percent of the coal miners in the Donbass–Dnepr Bend were Great Russians (Elwood, *Russian Social Democracy*, p. 9).

[27] One measure of peasant impoverishment was that in 1904 in the provinces of Orel, Voronezh, Tula, Tambov, and Riazan, over a quarter of the peasants did not own horses (Martin Gilbert, *Atlas of Russian History* [New York, 1972], p. 68).

ancestors, this meant that most central Russian peasant households were steadily losing their ability to live off the land and needed off-farm sources of income to buy additional land and livestock and to pay their taxes and redemption payments.[28]

In addition to the widespread rumors that it was possible to earn good wages in southern "pits" (*iamki*)—a message carried by the increasing number of villagers with firsthand experience—word was spread by recruiters and contractors, whose search for workers took them from the Donbass–Dnepr Bend "to Russia." They went from village to village promising the high wages Donbass–Dnepr Bend mines were compelled to offer.[29] In the 1890s, semiskilled factory workers in central Russia typically earned the pitiful sum of 40 to 60 kopecks a day. In contrast, the daily earnings of Donbass–Dnepr Bend miners averaged about 1.25 rubles. The *zaboishchiki*, miners who took pick to coal face, usually earned 1.25 to 1.60 rubles a day working piece rate, and at times as much as 2.00 rubles.[30]

While shunned by the local peasants, Donets Basin coal mining became the favored off-farm source of income in many districts of central Russia. A zemstvo study of villages in the Morshansk district in Tambov province during the early 1880s noted that "many homesteads during the winter were left in the care of women because most of the men in small families and all the able workers of large families went to the mines."[31] The Soviet study of the village of Viriatino in the Morshansk district reported that "after 1905 it was a rare peasant homestead that did not have at least one

[28] The Donbass–Dnepr Bend had relied on workers from outside the region since before the industrialization drive. Annually, for as long as anyone could remember—but on a particularly significant scale following the emancipation—migrants from the more densely populated provinces of central Russia went south to the fertile steppe in search of work as agricultural laborers on gentry estates. Since the southern harvest was slightly earlier than that in central Russia, migrant peasants had time both to earn some money and, if they hurried, make it back home in time to help with the completion of their own harvest. Toward the end of the nineteenth century, when industry was expanding in the Donbass–Dnepr Bend, the demand for agricultural laborers began to contract—which helped expand the pool of potential industrial workers. Many of the old gentry estates were breaking up, and peasants, who had less need for hired help, bought much of this land. Those large estates that remained were becoming even bigger, and they increasingly invested in laborsaving machinery (Semenov, "Rostov-na-Donu," p. 281; R. Munting, "Outside Earnings in the Russian Peasant Farm: The Case of Tula Province, 1900–1917," *Journal of Peasant Studies* 3 [1976]: 436).

[29] E. S. Kogan, "K voprosu o formirovanii proletariata v Donbasse," in *Istoriko-bytovye ekspeditsii*, ed. Pankratova, pp. 77–78; Sula Benet, ed. and trans., *The Village of Viriatino* (New York, 1970), pp. 37–38; Gessen, *Istoriia gornorabochikh*, p. 86.

[30] Even those miners working in the most poorly paid but easier and less dangerous auxiliary positions—above ground as sorters, for example—earned 80 to 90 kopecks a day (Avdakov, "O merakh," pp. 332, 334; Taskin, "K voprosu o privlechenii," p. 16).

[31] N. Romanov, "Krest'ianskoe khoziaistvo v Morshanskom uezde," in *Sbornik statisticheskikh svedenii po Tambovskoi gubernii*, vol. 3 (Tambov, 1882), p. 250.

worker in the mines, and in some villages there were two or three such migrants in every homestead."[32]

Migrants predominated in the iron and steel mills of the Donbass–Dnepr Bend in percentages comparable to those in the coal mines. According to the 1897 census, 79 percent of the workers employed by the mills were not Ukrainians.[33] While most were Great Russians, the specific origin of Donbass–Dnepr Bend steelworkers varied greatly from factory to factory.[34] The relatively small number of Ukrainians who worked in the mills, especially during the summer, were usually either *chernorabochie* (manual workers) or *dvorniki* (watchmen and yard-keepers).[35]

Central Russian peasants generally migrated to Donbass–Dnepr Bend mines and factories in groups known as *artels*. A small number migrated individually. Artels traditionally were formed from among the young males of one village or district by an organizer, or *starosta*—an "elder," a peasant with some industrial experience, often someone from a "better-situated family, which added to the authority of the *artel*."[36] Connected by *zemliachestvo*, the bond of a common regional background, these groups of anywhere from ten to fifty migrants signed a contract together. In Viriatino, it was traditional for each new member to present the artel with "a bucket of vodka":

> After an *artel* had been formed, the leader went in July to the Donbass and made an agreement there with the current administration about the working conditions and housing of his people. The members were called upon to appear at the mine at a certain time and had to find money for their journey. Some migrants were obliged to sell sheep or part of the harvest; others resorted to loans from priests, who sometimes played the village usurers, or from kulaks. In some in-

[32] Benet, *Village of Viriatino*, pp. 37–38. Other central Russian districts and provinces, from the 1880s to the 1910s, provide similar evidence. According to a 1911 zemstvo study from the Zadonsk district in Voronezh, "the departure of the district's workers to the Donets coal region is very great, encompassing nearly half of the total worker out-migration from the district" (*Otkhozhie promysly, pereselencheskoe i bogomol'cheskoe dvizhenie v Voronezhskoi gubernii v 1911 godu* [Voronezh, 1914], p. 86, cited in Rashin, *Formirovanie*, p. 445).

[33] Ivanov, "Pod"em," p. 356.

[34] The Polish and Western European contingent was often considerable. At the Dneprovsk steel factory in the first half of the 1890s, 55 percent of the workers were from Great Russian provinces, 27 percent were from Polish provinces, and only 15 percent were from Ukrainian provinces (manual day laborers are not included in these figures). The remaining 3 percent were foreigners. At the Briansk factory at that time, almost all of the 3,756 workers were from just five provinces: Orel, Kaluga, Smolensk, Tver', and, to a lesser extent, Vitebsk (E. I. Ragozin, *Zhelezo i ugol' na Iuge Rossii* [St. Petersburg, 1895], pp. 37–46).

[35] Bohdan Krawchenko, *Social Change and National Consciousness in Twentieth-Century Ukraine* (New York, 1985), p. 43.

[36] Benet, *Village of Viriatino*, p. 37. For a discussion of artels, see also Reginald E. Zelnik, *Labor and Society in Tsarist Russia: The Factory Workers of St. Petersburg, 1855–1870* (Stanford, 1971); and Johnson, *Peasant and Proletarian*.

stances, *artels* as a unit took a loan for all their members under a common voucher.[37]

At the coal mine, the elder represented the artel before the company management. The artel representative often conducted all the artel's business, sparing management tasks such as apportioning work assignments and distributing earnings, even supplying the workers of the artel with "all the necessities: clothes, boots, meals, and, of course, vodka."[38] Each member of the artel paid the *starosta* a part of his earnings. Over time, more and more artel leaders were actually contractors or subcontractors hired by the mine, rather than artel members.[39] More often than not, the original artel started to come apart as a working and living unit soon after arriving in the Donbass–Dnepr Bend, with new members constantly replacing old ones. Membership in the artel, however, usually continued to be restricted by place of origin, or *zemliachestvo*. Migrants strongly preferred to work and live with those they considered their own kind. Workers from different provinces did not mix if they could avoid it. *Zemliachestvo* served a positive function by cushioning the move from village to industrial life, but it also divided worker from worker and contributed to the fragmentation of the Donbass–Dnepr Bend working class.

Many of the soon-to-be miners and steelworkers arriving from central Russia reached their distant destination in a time-honored fashion: floating down the Dnepr on a handmade raft, or hitching up a cow or horse and riding an old village cart. Some migrants, such as K. I. Rusanov of Orel province, spent weeks traveling long distances on foot. In an oral history, Rusanov later recalled his journey: "After collecting nine rubles I decided to go [south] in search of a living. . . . I went on foot—840 kilometers in twenty-three days. I left New Year's Day and on the 23rd of January 1884 I arrived at the mine."[40] With the expansion of the railroad network in the 1880s and the added inducement of specially reduced ticket prices for workers, railroad stations became the gateways to the large Donbass–Dnepr Bend mines and mills. All year long, one human wave after another—with two tidal waves in the spring and fall—washed ashore at a few key railroad stations. At the Alchevsk station on the Ekaterinin line, for

[37] Benet, *Village of Viriatino*, p. 37. Before the turn of the century, recruiters and contractors often were able to offer their peasant recruits advances and travel money. Advances increased the number of migrants recruited from central Russia but did not solve the labor-shortage problem. The individual Donbass–Dnepr Bend enterprise paying the advance was often left holding the bag. Migrants learned shortly after arriving at a Donets Basin mine that they could switch with impunity to a neighboring mine whose need for workers was equally great and thereby escape working off their debt (Taskin, *K voprosu o privlechenii*, p. 16).

[38] Voroshilov, *Rasskazy o zhizni*, p. 131.

[39] Crisp, "Labour and Industrialization," p. 377.

[40] Quoted in McKay, *Pioneers for Profit*, p. 260.

instance, at peak times of the year hundreds of peasant migrants daily tumbled from the arriving third- or fourth-class wagons. By the late nineteenth century, most migrants made the long trip south in these smelly, dirty wagons, in which passengers either sat tightly packed together on the floor or—if they were not so lucky as to find a spot on which to sit—were forced to stand endlessly.[41]

There was no mistaking the peasant origins of migrant workers when they arrived in the Donbass–Dnepr Bend, clad as most of them were in homemade clothes. Numerous accounts testify to just how poor and ragged these peasant recruits usually appeared. Rusanov recounted how he prepared for his 840-kilometer journey south: "I bought bast [for shoes] and wove it myself. I put two pairs of underclothes and some dried bread in a satchel and I got a walking stick. I put on my coat, a cloth robe covered with sheep's wool—a belt made of twine and a wool cap, and I took off on foot."[42] In the central Russian village of Viriatino,

> informants remember that in the 1880s–1890s, when workers went off to the Donbass for seasonal mining, they left dressed in thick, crudely worked, linen shirts, with coats and pants of the same thick, crude material. They did not even take a change of clothes with them; seven months later they would return to the village in the same outfit, by then dirty and torn. The people used to call this outfit "miners' attire," and it was worn until it was actually falling off their bodies. Instead of the usual slippers, however, they wore leather work boots in the mines.[43]

By the end of the 1890s, miners were returning in "city clothes": "From the Donbass the miners brought back to the village not only the money they earned but also the clothing they bought. Every young miner tried to buy himself at least one new outfit."[44]

The weary migrant in search of work who had come south not in an artel but individually was on his own when he arrived. Donbass–Dnepr Bend enterprises were unable to coordinate and systematize the hiring process. For a number of reasons, particularly government prohibitions, repeated proposals by the Association of Southern Coal and Steel Producers to establish employment offices at railroad stations were never realized. At the Alchevsk station, some of the bedraggled new arrivals would linger in the nearby town of Zhilovsk in an attempt to orient themselves, to discover where workers were needed and where the best conditions could be found. But most just set off immediately to nearby mines in search of employment. With little money in their pockets, these newly arrived migrants

[41] *Ekaterinoslavskii listok*, May 3, 1904, p. 2.

[42] Quoted in McCaffray, "New Work," p. 108.

[43] Benet, *Village of Viriatino*, p. 84.

[44] Ibid.

were anxious to find work as soon as possible and usually were not at a loss as to where to start looking. They typically went looking "on the off-chance," as they called it, to mines employing their fellow *zemliaki*, often men from their own village, who almost invariably were able to get them hired. Such contacts were almost a necessity in the mill towns. Unless they were skilled, migrants looking for steady work in the mills usually needed kin to inform them of openings and persuade foremen and other supervisors to hire them. This led to concentrations of *zemliaki* in particular skill areas and departments of the mill.[45]

Donbass–Dnepr Bend industrialists failed to mold most of their workers into steady, long-term employees ambitious to raise themselves up through the job hierarchy, so that while recruiting an adequate labor supply was a major problem, retaining workers was an equally serious one.[46] Few of the recruited peasants migrated south with the intent of settling there. They generally considered their industrial employment to be temporary and were not inclined to stay long.[47]

Turnover in the mines was fantastically high, much higher than in the steel mills. Almost every mine suffered from a constant flux in its labor force.[48] G. D. Naviazhskii, a zemstvo doctor practicing in the Donbass–Dnepr Bend, wrote in 1908:

> Not one mine has a regular contingent of workers. I do not have in mind here those conditions of the marketplace common to all capitalist enterprises—the expansions and contractions of the work force caused by expansions and then contractions of production. No! I am speaking about a specific phenomenon, a peculiarity, apparently unique to our mines. This phenomenon consists in the fact that the mines do not have any sort of significant contingent of regular workers, workers who remain at one and the same enterprise for a more or less long stretch of time.[49]

A contemporary German authority on the Donbass–Dnepr Bend work force, O. Goebel, reported that among the Donbass–Dnepr Bend enterprises he investigated, "it was considered fortunate if one-tenth of the work force formed a permanent core."[50] Miners typically stayed put for so short

[45] G. D. Naviazhskii, "V ozhidanii kholery," *Vrachebnaia gazeta*, no. 38 (1908): 154; A. L. Smidovich, "Ob organizatsii," p. 751; Kogan, "K voprosu o formirovanii," pp. 77–78.

[46] Hardly an annual meeting of the Association of Southern Coal and Steel Producers passed in which the problem of worker turnover was not a primary topic for discussion.

[47] A. I. Fenin, "Neskol'ko slov o polozhenii rabochikh na kamennougol'nykh rudnikakh Iuga Rossii," *Izvestiia obshchestva gornykh inzhenerov* 2 (1896): 18.

[48] Boikov, "Otchet o kholernoi epidemii," p. 411.

[49] "V ozhidanii kholery," pp. 154–155.

[50] O. Goebel, *Entwicklungsgang der russischen Industriearbeiter bis zur ersten Revolution* (Leipzig, 1920), p. 13, quoted in McKay, *Pioneers for Profit*, p. 247.

a time that in some Donets Basin mines, up to 80 percent of miners worked just one, two, or three months before picking up and moving on—often simply to try their luck at another mine in the hope that conditions there might be better. In 1896, A. I. Fenin estimated in the national mining engineers' journal that 60 to 70 percent of the coal mining work force completely turned over every two to three years.[51] Fenin was complaining, but an estimate that as many as 30 to 40 percent of the region's miners were in relatively permanent jobs was exceptionally high. Naviazhskii stated that the percentage of miners at any particular mine who had been there for over a year was sometimes as low as 2 percent and rarely exceeded 20 percent.[52] As late as 1907, the Association of Southern Coal and Steel Producers estimated that the typical Donets Basin miner moved two to two and one-half times during the course of a year.[53]

Management generally blamed the peasant character of their workers for the high turnover (as would Soviet managers decades later). Indeed, many of the migrants were new to industrial employment as well as to the region; and, as we will see, they wanted to return to agriculture. But one should remember that moving on was one of the few ways workers could express discontent with their working and living conditions in a country where strikes and trade unions were illegal and where legal provisions for the settlement of grievances were almost nonexistent.

There was little to discourage miners from exchanging employment at one mine for a job at another or from returning to their village. The contractual agreements binding miner to mine generally went unenforced.[54] Nor was it expensive for the typical Donbass–Dnepr Bend migrant worker—young and free of the encumbrance of a family—to move between mines. As noted above, miners traveled light. Upon settling their account at one mine, miners often simply packed their meager belongings, went to the nearby train station, jumped aboard a passing freight train, and rode the rails to the next station.[55] The labor shortage put workers in a relatively strong position. In shortage conditions, employers could do little to discourage job-hopping—and with employers often competing with one another for labor, they unwittingly encouraged it.[56]

The high turnover rate reflected the fact that the labor shortages that

[51] "Neskol'ko slov," p. 18.

[52] "V ozhidanii kholery," p. 156.

[53] A. L. Smidovich, "Ob organizatsii," p. 750.

[54] Some mines, however, did withhold a half or even an entire month's pay if a worker failed to remain for the length of his contract (Parasun'ko, *Polozhenie i bor'ba*, p. 108).

[55] *Ekaterinoslavskii listok*, May 3, 1904, p. 2.

[56] Conversely, it is not surprising that turnover declined during the occasional periods when Donbass–Dnepr Bend industry experienced a downturn. The first three years of the twentieth century would prove to be by far the most significant such industrial downturn during the period covered by this study.

plagued Donbass–Dnepr Bend mines were largely seasonal. The yearlong swirl of workers moving from one enterprise to another, or to and from the countryside, was just an eddy compared to the two protracted waves of wholesale turnover that broke during the fall and spring.[57] Seasonal turnover was so entrenched in Russia that most mines as well as other industries hired workers seasonally, for six-month hitches.[58] Easter traditionally was the end of the fall–winter term. It was then that Donbass–Dnepr Bend mine operators had the most trouble replacing workers departing to work their own farmsteads or to work as agricultural laborers on southern estates.[59] During the summer, as underground shafts became increasingly hot and humid, "all sorts of riff-raff would be made to assemble to keep the mines going. A subcontractor would round up men in the market place from among the 'barefoot ones' [*sic*] (*bosiaki*) many of them retired soldiers, the work-shy, the dossers, etc., and would attempt to fashion them into some sort of work gang."[60]

The persistent appeal of agricultural work highlights the peasant character of Donbass–Dnepr Bend miners and their lack of identification with their role as workers.[61] Donbass–Dnepr Bend coal miners displayed even stronger ties to their rural roots than workers in other industrial regions in Russia. Peasants came to the Donbass–Dnepr Bend to become miners usually only because mine earnings were considered to be the most expedient way to earn supplementary income for their family's farmstead. The migrants attached great importance to the independence and security they associated with the land, although a minority were glad to leave behind rural life and domineering fathers.

Most Donbass–Dnepr Bend miners worked in the mines with the idea of saving money to improve their lot as peasants. That was the impression garnered by the doctor-publicist V. V. Veresaev during his stay in the Donbass–Dnepr Bend in the summer of 1890. Illiterate miners often approached him to read letters they had received or to help them write to their families. What struck Veresaev in the miners' correspondence was their attentiveness and concern with everything relating to their farmstead back in the village—for example, where and how to buy a horse cheaply or the necessity of covering the barn. According to Veresaev, the migrants

[57] Potolov, *Rabochie Donbassa*, p. 146.

[58] Avdakov, "O merakh," p. 331.

[59] In the 1870s, the mines themselves were often responsible for seasonal turnover. Most Donbass–Dnepr Bend mines then were still technically too primitive to remain open year-round. Spring rains would raise the water level in underground shafts so high that mining became impossible. Mines were forced to ask all but a few of their workers to leave while the mine was drained (Benet, *Village of Viriatino*, p. 34).

[60] Crisp, "Labour and Industrialization," p. 378.

[61] Taskin, *K voprosu o privlechenii*, p. 14.

"deny themselves necessities while working here in the mines, in order to save needed money—and then go from here, never to return."[62] According to most other observers, however, the migrant miners squandered most of what they earned. In any case, for middle-peasant households in central Russian villages, where subsistence agriculture still prevailed, whatever cash could be saved from working seasonally in Donbass–Dnepr Bend mines could go a long way toward buying more cattle and land.

Donbass–Dnepr Bend miners brought to the central Russian village household some of the niceties of life: "New furnishings were bought, and wooden beds appeared, along with iron pots and pans, tea cups, and plates. All these items were the result of new tastes and new needs acquired during stays at Donbass mines."[63] The construction of brick houses in villages where peasants had lived since time immemorial in one-room log huts was the most dramatic change in village life that miners' savings made possible. A new house built with bricks gave the miners' family status within the village, and "for this reason, migratory miners were eager to put the money they earned, before everything else, into building a brick house."[64]

By the turn of the century, observers noted progress toward the formation of a core of stable miners (at least by the standards of the Donbass–Dnepr Bend mining industry)—workers who mined nonstop for more than one full year. But even this minority of so-called long-term miners in most cases had not abandoned their peasant dreams. The attitude of Nikita Khrushchev's parents was typical of long-term mining families in the Donbass–Dnepr Bend. In the early years of the twentieth century, they finally abandoned their tiny farmstead in the village of Kalinovka in Kursk province and moved into a small house in the Uspenovskii mining village just outside Iuzovka, where for years Nikita's father had journeyed each autumn to work in the mines.[65] In his memoirs, Khrushchev recalled how "both my father and my mother, but particularly my mother, dreamed of the day when they could return to the village, to a little house, a horse, and a piece of land of their own. That's why I lived sometimes with my father at the pit and sometimes with my grandfather in a village in Kursk province."[66] Like the seasonal workers, long-term miners generally planned to return home; and most actually managed to save, little by little. Once they

[62] V. V. Veresaev, "Podzemnoe tsarstvo," *Nedel'* (September 1892): 42–43, quoted in Potolov, *Rabochie Donbassa*, p. 175.

[63] Benet, *Village of Viriatino*, p. 39.

[64] Ibid., pp. 63–64.

[65] P. Bogdanov et al., *Rasskaz o pochetnom shakhtere: N. S. Khrushchev v Donbasse* (Stalino, 1961), pp. 9–13.

[66] N. S. Khrushchev, *Khrushchev Remembers*, ed. and trans. Strobe Talbott (Boston, 1970), 1:267.

accumulated a sum sufficient to purchase a farmstead, they immediately headed back to their native village.[67]

Even steelworkers who had seemingly cut their rural ties often continued to cherish village dreams after settling their families in the Donbass–Dnepr Bend and working in the mills continuously for years. Illustrative of this is the history of the Polozhintsev family, as told by a member of the family to historians in the early 1950s. Like Khrushchev, F. I. Polozhintsev was born into peasant poverty in Kursk province. The Polozhintsev family held almost no land. A mere one and one-half desiatines divided into three separate strips was all this family of ten could call its own. Polozhintsev's father managed to lease some additional land by working for his better-off neighbors, but years of barely managing to keep the family fed made the prospect of a job at the New Russia Company's mill in Iuzovka look attractive. Polozhintsev's wife joined him before long to serve as the cook for an artel of twenty workers. It is impossible to know with any precision how common such a move was, but after a few years the Polozhintsev family managed to return to their central Russian village with enough money to build a hut and buy some land and a horse.[68] What is clear is that few of the young migrants working in the mines and mills wanted to remain for long in the Donbass–Dnepr Bend.

In the 1890s, Donbass–Dnepr Bend industrialists finally recognized publicly that working and living conditions at their enterprises bore some responsibility for workers' unwillingness to stay put for an extended period. Before then, industrialists had simply chosen to blame their high worker turnover on the restlessness of youth and the peasant character of the available labor force. Donbass–Dnepr Bend miners were indeed young.[69] In the Krivoi Rog iron mines, for example, 90 percent of miners were under thirty years old.[70] The mining industry insisted that since most Donbass–Dnepr Bend mines offered relatively good and roughly equivalent wages, their workers could not be continually moving in order to receive higher pay, as some commentators suggested.[71]

[67] I. L. Lisser, "Gornorabochie na zheleznykh rudnikakh Krivorozhskogo raiona," *Zhurnal Obshchestva russkikh vrachei v pamiat' N. I. Pirogov*, no. 8 (December 1907): 751.

[68] Kogan, "K voprosu o formirovanii," p. 73. In contrast to the peasant migrants whose move into industry ended with an improved farmstead back in their village, for some migrants the Donbass–Dnepr Bend was just a stopover in a journey that ended with a new life in the industrial centers of the United States, Canada, Brazil, Argentina, or Australia (Caroline Golab, "The Impact of the Industrial Experience on the Immigrant Family: The Huddled Masses Reconsidered," in *Immigrants in Industrial America, 1850–1920*, ed. Richard L. Ehrlich [Charlottesville, Va., 1977], pp. 6–7).

[69] Taskin, *K voprosu o privlechenii*, p. 9; Lisser, "Gornorabochie," p. 751.

[70] Crisp, "Labour and Industrialization," p. 366.

[71] Industrialists buttressed their view that monetary incentives did not explain the motiva-

Industrialists started to make more of an effort in the 1890s to entice workers to settle in the Donbass–Dnepr Bend and quit their nomadic lifestyle. The industrialists were well aware that a relatively permanent labor force would never be achieved until miners cut their rural ties and settled in the Donbass–Dnepr Bend, as the annual reports of the Association of Southern Coal and Steel Producers attest. As was noted in chapter 1, especially primitive living conditions awaited most migrant workers arriving in the new mining settlements and factory towns during the early years of the Donbass–Dnepr Bend industrialization drive. The labor shortage and turnover spawned a competition among the big enterprises to build improved housing during the 1890s. In addition to barracks, industrial companies began to build family housing to try to induce workers to bring their families to live with them.

Before the 1890s, few of the young migrants working in the mines and mills considered establishing families in the Donbass–Dnepr Bend. Married workers, planning to stay for only a short stretch, left their wives and children behind in their home villages.[72] The reasons that workers living with their families in the Donbass–Dnepr Bend proved less transient than workers unencumbered with wives and children are obvious. No longer separated from their families, these married workers had less cause to return to their native villages. Workers with families were also both more inclined to develop their skills and less likely to roam from mine to mine or mill to mill, especially as they advanced in age. In addition to lowering

---

tions of their peasant recruits by pointing to the counterproductive results of pay hikes. When wages were temporarily raised, workers responded by working less. For evidence, the industrialists referred to the early 1890s, when a particularly severe labor shortage hit the Donbass–Dnepr Bend and dramatically boosted wages. Then, the more a worker earned per day, the fewer days he worked. Miners were evidently content to earn the monthly income they had come to expect (E. Kolodub, *Trud i zhizn' gornorabochikh na Grushevskikh antratsitnykh rudnikakh*, 2d ed. [Moscow, 1907], p. 123; Taskin, *K voprosu o privlechenii*, p. 15). The industrialists' assertion should not be rejected out of hand. As such leading labor historians as Herbert Gutman and E. P. Thompson have pointed out in the American and British contexts, people entered industry with preindustrial ideas and work habits that shaped their responses to industrial life (Herbert G. Gutman, *Work, Culture, and Society in Industrializing America: Essays in American Working-Class and Social History* [New York, 1977]; E. P. Thompson, "Time, Work-Discipline, and Industrial Capitalism," *Past and Present* 38 [1967]: 56–97). It should also be noted that although Donbass–Dnepr Bend workers may have been slow to react to financial incentives intended to increase productivity, they were quick to act when wage rates were cut.

[72] This was particularly true among the miners in the Krivoi Rog. In the Donets Basin, some miners did live with their families, but not many. Of 1,623 Donets Basin miners surveyed in a zemstvo study in the mid-1880s, only 7.1 percent lived with their families (Potolov, *Rabochie Donbassa*, p. 147). According to a different source, by the early 1890s the percentage had risen to 10 to 15 percent. Only at the oldest mines, such as those of the New Russia Company, did the percentage of miners who had settled their families in the Donbass–Dnepr Bend approach 20 percent (Gessen, *Istoriia gornorabochikh*, p. 133).

turnover rates, workers with families had other advantages for employers. Saddled with responsibilities, they tended to be less likely than their single, generally younger coworkers to engage in activities related to labor unrest. Furthermore, mine operators or mill directors who had an unusually long-term perspective must have realized that when a worker's family became permanently settled at a mine, the miners' offspring could also be a future source of settled, skilled workers. Better housing appeared to be an obvious way to create a more stable, docile, and prolific work force.

Donbass–Dnepr Bend industry in the 1890s increasingly spent the capital necessary to build special family housing. Until then, workers' families generally had been forced to live in mud dugouts—the *zemlianki* described in chapter 1—or in barracks. Blankets hung up around a bed in the corner commonly provided the only privacy married couples enjoyed in barracks. In the 1890s, relatively comfortable family housing, which ranged from cottages to four-family dwellings, soon began to be a necessity if an enterprise hoped to compete with other enterprises trying to establish a more stable and skilled work force.

In addition to the shortage of appropriate housing, other considerations discouraged miners from bringing family members to the Donbass–Dnepr Bend—among them the difficulty of supporting a family on a miner's wages. Mining settlements offered women and children little opportunity to work.[73] Steel mills also had few jobs for women, but the wives of metallurgical workers had a much better chance of finding employment in the cities and towns where steel mills were located.[74] It is not necessary to dig

[73] Lisser, "Gornorabochie," pp. 755–756. While underemployment was the rule in central Russian villages, at least all able-bodied members of the household a miner left behind could presumably support themselves. Donbass–Dnepr Bend mining villages, however, were quintessential one-industry towns. Miners generally did not earn enough to support a family, and mines employed female labor to a very limited extent; and women were not eligible for work inside the mine shafts. And while a miner's wife might be lucky enough to secure one of the few aboveground mine jobs, such as sorting, a worker had almost no hope of finding work at a mine for any females other than his wife. Rather than working for the mine, a more likely and better source of income for a miner's wife was to serve as the cook, laundress, and housekeeper for her husband's artel (Kolodub, *Trud i zhizn'*, p. 124; I. N. Kavalerov, "O polozhenii bol'nykh zhenshchin-chlenov semeistv gornorabochikh na rudnikakh, zavodakh i drugikh promyshlennykh predpriiatiiakh, raspolozhennykh v raione Bakhmutskogo uezda Ekaterinoslavskoi gubernii," *Trudy IX pirogovskogo s"ezda* 4 [1905]: 406). Regarding juvenile members of the family, the law prohibited mines from employing those under the age of seventeen, although such laws commonly went unenforced. Fathers sometimes could obtain work at the mines even for their very young sons. The father of Kliment Voroshilov, the future military and political leader, found his then seven-year-old son employment inside a Donets Basin pit gathering pyrites for ten kopecks a day (Voroshilov, *Rasskazy o zhizni*, p. 27).

[74] Women worked, for example, in the small manufacturing shops that supplied the machine shops with "hinges, loops, spikes, wire sieves, and bolts" (Crisp, "Labour and Industrialization," p. 357).

very deep to uncover other reasons miners and steelworkers felt settling their families in the Donbass–Dnepr Bend was undesirable. As will be discussed in some detail in chapter 3, to enter Donbass–Dnepr Bend working-class life was to enter an overwhelmingly male environment, a rough world in which drinking, gambling, prostitution, and fighting were the social norm. Family life left much to be desired, no doubt even in comparison with what was left behind in the hardly idyllic central Russian village. One mine manager drew this lurid picture of a miner's family life in the Donbass–Dnepr Bend:

> Fathers, worn out from their backbreaking work in the mine and aware of their inability to in any way brighten their family's life, for the most part do not bring earnings home. Instead they squander them on drink. The children—neglected, half-naked, and perpetually hungry—"earn their living" through petty thievery. Not a small percent of them, upon reaching legal age, do not change their views about the inviolability of other people's property.[75]

Journalists who ventured into the mining settlements presented a similarly depressing picture. Despite mining enterprises' increased investments in housing, a journalist such as P. Surozhskii could still report in 1913 after a visit to the Briansk mines that "for those with families there was terrible overcrowding, deprivation, sick and querulous wives, and puny, emaciated children."[76]

Some Donbass–Dnepr Bend mining industrialists became so exasperated with their labor shortages that they decided to try to capitalize on their workers' preference for farming. Firms began to offer workers a small plot of land, usually adjacent to a worker's residence, if they settled at the mine with their families. Garden plots allowed a family to grow its own vegetables and provided a profitable activity in which a miner's wife and children could participate. Raising chickens and cattle even became possible.[77]

[75] Kolodub, *Trud i zhizn'*, pp. 124–125.

[76] P. Surozhskii, "Krai uglia i zheleza," *Sovremennik*, no. 4 (1913): 308, quoted in W. Bruce Lincoln, *Passage through Armageddon: The Russians in War and Revolution, 1914–1918* (New York, 1986), p. 223.

[77] The offer of land was the most radical and promising measure the mining industry tried in its attempt to establish a stable contingent of skilled miners. It was not, however, a novelty in Russia; mines in the Urals, long before the end of serfdom, granted plots of land to miners with families. Donbass–Dnepr Bend firms hoped miners would feel that they could have the best of both worlds—the income that mining made possible combined with a domestic situation reminiscent of village life. Furthermore, industrialists hoped that household farming would bring not only a more stable and experienced work force, but a more sober and disciplined one as well—that working garden plots would divert workers from the drunken revelry and violence in which they customarily indulged during their leisure time (Taskin, *K voprosu o privlechenii*, pp. 14–15; TsGIA, f. 23, op. 30, d. 47, p. 85). The minister of finance, Sergei

Worker garden plots never became widespread, but by the end of the century most of the bigger mines had built such amenities as chapels, hospitals, schools, and libraries in addition to housing, to encourage workers to think twice before leaving. As we saw in chapter 1, firms constructed comfortable housing for their more skilled workers to encourage these workers to settle down at the mine or factory. In the 1890s, the turnover rate in the Donbass–Dnepr Bend did begin to decrease. Even so, on the eve of 1905, the percentage of workers who had settled down with a family at a Donbass–Dnepr Bend enterprise was still low and turnover remained staggeringly high. Although the mills enjoyed considerably more success than the mines in establishing a stable core within their labor force, industrialists still felt they had not made much headway toward establishing a stable work force.

The Donbass–Dnepr Bend labor force continued to consist largely of young male migrants fresh from the countryside. Not unlike recruits initiated into industrial production elsewhere, the workers were ill prepared by life in the village and its agrarian work habits to become disciplined cogs in the wheels of Donbass–Dnepr Bend industry. It was a repellent environment in which the newly hired worker found himself when he went to work in the dark pits of the mines or in the cavernous, red-hot furnace sheds and rolling shops of the mills. As their outbursts of discontent will at least partly attest to, many in this motley labor force found it difficult to make the adjustment to mine and mill labor.

The distinctive manner in which the Donbass–Dnepr Bend working class formed—or, more precisely, the manner in which it was continually being

---

Witte, was among those quick to point out the basic obstacle to the wide implementation of this plan. Most Donbass–Dnepr Bend mining enterprises could not provide workers with land for the simple reason that their mines were located on leased land (TsGIA, f. 37, op. 58, d. 299 [*Dnevnik komissii A. A. Shtofa*], p. 89; TsGIA, f. 23, op. 30, d. 47 [ministry of finance report, December 9, 1899], p. 93). Nobles and peasant communes both commonly refused to offer interested corporations and entrepreneurs the option of purchasing the land they wanted to mine. Most enterprises were forced to sign thirty-six-year leases. These leases also discouraged enterprises from building more substantial worker housing. But even when firms owned the land on which their mines were located or when they worked out an arrangement with the owners, other snags in this labor-relations scheme quickly became apparent. Lack of water made plot cultivation difficult. Also, the amount of land allotted often failed to satisfy workers. If the scheme was to succeed in settling workers at a mine for the long term and on a large scale, plots granted by mines could not be perceived by workers as mere tokens; they had to serve as substitutes for what the workers in reality—or just in their hopes and dreams—thought they were abandoning in their native villages. But mine operators had no interest in offering miners truly viable pieces of farmland. From the perspective of the mining industry, granting miners the sort of plots they wanted would have been a cure worse than the disease. Mine operators perhaps justifiably feared that if they granted larger plots, the peasant-workers would devote their energy and time more to farming than to mining (TsGIA, f. 37, op. 58, d. 299 [*Dnevnik komissii A. A. Shtofa*], pp. 88–89).

formed—helped shape the Donbass–Dnepr Bend labor movement in many ways. Transience and the lack of a long-term commitment to their jobs prevented many workers from developing a working-class consciousness in the Donbass–Dnepr Bend, as elsewhere, although in switching jobs frequently some migrants gained a sense of the bigger picture. One radical *intelligent* active in the region noted that the "railway stations, so empty elsewhere in Russia, are like bazaars here. In 3rd class coaches the talk is of the latest strike, and of how the contractors and technical staff and the police rob the workers."[78] More important, the industrialists' recruiting difficulties gave workers in the Donbass–Dnepr Bend a sense of power. Skill was a cherished commodity in short supply in the region. But even the least-skilled mass of workers—namely, the miners—were also in short supply. When business was booming and jobs went begging, Donbass–Dnepr Bend workers did not feel as dispensable and were not as easy to intimidate as workers elsewhere in Russia. The managers of the Donbass–Dnepr Bend's steel mills and coal mines generally were more dependent on the goodwill of their workers than were employers elsewhere. But the fact that the work force was in a constant state of flux made organizing difficult for labor activists.

Jews employed in artisanal shops constituted the third major group of workers in the Donbass–Dnepr Bend, after the skilled factory and railroad workers and the miners and semiskilled or unskilled factory workers. Although they rarely appear in the available primary sources and Soviet histories, Jewish artisans played a large role in the Donbass–Dnepr Bend labor and revolutionary movements, as well as in the backlashes their involvement in these movements helped provoke.

Most artisans in the Donbass–Dnepr Bend worked as tailors, shoemakers, seamstresses, cap-makers, watchmakers, locksmiths, and bakers, and the overwhelming majority of them were Jewish. Basic statistical information on Donbass–Dnepr Bend artisans is scarce, but already by 1891 government investigators had counted 38,598 artisans in Ekaterinoslav province alone.[79] A large number of Jews also worked as salesclerks in the retail shops selling the artisans' wares or in other shops. During the 1890s, the small-scale sector of the economy continued to grow, albeit much more slowly than heavy industry.

Jews, even new arrivals, rarely worked in the booming industries that had drawn Great Russians to the Donbass–Dnepr Bend. As one contem-

[78] Levus, "Iz istorii revoliutsionnogo dvizheniia v Donetskim basseine," *Narodnoe delo*, no. 3 (1909): 44, quoted in Friedgut, *Iuzovka and Revolution*, p. 66.

[79] TsGIA, f. 1284, 1892, op. 223, d. 202, p. 80.

porary, the Labor Zionist writer Ber Borochov, noted with rhetorical flourish:

> The Jewish worker is kept away from the main moving power of the contemporary economy—from big industry. Neither in the depth of mines, nor by the burning furnace and not by the steam engine was his combative spirit and his class consciousness forged. In the narrow, suffocating shop, on the low stool, by the modest workbench were his aspirations born. Not in the smoke and noise of the factory was his body steeled to bear the hardships of struggle, but in the soot of small oil lamps and in the dampness of cellars.[80]

It was not the refusal of religious Jews to break the Sabbath rest and work on Saturday, as the socialist press in the Pale of Settlement asserted, that primarily accounts for why Jews entered artisanal rather than industrial occupations. This was especially true in the Donbass–Dnepr Bend, where Jews tended to be less religious than Jews in other parts of the Pale.[81] Some historians suggest industrial employers, including Jews, refused to hire members of the Jewish lower classes because physically they compared unfavorably with migrant Great Russian peasants or because they had a reputation for militance.[82] But the Jewish absence in the mills and mines of the Donbass–Dnepr Bend seems to have been a matter more of Jewish choice than of employer discrimination. As was the case with most Ukrainian peasants (and this may be all the two groups had in common), Jews acted on their aversion to industrial labor by refusing to work in mills and mines.[83]

While social status in the Jewish community generally coincided with income, industrial workers were the major exception. Jews placed such a premium on independence that even relatively well paid factory workers occupied the bottom of the social ladder.[84] Yet Jewish artisans themselves were becoming rapidly proletarianized. Not only did Jewish artisans generally earn less and work longer hours than their counterparts in the industrial work force (although conditions were better in the Donbass–Dnepr Bend than in the northwestern provinces of the Pale), for apprentices and journeymen the dream of becoming a master and making the transition from employee to employer was becoming increasingly difficult to realize as artisanal production had to face ever-increasing competition from

[80] Quoted in Yoav Peled, *Class and Ethnicity in the Pale: The Political Economy of Jewish Workers' Nationalism in Late Imperial Russia* (New York, 1989), p. xii.

[81] Ibid., p. 85.

[82] Ibid., pp. 75, 116.

[83] On the absence of Jews in industry in the Pale generally, see Ezra Mendelsohn, *Class Struggle in the Pale* (Cambridge, England, 1970), p. 20; and Peled, *Class and Ethnicity*, p. 28.

[84] Arcadius Kahan, *Essays in Jewish Social and Economic History*, ed. Roger Weiss (Chicago, 1986), pp. 26–27.

larger-scale, technically superior factories. The owners of artisanal workshops, for their part, were not much better off than their employees.[85] Jewish master craftsmen themselves often enjoyed only the appearance of independence. To eke out a livelihood, they and their families often worked on a consignment basis and joined whatever employees they hired in working long, long hours.

The small workshops were patriarchal, often oppressively so, and they paid but a fraction of what Russian workers earned in the large factories or even the mines of the Donbass–Dnepr Bend. A master craftsman commonly employed only one or two underlings, rarely more than a dozen; so while in some shops strong friendships formed between employer and employee, in others journeymen and apprentices were constantly under their master's thumb and were often subjected to the financially squeezed master's insults, if not blows. Although artisans became increasingly assertive and politically active away from work, keeping their jobs no doubt depended on taking their lumps without protesting. Given the labor surplus in the Donbass–Dnepr Bend Jewish communities, masters often treated the apprentices they hired as if they were servants, providing them with little opportunity to learn their crafts—a common complaint of apprentices swept up in the radical fervor of the 1905 Revolution.[86]

The generally young, single males employed in artisanal workshops typically ate and slept cheek by jowl in the same dark and dingy room where they spent as many as fourteen hours per day working. While it is difficult to imagine that the working and living conditions endured by most journeymen and apprentice artisans in the Donbass–Dnepr Bend could have been worse than those endured by miners and blast-furnace hands, they may have been, even though the typical workshop employee was more skilled and better educated than his industrial counterpart.[87] In 1905 workers in small, labor-intensive manufactories presented demands to improve an almost-unbelievable plight. For example, coopers—workers who made and repaired barrels and casks—demanded that instead of their eighteen-hour workday, a twelve-hour day be established and that their monthly wages of eight to ten rubles be increased to fifteen to twenty rubles.[88]

[85] *Sbornik materialov ob ekonomicheskom polozhenii evreev v Rossii*, 2 vols. (St. Petersburg, 1904); Peled, *Class and Ethnicity*, p. 36.

[86] TsGIA, f. 1282, d. 463 (Ekaterinoslav governor's annual report, 1900), pp. 6–7. Apprentices were usually under fourteen years of age when they began their apprenticeship (Isaac M. Rubinov, *The Economic Condition of the Jews in Russia* [New York, 1907], p. 524).

[87] Rubinov, *Economic Condition*; Lalaiants, "O moikh vstrechakh," p. 60; Mendelsohn, *Class Struggle*, p. 60; Weinberg, "Worker Organizations."

[88] *Pridneprovskii krai*, June 20, 1905, p. 4. By the late nineteenth century, most Donbass–Dnepr Bend industrial workers worked a ten-hour day, with an eight to nine-hour day on Saturdays and the eve of holidays (TsGIA, f. 37, op. 58, d. 306, p. 118).

Thus, though they rarely took jobs as industrial workers, Jews came to constitute a large part of the urban population in the Donbass–Dnepr Bend. Artisans and the mass of peddlers, as well as old-clothes dealers, street sellers of fruit and trinkets, repairmen and odd-jobbers, and merchants and their salesclerks were largely Jewish. Many professionals were Jewish as well. Jews accounted for an especially large share of the population—35 percent in 1897—in Ekaterinoslav, the oldest, largest, and economically most diverse city in the Donbass–Dnepr Bend.[89] Even in Iuzovka—the quintessential Donbass–Dnepr Bend industrial company town—one-fifth of the residents were Jewish.[90] In the small mining villages, as throughout the Donbass–Dnepr Bend, Jews owned most of the stores, inns, and taverns.[91]

As for the native ethnic population, we have seen that Ukrainians were a distinct minority in the working class and in the industrial cities and towns of the Donbass–Dnepr Bend. At the turn of the century, Ukrainians constituted only 16 percent of the population in Ekaterinoslav and accounted for only 21 percent of mill workers and 22 percent of miners.[92] In addition, many of the Ukrainian workers either tried to hide their Ukrainian identity or had become Russianized. The frustrations of the tiny Marxist Ukrainian nationalist movement illustrate this. As one Ukrainian Social Democratic Labor party activist complained in 1906: "The Ukrainian proletariat has become so Russianized that members of the Party working among them must first teach them the Ukrainian language."[93] Russian was the language used in the few schools and books to which workers had access.

The usual social gulf separating town and countryside during rapid industrialization was significantly widened in the Donbass–Dnepr Bend by ethnic cleavages. The ethnic composition of industrial cities and towns stood in sharp contrast to that of the surrounding countryside. While the

[89] Tsentral'nyi statisticheskii komitet Ministerstva vnutrennikh del, *Pervaia vseobshchaia perepis' naseleniia Rossiiskoi imperii, 1897 g.*, vol. 13, *Ekaterinoslavskaia guberniia*, ed. N. A. Troinitskii (St. Petersburg, 1904), pp. 119, 127. By 1904, 40 percent of Ekaterinoslav's population was Jewish (Tsentral'nyi statisticheskii komitet Ministerstva vnutrennikh del, *Goroda Rossii*, p. 391).

[90] According to a New Russia Company report, in 1913 only 14,000 of Iuzovka's 43,000 residents did not work for the company in one capacity or another. Of these 14,000 residents, 12,000 were Jewish (cited in Friedgut, *Iuzovka and Revolution*, pp. 86–87).

[91] TsGIA, f. 37, op. 58, d. 305, p. 298. Jews controlled the traffic in liquor throughout the Pale until state liquor stores were introduced at the end of the nineteenth century to replace privately owned taverns (Rogger, *Jewish Policies*, pp. 147–150, 156).

[92] Ivanov, "Pod"em," p. 356; Tsentral'nyi statisticheskii komitet Ministerstva vnutrennikh del, *Goroda Rossii*, pp. 210–211.

[93] Institut Marksizma-Leninizma pri TsK KPSS, *Chetvertyi (ob"edinitel'nyi) s"ezd RSDRP, aprel' (aprel'–mai) 1907 goda: Protokoly*, p. 33, quoted in Elwood, *Russian Social Democracy*, p. 10.

villages remained almost purely Ukrainian, the cities became primarily Great Russian and Jewish. The native rural Ukrainian population, except for those individuals who benefited financially, might be expected to have resented the flood of newcomers. And indeed, the local Ukrainian peasants regarded miners and Jews with particular suspicion and contempt and viewed the wealth and power of the urban centers with hostility and envy. The Bolshevik V. Skorovstanskii concisely summarized how he thought ethnic differences aggravated the Ukrainian peasants' unfavorable view of the city: "The city is aristocratic, foreign, not ours, not Ukrainian. Russian, Jewish, Polish—only not ours, not Ukrainian."[94]

Thus, one important consequence of the mass migration into the Donbass–Dnepr Bend was the unusual diversity of the work force and of the industrial cities and towns; in addition to Russians, Ukrainians, and Jews, there were sizable contingents of Belorussians and Poles and more than a smattering of Greeks, Gypsies, Tatars, and Turks. This heterogeneity meant that in addition to the usual difference between skilled and unskilled, there were other significant lines of cleavage among workers in the Donbass–Dnepr Bend.

Ethnic heterogeneity and differences in regional origins balkanized each enterprise's labor force and impeded workers' developing sense of class consciousness. To a large extent, the skilled ranks at many steel plants consisted of foreigners, paid much higher wages and offered much nicer housing than their Russian and Ukrainian counterparts. Such perquisites were necessary to lure foreign workers away from their native countries to a backwater such as the Donbass–Dnepr Bend. Even the Great Russian industrial workers lacked a shared identity. With few skills and with little inclination to abandon farming and settle in the Donbass–Dnepr Bend, central Russian migrants brought with them a strong sense of their *zemliak* identity, their identity as a member of one of a variety of distinct regional groupings. "What a variety of tribes, dialects, sensibilities!" is how P. Smidovich, a radical intellectual activist, characterized the southern metallurgical labor force with which he worked and lived.[95] The origin of the predominant group of workers varied from factory to factory and from mine to mine, but at seemingly every firm diversity led to clannishness rather than assimilation. The migrants brought with them the villager's suspicion of strangers and outsiders. Regional origins were rarely forgotten and were an integral feature of working-class life in the Donbass–Dnepr Bend, except perhaps among that small percentage of the work force that made the

[94] V. Skorovstanskii [V. Shakhrai], *Revoliutsiia na Ukraine* (Saratov, 1919), pp. 7–8, quoted in Krawchenko, *Social Change*, p. 20.

[95] "Rabochie massy," p. 167.

Donbass–Dnepr Bend its permanent new home and not just a place to make some money before moving on.

One aspect of the Donbass–Dnepr Bend's industrial boom that brought these diverse workers together and that helps explain why labor-management relations proved to be especially antagonistic in the region was the foreign ownership and management of most of the large enterprises. Most of the top administrators and, initially, most of the foremen had Western European backgrounds, were unable to speak Russian, and treated their workers with haughtiness. All this fed working-class xenophobia and created an explosive situation.[96] Members of the government could have no excuse for not being acutely aware of it. In 1900, for example, Ekaterinoslav province's senior factory inspector, S. Aksenov, repeatedly filed reports in which he expressed his concern over how foreign administrators viewed and treated Donbass–Dnepr Bend workers. In his major report for the year, Aksenov stated that the foreign administrators "detest or abhor Russian workers and often do not acknowledge their basic human rights. The workers pay them in their own coin. In this there is not the slightest exaggeration."[97] On those occasions when the foreign directors tried to learn more about working conditions than what they could see from their office windows, they often did so through Jewish translators, which only made matters worse—for, as we will see, Jews were the one group most workers resented more than foreigners. Aksenov goes on to note that while the foreign directors were ultimately responsible, it was the foreign foremen they hired who often directly provoked worker discontent:

> The directors always choose and evaluate foremen on the basis of their specialized knowledge. They completely disregard the level of their intellectual and moral development. Not many of these foremen speak even broken Russian; all most of them know in Russian are strong curses and some technical terms, or they are unable to speak Russian at all and communicate solely through mimicry. At the same time, since they are terribly uncultured, rude, and in most cases immoral, the worst foreign foremen are extremely familiar in their relations with Russian workers, as are the directors. They slight them in every way possible, swearing and often beating them; in the event an individual worker protests, foremen quickly, and without even attempting to mask their arbitrariness, impose various punitive measures: depriving the worker of his day's wages, downgrading his piecework, fining him for all sorts of arbitrary reasons.[98]

[96] Native engineers and spokesmen for the foreign-owned Donbass–Dnepr Bend coal and steel industries had perhaps become predominate by the end of the nineteenth century. Men whose surnames were Jewish, German, Polish, French, or English constituted just under half of the delegates at the 1905 meeting of the Association of Southern Coal and Steel Producers (McCaffray, "The Association," pp. 466–467).

[97] Quoted in Berkhin, *Luganskaia bol'shevistskaia organizatsiia*, p. 8.

[98] Ibid.

Shared hostility to foreign bosses should not be exaggerated, however. Ethnic and regional animosities within the working class, coupled with the transient character of the work force, played a crucial role in shaping the Donbass–Dnepr Bend labor movement. The variety of backgrounds among industrial workers and artisans limited the appeal of collective action and posed obstacles to solidarity and organization within worker ranks. One searches in vain for evidence to support Lenin's pronouncement that the industrial boom in the Donbass–Dnepr Bend was serving the historically progressive function of assimilating the Great Russian and Ukrainian proletariat: "Capitalism is putting in the place of the dull, toil-hardened, settled, beastly Great Russian or Ukrainian peasant a mobile proletariat, whose living conditions break down the national narrow-mindedness of both the Great Russians and Ukrainians."[99] Smidovich—who, unlike Lenin and other émigré radical *intelligenty*, was actually trying to organize Donbass–Dnepr Bend workers—recognized, much to his chagrin, that "life still has not assimilated them, has not given factory workers' lives a common coloration[,] . . . a consciousness of their common interests."[100] Workers clearly did have much in common, but despite Marxist theory and agitators' hopes, a unified working class was not automatically forged by shared workplace experiences or shared economic status. Worker transience and regional and ethnic prejudices interfered with cohesion.

Anti-Semitism was rife among Donbass–Dnepr Bend miners and metallurgical workers. It was a rare worker whose personal experiences prompted him to question his ethnic prejudices. When the then-young worker Kliment Voroshilov arrived in Lugansk, on the run from the police, he hid out in the large, poor household of a Jewish tailor. In his memoirs, Voroshilov recounted how the family's solicitude and kindness led him to ponder "who profits from setting Russian workers against Jewish workers, from the organization of pogroms and the inflaming of anti-Semitic passions." Voroshilov concluded that "this profits only the industrialists and the tsarist police, who fear most of all the solidarity of workers of different nationalities."[101] Be that as it may, at times anti-Semitism seemed to be the only unifying force within the ranks of industrial workers.

These features—workers' shallow roots in the region, rapid turnover, and ethnic heterogeneity—gave the Donbass–Dnepr Bend labor force its particular character and would help distinguish the labor movement there from movements in the northern capitals and other industrial cities. As we will see in the next chapter, the social context in which the Donbass–Dnepr

[99] Quoted in Ivanov, "Pod"em," p. 356.
[100] "Rabochie massy," p. 167.
[101] *Rasskazy o zhizni*, pp. 117–118.

Bend work force formed also shaped the labor movement. Rapid growth in this isolated agrarian region, coupled with the preponderance of male migrants fresh from the countryside, created industrial centers in the Donbass–Dnepr Bend that in many ways resembled the wild frontier towns of the nineteenth-century American West.

3

Working-Class Daily Life

> The Russian mine worker leads a generally drunken life, wallowing in filth. . . . The mine owner cannot change such a way of life as the worker leads—it is beyond his powers.
>
> (*Director of the Bogodukhov-Kalmius mine*)

> Anyone who knows the present life of miners and factory workers in the Donets Basin . . . will understand the hatred and bitterness that has been amassed in the chests of this 160,000 man army and all those irrepressible waves of riots that have rolled over the mining and metallurgical regions of the South.
>
> (*1903 report of the SD's Donets Union*)

THE DONBASS–DNEPR BEND labor movement reflected the everyday experiences of working-class life, both on and off the job, in factory cities and mine settlements. Donbass–Dnepr Bend industrial cities and towns had "a kind of rough-and-ready, boom-town atmosphere which had no parallel anywhere else in the empire."[1] Workers worked and lived in a world from which alcohol, gambling, prostitutes, and fighting provided the main escapes. In the rest of the country, most skilled workers, including those who recognized that change was impossible without class solidarity, felt contempt for the mass of workers, whom they considered uncouth and rowdy slackers. But in the Donbass–Dnepr Bend, it was difficult even for literate, skilled workers to, in the words of Tim McDaniel, "measure up to the conscious workers' new conception of the dignity of the working class."[2] Uplifting cultural or educational alternatives to the taverns were in short supply in the region's steel towns and pit villages. When labor unrest erupted in riots and pogroms, many in the Donbass–Dnepr Bend, including revolutionaries, were inclined to blame the degrading character of Donbass–Dnepr Bend industrial life and workers' ignorance and dissoluteness.

[1] Rieber, *Merchants and Entrepreneurs*, p. 222.

[2] *Autocracy, Capitalism, and Revolution*, p. 206.

The large concentrations of workers in isolated places where they constituted the largest social group fostered well-founded fears in government circles that if unrest erupted, it could quickly escalate to uncontrollable dimensions. Few cities anywhere in Russia matched the concentrated industrial character of towns and cities in the Donbass–Dnepr Bend. In Donets Basin mining settlements, three-fourths of the inhabitants worked in the mines in 1905. More than half the households in the steel towns of Iuzovka and Lugansk had at least one member employed in heavy industry.[3] In these cities and towns, most of the residents not employed in the factories or mines made a living catering in some way to working-class needs and tastes. The mostly Jewish shopkeepers, pawnbrokers, and owners and employees of taverns all served a predominantly working-class clientele.[4] In these cities, innumerable taverns and liquor stores sought to meet workers' prodigious demand for cheap alcohol. Less conspicuously, many residents illegally sold liquor out their door. And since most workers were single, or separated from the wives left behind in the village, prostitution thrived in the boomtowns. A landlord could transform his building into a brothel with a small investment paid under the table to the police, who were more than willing to supplement their meager salaries with such bribes.

As the earlier discussion of the haphazard growth of industrial towns in the Donbass–Dnepr Bend might have suggested, the governmental system in tsarist Russia was poorly equipped to moderate the political, social, and economic strains resulting from rapid industrialization and urbanization. Local government was little developed. City governments generally lacked the funds necessary to provide many of the most basic services because the central government restricted their power to tax property. Within this national context, a legal quirk left many industrial cities and settlements in the Donbass–Dnepr Bend even further disadvantaged. The autocracy failed to grant most of the new factory and mining centers in the Donbass–Dnepr Bend, despite populations in the tens of thousands, the legal status of a city, depriving them of the right to elect a city council, a *duma*.[5] The

[3] Rashin, *Formirovanie*, p. 511; Nikolaenko, *Revoliutsionnoe dvizhenie*, p. 3; Zaitsev, "Bol'sheviki Iuzovki," p. 156.

[4] *British Documents on Foreign Affairs: Reports and Papers from the Foreign Office*, part 1, series A, vol. 2, *Russia, 1881–1905*, ed. Domenic Lieven (Frederick, Md., 1982), p. 1.

[5] Iuzovka, for example, despite a population of over forty thousand in 1905, was not recognized as a city until the 1917 Revolution. Robert Lewis and Richard Rowland have noted that in the 1897 census, "thirty-five predominately mining and manufacturing centers with populations between 15,000 and 41,000 were not included in the urban population," while "very small *uezd* centers, which were little more than agricultural villages, were considered urban" (Robert A. Lewis and Richard Rowland, "Urbanization in Russia and the U.S.S.R., 1897–1966," *Annals of the Association of American Geographers* 59 [December 1969]: 778;

central government entrusted bureaucrats appointed by the governor with the governance of these towns.[6] Even many of these bureaucrats acknowledged in departmental reports that the failure to respond to major demographic changes meant that in boomtowns many of the most basic public services often were lacking or grossly neglected.[7]

Donbass–Dnepr Bend factory districts, including Ekaterinoslav's, lacked even the most elementary sanitary facilities—running water and a sewerage system.[8] For their water, most residents of industrial districts were forced to rely on wells, reservoirs, or rivers, which were often contaminated by industrial waste.[9] Cats, rats, and mice were fished out of the reservoirs and other drinking-water sources that served some working-class districts.[10] A good share of the uneducated migrant workers were not equipped to protect their health in such unsanitary conditions. Accustomed to village life, they did not heed warnings to boil water. Many persisted in going to the river to quench their thirst, as they had in their home villages. In addition to the poor water supply, in working-class districts densely filled with shanties, the only latrines were cesspools or outhouses. The workers themselves often had to build their own latrines; they commonly lacked doors, and by all appearances they were never cleaned.[11] The outhouses built by Donbass–Dnepr Bend mines to serve their worker barracks almost universally struck investigators as disgusting. To minimize sanitary problems, the mines located outhouses fifty to eighty steps from the barracks. Many workers responded by choosing not to make the trip. Excrement commonly littered the grounds. Conditions were not much cleaner indoors, where garbage could be seen lying everywhere.[12]

Given the combination of overcrowded housing and bad sanitation, along with diets barely adequate nutritionally and workers' debilitatingly

---

Roger L. Thiede, "Industry and Urbanization in New Russia from 1860 to 1910," in Hamm, *The City in Russian History*, pp. 125–126).

[6] In reality, company managers generally dominated company towns.

[7] TsGIA, f. 1282, 1901, op. 3, d. 463 (*Izvlechenie iz vsepoddanneishego otcheta za 1900 g. o sostoianii Ekaterinoslavskoi gubernii*), p. 5; Michael F. Hamm, "The Breakdown of Urban Modernization: A Prelude to the Revolutions of 1917," in Hamm, *The City in Russian History*, p. 196.

[8] Ekaterinoslav's city duma, which was the Donbass–Dnepr Bend's biggest and best-funded city government, was able to make a serious effort to meet the rapidly growing demand for city services. Ekaterinoslav was able to increase its budget as the city grew during the last half of the nineteenth century, from 95,000 rubles in 1870 to 1,028,500 rubles in 1905. But even in Ekaterinoslav, the city administration provided only a minimum of public sanitation and safety services.

[9] Tatarskii, "Otchet ob epidemii," p. 381; *Pridneprovskii krai*, March 28, 1900, p. 3.

[10] See, for example, the report regarding the reservoir that served the Mariia coal mine's settlement (*Syn otechestva*, October 29, 1905, p. 5).

[11] Cheremukhin, "Kak zhivut," p. 2; Fenin, "Neskol'ko slov," p. 26.

[12] Vartminskii, "K voprosu o zhilishchnykh usloviiakh," p. 504.

heavy labor, it should not be surprising to find that Donbass–Dnepr Bend working-class districts were disease-ridden. One contemporary study compared the prevalence of disease among peasants and miners in Ekaterinoslav province in 1908: "No one would argue that peasants live in good conditions . . . and peasants have a much larger percentage of people more susceptible to illness (children, the elderly, women) than miners, who consist largely of adult males. Yet figures show that illness among miners (leaving aside accidents) was two to three times higher than among peasants."[13] Typhus and cholera epidemics repeatedly swept through Donbass–Dnepr Bend working-class populations. When such an epidemic struck, the authorities, who had done so little to prevent these disasters, often responded in a manner that aggravated working-class anxieties and animosities.

The classic example of local-government mismanagement in the face of a health crisis occurred in Iuzovka during the 1892–93 cholera epidemic. When cholera—"the disease of the poor and hungry, the ignorant and superstitious, the symbol of backwardness"[14]—struck hundreds of the city's workers after first appearing in the neighboring mines, police and Cossacks quickly cordoned off Iuzovka's factory districts. This measure greatly agitated the miners, who, in addition to seeing fellow workers inexplicably stricken with the fatal scourge, were thereby deprived of access to the only major marketplaces in the area and cut off from friends who lived in the city. Within Iuzovka itself, workers grew increasingly agitated. In addition to the quarantine, the police, on orders from the local authorities, hastily began to demolish the unsanitary outhouses, confiscated the possessions of cholera victims and disinfected their residences, and prohibited the sale of any vegetables or fruits. All these preventive measures were implemented in a high-handed manner: the police failed to explain to the fearful workers why such measures were necessary. Making matters worse, unfounded rumors quickly spread through the working-class population. It was rumored, for example, that the cost of the temporary cholera barracks and special teahouses (*chainye*) being constructed would be deducted from workers' wages. Doctors were said to be treating cholera victims inhumanely. Because the anxiety and provocation resulting from the epidemic was coupled with workers' general discontent with their working and living conditions, the sending of a worker's sick wife to a cholera barracks against her will proved to be all that was necessary to touch off one of the major labor disturbances in Russia in the 1890s, the 1892 Iuzovka "cholera *bunt*."[15]

[13] P. Pokrovskii, "Kak zhivet donetskii shakhter," *Russkoe bogatstvo*, no. 12 (1913): 255.

[14] Nancy Mandelker Frieden, *Russian Physicians in an Era of Reform and Revolution, 1856–1905* (Princeton, 1981), p. 143.

[15] Potolov, *Rabochie Donbassa*, pp. 211–212; T. Kharechko, "Sotsial-demokraticheskii soiuz gornozavodskikh rabochikh (iz istorii revoliutsionnogo dvizheniia v Donbasse)," *Leto-*

Police departments in the Donbass–Dnepr Bend also failed to keep pace with the region's rapid development—at least until around the turn of the century, when pleas from industrialists and a sharp upsurge in the number and scope of labor disturbances in the Donbass–Dnepr Bend pushed the central government to enlarge police staffs in industrial areas. It was largely at industrialists' expense that the government began to increase police forces to levels commensurate with the region's rapid industrialization and urbanization, although the size of police forces varied from city to city.[16] When public services were increased in the Donbass–Dnepr Bend—and this was also true with regard to schools and medical care—the factories and mines either largely paid the bill or directly provided the service themselves.

Whatever the size of police forces in Donbass–Dnepr Bend cities, the quality of individual policemen was woefully low. As elsewhere in Russia, the police were not known for their professionalism or incorruptibility.[17] Donbass–Dnepr Bend police forces employed illiterates, offered little training, and suffered turnover rates rivaling those in the industrial labor force. Low pay and low status were primarily responsible for the low caliber of police recruits. On average, policemen earned even less than workers in the Donbass–Dnepr Bend, although the police received considerable income under the table. Still, on the eve of the 1905 Revolution, the gov-

---

pis' revoliutsii, no. 3 (1925): 10. The problem with the authorities' response to the cholera epidemic in Iuzovka was more a matter of implementation than methods. Containment of a cholera epidemic among the little-educated masses required compulsion. Workers distrusted and often hated doctors, seeing them as "part of the educated, privileged, and hostile establishment" (Friedgut, "Labor Violence," p. 251). Some sense of the obstacles facing authorities in their efforts to protect workers can be gleaned from a doctor's experience at the Rutchenkovka mine: "I often arrived at the residence of a cholera patient to see a gathering of his neighbors and acquaintances. This habit is difficult to eradicate because of the extreme ignorance of the worker masses at the mine. Typically, all reasoning regarding the danger of contamination met the argument that 'everything occurs according to God's will' " (Boikov, *Otchet o kholernoi epidemii*, p. 422).

[16] Factory and mine funds supported 524 of the 763 urban police officers serving in Ekaterinoslav province in 1901. In two industrial cities lacking official city status, Kamenskoe and Iuzovka, public services were particularly inadequate; yet the police forces had been so beefed up by the end of the century that the policeman-to-resident ratio exceeded the relatively high ratio in the capital city of Ekaterinoslav. In contrast, in Ekaterinoslav's working-class suburbs of Amur and Nizhnedneprovsk, there was only one policeman for every 1,252 residents; and in the factory city of Lugansk, the ratio was one policeman per 1,007 residents (Tsentral'nyi statisticheskii komitet Ministerstva vnutrennikh del, *Goroda Rossii*, pp. 196–197; Parasun'ko, *Polozhenie i bor'ba*, p. 525). Neil Weissman concluded that "shortfalls in police complements were a particular problem in the many new industrial centers" (Neil Weissman, "Regular Police in Tsarist Russia, 1900–1914," *Russian Review* 44, no. 1 [1985]: 46).

[17] Richard G. Robbins, *The Tsar's Viceroys: Russian Provincial Governors in the Last Years of the Empire* (Ithaca, N.Y., 1987), pp. 184–185; Weissman, "Regular Police."

ernor of Ekaterinoslav reported that police wages in the province created "a dangerous situation."[18]

The inadequacy of the Donbass–Dnepr Bend police was particularly felt in the poor and industrial districts. Despite paying the greater part of the cost for their city's police force, the large Donbass–Dnepr Bend companies did not consider relying solely on city police. These factories and mines had their own private security guards for protection. In Iuzovka, the New Russia Company employed a police force larger than that of the city itself—sixty-five guards at an annual cost of forty thousand rubles, compared to the sixty-four police on the city's payroll. It is not surprising to find that according to a government report, a factory in a Donbass–Dnepr Bend steel town normally was well policed, while in the streets just outside the factory gates, all sorts of thieves and "expropriators" reigned supreme.[19]

To police Donbass–Dnepr Bend streets was not easy. The continual influx of young peasants and transients into the industrial boomtowns created enormous problems that were even further aggravated during those occasional years when the opportunity for work slackened or contracted. Even though Donbass–Dnepr Bend industry generally suffered from a shortage of workers, the labor market did fluctuate. It was not always a seller's market.[20] During economic downturns, most of those thrown out of work returned to their native villages. In 1901, when the number of unemployed quickly reached 10,000, the government established special low railroad fares to help facilitate unemployed workers' immediate return to the countryside.[21] Many, however, stayed to join the increasingly large number of vagrants and thieves congregating in Donbass–Dnepr Bend industrial cities.

Raggedly clothed tramps became a fixture of Donbass–Dnepr Bend street life. In response, city governments tried to facilitate philanthropic endeavors by the local elite, including industrialists. By the late 1890s, in

[18] TsGIA, f. 1284, d. 111, p. 2. Throughout the period covered by this study, Donbass–Dnepr Bend police forces proved hopelessly inadequate in the face of any sizable disorder. To restore order, the governor repeatedly needed to call in troops.

[19] TsGAOR, DP 00, 4-e d-vo, f. 102, 1907, op. 116, d. 18, ch. 9 (*Po Ekaterinoslavskoi gub. obshchestvennoe nastroenie*), pp. 18, 113.

[20] A weak southern harvest was the usual reason for the temporary downturns in job opportunities in Donbass–Dnepr Bend industry. Southern agriculture and industry drew largely from the same pool for their unskilled labor. A poor harvest meant the number of laborers willing to work in industry during those summers increased. These seasonal fluctuations, though, were just brief deviations from the general sharp rise in the number of jobs created in the Donbass–Dnepr Bend from the 1870s to 1900. It was only during the years 1901 to 1903, when international economic conditions caused the mining and metallurgical industries to go from boom to bust, that workers' marketability underwent a dramatic turnabout.

[21] Peter I. Liashchenko, *History of the National Economy of Russia to 1917*, trans. L. M. Herman (New York, 1949), p. 656.

Ekaterinoslav at least, charity for the needy was thriving. Shelters, flophouses, and medical clinics, as well as inexpensive cafeterias, soup kitchens, and teahouses, received funding. Three kopecks bought a place for an indigent to spend the night with a roof overhead and a hot meal during the day.[22] Two soup kitchens in Ekaterinoslav served almost five hundred meals a day.[23] But these philanthropic efforts were never sufficient to meet the need. During the economic nosedive in the first years of the twentieth century, the number of poor and unemployed living on the streets of Donbass–Dnepr Bend cities mushroomed, and the programs designed to ameliorate the situation could not keep pace.[24]

The rapid growth of industrial towns in the Donbass–Dnepr Bend signified opportunity and attracted not just those in search of work, but all sorts of people, including adventurers and criminals. In addition, around the turn of the century, newspapers noted a sharp upsurge in the number of teenagers living on the streets. They survived through petty theft, prostitution, and begging. According to newspaper accounts, on Donbass–Dnepr Bend city streets any passerby at all well-dressed was sure to be approached by "ragamuffins" begging or soliciting. [25] Ekaterinoslav police arrested as many as twenty a day of these children of the streets.[26] The importunity and cavalier style of the girls especially was scandalous enough to be newsworthy. Readers of the Ekaterinoslav newspaper *Pridneprovskii krai* could find on January 15, 1900 a reporter's account of being besieged by seventeen different illicit requests and proposals during his evening stroll the day before. The article's tone was one of both outrage and exasperated helplessness. It ended, "Can nothing really be done to free our boulevards of this ulcer?"[27]

While workers generally left their families behind in the village, many did raise children in the Donbass–Dnepr Bend's rough working-class districts, often with unfortunate results. Before they were old enough to work, most such children spent their days left to their own devices. Along with children of the non-working-class poor, workers' children often

[22] A. E. Vartminskii, "Ob epidemii sypnogo i vozvratnogo tifov v g. Mariupole," *Vrachebno-sanitarnaia khronika Ekaterinoslavskoi gubernii*, no. 9 (September 1909): 352; *Ekaterinoslavskii listok*, May 4, 1904, p. 3.

[23] Naviazhskii, "V ozhidanii kholery," p. 172.

[24] TsGIA, f. 1263, op. 2, d. 5724 (*Izvlechenie iz vsepoddanneishego otcheta za 1892 g. o sostoianii Ekaterinoslavskoi gubernii*), pp. 84–86.

[25] *Donetskoe slovo*, July 9, 1906, p. 4.

[26] *Pridneprovskii krai*, January 22, 1900, p. 3.

[27] P. 3. Like the other social consequences of rapid industrialization and urbanization, such developments were hardly unique to the Donbass–Dnepr Bend. For a discussion of the "new crime" of hooliganism that focuses on St. Petersburg, see Joan Neuberger, "Crime and Culture."

joined the runaways living on the streets in petty theft, prostitution, and begging.[28]

The newspapers and local social critics placed much of the blame for juvenile delinquency on the government's feeble commitment to lower-class education. The Ekaterinoslav newspaper *Vestnik Iuga* argued dramatically that the absence of even a single school in the industrial suburb of Amur had dire consequences for the whole society and not just for the children deprived of an education:

> The majority of them degenerate into that sort of person it has become customary to call "hooligan." Already from the age of seven they begin stealing, often using violence. They become more and more embittered and, by the time they are fifteen, their experiences have produced glaring examples of that type of Black Hundred with a rich reserve of hatred toward all that is honest . . . bands of children aged seven to twelve have become notorious as the most awful cutthroats.[29]

The number of public schools in Donbass–Dnepr Bend cities proved far from sufficient to meet the growing mass demand (much of the middle class and the rich could, of course, afford private schools and tutors).[30] As in other matters, Ekaterinoslav was in a better financial position to support mass education than other industrial cities in the Donbass–Dnepr Bend. Even so, Ekaterinoslav, the city to which workers were most inclined to bring their families, could as late as 1905 muster only enough funding to operate twenty public schools, and these were often little more than one-room primary schools.[31]

Factories, along with churches, could not provide enough schools in the industrial towns of the Donbass–Dnepr Bend to take the place of an adequate public-school system. Factories made an effort, though, as they were required to do by the factory legislation of June 12, 1884.[32] By the first years of the twentieth century, schools existed at twenty-seven of the thirty-one largest mines and at fifteen of the region's twenty-two steel mills.[33] The total number of schools is misleading, however—at least from

[28] *Pridneprovskii krai*, January 22, 1900, p. 3.

[29] August 5, 1905, p. 3.

[30] Working-class districts and towns fell outside the purview of the zemstvos. Even though in Donbass–Dnepr Bend mining districts mines provided 40 to 50 percent of zemstvo funding, their workers did not benefit from the zemstvos' educational efforts (*Gorno-zavodskii listok*, October 16, 1904, p. 7249).

[31] *Pridneprovskii krai* reported that "only two of the schools have good, suitable rooms" (July 15, 1905, p. 3).

[32] Griffin, "Formative Years," p. 646.

[33] TsGIA, f. 37, op. 58, d. 299 (*Dnevnik komissii A. A. Shtofa*), p. 90; TsGAOR, f. 7952, op. 6, d. 86, p. 108; I. S. Rozental', "Dukhovnye zaprosy rabochikh Rossii posle revoliutsii 1905–1907 gg.," *Istoricheskie zapiski* 10 (1982): 73; Avdakov, "O merakh," p. 18.

the workers' perspective. Factory primary schools were often opened to meet the needs of a factory's foreign community, rather than those of its Russian workers. For example, the New Russia Company was considered by many to be a model firm in regard to education, but only one of the company's two primary schools in Iuzovka was truly open to the children of workers. The other one catered to the foreign population and conducted classes only in English. For a worker's child to attend one of the secondary schools that a few factories provided required an extraordinary commitment from the parents. Whereas company primary education was usually free or required nominal tuition, the tuition for secondary grades could equal an entire month's income for a steelworker. When the future Soviet leader Leonid Brezhnev attended the Southern Russia Company's *gimnaziia* in Kamenskoe, he was the only worker's son in his class of forty students.[34]

Donbass–Dnepr Bend workers who were determined to broaden their own horizons would have been hard-pressed to do so through legal channels. But for some workers, Sunday schools and night classes filled this gap.[35] As with other schools, the best place to be was Ekaterinoslav, where opportunities to learn exceeded those in other Donbass–Dnepr Bend industrial cities. In the smaller industrial towns, there was "almost no one willing to work in the area of enlightening the worker masses."[36]

Ekaterinoslav was one of only thirteen cities in Russia where philanthropic liberals, wishing to raise the "moral and intellectual level" of workers, established Sunday schools for adult workers in the early 1890s. As the local newspaper recognized, with the city's transformation from an insignificant small town to an industrial center "the character of the population changed significantly. Out of the earlier, formless and identical mass of poor emerged the 'worker,' in the contemporary sense of the word, complicating our lives and putting us face to face with the serious questions of life."[37] The sponsors and teachers of the Sunday school demonstrated considerable dedication toward their goal of bringing basic educational skills to the working classes. Their achievement was, nonetheless, quite limited in scope. Ekaterinoslav's Sunday school enrolled no more than one hundred workers in its separate courses for men and women, a much smaller number than the programs in the capitals and some of the other participating cities in Russia. Also, judging from who enrolled in the courses, this educational opportunity did not appeal to the mass of workers. Eka-

[34] TsGIA, f. 37, op. 58, d. 299 (*Dnevnik komissii A. A. Shtofa*), p. 96; John Dornberg, *Brezhnev: The Masks of Power* (New York, 1974), p. 43.

[35] Radical study groups, *kruzhki*, will be discussed in chapter 5.

[36] *Vestnik Iuga*, September 23, 1905, p. 4.

[37] *Pridneprovskii krai*, January 15, 1905, p. 2.

terinoslav's Sunday school students were drawn from among the city's skilled workers, artisans, and domestic servants.[38]

In 1905 local chapters of the Imperial Russian Technical Society began to offer night classes for workers in such Donbass–Dnepr Bend cities as Ekaterinoslav, Kamenskoe, and Iuzovka. For fifty kopecks a year, workers could attend two-hour classes that met four to six days a week. Courses were taught at six different levels in subjects ranging from reading and arithmetic for illiterate workers to physics, algebra, and literature for the most educated among them. Hundreds of students enrolled, but the revolutionary events of 1905 hurt daily attendance in the course's first year. When Kamenskoe was placed under martial law, attendance dwindled; workers were afraid they would be beaten by Cossacks if they were still on the street after 9 P.M.[39]

The government and the social elite in Donbass–Dnepr Bend cities and towns did not provide the financial support necessary for the establishment of a symphony, ballet, or other forms of high culture. Workers, of course, had never been exposed to the arts and would have had little interest in attending, even assuming they could have afforded the price of admission. But it was not just the more elite forms of culture that were lacking. Outside Ekaterinoslav, Donbass–Dnepr Bend cities did not even have daily newspapers.

The Donbass–Dnepr Bend did not offer much of what is thought to be wholesome "low" culture, either. Ekaterinoslav and the other steel cities and towns lacked the organized sports and plebeian entertainment already existing in similar cities outside Russia. In Pittsburgh, for example, steelworkers in the late nineteenth century commonly spent their leisure time participating in competitive sports such as bowling, baseball, and rowing. Workers packed the numerous halls that presented variety shows. Later, in the early twentieth century, Pittsburgh's workers attended professional baseball games and boxing matches.[40]

Whatever the larger industrial enterprises provided in the way of cultural opportunities was usually all that was available to Donbass–Dnepr Bend workers. As in the case of schools, Donbass–Dnepr Bend enterprises made various attempts to compensate for the absence of cultural or recreational programs for workers. Around the turn of the century, many companies started to spend the money necessary to offer workers what they considered to be uplifting alternatives to the ways in which workers usually spent

[38] Ia. V. Abramov, *Nashi voskresnye shkoly* (St. Petersburg, 1900), p. 246; *Pridneprovskii krai*, January 15, 1905, p. 2.

[39] *Zapiski Ekaterinoslavskogo otdeleniia Imperatorskogo russkogo tekhnicheskogo obshchestva*, no. 6–8 (1906): 1–12.

[40] Francis G. Couvares, *The Remaking of Pittsburgh: Class and Culture in an Industrializing City, 1877–1919* (Albany, N.Y., 1984), pp. 39–45, 120–124.

their free time. The Briansk factory in Ekaterinoslav was one of two mills in the region to build its own auditorium. But though the sign above the entrance proclaimed "The Workers' Auditorium," in practice it was primarily utilized by the administrative staff—at least until revolutionary groups and workers repeatedly seized the auditorium for themselves in 1905. Even so, the factory sponsored light-minded plays on the Briansk auditorium stage in which workers often performed alongside their superiors within the enterprise. These performances were much better attended by workers than other cultural programs, with audiences often reaching six to seven hundred in number. Twice a week, Briansk workers could enjoy music in the auditorium, or, if the weather was good, in the square outside. At these events, the factory administration sold pamphlets produced by literacy societies at an 80 percent discount. At such bargain prices, workers reportedly gobbled up these brochures "as if they were blintzes."[41]

Ten of the twenty-two large steel mills had opened libraries or reading rooms by 1913. For the mass of workers, the absence of a factory library meant that in addition to not having much to read, they had precious few places to sit in relative peace and quiet. As we have seen, most workers lived in crowded, noisy conditions, whether in private or factory housing. Company barracks were inexpensive or free, but for a worker interested in reading, they were a continual cause of frustration. Most unskilled workers, particularly the miners, could not spend their leisure time reading, even if they wanted to. Whereas 60 percent of Donbass–Dnepr Bend metallurgical workers were literate, according to the 1897 census, only 31 percent of miners were.[42] Of those who could read, few did.[43] Most observers of the miners would agree with the impression recorded by A. Shestakov, a Social Democratic organizer active in the Donets Basin in the first years of the twentieth century: "Donbass miners never read. They live to work and get drunk."[44]

As meager as the cultural offerings in most factory towns were, the situation was much worse at the isolated mining settlements dotting the Donets Basin. This is not to say that some mine operators did not make an effort to provide, at their own expense, leisure-time alternatives to drinking. If none of the mines built auditoriums, by the 1890s most of the larger

[41] TsGAOR, f. 7952, op. 6, d. 86 (*Izdatel'stvo "Istorii fabrik i zavodov"*), p. 109; *Pridneprovskii krai*, January 4, 1900, p. 3. One study of the budgets of 38 percent of the metallurgical workers at the Hartmann plant in Lugansk revealed that these relatively well paid workers spent six rubles annually on books and performances (V. Ovsiannikov, "Dovoennye biudzhety russkikh rabochikh, *Voprosy truda*, no. 10 [1925]: 61, cited in Rozental', "Dukhovnye zaprosy," p. 74).

[42] Potolov, *Rabochie Donbassa*, p. 133.

[43] Lisser, "Gornorabochie," pp. 759–760.

[44] A. Shestakov, "Na zare rabochego dvizheniia v Donbasse," *Proletarskaia revoliutsiia*, no. 1 (1921), p. 160.

enterprises did make some genteel recreation possible. Most provided large recreation rooms and some regular entertainment. After the turn of the century, many mines began to hold Sunday and holiday readings.[45] Some even managed to present plays or readings on a monthly basis, which attracted the whole community—although only those who were sober and had washed at the baths were permitted entrance.[46]

Going for a stroll was a favorite leisure activity in the larger Donbass–Dnepr Bend cities, as in all of urban Russia. In Ekaterinoslav, representatives of all social strata thronged Potemkin park in the center of town, where one could promenade to military music performed by a brass band. Fashionable society had not been scared away, thanks largely to the fee that served to limit the numbers admitted from the lower classes.[47] The scene was more raucous when the park built in the Briansk factory administration's residential colony was open to workers. The Briansk park opened its gates to workers just two days a week, and then only to those willing to pay a nominal fee. Until forced to leave at 2 A.M., most workers strolled, drank furtively, and rested on the park's benches. Others contributed to the racket that filled the air by beating bass drums or playing skittles and other games.[48]

Heavy drinking played a central role in Donbass–Dnepr Bend working-class life and generally provided the escape workers sought. It was also commonly thought to be the vice that underlay all of the workers' other vices. Most outside observers sounded patronizing, if generally sympathetic, when they discussed the cause of workers' drunkenness. Doctor N. Putiagin stated in his report to the 1908–9 congress of Don oblast doctors: "These unskilled people are the most ignorant workers in the world. Children of the dark village, mentally and morally wretched and generally helpless, they have fallen into what is for them an unaccustomed life and work situation. In response they become still more helpless, losing the ground under their feet. Degenerating morally and physically, a significant percentage of these workers become alcoholics."[49] Temperance societies, such as the two established at the turn of the century in Ekaterinoslav and Lugansk to check working-class alcoholism, were of little consequence.[50]

[45] Lisser, "Gornorabochie," p. 759; TsGIA, f. 37, op. 58, d. 299 (*Dnevnik komissii A. A. Shtofa*), p. 108.

[46] *Gorno-zavodskii listok*, June 3, 1906, p. 8537.

[47] Mashukov, *Vospominaniia*, p. 49.

[48] *Vestnik Iuga*, August 13, 1905, p. 3.

[49] Quoted in Kim Zelenskii, *Shakhtinskie gorniaki na putiakh k bol'shevizmu v 1905–1908 godakh* (Rostov-on-Don), p. 15. Government investigators could adopt a similarly patronizing, yet sympathetic, tone. See, for example, TsGAOR, DP OO, f. 102, 1907, d. 18, ch. 2, p. 138.

[50] Priimenko, *Legal'nye organizatsii*, p. 118.

Donbass–Dnepr Bend workers were, of course, hardly alone in their enthusiasm for drink. Russian men of all classes enjoyed a reputation as hard drinkers.[51] But while there is little hard evidence on which to base comparison, investigators and commentators usually were of the opinion that even within this national and class context of immoderate imbibing, Donbass–Dnepr Bend workers drank much more than their share.[52] Miners became widely renowned for their prodigious drinking habits. Especially on those Sundays that coincided with payday or were part of an extended holiday, workers traditionally abandoned themselves to a style of drinking that rarely stopped before stupor.

Any day off was the occasion for such a drinking binge that weekends and holidays were popularly known as "drunk days" (*p'ianye dni*).[53] There were more such days off than one might think. In the Donbass–Dnepr Bend, as in Russia generally, workers in theory worked a six-day week. In reality, the metallurgical workers and miners at best averaged a five-day workweek.[54] The large number of national and local religious holidays Donbass–Dnepr Bend industry felt compelled to observe, combined with the government-mandated half day on Saturdays, was not the only reason steelworkers and miners did not actually work the six-day week.[55] An inordinate amount of worker absenteeism following holidays—primarily due to continued heavy drinking or the need to sleep off their sprees—helped further whittle down the length of the average workweek.[56]

Rare indeed was the young worker who did not start seriously drinking immediately upon leaving work at two o'clock Saturday afternoon. Often, that meant workers started drinking while still on the street. Here and there in the dusty side alleys of the factory and mining towns, small clusters of workers could be seen huddled around a bottle. As today, the style in Russia was not to sip. One drank to get drunk. Workers passed around and

[51] For a discussion of Russian patterns of food and alcohol consumption, see R. E. F. Smith and David Christian, *Bread and Salt: A Social and Economic History of Food and Drink in Russia* (Cambridge, England, 1984).

[52] See, for example, Statisticheskii otdel Ekaterinoslavskogo gubernskogo zemstva, *Sbornik statisticheskikh svedenii po Ekaterinoslavskoi gubernii*, vol. 2, *Bakhmutskii uezd* (Ekaterinoslav, 1886), p. 322; and Lisser, "Gornorabochie," p. 759.

[53] *Sbornik po Ekaterinoslavskoi*, p. 323.

[54] N. S. Avdakov, *Doklad komissii po voprosu ob uluchshenii byta rabochikh na kamennougol'nykh kopiakh Iuzhnoi Rossii* (Khar'kov, 1900), p. 9; Seryi, *Rabochie*, p. 192. An 1884 zemstvo study found that Donets Basin miners who were employed year-round worked between 215 and 240 days a year. Sixteen years later, in 1900, an industry commission found that Donets Basin miners still worked only 250 days a year (Kir'ianov, *Zhiznennyi uroven'*, pp. 78–79).

[55] Taskin, *K voprosu o privlechenii*, p. 11.

[56] Many of those workers who did come to work following "drunk days" were suffering from such frightful hangovers that they risked injuring themselves and others, did little real work, and might as well have stayed away.

quickly downed a bottle—usually some variety or other of cheap alcohol, typically vodka low in quality but potent.[57]

Workers leaving work hardly needed to drink on the street. Taverns started opening for business near a new Donbass–Dnepr Bend industrial enterprise the day the first construction workers were hired. Taverns became so widespread in working-class districts that they could be found almost anywhere a worker's daily routine might take him. Steelworkers in Kamenskoe had a choice of sixteen different taverns within just fifty meters of the plant gate.[58] Bars and liquor stores practically abutted some workers' barracks. In the opinion of an 1894 industry commission that addressed the question of regulating the sale of vodka in mining districts, the close proximity of taverns to workers made worker drunkenness a foregone conclusion: "Since the underground labor of coal miners is such heavy, difficult work, they need to relax after work even more than other workers . . . if on the way to relaxation stand *kabaki*, with their doors always cordially open—the path to rest is direct."[59] Management could do little to restrict the accessibility of alcohol. Many mine operators even lacked the power to keep bars and liquor stores off the mine's property because the land was rented.[60] In addition, liquor sales were an important source of government revenue, making fiscal considerations a major obstacle to meaningful reform.[61] But the mining companies' failure to close nearby taverns was probably of much less consequence than the industrialists believed. The central government's decision in the 1890s to restrict the retail sale of alcohol to state stores and the few successful attempts by firms to restrict the number of places selling alcohol only seemed to increase the amount sold under the counter.[62]

[57] *Doklad komissii XVIII s"ezda gornopromyshlennikov Iuga Rossii* (Khar'kov, 1894), p. 332.

[58] Parasun'ko, *Polozhenie i bor'ba*, pp. 123, 383.

[59] Avdakov, "O merakh," p. 333.

[60] These mines had signed long-term contracts—thirty-six-year leases—in which their authority above ground often was circumscribed by their lessor's desire for additional income (ibid., pp. 332–333).

[61] In 1892, when doctors and mine inspectors demanded that taverns be closed after the cholera epidemic struck the Donbass–Dnepr Bend, the minister of finance, Sergei Witte, strongly objected and underscored the losses to the treasury if drinking establishments in Ekaterinoslav province were closed (Parasun'ko, *Polozhenie i bor'ba*, p. 383). When Witte introduced the reform designed to establish a total state monopoly of the liquor trade two years later, he sanctimoniously declared, "The reform must be directed, first of all towards increasing popular sobriety, and only then can it concern itself with the interests of the treasury" (Smith and Christian, *Bread and Salt*, pp. 313–315).

[62] The Ekaterinoslav governor's own report conceded that the reform failed to inhibit illegal sales of vodka and beer "in restaurants, cafés, teahouses, shops, secret dens of depravity [*pritonye razvraty*], and even private homes" (TsGIA, f. 1282, 1901, op. 3, d. 463 [*Izvlechenie iz vsepoddanneishego otcheta za 1900 g. o sostoianii Ekaterinoslavskoi gubernii*], p. 13; N. N. Shipov, *Alkogolizm i revoliutsiia* [St. Petersburg, 1908], p. 61).

Taverns offered workers a social environment all their own. Especially for workers living in company barracks, taverns served as informal social centers, the one place beyond the meddling of the bosses—the "colony people" (although company barracks had their full share of "drunkenness, fights, and even killings").[63] Spending free time in bleak barracks not surprisingly had little appeal compared to the conviviality, music, women, and gambling taverns could offer. Not that miners' and steelworkers' taverns were anything fancy; they were dirty and greasy, often a simple shack. Sex between the workers and the women they met in the taverns added venereal disease to the list of scourges of Donbass–Dnepr Bend working-class life. A few of the better taverns, however, boasted bright wallpaper and even tables covered with white tablecloths (at least when they first opened for the day). Skilled steelworkers often not only washed off the grime of the mills, but even changed into whatever was the current fashion of proletarian dandies before setting off for the taverns. In worker memoirs, the image of a worker in a tavern singing drinking ditties or tearful songs lamenting life's injustices to the accompaniment of an accordion, harmonica, balalaika, or guitar, in a room full of workers all drinking and singing along, provides a cherished (if romanticized) picture of Donbass–Dnepr Bend working-class camaraderie.[64]

Almost the entire working class participated in the weekend and holiday carousing, from highly skilled, highly paid lathe operators earning two to three hundred rubles a month to miners and unskilled steelworkers earning one-tenth as much.[65] In pit villages such as Gorlovka, "from the moment wages were paid Saturday until Monday evening the taverns there swarmed with workers."[66] At some mines, mass drunkenness continued on such a scale following a payday that large-scale absenteeism would force a mine to close down for two, three, or even four days. During these binges, some workers were sure to drink themselves into a state of delirium tremens. Some workers had histories of almost never making it to work on Mondays. In pursuit of oblivion, workers often squandered their entire pay, earned through such backbreaking and dangerous labor, or even went into debt to the tavern. A government report noted that of the 350,000

[63] Zaks, "Trud i byt," p. 93. The labor shortage in the Donbass–Dnepr Bend no doubt largely explains why industrialists there made little effort to enforce rules—unlike employers in Moscow, where workers were commonly fined for "drinking, loud talking, card playing, and singing" in company barracks, or even for failing "to keep their beds clean and tidy" (Johnson, *Peasant and Proletarian*, p. 85).

[64] A. N. Shcherban' and A. A. Rutenko, *Stranitsy letopisi donetskoi* (Kiev, 1963), p. 36; Zaks, "Trud i byt," p. 94; P. Kharlamov, *Rozhdenie zavoda (Probnaia glava iz istorii Dnepropetrovskogo metallurgicheskogo zavoda im. Petrovskogo)* (Khar'kov, 1934), p. 9.

[65] Shestakov, "Na zare," p. 157.

[66] Gessen, *Istoriia gornorabochikh*, p. 92.

rubles one Donbass–Dnepr Bend steel mill paid out to its workers every two weeks, 150,000 rubles were spent on alcohol.[67]

Up to a point, workers' squandering of their pay on alcohol may have served Donbass–Dnepr Bend industrialists' interests by limiting turnover somewhat, since most workers intended to return to their home villages only after they had saved some cash. On the other hand, all the industrialists complained about their workers' drinking and the resulting absenteeism, on-the-job accidents, and low output. In the words of one mine director, the mass drunkenness following paydays was "the scourge of mine life."[68] Management argued that in addition to the availability of alcohol in the Donbass–Dnepr Bend, the high pay scale was largely responsible for fostering worker drunkenness. The annual reports of the Association of Southern Coal and Steel Producers contained statements such as the following: "Nothing is more dangerous than to give the mass of the common people so much money. They can spare almost half of what they earn, which hardly induces them to treat their wages judiciously."[69] The church chimed in. The pastor of the Preobrazhenskii Church in Iuzovka deplored how "good pay gave the worker the opportunity to satisfy every desire, and speculators of every sort served up the means of pandering to the lowest tendencies of the worker, who, even without this, did not have the most honorable code."[70]

Other than illegally keeping paydays infrequent, management usually felt it had no alternative besides fines to combat absenteeism on Mondays or other days following holidays and paydays, since the labor shortage dis-

[67] Avdakov, "O merakh," p. 333; Fenin, *Vospominaniia*, p. 53; *Sbornik po Ekaterinoslavskoi*, pp. 322–323; Nikolaenko, *Revoliutsionnoe dvizhenie*, p. 53; TsGIA, f. 23, op. 30, d. 47 (*Izvlechenie iz vsepoddanneishego otcheta za 1898 g. o sostoianii Ekaterinoslavskoi gubernii*), p. 149; Kharlamov, *Rozhdenie zavoda*, p. 9; Fenin, "Neskol'ko slov," p. 33; Lisser, *Gornorabochie*, p. 759; TsGAOR, DP OO, 4-e d-vo, f. 102, 1907, op. 116, d. 18, ch. 9 (*Po Ekaterinoslavskoi gub. obshchestvennoe nastroenie*), pp. 15–16.

[68] Fenin, *Vospominaniia*, p. 53.

[69] Fenin, "Neskol'ko slov," p. 34. Because payday lent itself to the greatest excesses, many enterprises petitioned the government to allow them to pay workers either indirectly or less frequently. The government denied such requests (Rubin, *Rabochii vopros*, pp. 21–22). Mines already had a reputation for cheating workers out of what they owed them. A few mines and mills nonetheless managed to disregard the law and give workers only a portion of their monthly wage. The rest of their monthly earnings were either sent home then or held by the enterprise until the semiannual holidays—Easter in the spring and the autumn saint's day *Pokrov den'*—when the work force customarily turned over and workers returned to their village homes. According to mine administrator Fenin, "this illegal action was the most effective measure in the struggle against drunkenness; however, it did give the management a lot of extra trouble" (*Vospominaniia*, p. 53). Of course, infrequent paydays also allowed many companies to increase their profits, since this practice commonly forced workers to buy on credit at the overpriced company stores.

[70] Quoted in Friedgut, *Iuzovka and Revolution*, pp. 71–72.

couraged firing workers. Given that mine jobs were so often plentiful, a partial explanation for the absentee problem may be that miners were collectively flaunting their power over their employers in one area where they could do so.[71] Foremen fined workers for unexcused absences at some risk to themselves. For example, on February 6, 1903, when a Briansk factory foreman refused to excuse Vasilii Vologuchev after the still-drunk worker finally appeared at work following a three-day absence, the worker went after him with a knife. The foreman escaped with his life only because the cigarette case in his pocket deflected the blow from his heart.[72] Fining workers put not only the individual foreman at risk. Paydays could be especially explosive when workers saw how much had been deducted from their pay. During work stoppages, striking workers typically demanded the elimination of fines.

The medical investigator I. L. Lisser stated that iron miners in the Krivoi Rog generally did not drink during the week, but this was not the consensus.[73] In fact, Lisser probably would have been hard-pressed to find anyone else familiar with Donbass–Dnepr Bend working-class drinking habits to agree with him. Most sources report that Donbass–Dnepr Bend workers not only drank during the week, but also often disregarded company rules and drank on the job. The skilled steelworker Kostia Norinskii remembered that during water breaks, workers, especially blast-furnace workers, quenched their thirst surreptitiously with vodka, which was always hidden somewhere near the water bucket.[74] Many workers justified on-the-job drinking with the belief that alcohol helped to counter the effects of laboring in cold or wet conditions, as in the damp underground mines.[75] Drinking in the mines was, of course, hardly healthful, since it contributed to the extraordinarily high accident rate. Doctor Putiagin not only stated that workers drank on the job, but claimed that if workers were not drinking during work shifts, it was only because they were using work as a time to sober up.[76] What is indisputable is that come the weekend or a holiday, workers loved nothing more than to gather together to drink. It was no coincidence that the most riotous labor disturbances usually began on weekends or holidays.

What workers did not spend on alcohol might be lost in gambling.

[71] The high rates of absenteeism in the Donbass–Dnepr Bend can also be attributed simply to the difficulty peasant recruits experienced in adjusting to industrial labor, the benefits of *zemliachestvo* notwithstanding. Absenteeism is common internationally during the initial stages of industrialization.

[72] *Ekaterinoslavskii listok*, May 13, 1904, p. 3.

[73] Lisser, *Gornorabochie*, p. 759.

[74] K. M. Norinskii, "Na svoikh khlebakh," *Istoriia ekaterinoslavskoi*, p. 38.

[75] I. Kuznetsov, "Rabochii klass i alkogol'naia problema," *Gornorabochii*, no. 7–8 (1922): 43.

[76] Zelenskii, *Shakhtinskie gorniaki*, p. 15.

Workers' card games lasted into the small hours of the morning. They played for serious stakes and could be "cleaned out down to their last dime." Of course, by the same token, some workers picked up extra cash. Every so often, a worker was said to have returned to his village to buy land after hitting a jackpot.[77] The winning and losing, however, were not necessarily kept within the family, so to speak. Even within the barracks, outsiders joined workers' card games. Usually these outsiders consisted of young peasants from neighboring villages. However, cardsharps clandestinely working in tandem also descended on workers' payday card games. These hustlers considered workers simpletons, easy prey. And indeed, workers were no match for such professionals. It was not unheard of for a cardsharp to walk away from a factory or mine with a haul of thousands of rubles.[78]

A small minority of workers looked with disdain upon all this carousing. Some of these workers joined the revolutionary movement. In his memoirs, A. I. Smirnov, a Briansk factory worker active in the embryonic social-democratic movement during the 1890s, did not credit hatred of the autocracy, poor working and living conditions, or a reading of Marx for pushing him to become involved in the radical movement, but rather a revulsion toward working-class alcoholism. In an emotional account that has the overtones of a religious conversion, Smirnov recalled a crucial juncture in his and another seventeen-year-old Briansk factory worker's path toward becoming Social Democrats:

> Our fathers worked together in the rail-rolling shop at the Briansk factory. One night around midnight, the two of us arrived simultaneously at the "Krasnoe selo," a tavern in the factory quarter in which our fathers' artel chose to squander their wages. We had both come to retrieve our fathers. But all our requests to leave were met with slaps. We could not simply leave because we knew when we arrived home we would be told to return for our fathers. So we just stood on the street near the tavern and waited for our fathers to leave. They drank and ate for a long while, which gave us time to do a great deal of thinking and to ask ourselves why workers needed to get drunk and who profited from it. We decided then and there to devote ourselves to struggling for these wretched, ignorant, oppressed people who were destroying their health in factories and taverns. From this memorable night, we began to look for people who could show us the true path, who could show us how to unite all workers.[79]

[77] Algasov and Pakentreiger, *Brianskie razboiniki*, p. 15. Such stories may well have been legends.

[78] Ibid.

[79] A. I. Smirnov, "Vospominanie o 1-om kruzhke s.-d. rabochei partii g. Ekaterinoslava v 1894 g.," *Istoriia ekaterinoslavskoi*, p. 12.

Not only did many of the workers drawn to the revolutionary movement look with disdain upon the drinking of their fellow workers, they often refrained from smoking and swearing and were expected to stop visiting prostitutes. There was pressure not to marry, since revolutionaries argued from experience that family commitments impeded revolutionary activism. The single-mindedness and asceticism for which radical workers strove, as well as their sexism, is conveyed by an incident the radical worker Ivan Babushkin included in his memoirs. Babushkin rejected two women's request to join his social-democratic reading circle after asking himself, "Would the presence of attractive members of the opposite sex not have a retarding effect on our studies?"[80]

Just how prevalent Donbass–Dnepr Bend workers' penchant for carousing was may be judged by the following: It was suspect for a group of workers to ever get together and not drink, gamble, and generally make a racket. A. Maleev, a Donbass–Dnepr Bend social-democratic organizer, remembered that a radical worker *kruzhok*, or circle, meeting in a worker's apartment was sure to attract dangerous attention if curious eavesdroppers did not see alcohol and cards on the table. To deflect suspicion, Maleev's kruzhok established a rule that: at every meeting there should be a quart of vodka, some bottles of beer, and an accordion on the table.[81]

Such appearances of alcohol at kruzhok meetings were not always for show. While the most politically committed workers in the Donbass–Dnepr Bend often shared with radical students puritanical ideas, the less-committed workers within the movement showed no interest in abandoning customary ways. Babushkin recalled how in his Ekaterinoslav circle workers might be attentive for a couple of hours, but then "the listeners began to falter, asking me to excuse them, but they'd like to have a drink! Of course, most of them were fathers of families, or old enough to be, and I knew quite well that before I met them they spent most of their time in a saloon. And so I had to work with men who were a bit weak in the knees."[82] The much-traveled activist L. Shklovskii was surprised to learn when he arrived in Lugansk in 1905 that "carousing was not considered reprehensible by members of the organization"; that at social-democratic gatherings in which workers predominated, there was no shortage of alcohol.[83] Many Donbass–Dnepr Bend activists shared the experience of a

[80] I. V. Babushkin, *Recollections of Ivan Vasilyevich Babushkin, 1893–1900* (Moscow, 1957), p. 76.

[81] A. Maleev, "Aleksandrovskaia organizatsiia RSDRP v 1900–1905 gg.," in *Na barrikadakh: 1905 god v Aleksandrovske*, ed. M. L'vovskii (Zaporozhe, 1925), p. 5.

[82] *Recollections*, p. 138.

[83] L. Shklovskii, "Vospominaniia o 1905 gode," *Proletarskaia revoliutsiia*, no. 48 (1926): 196.

Jewish activist in Minsk, who drank to win the confidence of the Christian workers he sought to radicalize. "I had to drink along with them, otherwise I would not have been a 'good brother.' I hoped that by becoming their 'good brother' I would be able to make them class conscious. In the end neither of us achieved anything. They could not make me a drunkard, and I could not make them class conscious."[84]

Daily life was violent in the rapidly growing Donbass–Dnepr Bend cities and towns. Hostile relations between working-class barracks, streets, and neighborhoods, sometimes a result of different ethnic or regional compositions, created sharply defined and forcibly defended territories.[85] Strangers entering a neighborhood ran a risk of being assaulted and robbed by young neighborhood toughs. In addition to those with a despised ethnic or regional background, outsiders carrying the markings of the privileged and educated classes—including those who thought of themselves as fighters for the workers' cause—were subject to threatening taunts and merciless mockery, if not blows and knifings, by working-class toughs. Workers may not have been prime targets, but they, too, were subjected to assaults and muggings, especially on paydays and holidays. The mostly working-class residents in the district neighboring the Briansk factory in Ekaterinoslav complained continually of the street theft perpetrated by small gangs. Typically, four to five "drunk idlers" (in the words of a newspaper report) would gather on a street during the evening and simply knock passersby off their feet before robbing them.[86] One former resident of Lugansk remembered that gangs commonly beat their victims so badly that "for the next two weeks they were ashamed to show their faces at the factory."[87] If the toughs occasionally allowed their cornered prey to escape unharmed, it was rarely without first forcing them to grovel.

Nights, not surprisingly, were particularly dangerous in Donbass–Dnepr Bend cities and towns. Whatever order the police maintained during the day literally disappeared with nightfall, when police vacated their street posts. Already by the 1880s, working-class toughs controlled the streets in industrial towns after dark. They robbed people at knifepoint, or even gunpoint. The Lugansk gendarme officer reported in 1886 that "policemen fear going about at nighttime because of conflicts with wandering groups of young workers who go about the streets for some reason always

[84] Sholem Levin, *Untererdishe Kemfer* (New York, 1946), p. 151, quoted in Mendelsohn, *Class Struggle*, p. 33.

[85] Voroshilov, *Rasskazy o zhizni*, p. 122.

[86] *Pridneprovskii krai*, October 6, 1901, p. 2.

[87] Nikolaenko, *Revoliutsionnoe dvizhenie*, p. 7.

armed with revolvers and fire on police patrols."[88] Residents thought many workers appeared to enjoy terrorizing passersby just for the amusement. Even those closely acquainted with workers shared this view. From 1898 to 1905, I. Polonskii was a social-democratic activist in Ekaterinoslav. To illustrate the "low level of consciousness" he confronted when trying to organize workers, Polonskii wrote in his memoirs that "for entertainment, factory youths very often engaged in street violence. Even workers were afraid to walk many working-class city streets at night because they feared attack by dangerous 'pranksters' [*ozorniki*]."[89] Isolated comments in Ivan Babushkin's memoirs speak to the crime problem in Ekaterinoslav at night, when there was not "a soul about" and it was not safe to be on the streets.[90] Babushkin remembered the danger he felt whenever he returned to Ekaterinoslav after staying until midnight or thereabouts in the industrial suburbs. As crime reports in the daily press made clear, the area around the bridge across the Dnepr, which separated the city from its industrial suburbs of Amur and Nizhnedneprovsk, was a favorite spot from which to mug passersby.[91] Babushkin recalled, "I would set off for home, escorted by a number of the boys, to a place near the Dnepr, where there was a steep bank; from here I went on alone towards the river, shivering in the sharp, piercing wind and frost, holding a sharp dagger in my hand because it was dangerous in these parts, as I had found out once for myself when I was robbed of money and other belongings."[92]

Besides individual thugs and numerous petty gangs, gangs of professional thieves menaced Donbass–Dnepr Bend cities and mining settlements.[93] Iuzovka was the home of two large gangs led by the Cossack atamans Malakhov and Sibiriako. Attacks perpetrated by these toughs were particularly vicious and often left their victims dead. Gang murders went unpunished in the majority of cases. Because the victims were largely migrant workers, far from their families, there was no one to press the case on their behalf. Even if the police apprehended a suspect, a bribe of twenty-five to fifty rubles was reputedly sufficient to set the killer free.[94]

Fighting and violence were so prevalent in the Donbass–Dnepr Bend that street fights figure prominently in accounts written by visiting authors

[88] TsGAOR, f. 102, 1887, d. 9, ch. 21, p. 43, quoted in Brower, "Labor Violence," p. 427. That workers were armed with revolvers as early as 1886 is surprising.

[89] I. B. Polonskii, "Iz zhizni partiinoi organizatsii (1898–1900 gg.)," *Istoriia ekaterinoslavskoi*, p. 139.

[90] *Recollections*, p. 113. Babushkin, perhaps the most famous prerevolutionary organizer of worker rather than intellectual origin, was active in Ekaterinoslav during the late 1890s.

[91] *Ekaterinoslavskii listok*, May 4, 1904, p. 3.

[92] *Recollections*, p. 111.

[93] Mine safes were a favorite target for night raids by gangs, which could consist of wildly shouting and shooting gypsies (Fenin, *Vospominaniia*, p. 88).

[94] Zaitsev, "Bol'sheviki Iuzovki," p. 156.

trying to give their readers a general sense of industrial cities there. The 1898 inaugural issue of a new Ekaterinoslav city publication, *Ekaterinoslavskii kalendar'*, which might have been expected to put the city's best foot forward, featured in its main article a vicious, bloody street fight. The author of the article was presented to the reader as an anonymous foreign visitor who had spent one week the previous summer in an unidentified Donbass–Dnepr Bend city, apparently Ekaterinoslav. He recounted a beating he had witnessed during his stay there and tried to convey the impression that such scenes were nothing out of the ordinary:

> Returning to my hotel, I witnessed . . . a melee on Cossack Street. The uproar, complete with the yelling and weeping of women and children, was the picture of a pogrom. I asked what was happening and was told, "Drunks are going at each other." I saw a crowd of twenty to thirty people pummeling one man in broad daylight. It was impossible for the victim to defend himself. . . . Those involved in the fighting were workers. A gang of urchins accompanied these workers when they decided to make their triumphant departure. The victim of their violence was disfigured. All sorts of cuts and bruises were visible through what remained of his clothing. When this idler stood, . . . half his face was covered with blood. His arms dangled like whips. . . . Not seeing any police, I wondered—in what sort of place am I?[95]

Indeed, in what sort of place was he? Another answer is provided by the writer Konstantin Paustovsky, who briefly worked in the New Russia Company mill. In his capsule portrait of Iuzovka, Paustovsky included the following scene:

> As soon as two women had grabbed each other's hair with animal shrieks, a crowd would form around them and the fight would be turned into a gambling game: bets of two kopecks were placed on which one would win. Old drunkards of the neighborhood were always the bankers. They would hold the money in a torn cap. The women were deliberately provoked to this fighting. Sometimes a fight would spread to include a whole street. Shirt-sleeved men would join in, using brass knuckles and lead-tipped whips, and cartilages would crack and blood would flow. Then a patrol of Cossacks would ride up at a trot from *Novyi Svet*, where the administration of the mines and factories lived, and disperse the crowd with knouts.[96]

Workers themselves shared this picture of Donbass–Dnepr Bend streets. Polonskii noted in his memoirs that factory youths often fought on the streets just for the excitement of it.[97]

[95] "Rotozei, ekskursiia znatnogo inostrantsa v malovazhnyi russkii tsentr," in *Ekaterinoslavskii kalendar'—al'manakh na 1898 god* (Ekaterinoslav, 1897), p. 59.

[96] *Story of a Life*, p. 430.

[97] Polonskii, "Iz zhizni," p. 139; see also Brower, "Labor Violence."

Newspaper and memoir accounts of Donbass–Dnepr Bend working-class cities and mining settlements paint a picture of a violent, lawless scene. The statistical evidence supports these accounts, but the statistics themselves present problems in analysis. Evidence from the justice of the peace court—the *mirovoi sud*, in which cases of muggings, public drunkenness, and brawling were heard—is unavailable. Judicial statistics from the circuit court—the *okruzhnyi sud*, which tried more serious cases of assault, robbery, and murder—were published but are also problematical. Circuit-court statistics for convictions and acquittals include whole provinces, making analysis of industrial centers and comparisons with other urban centers difficult. However, these crime statistics merit a brief examination.

The court records indicate that Ekaterinoslav province's rate of violent crime was indeed high. During the years 1898 to 1906, the province had the second-highest number of convictions for murder (committed without any mitigating circumstances), assault, and murder resulting from the use of excessive force in fights (see table 3). The rate for these crimes was higher only in St. Petersburg province; and in the case of rape, Ekaterinoslav exceeded even St. Petersburg. This is remarkable, considering that the level of urbanization in Ekaterinoslav province was far lower than in St. Petersburg.[98] The statistics suggest that the level of violence in the industrial cities of the Donbass–Dnepr Bend exceeded that in the central Russian industrial provinces of Moscow and Vladimir. Poltava, the least industrialized and urbanized of the five provinces examined, had a much lower level of violent crime.[99]

Popular violence was deeply ingrained in Russian lower-class culture. Street fights provided a favorite pastime and emotional outlet for the working class in the Donbass–Dnepr Bend. Of course, fighting has played this role to varying degrees almost everywhere workers have lived in similar conditions; furthermore, it was not a strictly working-class phenomenon. Daniel Brower has suggested, however, that Russia possessed an extraordinary tradition of working-class violence.[100] Unfortunately, the fragmentary and impressionistic nature of the evidence to which Brower refers, as well as of that presented here, makes it difficult to assess the level of violence in the Donbass–Dnepr Bend in comparison with other Russian

[98] The cities of St. Petersburg and Moscow accounted for 60 and 42 percent of the population in their respective provinces in 1897. Only 12 percent of Ekaterinoslav province's population was urban (Thomas Stanley Fedor, *Patterns of Urban Growth in the Russian Empire during the Nineteenth Century* [Chicago, 1975], pp. 186–187).

[99] For perspective, the absolute population figures from the 1897 census for these five provinces are as follows: Poltava, 2,778,151; Moscow, 2,430,581; Ekaterinoslav, 2,113,674; St. Petersburg, 2,112,033; and Vladimir, 1,515,691.

[100] "Labor Violence," pp. 417–453.

TABLE 3
Provincial Crime Rates, 1898–1906

Category and Province	*Number of Convictions*	*Percentage of Total Convictions for Category*	*Ranking per Capita*
Murder			
St. Petersburg	353	32.6	1
Moscow	187	17.3	4
Ekaterinoslav	243	22.5	2
Vladimir	149	13.8	3
Poltava	150	13.9	5
Serious Assault			
St. Petersburg	1,192	30.6	1
Moscow	682	17.5	4
Ekaterinoslav	752	19.3	2
Vladimir	531	13.6	3
Poltava	743	19.0	5
Rape			
St. Petersburg	73	27.7	2
Moscow	37	14.1	4
Ekaterinoslav	77	29.3	1
Vladimir	45	17.1	3
Poltava	31	11.8	5
Murder Resulting from Fights			
St. Petersburg	548	33.1	1
Moscow	335	20.3	4
Ekaterinoslav	449	27.1	2
Vladimir	209	12.6	3
Poltava	113	06.8	5

Source: Data for this table are derived from *Svod statisticheskikh svedenii opodsudimykh, opravdannykh, i osuzhdennykh* (St. Petersburg, 1898–1906).

working-class regions. There is no question, however, that Donbass–Dnepr Bend workers partook of this national tradition with gusto. This is supported by statistical evidence for the number of convictions for murders committed during fights. The number of defendants convicted of murder for using egregious force in fights (force considered unjustifiable on the grounds of self-defense) was extremely high in Ekaterinoslav province.

On paydays or holidays, Donbass–Dnepr Bend workers not only drank to great excess, but also became extremely rowdy. Newspapers regularly reported on drunken brawls in taverns, barracks, or wherever workers gathered to celebrate their days off. Such brawls often spilled out onto the streets and resulted in serious injury, sometimes even growing into riots and looting.[101] When Soviet historians in the early 1950s interviewed old Donbass–Dnepr Bend workers about their prerevolutionary life, many recalled that "there were fights all the time."[102] In working-class parishes, even church services were not immune from an occasional fistfight.[103] An aside by a journalist covering the Donbass–Dnepr Bend labor movement in 1906 reveals just how expected it was that workers would fight during holidays. During the holidays that coincided with May Day that year, strikes and other labor disturbances were anticipated. When the day passed rather uneventfully, a newspaper report on the labor scene in Grushevka remarked that "the holidays passed peacefully, if one does not count the usual fights and other holiday amusements of the drunken crowd."[104] The miner T. Kalashnikov recalled that during his days at the Briansk mine, "payday never passed without fights, which often ended in death. These fights would break out between lone individuals, artels, and even barracks. Such brawls resulted in broken windows, frames, and doors, injuries, and even death. Those guilty had to work off the damages."[105]

A promised fight was much anticipated. Workers engaged in the least-serious fights simply for "pleasure." These fights had more in common with boxing matches than mass brawls. Fighters simply rolled up their sleeves and went at each other, flailing away until one side was hurt badly enough to concede defeat. Workers considered such fights great entertainment. A well-placed blow elicited laughter and cheers from the onlookers. As in the case cited above, bets were placed on who would win. Spectators often expressed strong loyalties for one side or the other, in which case they were referred to as "patriots." They egged on their fellows until, in the case of a mass fight, they themselves joined in the fighting.[106]

In the absence of company-organized sports, payday and holiday fighting often took the form of particularly brutal, ritualized brawls. The workers' bigger, more-organized mass fights or brawls were called "wars." Only recently have Western historians discussed such "wars," which had long been a part of Donbass–Dnepr Bend working-class life and lower-class culture elsewhere in the empire.[107] The Donbass–Dnepr Bend workers who became Social Democrats and who were in a position to have their mem-

[101] *Vestnik Iuga*, September 4, 1905, p. 5; Avdakov, "O merakh," p. 332; *Iuzhnaia zaria*, August 15, 1906, p. 3.

[102] Zaks, "Trud i byt," p. 94.

[103] Nikolaenko, *Revoliutsionnoe dvizhenie*, p. 8.

[104] *Gorno-zavodskii listok*, April 29, 1906, p. 8487.

[105] Kirzner, *Gornorabochie*, p. 16.

[106] Kharlamov, *Rozhdenie zavoda*, p. 9.

[107] See Brower, "Labor Violence"; and Neuberger, "Crime and Culture," chap. 2.

oirs published (in the 1920s, following the Bolshevik Revolution) were reluctant to discuss the frequent and bloody working-class brawls. Kliment Voroshilov did so only after stating that "the truth is the truth" and conceding that workers were "still far-from-conscious fighters for proletarian solidarity."[108] One early Soviet historian of the Donbass–Dnepr Bend labor movement, I. Nikolaenko, like Voroshilov worked in Lugansk in his youth. Later he remembered trying to ascertain the origin of workers' love for fighting there. He had asked some old-timers when and how such battles had got their start. All they knew was that the "wars" were already a fixture in working-class life when they were young. Nikolaenko noted that just thinking about the "wars" clearly brought back fond memories and excited these old workers: "It was obvious from their faces that they burned with a desire to take part once again."[109]

One of the many everyday scuffles that broke out between young workers during the course of any week might be sufficient to touch off a weekend "war." In such instances, the weekday fight concluded with a pact to return en masse to battle on Sunday at some named hill or ravine outside town. During winter, a frozen river was the more appropriate arena for a brawl. In a "war," two opposing "walls" formed. The number of workers participating in these organized brawls could be staggeringly high, as those of "a quite venerable age" joined youths in one of the "walls."[110] The total number of fighters often reached a thousand or more. Rules for these "wars" existed; they were not supposed to be free-for-alls. For example, it was against the rules to use anything but one's fists, or to strike an opponent once he was down. But if the two sides became agitated, as was usual, the fighters quickly abandoned any pretense of observing rules.

A short description of a typical "war" makes it obvious how participants might become agitated. At first the two sides lined up opposite one another, content to stand and hurl insults across a neutral zone. The actual "war" usually began when one of the younger workers, a teenager, threw a rock at the opposing side. This elicited a like response, and before long rivets and nuts as well as rocks were flying back and forth. Inevitably, someone received a serious head wound. Just as predictably, tempers then flared and both sides charged the middle with what appeared to be a wild disregard for the risks. In the hand-to-hand combat that followed, if the sense of grievance or hatred was strong, one could expect to see chains and knives. Such fighting often ended in serious wounds and fatalities.[111]

[108] *Rasskazy o zhizni*, pp. 121–122.

[109] *Revoliutsionnoe dvizhenie*, p. 7.

[110] Voroshilov, *Rasskazy o zhizni*, p. 121.

[111] V. M. Stanislavskii, "K voprosu o sanitarnykh usloviiakh zhilishch gornorabochikh Donetskogo raiona," *Vrachebno-sanitarnaia khronika Ekaterinoslavskoi gubernii*, no. 10 (October

The Donbass–Dnepr Bend "wars" often pitted mine against neighboring mine or factory against factory.[112] In these instances, fighting might be seen as helping to cement bonds within an enterprise. But these were not the only divisions within the working class that determined who fought whom in "wars." Whatever the pretext or reason for a particular "war," be it a petty scuffle or a long-planned confrontation, working-class fighting often expressed ethnic and regional animosities. The "wars," as well as the smaller brawls, usually pitted *zemliaki* (workers from the same province or region) against workers from another province—the workers from Tula, for example, against those from Smolensk. As has been noted, this sort of clannishness provided the mass of workers in the Donbass–Dnepr Bend with their primary social identity and support. "Wars" sometimes pitted one worker barrack against another. This, too, often reflected *zemliak* allegiances, since Donbass–Dnepr Bend barracks commonly were segregated along ethnic and regional lines. Serious fights also tended to pit the major ethnic groups against one another. In these battles, groups of migrant Great Russian workers might unite to fight against fellow workers who were Tatars or Ukrainians, or against the neighboring Ukrainian peasants. According to Nikolaenko (no doubt guilty here of Ukrainian chauvinism), during holidays in Lugansk, in the fights held near the Hartmann factory, four or five Ukrainian city toughs could get the better of up to twenty-five Russians.[113] In brawls, and in other contexts, ethnic and regional animosities split the Donbass–Dnepr Bend working class asunder.[114] Brawls were just one of the many forms in which this disunity surfaced.

The authorities responded quite casually to the brawls, preoccupied as they were with protecting property and maintaining order in the city centers. Typically, the police showed no interest in stopping workers' "wars" and did not intervene until battles were on the wane. If the mounted police happened to gallop up when one or the other side of combatants had yet to gain the upper hand, they would stop and try to bide their time if the fighting was still fierce. Even so, the police sometimes misjudged when it was safe to make a move toward dispersing the crowd and perhaps securing a handful of arrests. The police then got caught in the middle and often were forced into an embarrassing retreat. The police were as impotent in

1909): 470; Nikolaenko, *Revoliutsionnoe dvizhenie*, pp. 6–7; Kharlamov, *Rozhdenie zavoda*, p. 9; Voroshilov, *Rasskazy o zhizni*, p. 121.

[112] Zaks, "Trud i byt," p. 94.

[113] *Revoliutsionnoe dvizhenie*, pp. 6–7, 12.

[114] Kirzner, *Gornorabochie*, p. 16; Zaitsev, "Bol'sheviki Iuzovki," p. 156; Lisser, "Gornorabochie," p. 749; Kharlamov, *Rozhdenie zavoda*, p. 9; TsGAOR, DP OO, f. 102, d. 4, ch. 18, l. A (*Volneniiakh i stachkakh sredi rabochikh v Ekaterinoslavskoi gubernii*, gendarme report, April 27, 1899), pp. 15–17.

quelling the politically nonthreatening violence of large-scale working-class fighting as they proved to be when it came to controlling factory rioting or pogroms.[115]

By the turn of the twentieth century, the days when Donbass–Dnepr Bend cities and towns could all be described as sleepy backwaters were long gone. The industrial boom brought a rough new world in its wake, and the Donbass–Dnepr Bend became notorious for its squalid, menacing working-class settlements. Peasant migrants arriving to work in the region's relatively well paying mining and metallurgical enterprises entered burgeoning cities and company towns suffering from overcrowding, inadequate public services, and rampant crime. The grave social problems racking Donbass–Dnepr Bend industrial centers often were a focus of concern on the part of the local authorities and social elite; but, not surprisingly, tsarist Russia proved unequal to the task of alleviating the strains resulting from rapid industrialization and urbanization, leaving workers' health and welfare at serious risk. The time spent brawling and "in a drunken stupor, with stinking, infected whores" (as one writer delicately put it),[116] only further increased the sickness and death Donbass–Dnepr Bend miners and steelworkers already suffered from bad drinking water; woefully inadequate toilet and sewage facilities; filthy, parasite-infested, and crammed housing; and the most dangerous jobs in industry. Private educational and cultural programs enjoyed some support, but the earnest efforts to "civilize" the new mass of workers had little impact. Workers continued to seek escape from their heavy lot in drunkenness, prostitutes, gambling, and fighting. And as we will now see, their discontent with conditions in the Donbass–Dnepr Bend boiled over into collective forms of mass unrest as well. To his colleagues at the ministry of internal affairs, finance minister Sergei Witte's greatest economic success—the development of the Donbass–Dnepr Bend—presented an equally great source of trouble.

[115] Nikolaenko, *Revoliutsionnoe dvizhenie*, p. 7.

[116] P. Surozhskii, "Krai uglia i zheleza," *Sovremennik*, no. 4 (1913): 308, quoted in W. Bruce Lincoln, *Passage through Armageddon: The Russians in War and Revolution, 1914–1918* (New York, 1986), p. 223.

Part Two

THE LABOR AND REVOLUTIONARY MOVEMENTS

4

Late-Nineteenth-Century Unrest

> All of cultured society has experienced the moral and material harm caused by mass *temnota* [benighted ignorance]. From time to time because of the *temnota* of the bottom strata of the worker population, the city is hit with ghastly Jewish pogroms, plagues such as cholera, and other disorders.
>
> (*Ekaterinoslav Commission for Popular Readings*)

UNTIL THE first years of the twentieth century, workers in the Donbass–Dnepr Bend, like workers throughout the Russian empire, offered little encouragement to those who sought to base a revolution on the discontent of a class-conscious proletariat. During the late nineteenth century, the labor movement in the Donbass–Dnepr Bend—as throughout Russia—exhibited few signs that the rise of a coordinated mass movement might be imminent, even though many revolutionary activists worked hard to mine the rich veins of worker discontent. In the decades preceding the 1903 general strike and the 1905 Revolution, workers in the Donbass–Dnepr Bend, as elsewhere in Russia, displayed their capacity for collective action only on rare occasions. When unrest did occur, it was exceptionally explosive and violent.

During the initial stages of the Donbass–Dnepr Bend boom, most workers appeared to have resigned themselves to enduring the hardships without protest. While boisterous among themselves, workers generally appeared docile and deferential before their bosses, behavior characteristic of the Russian peasantry. Their employers, like the nobility back in the countryside, expected as much. For a worker to smoke a cigarette or fail to remove his hat in the presence of an administrator was viewed as insolent insubordination.[1] As late as the mid-1890s, most "conscious" workers considered the prospects for organizing their fellow workers into a unified, powerful force to be all but hopeless. One such activist, Georgii Petrovskii, later recalled how workers were so embroiled in an "animalistic struggle

[1] Fenin, *Vospominaniia*, p. 53.

for survival" that they "almost entirely lacked solidarity and cohesion in the struggle against oppression at the factory."[2] Of course, workers lacked any legal means to seek redress. The tsarist government denied Russian workers the safety valves widely available to workers in the West: the right to organize into trade unions and bargain collectively with their employers. The tsarist government viewed any strike as a revolutionary act. Russians who walked off the job to rectify some wrong or to improve wages were engaged in a serious matter. Not only did workers lose wages and risk being fired, strikes invited the possibility of prison.[3] Local governmental authorities did not hesitate to call in troops to end "the disorders" and arrest ringleaders.

Uncommitted to a permanent life in the mines or mills and intent on accumulating some money quickly, the mass of migrants generally did not find appeals to strike attractive. Workers most commonly expressed their discontent by simply quitting their jobs individually and either moving to another job or returning to their home village. Although laboring in mines and mills produced some worker solidarity, high turnover, coupled with the subdivision of workers into separate mine chambers and factory departments and into separate ethno-regional groups, made it extremely difficult for workers at a mine or mill to organize a strike committee that could set a date, draw up demands, and mobilize the support of the company's labor force, all the while escaping management's notice. It was no easier for members of the revolutionary underground. Migrants brought to Donbass–Dnepr Bend industry peasants' traditional distrust of "outsiders."[4]

One should also keep in mind that, hard as life was in the mills and mines, most workers compared it to life in the poverty-stricken Russian countryside. Those recruited into the Donbass–Dnepr Bend labor force had long been inured to physical hardships and privations. Yet, at the same time, the generally fatalistic and submissive Russian peasantry was famous for occasionally resolving en masse to endure no more. Violence then erupted and swept across the countryside, with peasants sacking noble estates and raping and killing their inhabitants. Those recruited to work in Donbass–Dnepr Bend industry brought this tradition of rebellion with them to the mines and mills, along with their outward obsequiousness.

[2] G. I. Petrovskii, "S 1893 g. po 1905 g.," *Istoriia ekaterinoslavskoi*, p. 49.

[3] Workers convicted of instigating a strike that resulted in property damage and included threats against unwilling workers faced jail sentences of eight to sixteen months (Ascher, *Revolution of 1905*, p. 22; Gaston V. Rimlinger, "The Management of Labor Protest in Tsarist Russia, 1870–1905," *International Review of Social History* 5 [1960]: 226–248).

[4] In the countryside, peasants distrusted everyone outside their own commune, beginning with peasants in the neighboring village (Robert Edelman, *Proletarian Peasants: The Revolution of 1905 in Russia's Southwest* [Ithaca, N.Y., 1987]).

The threat of labor violence hung over the Donbass–Dnepr Bend throughout the period covered in this study. As we will see, when migrant workers considered risking illegal action, rioting was often the favored form of action.

Donbass–Dnepr Bend labor unrest did slowly take root soon after the first large, foreign-owned coal mine opened. From 1873 until the last years of the century, the number and size of disturbances and work stoppages grew with the development of heavy industry. During the 1870s and 1880s, growing labor discontent in the region was mainly confined to isolated disturbances in mining settlements. In the 1890s, when the metallurgical as well as the mining industries grew so dramatically, Donbass–Dnepr Bend workers increasingly began to shake off their docility. As steelworkers became active, the pace of outbreaks of worker unrest quickened. Most major instances of labor unrest in the region during the last decades of the nineteenth century occurred at the Briansk steel mill in Ekaterinoslav or at the mines and mills owned by the New Russia Company in Iuzovka. In addition, Donbass–Dnepr Bend artisans increasingly organized strikes "over narrow, everyday needs and interests." As the veteran Ekaterinoslav Social Democrat I. Kh. Lalaiants recalled, Jewish artisans proved more receptive to revolutionary agitators. "So far as such strikes ended successfully, they aroused others to follow suit."[5] However, the small number of workers involved even in the larger artisanal strikes and the fact that these strikers were artisans and generally Jewish led revolutionaries to place little stock in such strikes as the foundation for a larger revolutionary movement.

To understand working-class consciousness in the Donbass–Dnepr Bend, it is important to examine how the mass of miners and steelworkers expressed their discontent. Historians of other Russian regions have emphasized the nonviolent character of Russian labor unrest during the late nineteenth century.[6] In the Donbass–Dnepr Bend, while labor unrest usually consisted of brief, nonviolent work stoppages, destructive riots also were common. Workers' readiness to resort to violence proved to be the feature that most distinguished the labor movement in the Donbass–Dnepr Bend during the late nineteenth century. On a number of occasions, particularly in the 1890s, workers expressed their discontent in enormous outbursts of violent, destructive rioting. Spontaneously, without any preliminary discussion or clear leadership, workers en masse broke windows, destroyed machines, looted shops, and assaulted any factory foremen,

[5] Lalaiants, "O moikh vstrechakh," p. 60. Because artisanal employees recognized that their employers could not significantly raise wages and remain in business, given the uncompetitiveness of most artisanal workshops with factory production, artisans focused their efforts on reducing the length of their workday rather than on increasing wages.

[6] See, for example, Johnson, *Peasant and Proletarian*.

guards, and managers or any neighboring Jews they could get their hands on. The growth of the socialist movement during the 1880s and 1890s (which is examined in the next chapter) failed to produce a "conscious" labor movement during the late nineteenth century. The industrial boom meant that the few "acclimatized workers" were swamped by waves of "new, uncultured elements,"[7] who were still intent in the late 1890s on expressing their discontent in "arson, murder, and the destruction of machines and buildings."[8] The early Soviet historian M. A. Rubach referred to the 1898 "riot" (*bunt*) at the Briansk factory in Ekaterinoslav as the "highest expression of the whole epoch . . . the epoch of the spontaneous movement."[9] Ekaterinoslav province was the only province the ministry of internal affairs placed in a state of "heightened security" (*usilennaia okhrana*) during the 1890s (joining the six provinces in this state since 1881).[10]

According to Soviet figures, such as those compiled by O. A. Parasun'ko and shown in table 4, the Donbass–Dnepr Bend labor movement during the late nineteenth century was dominated quantitatively by nonviolent work stoppages. While large-scale rioting distinguished the Donbass–Dnepr Bend labor movement from labor movements elsewhere in Russia, most labor disturbances in the region were relatively nonviolent during this period.[11] To divide this unrest into the two separate categories of

TABLE 4
Number of Strikes and Riots in Ekaterinoslav Province, 1870–1899

	Strikes	*Riots*
1870–1875	8	3
1876–1880	2	0
1881–1885	8	0
1886–1890	20	3
1891–1895	14	6
1896–1899	107	9

Source: Compiled from tables in O. A. Parasun'ko, *Polozhenie i bor'ba rabochego klassa Ukrainy, 1860–90-e gody XIX v.* (Kiev, 1963), pp. 282, 390, 393, 562.

[7] G. Novopolin, "Iz istorii rabochego dvizheniia (1800–1903)," *Letopis' revoliutsii*, no. 2 (1923), p. 22.

[8] *Istoriia ekaterinoslavskoi*, p. xxiii.

[9] Ibid., p. xxii.

[10] The state of "heightened security" gave Ekaterinoslav's governor the power to suspend civil liberties and personally fine or incarcerate offenders "to preserve state order and public tranquility" (Robbins, *The Tsar's Viceroys*, pp. 181–182).

[11] It is clear, however, that Soviet sources have minimized the extent of worker violence. To give just one example, in the listing of incidents of labor unrest in *Rabochee dvizhenie v*

strikes and riots, or disturbances (*volneniia*), is, however, somewhat misleading. Soviet historians' use of the two distinct categories to differentiate types of working-class protest obscures the extent to which strikes and riots overlapped. Work stoppages in the Donbass–Dnepr Bend during this period commonly included some destruction, rocks thrown through windows, personal attacks, and looting of shops; or, to look at it conversely, working-class riots often began as nonviolent work stoppages. Even according to Parasun'ko's figures, during most of this period (from 1880 to 1894), 40,750 workers in Ekaterinoslav province rioted, compared to the 15,480 workers who participated in strikes.[12]

Donbass–Dnepr Bend labor actions, especially in the early years, generally followed a few basic patterns. They usually did not involve an enterprise's entire work force, but rather one department or even just a group of workers. In most instances, they lasted only one to three days. Typically, after refusing to start work or stopping during a shift, disgruntled workers gathered in front of the company office to confront a company representative with their grievances. The tsarist government's prohibition of trade unions, and even of open meetings to air grievances, largely explains why the workers in such instances did not present written lists of demands. The exchange between the assembled workers and the enterprise representative commonly resembled a shouting match. Such strikes were most likely to occur in the spring, especially after the mines announced their spring–summer pay rate.[13] Given that most workers were peasant migrants who viewed themselves as short-term workers, issues concerning pay not surprisingly provoked more strikes than any other cause.[14] As in the case of artisans, miners and steelworkers also struck over the length of the workday or the length of their lunch and other breaks, or to improve some other aspect of working conditions. Many work stoppages were defensive in

---

Rossii v XIX veke, the large-scale riot in 1898 at the Briansk mill in Ekaterinoslav was labeled a strike (*Rabochee dvizhenie v Rossii v XIX veke: Sbornik dokumentov i materialov*, vol. 4, ed. L. M. Ivanov [Moscow-Leningrad, 1963], pt. 2:776). It was a study of this chronicle of labor unrest that led Robert Johnson to conclude in *Peasant and Proletarian* that Russian labor unrest was disciplined and nonviolent. See also Brower, "Labor Violence"; and Joan Neuberger, "Hooliganism: Crime, Culture, and Power in Imperial Russia, St. Petersburg, 1900–1914" (unpublished manuscript).

[12] *Polozhenie i bor'ba*, p. 393. According to Parasun'ko's figures, from 1895 to 1899 far more workers struck than rioted—82,248 compared to 11,168 (ibid., p. 562). But the failure by the tsarist government, Donbass–Dnepr Bend management, and Soviet historians to include many working-class riots as instances of labor unrest makes quantitative analysis based on these statistics of dubious value. The statistics can be considered only a general indicator of some trends in the labor movement.

[13] Coal-mine operators' failure to fulfill anticipated pay hikes in the spring had produced unrest ever since the construction of the first large mines in the 1870s (ibid., p. 255).

[14] Issues concerning pay, of course, provoked unrest throughout industrial Russia, including regions with less worker turnover.

character. Workers stopped work to protest the lowering of the piece rate or an increase in overtime work. Less predictable sources of discontent also triggered labor actions. Workers repeatedly were spurred into action when their enterprise did not receive its payroll on time and therefore could not distribute wages on the agreed-upon day. By the end of the century, a foreman's insults could also be sufficient cause for workers to walk off the job, especially if the foreman was a foreigner.

Roughly half the work stoppages of the period achieved some concessions from the firm, as was the case in Grushev in 1879 at the mines owned by the Russian Steamship and Trade Company (ROPIT). With a work force of about a thousand miners, the Grushev coal mines were among the largest in the region at the time.[15] After the strike began, some of ROPIT's miners seized the company's scales and surrounded the home of the mine engineer. The strikers claimed the company cheated them by using scales that underweighed the amount of coal they mined, and they refused to return to work until the mine paid them what they insisted they were due. In an unusually long strike, the mine stayed closed for five days. Cossacks ultimately were called in and the strike ended, but a government investigation upheld the workers' claims.[16]

At a few mines, work stoppages apparently became regular seasonal rituals. The mine engineer Aleksandr Fenin recalled in his memoirs that when he managed the Makeevka mine in the 1890s, it was an annual spring event for workers at the mine to strike before Whitsunday, or the *Troitsa* holiday. Each year, according to this unusual account, during the week before the holiday, most of the mine's work force packed up their paltry belongings and moved from the company barracks to the open steppe outside the mining village. There the miners set up camp. Entire families joined the move. The strike often lasted a full week, during which time the miners, according to Fenin, "spent the evenings playing cards, wildly hooting, whistling, and cavorting about" as if the strike were some sort of annual festival. Fenin "would tell them their demands were unreasonable—that wages had been set at Easter for the whole summer and they had agreed to them." One might assume the strike tradition at the Makeevka mine stemmed from an initial success, but it continued year after year under Fenin's management, even though the mine refused to make any concessions to the strikers. (Perhaps it was a de facto demand for vacation time.) Each year the workers eventually conceded defeat and peacefully returned to the bar-

[15] Mines were, of course, much bigger in later years. In 1900 the South Russian Coal Company employed 6,430 workers at its mines near Gorlovka, and the New Russia Company employed 5,839 at its mines near Iuzovka (Potolov, *Rabochie Donbassa*, p. 125).

[16] Ibid., p. 184.

racks, although once it was necessary for Cossacks to make an appearance before they finally broke camp.[17]

For Donbass–Dnepr Bend miners to walk off the job and close down a mine during this period for as long as five days, as they also did in the ROPIT work stoppage, was rare. Before the great strike waves of 1903 and 1905, the government could quickly deploy troops to quell labor unrest. Lacking organized leadership, workers had difficulty sustaining a strike. Work stoppages were often so brief management did not even bother to report them to governmental authorities. A short work stoppage with some relatively minor destruction did bring egregious abuses out into the open and often succeeded in rectifying gross mistreatment, but such actions rarely achieved major changes or wage increases. Generally, instances of labor unrest in the Donbass–Dnepr Bend during the late nineteenth century lacked continuity with previous strikes and occurred in isolation. For Donbass–Dnepr Bend workers to establish any continuity from year to year was extremely difficult, given the labor force's transience.

Many peaceful work stoppages were quickly transformed into destructive riots. When faced with a crowd of angry workers, management invariably demanded that workers select representatives from their ranks so that orderly negotiations could be conducted, a demand workers usually rejected. Past experience had taught them that following the restoration of order, the worker representatives were likely to be singled out and arrested for instigating the strike.[18] At this critical juncture, if no concessions from management were forthcoming and workers refused to end the strike—and troops or Cossacks had not yet arrived—workers often began to riot.

Management generally could pacify workers by adopting delaying tactics that paid lip service to the workers' demands. Confident of government support and workers' normal obsequiousness and quiescence, management told workers their demands had merit and would be granted if at all possible. Management correctly believed that if it could temporarily defuse the crowd, real concessions could be avoided in most cases. Such tactics were risky, though. A crowd of agitated workers often saw the management's false promises for what they were, and their anger and frustration exploded in destruction and looting. It was in this way that work stoppages in the Donbass–Dnepr Bend could evolve into drunken rampages marked by arson, machine smashing, and personal attacks. These factory or mine uprisings were more akin to the traditional, uncoordinated, and terrifying outbursts of Russian rural violence known as *bunt*s than to strikes seeking

[17] Fenin, *Vospominaniia*, pp. 51–52.

[18] For management and the police to ask workers to elect representatives for negotiations, only to fire or arrest these representatives after order was restored, was common throughout Russia. See Oskar Anweiler, *The Soviets: The Russian Workers, Peasants, and Soldiers Councils, 1905–1921*, trans. Ruth Hein (New York, 1974), p. 24.

specific and limited economic gains. Taverns and shops (especially those owned by Jews), as well as mine and factory property, might be attacked. During most of these riots, the amount of damage workers wreaked was fairly modest.

Labor unrest in the Donbass–Dnepr Bend during the 1870s and 1880s erupted among the work crews laying the railroad lines, but it was concentrated at the mines owned by foreigners. The New Russia Company, the enterprise that Welshman John Hughes had opened in the early 1870s, was a primary target. Just as the New Russia Company had pioneered the foreign industrial development of the region, the miners and steelworkers employed by this company proved to be "the pioneers of Donbass–Dnepr Bend mass actions."[19] Work stoppages repeatedly occurred there and often culminated in attacks on shops, taverns, and company offices.[20]

One incident at the New Russia Company's mines provides a classic example of the disturbances in the Donbass–Dnepr Bend labor movement during this early period. On April 12, 1875, the New Russia Company faced an agitated work force when payday arrived and the company lacked the funds necessary to pay its workers. Because of their isolation, Donbass–Dnepr Bend enterprises frequently failed to receive their payroll on time, which understandably outraged workers and always created the possibility of serious trouble.[21] Paydays were a much-anticipated time of drinking and carousing—especially for employees at a company such as the New Russia Company, which illegally paid its workers only once every two months. In this particular instance, the mine administration temporarily pacified its infuriated miners and steelworkers by paying each of them a few rubles and assuring them their wages were sure to arrive within a few days.

The workers demonstrated unusual patience, but their mood became increasingly agitated as two weeks passed and they still had not received their pay. Workers began to stay away from work, and many threatened to quit. Following work on Saturday, April 26, a group of the miners made the short trip from the mines to the New Russia Company's main office, which was located at the company's steel mill in Iuzovka. Some of the factory workers there joined the miners, who assembled inside the factory office to demand immediate payment of their wages. They declared "they would not leave the office until they were paid, since they did not have any money and no one would lend them any."[22] They did leave after nightfall, but they returned to occupy the office again the next day. Hughes's proposal to give them an authorized note for credit purchases at the local

[19] Potolov, *Rabochie Donbassa*, p. 179.

[20] Kharechko, "Sotsial-demokraticheskii soiuz," p. 9; Parasun'ko, *Polozhenie i bor'ba*, pp. 255–257.

[21] TsGIA, f. 37, op. 58, d. 307, p. 7.

[22] Police report, quoted in Potolov, *Rabochie Donbassa*, p. 183.

shops touched a sore spot and only angered the workers more. The workers felt local merchants exploited them by inflating prices on credit purchases. They believed that in purchases with these credit notes, "they would lose at least half."[23] The agitated miners and factory workers finally had had enough and went on a drunken rampage, attacking first the company administration. They broke the windows of the Hughes family mansion. Otherwise, the workers did not damage company property. Hughes and the other British members of the administration managed to hide and escape personal attack before the workers turned to looting taverns and small shops at the city market. The payroll finally arrived a few days later and the wages were issued, but not before troops had been called in for protection and thirty workers arrested.[24]

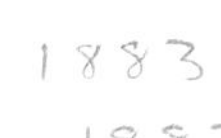

Except for the 1883 pogrom (discussed below), a strike in 1887 at the mines of the Rutchenko Coal Company in Rutchenkovka was the first large-scale labor disturbance in the Donbass–Dnepr Bend. For the first time, Donets Basin miners demonstrated considerable organization and solidarity. The Rutchenkovka strike began after the mine announced that during the summer season miners would earn twenty-two kopecks per wagon of coal, up just two kopecks from the twenty paid during the winter. Workers had expected more, and on May 4, four hundred miners working in the company's eastern mine—mine No. 19—struck. Confronted with a closed mine, the administration agreed to pay twenty-four kopecks per wagon at the mine. Still not satisfied, the five artels of migrants from Smolensk province who had instigated the strike demanded twenty-five kopecks.[25] When the administration refused, the strikers marched round to the western mines, Nos. 11 and 13, which promptly joined the strike. The next day, almost the entire fifteen hundred workers employed at the Rutchenko mines assembled in front of the mine office. In addition to more pay, the workers demanded that the administration fire a paramedic (*fel'dsher*) and some contractors and foremen hated for how they treated workers, and that the sale of inferior meat at the company store be stopped. A mine spokesman, a Frenchman by the name of Vensage, addressed the miners. To soothe the workers and defuse the threat of violence, Vensage agreed to all the strikers' demands, a promise he evidently had no intention of fulfilling.

The next day, May 6, when the mine believed it had regained control over its work force, the administration not only reneged on its promises,

[23] Report of the mine engineer Lebedev, quoted in Potolov, *Rabochie Donbassa*, p. 183.

[24] Levus, "Iz istorii," p. 50.

[25] Iu. Z. Polevoi, *Zarozhdenie marksizma v Rossii, 1883–1894* (Moscow, 1959), pp. 105–106. Here we see an example of how *zemliachestvo* facilitated outbreaks of labor unrest. Robert Johnson concluded in his study of Moscow province that "clusters of *zemliaki* formed a nucleus out of which grew larger strikes" (*Peasant and Proletarian*, p. 159).

but also fired the workers thought to be responsible for the strike. That night, an outraged crowd of miners went on a rampage. Armed with *kaili*, the hacks used for mining, the crowd attacked the company office. After breaking the office's windows and furniture, the miners decided to move on to the company's brewery and nearby taverns and inns. At the first tavern, workers who were opposed to this turn of events and sought to avoid drunkenness among the strikers smashed the vodka barrel, but the mass of workers were not to be denied. They simply proceeded to the brewery, where they reportedly drank thirty-two hundred gallons of beer![26] Later that night, many of the miners managed to make the five-verst trek to Iuzovka, where they hoped to loot and induce steelworkers at the New Russia Company to join their protest.

In Iuzovka, the New Russia Company thwarted the miners by successfully pitting steelworker against miner, foreigner against Russian.[27] At the behest of Arthur Hughes himself, son of the founder, the company armed with guns and put on horseback fifty steelworkers, mostly highly paid skilled workers imported from England. They charged the miners and sent them running.[28]

The next day, Ekaterinoslav's vice-governor and two battalions of soldiers arrived in Rutchenkovka and put an end to the disorders there, as well as the small protests and disturbances that the Rutchenko miners' uprising had sparked at nearby mines. The unrest succeeded in drawing the government's attention to the miners' grievances, but mass arrests rather than improvements followed. In his report, Ekaterinoslav's governor supported the mine. Instead of blaming working and living conditions for this outburst of worker discontent, His Excellency emphasized the peasant origins of the miners, arguing that the miners brought to the mines the troubles of the central Russian village.[29]

[26] G. Novopolin, "Pervye 'bezporiadki' gornorabochikh (1887)," *Letopis' revoliutsii*, no. 2 (1923): 11.

[27] This was a tactic the company had successfully employed earlier, in 1874 (Parasun'ko, *Polozhenie i bor'ba*, p. 256).

[28] Despite their role in this incident, the skilled foreign workers employed in the Donbass–Dnepr Bend commonly encouraged Russian workers to question the tsarist order. I. Shevchenko later recounted how he and ten or so other teenage boys went to work early each day to listen "with bated breath" to a skilled German worker tell stories "about foreign cities and the lives workers lived in other countries" and discuss the advantages of a democratic form of government. When rumors spread that government officials had authorized three days of pogromist looting, the German "persuaded not only us, but adults as well" to not participate (I. Shevchenko, "Moi vospominaniia," *Istoriia ekaterinoslavskoi*, pp. 56–57).

[29] TsGAOR, DP OO, f. 102, 1896, d. 606, ch. 3, pp. 23–24; Gessen, *Istoriia gornorabochikh*, pp. 124–126; Potolov, *Rabochie Donbassa*, pp. 200–203; Novopolin, "Pervye 'bezporiadki,' " pp. 10–11. The troops arrested all 366 workers at Rutchenko mine No. 19; 62 of them had to stand trial, while the rest were sent home to their native villages.

Government officials often evaluated the situation differently. When late-nineteenth-century work stoppages and riots achieved improvements in working conditions, it was usually due to government pressure on the enterprise. In their desire to ensure that disorders not be repeated, government officials often took the workers' side. This had been the Rutchenko workers' hope, as a local gendarme official noted after the riot. "Not knowing where to turn for help and protection, the workers decided to protest all together, not separately . . . they presume that they will be punished for the disorders but at the very least others will understand their situation and improve it, even if just a little."[30]

Social Democrats later evaluated as "backward" such incidents as the work stoppage and small riot by the workers at the New Russia Company in 1875 and at the Rutchenko mines in 1887. Social Democrats judged the labor movement to be in its infancy, since discontented workers rioted. This evaluation of the Donbass–Dnepr Bend labor movement was strongly influenced by three much larger violent outbreaks of labor unrest (which will be examined below). G. Novopolin, a social-democratic activist who wrote one of the first Soviet historical accounts of the Donbass–Dnepr Bend revolutionary movement, expressed the interpretation Social Democrats generally shared at the time. Novopolin argued that the composition of the work force in the Donbass–Dnepr Bend in the late nineteenth century kept the labor movement from rising above a "primitive" level:

> Skilled workers . . . were drowned in an uncultured mass of *chernorabochie* . . . but because working conditions in the "blessed" south differed little from conditions in the north, before long the labor movement in the south also assumed a revolutionary character. The revolutionary mood, because of the uncultured and unconscious character of the mass of workers, assumed at first a violent and pogromist character, which the isolated *intelligenty* and conscious workers failed to control or direct into proper channels.[31]

To appreciate the Social Democrats' view that the Donbass–Dnepr Bend labor movement could easily degenerate into riotous violence, a view that persisted among Social Democrats into the twentieth century and that influenced tactical decisions during "revolutionary situations," it is necessary to place the late-nineteenth-century Donbass–Dnepr Bend labor movement in the larger context of other forms of collective working-class violence besides strikes and work stoppages.

[30] *Rabochee dvizhenie v Rossii v XIX veke*, vol. 3, ed. A. M. Pankratova (Moscow, 1963), pt. 1:503, quoted in Brower, "Labor Violence," p. 421.

[31] "Iz istorii rabochego dvizheniia," pp. 16–17.

In addition to the rioting that often accompanied work stoppages in the Donbass–Dnepr Bend, on a few occasions during the late nineteenth century, worker discontent erupted in violent rampages unconnected to any attempt to first pursue peaceful means. These labor actions were atypical, but they reveal a side of the Russian working class that has been little appreciated since that era. At the time, radical organizers in the Donbass–Dnepr Bend continually denounced workers' proclivity for destruction and violence. Social Democrats particularly thought such mass actions hurt the labor movement. They viewed riots as mindless outbursts that posed no threat to the social or political order. Management and government authorities were not so sure. But despite government repression and radicals' efforts to curb workers' violence, this side of labor unrest would continue to play a role during the revolutionary years 1903–1905.

Three major outbursts of working-class violence and rioting occurred in the Donbass–Dnepr Bend during the last two decades of the nineteenth century—in 1883, 1892, and 1898. Each of these powerful displays of labor violence attracted national attention because the rampaging workers wreaked enormous destruction and because the riots were pogroms—violence directed at local Jews and Jewish enterprises. The first riot occurred in 1883 in Ekaterinoslav. Unlike the other two, this was a classic pogrom, the last big rampage in the wave of pogroms that rolled across southern Russia during the early 1880s.[32] Although this pogrom has not been considered a working-class disturbance, it should be. Workers constituted the bulk of the rioters; and when seen in the context of the labor movement, the pogrom clearly shares many features of later Donbass–Dnepr Bend labor disturbances. This is not to diminish the importance of anti-Semitism in the origins of the 1883 pogrom. On the contrary, viewing the pogrom in the context of labor unrest indicates the depth of anti-Semitism among Donbass–Dnepr Bend workers and the reason anti-Semitism could assume such importance in other labor disturbances. In the 1883 pogrom, Donbass–Dnepr Bend workers displayed the violent and pogromist proclivities that characterized labor unrest there on many later occasions. The other two major nineteenth-century Donbass–Dnepr Bend riots, which occurred in Iuzovka in 1892 and in Ekaterinoslav in 1898, were by contrast always recognized as instances of labor unrest. Worker anger at government handling of an epidemic in 1892 and at factory guards in 1898 provoked these two rampages, which both then degenerated into pogromist

[32] Prior to the wave of pogroms that began in 1881, only three relatively small-scale pogroms had erupted in Russia. All three occurred in the city of Odessa, in 1820, 1859, and 1871 (Louis Greenberg, *The Jews in Russia: The Struggle for Emancipation*, vol. 2 [New Haven, 1951], p. 19).

violence against Jews. All three of these mass labor actions will be examined in detail below. They established patterns of working-class violence that link labor unrest and pogroms. They also provide background for understanding the political consciousness of Donbass–Dnepr Bend workers and the crucial political events of 1903 and 1905.

The first of these riots occurred in July 1883 on the streets of Ekaterinoslav. Because the pogrom occurred in the early stages of the industrialization drive, the migrant workers from central Russia who accounted for the bulk of the pogromists were railroad workers, rather than miners or steelworkers. The construction of the Ekaterinin railroad line through Ekaterinoslav in the early 1880s brought thousands of migrant workers to the city and surrounding area.

Until recently, students of pogroms showed little interest in discovering who actually participated in pogroms. Outraged by the pattern of Cossacks' and troops' refusal to protect the Jewish populace from rampaging mobs, most scholars concentrated on trying to demonstrate local and central government involvement. But rather than being directed from on high, the pogroms of the early 1880s occurred in several spontaneous waves. I. Michael Aronson has convincingly showed that the pogroms spread spontaneously from towns to settlements to villages, moving along railroad lines, major highways, and rivers. Railroad workers were primarily responsible for spreading the pogroms throughout the Ukraine, but they were joined by other migrant workers, peasants, and lower-middle-class business competitors of the Jews.[33]

Ekaterinoslav was one of Russia's major Jewish centers. Jews accounted for over a third (35.4 percent) of the city's population by 1897. The Jewish presence in Ekaterinoslav was greater than the numbers suggest. Jews were the most settled inhabitants among the city's population. While Great Russians constituted the largest ethnic group, with 41.8 percent, this number included many of the community's most transient members—notably workers and garrisoned soldiers. And while most of Ekaterinoslav's Jews were poor artisans and petty traders, Jews also played a leading role in the city's commerce, with a handful of wealthy Jews attaining social and civic prominence.[34]

[33] "Geographical and Socioeconomic Factors," p. 31. Aronson argues that the 1881 pogroms reflected the surge of violence in towns at this time resulting primarily from Russia's modernization and industrialization. Recent scholarship concerning the pogroms during 1903–6 also minimizes the conventional emphasis on government conspiracy and complicity (Lambroza, "Pogrom Movement").

[34] Tsentral'nyi statisticheskii komitet Ministerstva vnutrennikh del, *Pervaia vseobshchaia perepis' naseleniia*, 13:3; Salo W. Baron, *The Russian Jew under Tsars and Soviets* (New York, 1964), p. 68.

The storm of anti-Semitic violence that swept across the Ukraine following the assassination of Alexander II on March 1, 1881 was the greatest expression of popular violence to hit Russia since the Pugachev rebellion in the late eighteenth century. Ekaterinoslav's major pogrom took place relatively late in the storm, after most of the pogroms had already occurred. In 1881–82, Jewish lives and property were attacked in 259 towns and villages in southern Russia.[35] The seriousness of these pogroms varied greatly. In the worst incidents, pogromists murdered, raped, and mutilated Jews of all ages and plundered and destroyed private and commercial property on a mass scale. In Kiev, pogromists killed approximately forty Jews, with hundreds more wounded. Losses in Kiev equaled 2.5 million rubles. But most of the pogroms involved no more than the shattering of windowpanes in Jewish shops and homes and the stealing of liquor from Jewish taverns.[36]

Ekaterinoslav experienced one of the many small pogroms on May 1, 1881, when, according to the official government report, "the workmen employed on the railway attacked and pillaged several shops belonging to Jews."[37] A major pogrom seemed imminent, but the city's large Jewish community managed to survive all the rumors and scares relatively unscathed. More serious disturbances may have been avoided at this time because the local authorities adopted an unusually strong antipogrom posture. The governor issued a proclamation, posted around the city, which declared Jews to be "subjects of the tsar" and entitled to the protection of their property. The seriousness of the government's position was reinforced by four companies of troops.[38] Despite these government measures, the threat of a pogrom equal to those occurring elsewhere in the Ukraine remained great. Reuters reported on May 8, 1881 that "the terror of the Jews in Ekaterinoslav is so great that on Wednesday last the authorities forbade the use of the boulevard as a public promenade, and took other precautionary measures."[39] Ekaterinoslav's city duma unanimously adopted a proposal to start a campaign to educate city residents that attacks on Jews hurt not only the Jews, but the welfare and finances of the empire as well. The duma also urged the bishop of Ekaterinoslav to join in the efforts to preserve order by speaking out against the evil of attacking

[35] The lives of those who lacked the wherewithal to recover were ruined. Almost one hundred thousand Jews were impoverished and twenty thousand were left homeless as a result of all the pogroms (Shlomo Lambroza, "Jewish Responses to Pogroms in Late Imperial Russia," in *Living with Antisemitism: Modern Jewish Responses*, ed. Jehuda Reinharz [Hanover, 1987], p. 259).

[36] Aronson, "Geographical and Socioeconomic Factors," p. 19; Baron, *The Russian Jew*, p. 53; Jonathan Frankel, *Prophecy and Politics: Socialism, Nationalism, and the Russian Jews, 1862–1917* (Cambridge, England, 1981), p. 52.

[37] *Jewish Chronicle*, no. 634 (May 20, 1881): 13.

[38] *Jewish Chronicle*, no. 668 (January 13, 1882): 8 and no. 634 (May 20, 1881): 14.

[39] Reprinted in *Jewish Chronicle*, no. 633 (May 13, 1881): 8.

Jews.[40] But this unusual level of antipogrom activity by the local authorities ultimately failed to save Ekaterinoslav's Jews from the workers and others in the city itching for a full-blown pogrom.

"A single spark can start a prairie fire," in the words of Mao Zedong. Ekaterinoslav's 1883 pogrom, one of the worst of the nineteenth century, was set in motion on July 20 by nothing more than the cries of a peasant woman at the market. A petty incident could trigger a massive pogrom partly because July 20 was the Russian Orthodox holiday of St. Elias (Elijah).[41] On holidays the city filled with workers and peasants who had come to shop and drink. The woman had run out of a Jewish shop howling as if in pain after the salesclerk smacked her son when he tried to steal the store's scale.[42] The woman's cries drew a large crowd consisting primarily of two hundred "laborers." The crowd eagerly took vengeance on the shop. They beat the clerk so badly he died the following day; then they plundered the shop and destroyed anything too large to carry off.[43]

This violence and plunder proved to be just the beginning. The rioters shouted "Beat the yids!" and proceeded to sack neighboring shops and a liquor store. After quickly drinking their fill, the crowd moved on to the quarter where most of Ekaterinoslav's Jewish businesses and artisanal workshops were located. By then the crowd had swelled tremendously, as approximately three thousand railroad workers joined in the rampage. Groups of one hundred and more, armed with crowbars and hammers, stormed Jewish shops and residences. The city market, the synagogue, and prayer houses suffered enormous damage. To capitalize on the pogrom, townspeople and peasants, many of them women, followed behind the rampaging workers carrying sacks and boxes, into which they stuffed as many Jewish belongings as they could.[44]

No police were to be seen when the pogrom erupted because it was before 9 A.M., the hour the police went on duty. By the time the police arrived, they were badly overmatched. They did try to stop the pogrom, however. In contrast to their reported performance during pogroms in other southern cities, Ekaterinoslav's police persistently tried to pacify and disperse the rioters. But, unwilling to shoot pogromists, they could do little except arrest isolated rioters.[45]

[40] Ibid., no. 646 (August 12, 1881): 6.

[41] Simon Dubnov, *History of the Jews*, translated and revised by Moshe Spiegel (New York, 1973), 4:547.

[42] Workers and peasants commonly distrusted the accuracy of Jewish shopkeepers' weights and measures.

[43] *Jewish Chronicle*, no. 752 (August 24, 1883): 6.

[44] *Jewish Chronicle*, no. 751 (August 17, 1883): 6 and no. 752 (August 24, 1883): 6; Novopolin, "Iz istorii rabochego dvizheniia," p. 19.

[45] An attempt to disperse the pogromists by attacking them with the fire-brigade hose backfired. July 20 was so hot that while the hoses' powerful spray temporarily forced pogromists

Troops offered the only realistic hope to suppress the rioting mob quickly.[46] But few troops were immediately available July 20 to stop the pogrom, even though a garrison was located in Ekaterinoslav. The pogromists were probably aware that most of the army had left for its summer encampment. Of those soldiers left behind, a large number had gone to work in the fields outside town and therefore were not available to suppress the sudden outburst of rioting. The first troops to appear concentrated on Ekaterininskii Prospekt, the city's principal boulevard; they managed to protect the Jewish businesses there. When reinforcements from surrounding localities finally arrived, the troops descended on the largest concentration of pogromists. The command to fire was given and the troops fired a volley of blanks. Unintimidated, workers jeered at the soldiers and continued to riot, convinced the soldiers would never kill fellow Russians to protect Jews. The troops proved the pogromists wrong when they fired again, this time with live ammunition. Although most of the troops fired over the heads of the crowd, more than a few pogromists were hit. Even the sight of fallen bodies failed to disperse the rioters immediately. The incensed crowd heaved a shower of rocks toward the troops, hitting forty privates, four officers, and several policemen. The troops fired again. This second volley finally dispersed the crowd, but the rioting continued elsewhere in the city; and later that night the soldiers fired again at pogromists.[47]

The Jewish community in Ekaterinoslav, until then one of the wealthiest in southern Russia, was devastated by the pogrom. The pogromists had plundered and demolished 846 residences. Nearly 2,000 Jewish families were impoverished, and total damage was estimated at between 600,000 and 1 million rubles. Their loss was more monetary than physical, as Ekaterinoslav's Jews generally managed to escape personal assaults by fleeing the city once the pogrom began. Women were raped and Jewish blood was shed; but other than the shop clerk, it was pogromists who died during the pogrom. The soldiers killed twenty-eight rioters and seriously wounded many more.[48]

The threat of renewed pogromist outbreaks followed the July pogrom. On at least two occasions later in the year, another major pogrom might

to retreat, the cold shower also seemed to invigorate the drunken rioters. They simply moved their attacks on Jewish homes and businesses to a neighboring street.

[46] Whether the military would actually act to quell the disorders was another question. In many instances, once pogroms got under way, troops and Cossacks were less inclined to attack pogromists than acts of Jewish resistance, since they did not want to be viewed as attacking Russians to protect Jews.

[47] *Jewish Chronicle*, no. 752 (August 24, 1883): 6.

[48] Ibid.; *Jewish Chronicle*, no. 753 (August 31, 1883): 10–11. Of the 327 people arrested for their participation in the pogrom, 153 were soon freed. Of the 107 arraigned, only 67 stood trial.

have erupted in Ekaterinoslav if the local government and Cossacks had not taken immediate preemptive action. As it was, the rioters succeeded only in wrecking a shop or two before these pogroms were stopped.[49]

Ekaterinoslav's 1883 pogrom revealed that workers were prone to engage in pogromist actions as well as strikes and attacks on their company's property and personnel. In the 1890s, Donbass–Dnepr Bend workers repeatedly engaged in violent rioting that had a pogromist component as one of its central features. In later years, these outbursts of pogromist rioting were more closely connected to traditional forms of labor violence than was the pogrom of 1883. Unlike the pogromist wave of the early 1880s, pogromist activities in the 1890s occurred as offshoots of factory disturbances.

During the rest of the 1880s, with the exception of the miners' uprising in Rutchenko in 1887, the Donbass–Dnepr Bend labor movement continued to consist primarily of isolated work stoppages that attracted little national attention. After a decade of general labor quiet, Donbass–Dnepr Bend workers' discontent exploded violently in August 1892. Angry workers in Iuzovka and the surrounding area went on a destructive two-day rampage. The government dubbed this riot the "cholera *bunt*" because it was sparked by the cholera epidemic that afflicted Donbass–Dnepr Bend miners in conjunction with the 1891–92 famine and by rumors of cholera-related disturbances along the Volga River. The bloodiest industrial conflict in Russia in the 1890s, the Iuzovka riot created a sensation not only in the Donbass–Dnepr Bend, but throughout the country.

Iuzovka's working-class population was primed to explode just weeks after the cholera epidemic claimed its first victim in the area. The government had implemented a number of preventive measures that angered workers.[50] A minor, seemingly insignificant confrontation on Sunday, August 2 touched off the riot. A group of workers, probably drunk—it was midafternoon on Sunday—refused to allow the authorities to take the cholera-infected wife of one of the workers to the dreaded cholera barracks (where they had good reason to believe she would die, far from her family). When a member of the cholera commission charged with hospitalizing the woman returned to the victim's working-class slum accompanied by the police inspector, workers greeted their arrival with an onslaught of jeers and rocks. "Complaints were shouted about 'Jew doctors' who had supposedly come from Rostov and were 'poisoning our brothers,' and the officials were asked why only Russians died, while the English and Jews did not even fall ill."[51] The workers' resistance forced the authorities to retreat.

[49] *Jewish Chronicle*, no. 763 (November 16, 1883): 7 and no. 752 (August 24, 1884): 7.

[50] See chapter 3; and Potolov, *Rabochie Donbassa*, pp. 211–212.

[51] *Russkie vedomosti*, no. 326 (November 25, 1892): 4, quoted in Friedgut, "Labor Vio-

The combination of workers' anti-Semitism, recent death tolls, and fear of doctors ignited long-standing grievances. As nightfall approached, the neighborhood became increasingly agitated. A crowd of workers began to make their way toward the cholera barracks, which they clearly intended to destroy, when they stopped at the district marketplace, "Novyi svet" (New World). Police confronted the crowd but, feeling overwhelmed, failed to take any action to disperse them. The workers lost sight of their original target and began to sack Jewish shops and taverns. Flames soon engulfed parts of the marketplace. On this first day of rioting, the rampaging crowd attacked only Jewish shops. They left unscathed shops whose owners, by displaying an icon, could indicate they were not Jewish.[52] Some skilled workers did make a futile effort to stop the pogrom.[53]

Even Cossack bullets failed to stop the rioting workers. A Cossack squadron had been permanently garrisoned in Iuzovka after a wave of strikes in 1888.[54] Therefore, only a short time elapsed between the beginning of the rioting at the marketplace and the arrival of the Cossack squadron; but by then the number of workers and other local residents flowing into the market to join the riot already approached five thousand. This crowd greeted the Cossacks' arrival with a shower of rocks. Threatened and enraged, the Cossacks wasted no time in abandoning the whip for the rifle and firing a volley into the crowd. The crowd did not disperse until shots rang out again, spilling more blood.[55] The Cossacks killed between fifty and two hundred workers, with the wounded probably numbering many times that. At least twenty-five officers and soldiers suffered wounds.[56] It was the worst civilian massacre until Bloody Sunday.

The disturbance did not end with the Cossack attack. The rioters continued to give vent to their fury the next day, August 3. That morning, workers at the Iuzovka steel factory continuously sounded the factory whistle, which could be heard for miles. Miners from the eleven large mines nearby heeded the call and arrived to join the factory workers. The number of participants in that day's disturbances was estimated to be at least fifteen thousand. The size of the crowd may even have reached thirty thousand.[57]

---

lence," p. 255. Cholera victims in Russia typically came almost entirely from the lower classes (Frieden, *Russian Physicians*, p. 144).

[52] TsGIA, f. 1405, op. 93, ed. khr. 8555, p. 42, cited in Friedgut, *Iuzovka and Revolution*, 1:201.

[53] Kharechko, "Sotsial-demokraticheskii soiuz," p. 10.

[54] John Bushnell, *Mutiny amid Repression: Russian Soldiers in the Revolution of 1905–1906* (Bloomington, Ind., 1985), p. 27.

[55] TsGIA, f. 1405, op. 93, d. 8555, p. 125.

[56] *Rabochee dvizhenie v Rossii v XIX veke*, vol. 3, pt. 2:211; TsGIA, f. 1405, op. 93, d. 8555, pp. 43, 50; Potolov, *Rabochie Donbassa*, pp. 212–213; Bushnell, *Mutiny amid Repression*, p. 27.

[57] Levus, "Iz istorii," p. 51.

The disorder engulfed the entire Iuzovka district. For all practical purposes, Iuzovka briefly found itself at the mercy of rioting miners and unskilled factory workers. They destroyed other parts of the city besides Novyi svet—primarily shops and taverns in and around the Larinskii marketplace. The Cossacks did not fire into the crowd again, apparently content to disperse groups of rioters periodically and to protect the police station and some church, postal, and administrative buildings while they awaited the arrival of reinforcements.[58]

The disorders stopped almost as suddenly as they had started. In the afternoon of the second day, workers began drifting home, and the disturbances had almost completely ceased when the Ekaterinoslav vice-governor arrived with two infantry battalions. Three more squadrons of Cossacks arrived the next day, August 4.

By the time the riots finally ended, the rampaging workers had looted and ravaged 180 stores, 12 taverns, 7 residential buildings, and a synagogue, wreaking approximately 1.5 million rubles' worth of damage.[59] Over five hundred workers and members of their families were arrested. On August 8, Ekaterinoslav's governor, V. K. Shlippe, arrived in Iuzovka. Implementing the directive sent by Alexander III, the governor ordered the public flogging of 190 people, including 14 women.[60] Among the sixty-six workers convicted in court, four were singled out and sentenced to death for instigating and leading the riot. Their sentences were later commuted to life imprisonment.[61]

Although it was common for death sentences to be commuted, the reason in this case may have been that even the authorities recognized that a handful of ringleaders could not be held responsible for such mass fury. In his report to the minister of internal affairs, the governor himself attributed the riot to Donbass–Dnepr Bend working and living conditions. "The miners' quarters are in dank, crowded dugouts. They meet solely with their fellows, with benighted folk, and this only on their free day and in the tavern. In such circumstances the mine workers have no opportunity to hear wise counsel of an honorable nature. They are surrounded by everything that leads to degradation and there is nothing to refine their customs."[62] Following the riot, Donbass–Dnepr Bend workers' living conditions attracted the attention of privileged society, as well as the government's concern, which led to the formation of a special commission

[58] *Vtoroi s"ezd RSDRP: Protokoly*, July–August 1903 (Moscow, 1959), p. 535.

[59] Brower, "Labor Violence," p. 417; Potolov, *Rabochie Donbassa*, p. 212.

[60] The 100–150 lashes were intended to inflict "serious physical pain" (Iu. Iu. Kondufor, ed., *Istoriia rabochikh Donbassa* [Kiev, 1981], 1:57).

[61] Potolov, *Rabochie Donbassa*, pp. 214–215.

[62] *Rabochee dvizhenie v Rossii v XIX veke*, vol. 3, pt. 2:561, quoted in Friedgut, "Labor Violence," p. 255.

to investigate housing and living conditions in the region.[63] The provincial commander of Ekaterinoslav's gendarmes, D. I. Boginskii, recognized that in addition to "discontent with decrees regarding cholera," it was infrequent pay, "the rising cost of necessities in the settlement [Iuzovka], actually higher than in the district capitals or even the provincial capital," and the "discontent of Russian workers with the foreign workers and foremen in the factories" that were responsible for triggering the massive riot. Boginskii proceeded to predict that "such disorders will be repeated annually, to a greater or lesser degree . . . because the mine owners all without exception, and in particular the French companies, as well as the merchants, exploit the workers."[64] Such long-term industrial conditions certainly contributed to the disturbances, as did working-class anti-Semitism. Any serious search for the cause of the riot could not and did not stop with the cholera epidemic.

The factory administration chose to take comfort from the fact that demands addressing working and living conditions were never raised during the riot. The report presented at the annual conference of the Association of Southern Coal and Steel Producers tried to shift all responsibility for the disorders from industrialists onto phantom organizers. The industrialists' report argued that the riot

> was prepared beforehand by unknown instigators. . . . The workers are migrants . . . for the most part landless . . . and [the miners] are especially dissolute and undisciplined, easy to incite to engage in all sorts of riots; workers from most of the [nearby] mines participated in the Hughes factory disorders. The workers did not request an increase in wages or anything else from their bosses, but simply gave themselves up to theft and violence, encouraged and quite obviously led by experienced hands.[65]

To the industrialists, what was needed was more force.[66]

In refusing to accept any responsibility for the most destructive riot to erupt in the Russian empire since the pogroms of the early 1880s, the industrialists fooled no one, except perhaps themselves. The response of the ministry of internal affairs to the industrialists' assertion that the riot was

[63] *Vtoroi s"ezd RSDRP: Protokoly*, p. 537. It was following the "cholera riot" that many mines began to build better housing.

[64] *Rabochee dvizhenie v Rossii v XIX veke*, vol. 3, pt. 2:214.

[65] Kolpenskii, "Kholernyi bunt'," p. 112.

[66] The industrialists demanded that Ekaterinoslav's governor provide increased protection. The government agreed to billet more troops in Donbass–Dnepr Bend industrial districts on the condition that the factories and mines assume the cost of building barracks and other military housing. Many enterprises, chiefly the smaller ones, balked and ultimately refused to contribute. As a result, additional troops still had not been stationed in the Donbass–Dnepr Bend when the century ended.

inspired by some guiding hand was "Where, then, is this hand?"[67] But as was true of the other working-class riots that followed during the 1890s, the industrialists were not solely to blame. As the 1892 gendarme report correctly suggested, Donbass–Dnepr Bend labor unrest was a complex phenomenon. The explanation must be sought in the multiplicity of strains and injustices in Donbass–Dnepr Bend working-class life. In 1892, the cholera epidemic and the increase in the cost of food resulting from the 1891 famine only aggravated all the other strains the mass of predominantly young migrant workers experienced in Donbass–Dnepr Bend industrial centers. As in other working-class riots, the mixture of causes led to violent rampages in which workers vented their pent-up hostilities on a mixture of targets.

The "cholera riot" foreshadowed the other major working-class riot in Russia during the 1890s. Some of the elements of the earlier unrest, particularly the cleavage between skilled and unskilled evident in the "cholera riot," came to the fore in the disturbance that erupted at Ekaterinoslav's enormous Briansk mill in May 1898. The Briansk riot provides some final background to the politically more significant labor actions that followed in the twentieth century.

The Briansk riot took place during the sharp upturn in labor unrest that occurred in the Donbass–Dnepr Bend between 1895 and 1899. It was the first instance in which Donbass–Dnepr Bend labor unrest can be linked to radical agitation. There is no evidence to support the authorities' tendency to blame outside agitators for previous strikes and riots.

The first mass social-democratic agitation campaign in the Donbass–Dnepr Bend preceded the Briansk riot. For months, Social Democrats distributed leaflets that for the first time brought out into the open workers' just complaints and grievances.[68] But as the Briansk riot demonstrated, the Social Democrats were not in a position to lead an outbreak of industrial unrest in the city. While the riot coincided with the origin of mass social-democratic agitation in the Donbass–Dnepr Bend and demonstrated that revolutionaries could play some role in inciting workers to act, the Briansk workers rejected the revolutionaries' calls for nonviolent demonstration of their discontent. The leaflets called for workers to present demands and peacefully walk off the job. The workers' response was to reaffirm their traditional preference for more violent expressions of discontent. The Briansk working-class riot proved to be even more spontaneous and violent than Iuzovka's "cholera riot."

[67] Quoted in Friedgut, "Labor Violence," p. 256.

[68] Ekaterinoslav's growing social-democratic movement managed to include more than one hundred workers in its circles in the years 1896–97 (see chapter 5).

Following the formation in December 1897 of Ekaterinoslav's Soiuz bor'by za osvobozhdenie truda (Union of Struggle for the Emancipation of Labor), the city's Social Democrats concentrated their main efforts on a leaflet campaign. During the first few months of 1898, Ekaterinoslav's Social Democrats distributed leaflets among the city's workers on an unprecedented scale. On a simple hand press, they cranked out thousands of copies of eight different leaflets, which they distributed around the factories and working-class quarters. On a single night in February, Social Democrats clandestinely distributed three thousand copies of a leaflet that attacked conditions at the seven largest factories in Ekaterinoslav.[69] Such a large-scale effort created a stir within the factories. "Some were explaining that there must have been many of 'them' to give out so many leaflets in so many places in one night, and there were various conjectures about the power and strength of 'these people,' their courage, and so on."[70]

The Soiuz bor'by leaflet campaign focused on workers' everyday concerns. The social-democratic activists appreciated the political conservatism of the mass of workers in Ekaterinoslav, who "en masse were distinguished by their devotion to the tsar."[71] Not one political word appeared in the leaflets. Only the most skilled workers showed much interest in thinking about politics, and they were as likely to be drawn to the right as to the left, according to Georgii Petrovskii, who worked at the Briansk factory in the 1890s. Petrovskii noted that many of his fellow workers later did join the reactionary, virulently anti-Semitic Black Hundreds' Union of Russian People.[72]

The Soiuz bor'by's politically neutral leaflets appeared to be a great success. For many Ekaterinoslav workers, the leaflets at last articulated grievances that had long angered them. The demands were modest, as is clear from this summary of the demands in the leaflet distributed among the workers at the Kamensk, Gallershtein, and Esau factories and in the railroad machine shops (note that no mention is made of a wage increase):

1. That the factories permit workers, "who work day and night in dust and smoke," to use the factory baths, which now are restricted to the foremen.

2. That the factory doctors be present during the posted hours and stop charging patients for medicine during home visits.

3. That the processing of accident claims be timely.

4. That an emergency hospital facility be constructed within the factory. As it

[69] Petrovskii, "S 1893 g. po 1905 g.," pp. 50–51.

[70] Babushkin, *Recollections*, p. 115.

[71] I. B. Polonskii, "Iz zhizni partiinoi organizatsii (1898–1900 gg.)," *Istoriia ekaterinoslavskoi*, p. 139.

[72] "S 1893 g. po 1905 g.," p. 51.

is, maimed workers risk dying from the loss of blood that occurs during transport to the hospital miles away.

5. That the exit gates be opened at supper and after work.[73]

6. That workers be guaranteed one twenty-four-hour period every week when they do not have to work.

7. That the factories observe the law and stop work at 2 P.M. on the eve of Sundays and holidays.

8. That wages be paid every other Saturday and in full. As it is, workers are forced to go into debt to shopkeepers, who use credit purchases to sell inferior goods at inflated prices.

9. That piece rates be clearly stipulated and paid according to piece-rate agreements.[74]

The leaflet did end on a militant note. The Soiuz bor'by proclaimed: "Here is not just an adversarial relationship between capitalists and workers. The capitalists lack simple humanity. They treat workers like dogs. . . . The administration enjoys all the comforts of life, while for their workers, they think a dog's life is good enough."[75]

Social Democrats working inside the Briansk mill reported that workers there were discussing the leaflets. These workers were especially impressed when management at a couple of the smaller factories, fearing a strike, quickly implemented some of the demands the leaflets presented.[76] The workers, however, showed no interest in the Social Democrats' tactical advice. The worker-activist Ivan Babushkin recalled how workers refused to follow the radicals' call to strike peacefully and present demands to the factory administration. They instead expressed a desire to wreck the factory offices and to beat foremen and factory guards:

> It was strange to hear the rumors among the workers about a revolt, in complete contrast to the message given in the leaflets, which said clearly that a rising was undesirable and could bring nothing but harm to the workers. They had read something different in the leaflet and nothing could change their belief that a revolt had been ordered. Old methods of struggle die hard; the workers couldn't think of a strike unless it entailed the beating up of a foreman or the wrecking of the factory offices.[77]

[73] For security reasons, workers were allowed to leave work every day only through a narrow opening in the gates. This funnel created a potentially dangerous mob scene as workers in the crowd crushed one another and knocked over those who gathered outside the gate.

[74] *Listok rabotnika*, no. 9–10 (November 1898): 15–17. Workers complained that management often told them they were working for a piece rate so they would work harder, but then paid workers only the regular day wage.

[75] Ibid., p. 17.

[76] Soiuz russkikh sotsial'demokratov, *Rabochee dvizhenie v Ekaterinoslave* (Geneva, 1900), p. 4.

[77] *Recollections*, p. 108.

Tensions were already high at the Briansk factory when the death of a worker, killed in a scuffle with a Circassian factory guard, triggered the riot. As in the 1883 pogrom and the 1892 riot in Iuzovka, a relatively minor confrontation unleashed the workers' pent-up hostilities.

Animosity between workers and company guards had been festering for some time and was an important cause of the Briansk riot. Workers throughout the Donbass–Dnepr Bend hated the mountaineers from the Caucasus Mountains hired as guards by many factories and mines to control theft and general unruliness.[78] The Briansk factory management hired eighty Circassian guards in 1896.[79] From management's perspective, the Circassians made excellent guards. Learning from the government's example in its use of Cossack troops, the factory administration correctly thought the Circassian guards would not identify with the ethnically different work force and if necessary would not refrain from shooting at a crowd of workers for fear of killing one of their compatriots.[80]

Workers thought Circassian guards performed their duties with unnecessary zeal, and a large group of Briansk workers made their enmity toward the Circassians well known to the management and to everyone else at the factory. The question of the guards' treatment of the workers notwithstanding, prejudice largely explains the workers' antagonism toward the Circassians. The workers disparaged the Circassians as a backward lot who did not even speak Russian. Many workers simply could not tolerate having these "inferior aliens ruling over us 'Russian people'."[81] Workers complained repeatedly to the Briansk administration about their hiring Circassians "while Russians go hungry."[82]

The enmity Donbass–Dnepr Bend workers harbored toward the Circassians was normally bridled by fear. Fights occasionally broke out between the Circassians and the workers, but generally the workers were intimidated, afraid to stand up to the Circassians, whom they considered "wild savages." Nonetheless, the workers' animosity could explode following an instance of perceived Circassian brutality. This was evident even before the death of a worker at the hands of a Circassian guard sparked the 1898 riot

[78] Until the introduction of Circassians in the Donbass–Dnepr Bend in the 1890s, many of the large foreign firms had recruited guards from among the same pool of applicants that provided the mass of their unskilled labor. Factory guards were poorly paid and were often said to be accomplices to theft rings. At the Briansk factory, guards on average earned only fifteen rubles a month in the 1890s, a wage well below what workers possessing the most elementary skills earned (this sum did not, however, include the supplementary income bribes no doubt provided).

[79] Many of the guards were actually Ossetian Cossacks, but they were referred to as Circassians.

[80] *Pridneprovskii krai*, January 29, 1900, p. 4; *Istoriia ekaterinoslavskoi*, p. 113.

[81] *Pridneprovskii krai*, January 26, 1900, p. 3.

[82] Novopolin, "Iz istorii rabochego dvizheniia," p. 20.

in Ekaterinoslav. When another Circassian guard stabbed a young miner during a walkout in 1895 at the Gorlovka mines, one of the largest enterprises in the Donbass–Dnepr Bend, what had been a peaceful wage dispute quickly turned violent. Although the worker was not seriously wounded, word of the knifing enraged the miners. A crowd of five hundred miners went on a window-smashing spree. The rampage stopped before it did extensive damage only because the workers' anger dissipated when an attempt to force their way into the mine (where they intended to destroy machinery) was thwarted by locked, steel-reinforced doors.[83] A similar "strike" and clash with the guards occurred at the Briansk mill two years before the 1898 riot.[84]

The 1898 Briansk riot began on May 29 when a young worker employed at a nearby factory tore a board off the fence surrounding the Briansk factory, shortly after the factory whistle signaled the end of the workday. The worker, Nikita S. Kutilin, a migrant from Kursk province, was on his way home from work. While Soviet historical accounts have portrayed this theft as an act of desperation by a worker without other means of heating his hut, contemporary sources, including the revolutionary press, state that Kutilin pried the board loose to taunt a guard on duty nearby.[85] Whatever his motivation, within seconds the guard and Kutilin were at each other's throats. After kicking and knocking the guard down, Kutilin was more than holding his own when another guard jumped into the melee. The fight immediately attracted a crowd of onlookers from among the workers and hangers-on who happened to be milling around nearby. But before they knew what happened, the worker Kutilin lay dead, the victim of a dagger jab to the gut.

The sight of their slain fellow left sprawled on the ground drove the crowd wild with fury. They attacked and unmercifully beat the hated Circassian guards—first the two at hand, then those that came running to their defense. The guards managed to escape with their lives, but the workers continued to lash out at the immediate cause of their rage by setting fire to sentry boxes and destroying the guards' belongings. Far from satiated after this retaliation, the workers were intent on a full-scale riot. The flames and shouting acted as magnets, and the crowd quickly swelled to some two

[83] Gessen, *Istoriia gornorabochikh*, p. 141; Levus, "Iz istorii," p. 53.

[84] A. Smirnov, "Vospominanie o I s.-d. rabochem kruzhke Ekaterinoslava v 1894 g.," *Istoriia ekaterinoslavskoi*, p. 20.

[85] This account of the ensuing events is based on the following sources: TsGIA, f. 23, op. 30, d. 47, pp. 7, 15, 149; *Pridneprovskii krai*, Jan. 26, 1900, p. 3; *Rabochee delo*, no. 1 (April 1, 1899); *Istoriia ekaterinoslavskoi*, pp. 109–110; Novopolin, "Iz istorii rabochego dvizheniia," p. 20; G. Petrovskii, "Vospominaniia o rabote na Brianskom zavode v devianostykh godakh," *Letopis' revoliutsii*, no. 2 (1923): 32–33; Babushkin, *Recollections*, p. 133; Knyshev, *Zarevo nad Brianskoi*, pp. 22–23.

thousand rioters, according to conservative estimates. Most of this crowd knew nothing of the circumstances provoking the riot except that a Circassian guard had killed a worker. Spurred on by a few leaders, the howling crowd turned its sights on the factory itself and rushed in through the now-unguarded gates. In a flash, part of the crowd surrounded the factory office. Emboldened by the cloak of nightfall, workers fetched a sledgehammer, cracked open the safe, and threw five thousand rubles to the crowd. They poured kerosene and set the factory office afire; within minutes it was enveloped by flames. The sight of the factory office going up in smoke further excited the crowd; they looted the factory store and sacked the apartments of some of the white-collar employees, primarily those apartments occupied by foreigners. Many of the rioters then tried to enter the factory proper and wreak the same havoc there, but they were prevented from doing so by workers on the night shift. Even so, within one hour the rampaging crowd had inflicted over 150,000 rubles' worth of damage on the factory.

During all this time, few of the local police were anywhere to be seen. In the face of such a large crowd, so quickly amassed, the police force fell into complete disarray. When the police chief eventually arrived and moved in among the rioters in an attempt to use his presence and powers of persuasion to calm the crowd, one of the workers shouted out, "Your Honor, go away. Let us have our rampage! Let us have our fun!"[86] According to a Social Democratic account, these words expressed the mood of these people, who "like deprived convicts wanted one day to rampage and burn as they pleased."[87] When the chief persisted in his attempt to calm the workers, someone threw a rock that hit him smack on the head, to the delight of the crowd. The chief collapsed and had to be carried away.

Meeting no resistance, the crowd moved on to Kaidaka, an adjacent working-class quarter, where it continued beating, looting, and burning. Initially, when the rampage was still confined to the Briansk grounds, the crowd vented its anger solely on factory representatives, symbols, and institutions the workers particularly hated. But as the disorders continued, they assumed a different character. After the first target in Kaidaka—a government liquor store—had been sacked and the vodka downed, someone shouted, "We have vodka. Now we need *zakuski* [appetizers]—let's go for the yids' stores!"[88] As the crowd of workers, many of whom were armed with crowbars and assorted metal rods, approached a row of small shops, shouts were heard: "Attack! This is a yid's shop!"[89] The now wildly drunk

[86] Rossiiskaia sotsial-demokraticheskaia rabochaia partiia, *Sud nad brianskimi rabochimi* (Geneva, 1901), pp. 11–12.

[87] Ibid.

[88] *Pridneprovskii krai*, January 31, 1900, p. 3.

[89] *Pridneprovskii krai*, January 30, 1900, p. 3.

crowd—"fuddled and fuming with drink," in Babushkin's words—displayed selectivity in choosing which shops to sack and pillage.[90] Next, they terrorized the Jews living near the Briansk factory, smashing and plundering a Jewish prayer house along with dozens of homes, shanties, and shops. One Russian resident of this district later testified that he happened to recognize one of the workers among a group of rioters destroying seemingly everything in sight. He implored the worker to stop. The worker told him not to worry. "We aren't touching Russians' property, only that which belongs to the yids."[91] One day laborer testified that when he saw the crowd sacking Jewish shops, dragging out men, women, and children, he tried to dissuade them. In response, someone in the crowd quickly shouted, "He who defends yids is himself undoubtedly a yid." The would-be peacemaker escaped attack only by unbuttoning his jacket to show a cross.[92]

When troops finally arrived, they cordoned off the factory and parts of the city. Confronted by the troops, workers threw a few rocks; but skirmishes were brief and the crowd quickly dispersed—although it was not until the early hours of the morning that the last of the rioters dragged themselves home. By then, searches in the working-class neighborhoods had already begun. Police and soldiers arrested anyone with an unusual quantity of groceries, often as little as a pound of sugar or one-eighth of a pound of tea. Within twenty-four hours they arrested twelve hundred people. Over five hundred of those arrested were immediately exiled to their native villages. For seventy-three of the accused, there was thought to be sufficient evidence to place them on trial. Thirty-four of these were left in prison until brought into court almost two years later.

The authorities' response to the riot, however, was not limited to repressive measures. The workers who escaped arrest and exile enjoyed such concessions as a reduction in Briansk factory work shifts to ten and a half hours, the introduction of accident insurance, and the use of former soldiers instead of Circassians as factory guards.[93]

Around seven thousand workers were employed at the Briansk factory at the time of the riot. Who was it that participated? In such disorders, participant identification is always difficult, but this working-class riot is

[90] Babushkin, *Recollections*, p. 134.

[91] *Pridneprovskii krai*, February 1, 1900, p. 3.

[92] *Pridneprovskii krai*, January 31, 1900, p. 3. Such an attempt to dissuade a crowd of workers bent on a pogrom was not necessarily futile, especially if undertaken before the crowd began rampaging. A year later, following the arrest of some workers for leading a walkout, a crowd of agitated workers began to vent their anger by throwing rocks at some Jewish artisans returning home from work. A "simple word from a conscious worker was sufficient to stop the uproar," according to one account (Novopolin, "Iz istorii rabochego dvizheniia," p. 24).

[93] Parasun'ko, *Polozhenie i bor'ba*, p. 491.

relatively well documented because the riot and subsequent trial attracted national attention. The evidence, which includes trial testimony, worker memoirs, police and government reports, and the radical and daily press, indicates that the skilled Briansk work force was not to any significant extent responsible for the destruction. Many skilled workers not only refused to join in the violence, but acted to restrict its scope. When the rioters were looting and burning the factory office buildings, and the overwhelmed factory guards and local police could exert no control over the crowd, the factory itself—the machinery and workshops—was protected by skilled workers, albeit halfheartedly. In his trial testimony, the engineer M. A. Kokh stated that without the "fortunate development" of workers' defense of the factory, the *bunt* would have escalated into "a horribly bloody catastrophe." Kokh, as manager of the rolling and puddling works, was in charge of almost one-third of the Briansk work force. In his testimony, he recounted what happened in his section of the factory:

> Into my shop rushed workers who urged my workers to stop work, burn the building, and slaughter the administration. One of the senior workers of my shop, a person with great authority among his comrades—the foreman obviously did not command such respect—took a crowbar and began to threaten the rabble-rousers, then turned to the workers of my shop and exhorted them not to listen to the *buntovshchiki*. The workers wavered before they all acquiesced. Without this bit of luck it would have been very bad.[94]

The sources repeatedly emphasize that the major role in the Briansk disorders was played by drunken working-class youths.[95] Witnesses from the Briansk factory management identified the participants as young "backward workers," those who especially "loved to drink" and "yielded easily to any outside influence."[96] All in all, the weight of the evidence on the riot indicates that the rioters and looters consisted primarily of young, unskilled Briansk workers who were joined in the rampaging crowd by large numbers of similar workers from neighboring factories, along with more than a few of the unemployed or irregularly employed workers and vagabonds who habitually milled around the factories.[97] Even Kutilin, the

[94] *Pridneprovskii krai*, January 26, 1900, p. 3. There are other reports of such displays of worker resistance (Babushkin, *Recollections*, p. 134; *Pridneprovskii krai*, January 29, 1900, p. 3).

[95] *Pridneprovskii krai*, January 30, 1900, p. 3.

[96] *Pridneprovskii krai*, January 26, 1900, p. 3; January 29, 1900, p. 3; January 30, 1900, p. 3; January 31, 1900, p. 3.

[97] TsGIA, f. 23, op. 30, d. 47, p. 7. In a similar (if less destructive) riot a few months later at the Providence factory in Mariupol', hundreds of *chernorabochie* upset over their winter wage "together with other people and some beggars" destroyed some factory property and numerous shops (*Rabochee dvizhenie v Rossii v XIX veke*, vol. 4, pt. 2 [gendarme report, November 4, 1898]: 211–213).

worker whose slaying triggered the riot, was not a Briansk worker. The report on the riot in the official government press went so far as to flatly state that the Briansk workers themselves did not take part in the destruction. No doubt the explanation for that statement is largely semantic, a matter of convention; the reporter probably considered the large number of day laborers and other unskilled workers employed at the Briansk factory to be *chernorabochie*, not *rabochie*—that is, temporary, not full-time, regular Briansk employees.[98] One of the workers on trial as a ringleader was said to have worked only occasionally in the factory, since his winnings from other workers at cards and pitch-and-toss meant he usually did not need factory wages.[99]

As in the case of the Iuzovka "cholera riot," opinions varied on the causes of the Briansk riot. One official report described the rampaging crowd as "out of control. It did not understand what it was doing."[100] One witness to the disorders, when asked in court to identify those sitting in the dock, answered, "How can I recognize them now, Your Honor? Now they are so peaceful and meek, but then they all looked to me like giants, tripled in stature."[101] These impressions of the Briansk riot reflected a popular belief that such worker disorders could be explained by mob psychology and the ignorant workers' propensity for violent drunkenness. Most reports, however, official and nonofficial alike, did consider factory conditions—such as recent fluctuations in the length of the working day, deductions from workers' earnings, and late issuance of pay—to be leading causes of the outburst. How, then, is the working-class attack on Jews in all these instances to be understood?

Before the 1898 Briansk factory disorders, workers repeatedly made known their resentment of the neighboring Jewish population. Donbass–Dnepr Bend workers, particularly the less-skilled, were virulently anti-Semitic. I. Polonskii, who was active in the years 1898–1900 in Ekaterinoslav's embryonic Social Democratic organization, wrote in his memoirs that the mass of Ekaterinoslav's workers were "notable for spontaneous chauvinism, in particular their anti-Semitism."[102] In the 1890s, however, liberals and radicals had reason to argue that workers' pogromist outbursts stemmed more from class conflict, or from a hostility toward exploiters rooted in workers' personal experience, than from an age-old prejudice. This was the rationale pursued by the counsel for the defense at the Briansk

[98] TsGIA, f. 23, op. 30, d. 47 (Report from *Ekaterinoslavskie gubernskie vedomosti*, May 31, 1898), p. 15.

[99] *Pridneprovskii krai*, January 31, 1900, p. 3.

[100] TsGIA, f. 23, op. 30, d. 47 (Ekaterinoslav governor's annual report, 1898), p. 149.

[101] Rossiiskaia sotsial-demokraticheskaia rabochaia partiia, *Sud nad brianskimi rabochimi*, p. 12.

[102] I. B. Polonskii, "Iz vospominanii partiinogo tipografa," *Istoriia ekaterinoslavskoi*, p. 140.

trial. F. N. Plevako, V. A. Maklakov, A. M. Aleksandrov, and N. K. Murav'ev, some of the most illustrious trial lawyers in Russia, were attracted by the case and helped defend the accused Briansk rioters.[103]

Workers claimed the Jewish shopkeepers cheated them. In rough working-class neighborhoods and settlements such as that bordering the Briansk factory, workers' interaction with Jews was essentially limited to their dealings with the local shopkeepers, who were almost all Jewish. The trial defense asserted that shady business practices, overpricing, and usury by the Jewish shopkeepers understandably provoked the workers' rage. The defense lawyers presented the pogromist rampage as an attempt by the powerless to right past wrongs, a line of argument similar to that usually favored by the government when it explained what caused pogroms. The Jewish victims were held to share responsibility with their working-class attackers: "Compare, gentlemen of the court, these two types of people, compare the moral makeup of some of those shopkeepers with those sitting in front of you in the dock—and you will be able to agree with me that these people could exchange places freely . . . for between them is just the force of circumstance, the significance of which you will determine in your sentence."[104] Thanks partly to the lawyers' portrayal of the Jewish shopkeepers, the seventy-three defendants all received light sentences. Not one of the guilty rioters was sentenced to more than two years, even though evidence for the argument of the defense was slim.

Although shopkeepers in Russia, whatever their ethnic background, were commonly accused of overpricing and selling shoddy merchandise, Jewish store prices should not have been especially provocative. Prices in the factory stores, the Jews' competition, were higher, and workers had long complained of the poor quality of goods in factory stores.[105] While there were repeated accusations that Jewish shopkeepers "exploited the working population by cheating when measuring weights," the main source of tension seems to have been the Jewish shopkeepers' practice of giving credit or loans at high interest, as well as buying whatever workers had to sell. Workers, particularly those who worked irregularly and were always short on cash,[106] were able to buy basic necessities and items such

[103] These liberal lawyers were renowned partly for their oratory in defense of revolutionaries and rebellious workers and peasants. Lawyers could say in court—and have printed in the local legal press—what the censors otherwise would never permit to be published in tsarist Russia. The Briansk lawyers' speeches were considered sufficiently radical for the Social Democrats to publish and disseminate them in the underground pamphlet *Sud nad brianskimi rabochimi*.

[104] This statement is from Aleksandrov's concluding remarks to the court (*Istoriia ekaterinoslavskoi*, p. 130).

[105] One factory store was also looted during the riot.

[106] These were the "dregs" (*podonki*) of the worker population, in the words of A. M. Gor-

as sugar, tea, and tobacco on credit at the factory store. They then often went to the Jewish stores and exchanged these items for cash at a rate, of course, far below what they had originally paid. Customarily, the purpose of these exchanges was to buy vodka. This trading of groceries for liquor increased the workers' debt. Later, when workers received their pay and saw the amount deducted for credit purchases, they were prone to blame "the greedy Jews," whom they identified with the merchants.[107]

The three instances of mass working-class unrest examined in this chapter highlight Donbass–Dnepr Bend workers' proclivity to riot. Contrary to the prevailing view of Russian labor historians, late-nineteenth-century labor unrest often proved to be violent, at least in the Donbass–Dnepr Bend. A mix of causes—the strains produced by rapid industrialization, frontier social conditions, and ethnic animosity—were responsible for widespread discontent in the Donbass–Dnepr Bend. Mass drunkenness, brutal brawls, and the regularly exercised option of moving on, either to another job or to and from the countryside, did not serve as sufficient outlets for workers' frustrations. Workers' collective action, as elsewhere in Russia, most commonly took the form of relatively peaceful work stoppages. But from the beginning of the 1880s, Donbass–Dnepr Bend workers repeatedly expressed their discontent in mass destruction and violence.

Riots usually began with workers attacking their factory or mine and the residences and persons of their superiors. As riots spread, workers attacked targets unconnected with the grievance that precipitated their collective action. In Ekaterinoslav in 1898, an attack on the factory guards spontaneously degenerated into a pogrom. In the case of pogroms, the promise of loot and violent excess, as well as ethnic animosity, accounts for the workers' motivation.

In these mass rampages, a stratification of workers is evident where it is possible to identify participants. It was the young, unskilled elements from the working-class districts that were the main component in pogromist crowds. Drawn to the mines and mills by the opportunity to work for relatively high wages, the tens of thousands of young peasant males who largely composed the Donbass–Dnepr Bend working class proved to be poor recruits for the sort of nonviolent, organized activity favored by the

iainov, the Briansk plant manager (from his trial testimony as reported in *Pridneprovskii krai*, January 29, 1900, p. 4).

[107] *Pridneprovskii krai*, January 26, 1900, pp. 3–4. Shopkeepers also were accused of paying workers for factory property slipped past guards and of supporting those who preyed on workers by knowingly cashing stolen paychecks for a price (*Pridneprovskii krai*, January 27, 1900, p. 3; January 29, 1900, p. 4).

revolutionary parties. When they were provoked to express their discontent, rioting held far more appeal than illegal work stoppages. They had no interest in sacrificing for a long-term goal such as political change. Immediate problems loomed larger in their minds, so that when the mass of workers did peacefully walk off the job in the late nineteenth century, it was to achieve bread-and-butter improvements. The workers' main concern was an increase in wages, followed by a reduction in working hours and an improvement in working and living conditions.

The dramatic upsurge in labor unrest in the last years of the nineteenth century did provide some encouragement for radical activists. Strikes, even by miners, increasingly followed the distribution of radical leaflets.[108] But rather than emphasizing workers' growing combativeness, the memoirs Social Democrats published decades later, following the Bolshevik seizure of power, emphasize Donbass–Dnepr Bend workers' low political consciousness during this period. A summation of the problems the Donbass–Dnepr Bend labor force posed for radical organizers is provided by P. Smidovich, who hid his privileged background, trained to be a factory electrician, and went to work at the Briansk plant in 1898. Smidovich not only intended "to live their life, to experience their suffering, their joy," but hoped to be able to propagandize the work force from within.[109] His aborted effort to galvanize the Briansk workers into organized, nonviolent action produced only frustration and this description of the workers:

> If the boss presses down too hard the workers riot, burn the office, and beat the director—but they are not able to formulate their demands and stand up for themselves. . . . The workers themselves are still unable to create an organization. Their godforsaken, hard lives weigh on their personalities and prevent their development. . . . The people do not live and are not able to live with a clear head in this situation. They block out consciousness of their heavy lot with tobacco and liquor. They drink frightfully.[110]

That Donbass–Dnepr Bend workers en masse failed to demand fundamental social, economic, and political changes seems to underscore Lenin's thesis that the mass of workers, left to themselves, were incapable of becoming an organized, class-conscious, revolutionary force. In the Donbass–Dnepr Bend, as elsewhere in Russia (and Western Europe, for that matter), workers for the most part shunned politics and proved difficult to organize, though on occasion they were receptive to appeals to strike for improved wages and working conditions. Not just miners, but steelworkers too—such as those at the Briansk factory—voiced their opposition to

[108] This was the case, for example, in October 1898 at the New Russia Company coal mines (*Rabochee dvizhenie v Rossii v XIX veke*, vol. 4, pt. 2:207).

[109] P. Smidovich, "Rabochie massy," p. 162.

[110] Ibid., pp. 164–165.

anyone who held the tsar "responsible for the bad position of the workers, rather [than] the *chinovniki* [bureaucrats] and capitalists."[111] Only a smattering of the more skilled, longtime workers within the ranks of the Donbass–Dnepr Bend industrial work force were receptive to the growing revolutionary movement's propaganda and agitation and opposed the rioting favored by the mass of workers.

The efforts of radicals to cultivate political protest within the Donbass–Dnepr Bend, which will be examined in the next chapter, became fruitful only after the turn of the century and then primarily because of the radicalization of artisanal rather than industrial workers. An explicitly political movement willing to go into the streets first appeared in Ekaterinoslav in 1901 and 1902, when street demonstrations followed leaflet campaigns by the local Social Democrats. On December 15, 1901, in a demonstration similar to those that had occurred earlier that year in Moscow, St. Petersburg, Khar'kov, Kazan, and Kishinev, a few hundred demonstrators, many wearing red jackets and red ties, defiantly ignored the governor's promise to suppress with force even the smallest demonstration and began marching on the central boulevard of Ekaterinoslav, singing the "Marseillaise," waving a red banner, and shouting "Long live political freedom!" and "Down with the autocracy!" The crowd swelled as sympathetic bystanders added their support before Cossacks wielding bullwhips and sabers broke up the demonstration. In 1902 Ekaterinoslav witnessed smaller, but similar, demonstrations during February and on May Day.[112]

This progress toward the politicization of the Donbass–Dnepr Bend working class was achieved at that time largely because artisans in the region played a central role in the emergence of a mass labor movement, just as they had earlier in Western Europe. In contrast to the predominantly Great Russian industrial workers and miners, a great number of the mostly Jewish artisans—suffering doubly because of factory competition on the one hand and anti-Semitic governmental discrimination and popular hostility on the other—were ready to support revolutionaries shouting "Down with the autocracy!" It was artisans, along with students—not industrial workers—who accounted for the bulk of the crowd when Ekaterinoslav saw Ekaterininskii Prospekt fill with demonstrators in 1901 and 1902.[113]

[111] Lane, *Roots*, p. 165.

[112] F. I. Dan, *Iz istorii rabochego dvizheniia i sotsial-demokratii v Rossii, 1900–1904 gg*. (Rostov-on-Don, n.d.), p. 20; D. Kol'tsov, "Rabochie v 1890–1904 gg.," in Martov, Maslov, and Potresov, *Obshchestvennoe dvizhenie*, 206; "Studencheskie volneniia v 1901–1902 gg.," *Krasnyi arkhiv*, no. 89–90 (1938): 269; E. Adamovich, "Vospominaniia starogo bol'shevika," *Istoriia ekaterinoslavskoi*, p. 228; *Iskra*, no. 14 (January 1, 1902): 1 and no. 15 (January 15, 1902): 1.

[113] The demonstrators demanded constitutional freedoms, but what in particular motivated student radicals to organize the 1901 demonstration was the beating of demonstrators in

The Jewish artisans maintained the continuity of the Social Democratic influence in Ekaterinoslav during the first years of the new century, when it was especially tenuous among the Great Russian steelworkers and railroad workers. Skilled workers active in the revolutionary movement did participate in the 1901 and 1902 demonstrations, but they were a distinct minority and stayed in the background. Not one industrial worker was among the fifty arrested in the 1901 demonstration.[114] While it is true that industrial workers' quiescence throughout the Donbass–Dnepr Bend during the first years of the twentieth century could be attributed to the dramatic downturn in the mining and metallurgical industries between 1901 and 1903,[115] since workers generally prove much less willing to take action when the job market tightens, more important were the still-powerful hold on workers of the myth of the "good tsar" and their animosity toward Jews and students. Some of the skilled workers were becoming increasingly responsive to the growing revolutionary propaganda and agitation in the Donbass–Dnepr Bend. But even with their growing strength in the ranks of the skilled, revolutionaries were in no position to direct mass labor unrest. As the next chapter shows, the revolutionary movement's penchant for centralization and hierarchical forms of organization, which excluded workers, also helps to explain its continued failure to capitalize on the discontent of Donbass–Dnepr Bend industrial workers and miners.

Khar'kov on December 2 and the 1899 "provisional regulations" of universities, which made assignment to army disciplinary battalions the penalty for student insubordination.

[114] Dan, *Iz istorii rabochego dvizheniia*, p. 20.

[115] Between 1901 and 1903, Russian industry went into a tailspin. The Donbass–Dnepr Bend labor force suffered mass layoffs and pay cuts as industrialists reduced their work force and payroll by about 25 percent. They also reduced workweeks and significantly lowered pay scales, often by 25 percent (*Vtoroi s"ezd RSDRP: Protokoly*, p. 544). Most of the workers fired during the industrial depression left the Donbass–Dnepr Bend.

1. The central avenue of Makeevka. Note the proximity of the French-owned Makeevka Company's steel mill and coal mines to the town center.

2. The New Russia Company's steel mill in Iuzovka. In the foreground is the model company housing available to some skilled workers with families.

3. A group of coal hewers posing in front of a mine shaft.

4. A “sled man” hauling coal in a mine.

5. Loading coal by hand into railroad wagons at the Gorsko-Ivanovskii mine.

6. Unloading coal for the blast furnaces at the New Russia Company's steel mill.

7. Briansk rolling mill workers and management.

8. A crew of pattern-makers posing with shop foremen and managers at the Briansk steel mill.

A. Smirnov

I. Mazanov

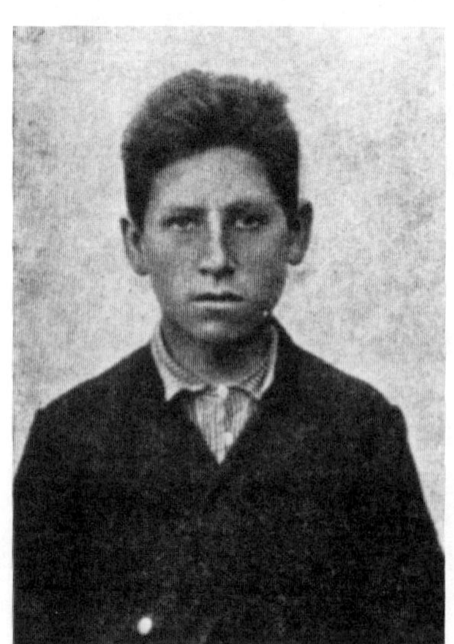

Afanasev

G. Metlitskii

9. Ekaterinoslav worker-*intelligents* active in Briansk steel mill Social Democratic kruzhki during the 1890s.

10. A reunion in the early 1920s of former workers who had been Bolshevik members of the Ekaterinoslav Social Democratic party. *Left to right*: I. Zakharenko, I. Merenkov, I. Shevchenko, G. Petrovskii.

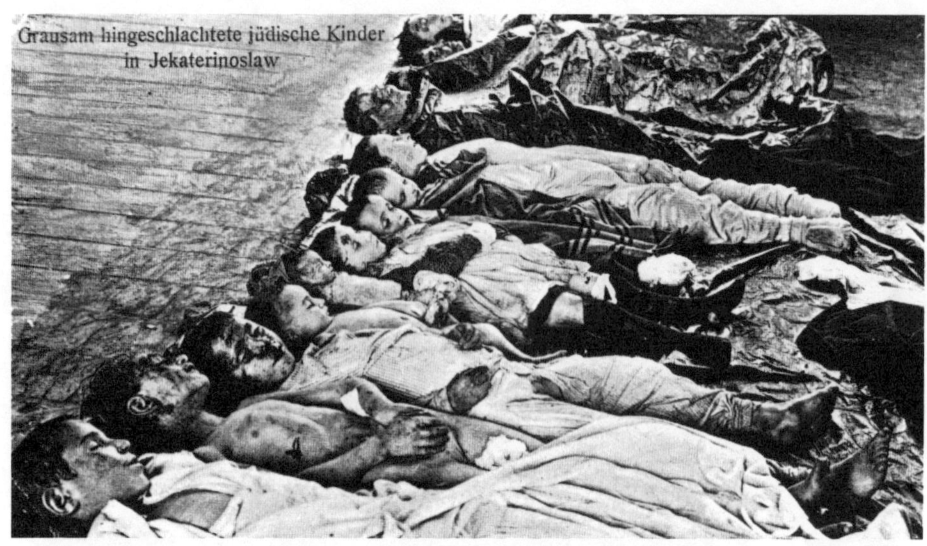

11. Victims of 1905 pogroms in Ekaterinoslav. Postcards published by the self-defense organization of the Labor Zionist party. From the Archives of the YIVO Institute for Jewish Research.

5

The Rise of Political Radicalism

> The worker who, despite all the danger, comes to our circles is above all a warrior . . . and our task is to release the powers and talents of that warrior, to place the sharply honed weapon of revolutionary socialism into his hands and teach him to use it.
>
> (*Iskra*)

THE STRAINS of rapid industrialization in the Donbass–Dnepr Bend proved insufficient to generate a mass outbreak of explicitly political working-class action. Workers' lack of education and general "backwardness," their faith in the tsar, and the determination of some workers to make the transition from skilled worker to foreman (or, in the case of artisans, from employee to employer) were all daunting obstacles for the revolutionary movement. An additional disincentive was that any involvement in underground political activity was forbidden by the government and harshly punished. All the same, radical activism did grow throughout the last decades of the century. Through study circles, or *kruzhki*, Donbass–Dnepr Bend activists enjoyed some success in their persistent efforts to radicalize workers and encourage them to act collectively. Activists worked hard to establish alliances across ethnic and regional lines, alliances based on common class interests. Many individual skilled workers and artisans responded to the revolutionary message and entered the radical underground. But the Donbass–Dnepr Bend revolutionary movement in the late nineteenth century failed to develop a strong base within the working class, or even a large number of factory contacts. It is not surprising, therefore, that the early history of the revolutionary movement was fitful and fraught with internal tensions, often between working-class recruits and their *intelligenty* leaders. Police sweeps repeatedly erased much progress.

The early decades of radical activity finally bore fruit between 1903 and 1905, following the emergence of revolutionary political parties around the turn of the twentieth century. Donbass–Dnepr Bend workers appeared to appreciate the need for organization and leadership and supported the revolutionaries' calls for general strikes en masse. During the 1905 Revolution, the Donbass–Dnepr Bend revolutionary movement, although faction-ridden and troubled by class tensions, emerged as a powerful force.

The transition to revolutionary activism was not as smooth as mass support for general strikes suggests. Although Donbass–Dnepr Bend workers felt exploited and responded to those promising that collective actions would alleviate their plight, they viewed with suspicion abstract notions of class solidarity and any emphasis on political rather than immediate economic change, especially when expounded by Jews and *intelligenty*. Even during the revolutionary year of 1905, working-class political radicalism coexisted with a deep reactionary strain. As we will see later, the mass of workers remained an extremely volatile group.

It was not a matter of chance that Ekaterinoslav was the one Donbass–Dnepr Bend city to join Russia's first general-strike wave, which swept across southern Russia in 1903. Ekaterinoslav had always been the center of revolutionary activity in the Donbass–Dnepr Bend. During the years leading up to the 1905 Revolution, Ekaterinoslav became a hotbed of radical underground activity—not just in comparison with cities in the Donbass–Dnepr Bend, but with cities throughout Russia. By the beginning of 1905, all of the three major revolutionary parties or movements—the Social Democrats, the Socialist Revolutionaries, and the Anarchists—enjoyed as strong a base in Ekaterinoslav as anywhere in the country.

The revolutionaries' numerical strength in Ekaterinoslav, however, meant nothing until they could elicit mass support from workers for general strikes, which would provide the revolutionary movement with its power. As one of Ekaterinoslav's Social Democrats recalled in 1905:

> For a long time, a very long time, we were forced to struggle in the darkness of political oppression. Under the threat of prison and exile, we withdrew into tight study circles, observing strict secrecy. Every step we took was done conspiratorially; all our work was conducted underground. From this underground our message had difficulty reaching the wide mass of workers, enormous difficulty. We suffered many arrests and succeeded in filling our ranks only with lone individuals from the ranks of conscious workers. The masses remained on the side, and only a grain of our teaching reached them. . . . Under the leaden lid of the autocratic order, as in the grave, all living forces in the country slumbered, and only the muffled voice of the revolutionaries from the underground disturbed the general quiet. This voice did trouble the reactionary forces, though, which felt that here was a growing enemy and which met each of our steps with furious blows. Victim after victim fell, but the SDs did not surrender and stubbornly carried out their underground work in anticipation of better days.[1]

[1] *Sotsial' demokrat*, no. 12 (August 18, 1905): 10.

Radical activities in the Donbass–Dnepr Bend began during the Populist era. In the 1870s and 1880s, as throughout Russia, the small number of locally active radicals shared a Populist orientation and concentrated their efforts on the peasantry rather than the working class. But while peasants were the Populists' primary target, many organizers continued their propaganda work after the harvest in places such as Iuzovka, where they tried to make contact with the workers employed in the recently opened steel mill and surrounding mines.[2] Discouraged by their reception in the countryside, many Populists thought Donbass–Dnepr Bend workers' continual movement back and forth between agriculture and industry meant that they could serve as a conduit for bringing the Populist message into the village.

Propaganda activity in the Donbass–Dnepr Bend was sporadic and its impact minimal during the 1870s and early 1880s. Populist ranks, small to start with, suffered wholesale arrests during the "Going to the People" movement and then were further depleted by the disillusionment following that failure. Worker circles did appear in Ekaterinoslav and Iuzovka, but the primary centers of Populist propaganda in southern Russia were located just outside the Donbass–Dnepr Bend, in Khar'kov and Rostov-on-Don. Khar'kov and Rostov did provide some cross-fertilization, as students and workers introduced to radical ideas there occasionally traveled to the Donbass–Dnepr Bend. One such activist was a worker with the pseudonym of Leon Andreev, who left Rostov in 1876 to work at the Posokhov mine. Andreev immediately organized a kruzhok consisting of a handful of the Posokhov workers. Such rare contact usually proved short-lived. It took the police just five days to learn of the kruzhok's evening meetings and Andreev's message to the miners: "There is no God. . . . capital and government bureaucrats oppress workers and prevent them from enjoying a better life. Everyone should be equal so there would be no rich men or bosses."[3] Occasionally a Populist organizer, if he did not overextend his stay, went undetected and achieved an extraordinary rapport with workers. Nikolai Bykovtsev, for example, went to work in the Grushevsk mines in 1876. His account suggests how *zemliachestvo*, the solidarity among workers of one region, could serve to protect radical organizers. Bykovtsev found in his short stay at the Grushevsk mines that workers would tolerate a radical in their midst rather than betray a brother *zemliak*:

> Among the mass of workers, of whom most were passportless migrants from Tambov, it was unnecessary to be especially secretive or restrained, since every-

[2] Potolov, *Rabochie Donbassa*, p. 190.

[3] *Byloe*, no. 8 (1907): 104–106, quoted in Potolov, *Rabochie Donbassa*, p. 109.

> one working in the mines knows very well that to live with wolves it is necessary to howl with wolves. In other words, those who did not like revolutionary conversations did not have to participate in them, but to violate the rules of the wandering brotherhood in one's devotion to the legal order meant to risk one's head.[4]

Such isolated, brief, and superficial contact by early Populist activists left no imprint on the Donbass–Dnepr Bend labor movement. There is no evidence linking Populist propaganda with Donbass–Dnepr Bend labor activity during the 1870s.[5]

In the early 1880s, Lugansk suddenly became a center of activity for Narodnaia Volia, "the People's Will," following the arrival of student activists from Khar'kov, Rostov, and Odessa and their success at recruiting workers into kruzhki in 1883. In 1884 Lugansk became one of the nation's main Narodnaia Volia printing centers and bomb factories. The exploits of the local *narodovol'tsy* also included armed robberies to raise money for the financially strapped and beleaguered movement after the assassination of Alexander II. But near the end of 1884, the movement suffered a near-fatal blow. The arrest of members of Narodnaia Volia's central organization in St. Petersburg provided the police with the names and addresses of activists in Lugansk. During the next few years, the Lugansk movement just barely managed to survive.[6] Then, on the night of April 14, 1887, the police seized most of the remaining members.[7]

The Populist movement in Ekaterinoslav also briefly achieved success during the 1880s. Ekaterinoslav's Narodnaia Volia movement became in 1884 the best organized and most effective of all the *narodovol'tsy* groups in the empire; and during the following year, Narodnaia Volia established its national headquarters in this still-embryonic industrial city.[8] The autocracy's practice of exiling arrested *narodovol'tsy* to provincial centers in the south and southwest helps explain why the movement's remaining leaders chose Ekaterinoslav as the place to resurrect the party following the police's decimation of the central organization in 1884. Ekaterinoslav's time in the radical limelight proved short, however. In 1886 the police arrested the *narodovol'tsy* in Ekaterinoslav, just as they had earlier in St. Petersburg and Lugansk. Following the police sweeps in Ekaterinoslav and Lugansk, the Populist movement in the Donbass–Dnepr Bend exhibited occasional signs of life, but it never truly recovered until the rise of the Socialist Rev-

[4] M. R. Popov, *Zapiski zemlevol'tsa* (Moscow, 1933), pp. 157–158.

[5] Potolov, *Rabochie Donbassa*, pp. 189–190.

[6] TsGIA, f. 1405, op. 88, d. 9998, p. 58.

[7] Potolov, *Rabochie Donbassa*, pp. 192–199.

[8] Norman M. Naimark, *Terrorists and Social Democrats: The Russian Revolutionary Movement under Alexander III* (Cambridge, Mass., 1983), p. 98.

olutionary party in the first years of the next century.[9] The few workers involved in Ekaterinoslav and Lugansk Populist circles during the 1880s exerted no appreciable influence on their fellow workers.[10]

Even though most of the few revolutionaries active in the Donbass–Dnepr Bend continued to be Populists, beginning in the late 1880s, radicals in Ekaterinoslav—as elsewhere in Russia—began to identify themselves as Marxists and their cause as social democratic.[11] The history of social democracy in the Donbass–Dnepr Bend dates back well before a Social Democratic party was formally organized in Russia in 1898. Social democracy received a boost during the early 1890s, when the rapid growth of the working class was coupled with further cause for disillusionment with the peasantry—namely, peasant passivity during the 1891 famine. The increasing number of strikes, plus workers' forceful response to the cholera epidemic in Iuzovka's 1892 "cholera *bunt*," stood in sharp contrast to peasant quiescence. While Donbass–Dnepr Bend radicals were appalled at the miners' and factory workers' rioting, anti-Semitism, and general lack of "consciousness," their spirits nonetheless could not help but be bolstered by these outbursts and other signs of the workers' growing discontent and penchant for mass action. With the industrialization of the region, Populism's emphasis on the peasantry seemed outmoded to most radical activists in the Donbass–Dnepr Bend eager to win mass support.

As in the case of the Populist movement, it was radical *intelligenty*, typically from middle- and upper-class backgrounds—the proverbial outside agitators—who first introduced Donbass–Dnepr Bend workers to social-democratic ideas and encouraged them to abandon uncoordinated riots and work stoppages to engage in more "conscious" actions. They were outsiders not just in the sense that they came from outside of the working class. Many of the first Marxist activists also arrived in the Donbass–Dnepr Bend from elsewhere in Russia. It is ironic, since the police and government authorities were so quick to blame these activists for worker discontent, that it was partly the government's own policy that sent many of these so-called outside agitators to the Donbass–Dnepr Bend. For all their success at penetrating revolutionary organizations with informers and wreaking havoc through mass arrests, the police in tsarist Russia also unintentionally helped spread social-democratic activities to cities such as Ekaterinoslav, just as it had earlier facilitated the spread of Populism. The government punished political offenders convicted of crimes not serious enough to

[9] Novopolin, "Iz istorii rabochego dvizheniia," p. 21; *Istoriia ekaterinoslavskoi*, p. xvi; Naimark, *Terrorists*, pp. 99–100; *Dnepropetrovsku*, p. 7.

[10] Naimark, *Terrorists*, pp. 48, 91–94.

[11] A. N. Vinokurov, "Vospominaniia o partiinoi rabote v Ekaterinoslave," *Proletarskaia revoliutsiia*, no. 1 (1921): 165.

warrant Siberian exile by banishing them to administrative exile within European Russia. Subject to the authorities' approval, political convicts could choose any non-university town as their place of exile—including cities with a large working-class population and an active radical underground, such as Ekaterinoslav.[12]

Social Democratic activity in Ekaterinoslav began to flourish in the early 1890s, much as the Populist movement had during the 1880s. Social Democrats (SDs) in Ekaterinoslav were among the first to organize Marxist study circles. These kruzhki differed little from the Populist circles they emulated. As an activist elsewhere later recalled, it seemed the logical way to proceed. The organizers of SD kruzhki thought that "gradually the number of workers studying Marx would increase, and that they would bring into their circles still more new members. With time, all of Russia would be covered with such study circles and we would form a socialist workers' party."[13] SD organizers enjoyed more success in Ekaterinoslav than in larger industrial centers, such as Khar'kov. By the mid-1890s, a handful of kruzhki existed in various places around the city. Despite the danger, selected students, artisans, and skilled workers from some of the city's factories chose to participate in the kruzhki organized by exiles.[14] Even so, the movement's significance at this time should not be exaggerated. To provide some context in which to measure the Social Democratic view of success, when the "Briansk kruzhok" consisted of a dozen members in 1894, it was considered a great success even though there were five hundred times that many workers employed at the Briansk mill who "did not even dream about political and social questions; among them 'darkness' reigned in the full sense of the word."[15] In addition, almost half of the circle's participants actually were not Briansk workers, but local Jewish artisans or students and young professionals.[16] In addition, the few factory

[12] Rimlinger, "Management of Labor Protest," p. 232; I. B. Polonskii, "Iz zhizni partiinoi organizatsii (1898–1900 gg.)," *Istoriia ekaterinoslavskoi*, pp. 131–132. As late as 1905, Russia still had only ten universities. None was located in the Donbass–Dnepr Bend. Radical students from Kiev and Khar'kov universities, as well as from Ekaterinoslav's Higher Mining Institute, were active in the Donbass–Dnepr Bend.

[13] S. I. Mitskevich, *Revoliutsionnaia Moskva, 1888–1905* (Moscow, 1940), p. 143, quoted in W. Bruce Lincoln, *In War's Dark Shadow: The Russians before the Great War* (New York, 1983), p. 178.

[14] Polevoi, *Zarozhdenie marksizma*, p. 487; Naimark, *Terrorists*, p. 210; R. Freidel', "Iz vospominanii o 1-om rabochem s.-d. organizatsii v Ekaterinoslave," *Istoriia ekaterinoslavskoi*, p. 7.

[15] S. Belkin, "Vospominaniia briantsa o pervoi s.-d. organizatsii v Ekaterinoslave," *Istoriia ekaterinoslavskoi*, p. 29. It is important to recognize, however, that kruzhki organizers focused more on recruiting individual workers with leadership qualities or potential than on recruiting large numbers of workers (Weinberg, "Social Democracy," p. 6).

[16] A. Smirnov, "Vospominanie o pervom kruzhke sots.-dem. rabochei partii g. Ekaterinoslava v 1894 godu," *Letopis' revoliutsii*, no. 2 (1923): 39.

workers who became involved in the Social Democratic movement often did so without much forethought. I. Mazanov, one of the young skilled workers in the Briansk circle, later recalled, "A friend of mine, A. Smirnov, one day 'simply' asked me if I wanted to read a banned booklet. Whether I read it then I don't recall, but the fact is that within a short time I already was in a kruzhok and had become a 'socialist.' I didn't understand at all the seriousness of the proposition. It simply tickled my vanity that I would be the kind of guy who knew socialists!"[17] At least partly because circle leaders did not want to alienate their few working-class recruits, Mazanov's understanding of socialism remained superficial. After being arrested and thrown into prison, Mazanov's religious upbringing quickly reasserted itself. "On Sundays I went to the prison chapel, confessed my sins, and received communion. The night before Easter I lit an icon candle and touchingly prayed 'on my knees' for the world of socialism. . . . Absurd, but that's how it was."[18] Mazanov's continued religious observance was not unusual, at least at this stage in the history of the Donbass–Dnepr Bend Social Democratic movement. The few workers the Social Democrats recruited from the Briansk mill continued to celebrate religious holidays by attending church services, after which they caroused and got drunk.[19]

Many of the Social Democrats' followers had at most a rudimentary understanding of the ideology, but by 1895 the movement in Ekaterinoslav appeared to be making significant progress. The Social Democrats could boast that they had gathered over one hundred people in a forest outside the city to celebrate May Day with speeches and the singing of socialist songs.[20] But the Social Democratic movement, like the Populist movement before it, proved to be vulnerable to arrests. The secret police used their own agents and workers they recruited to infiltrate the radical underground. In 1895 the police rounded up most of the participants in Ekaterinoslav's Social Democratic movement. From 1895 until the 1905 Revolution, police repression meant the fortunes of Ekaterinoslav's Social Democratic movement rose and fell dramatically. Each upsurge in the movement sooner or later led to a wave of arrests. As a result, Social Democratic activity in what had been a thriving center could slow to a crawl. The temporary lulls in revolutionary activity following mass arrests explain, at least partly, why to the small number of workers interested in

[17] I. Mazanov, "Pamiatka rabochego sotsialista," *Istoriia ekaterinoslavskoi*, p. 22.

[18] Ibid., p. 23.

[19] G. I. Petrovskii, "S 1893 g. po 1895 g.," *Istoriia ekaterinoslavskoi*, p. 49. Skilled, "conscious" workers in St. Petersburg, such as Semen Kanatchikov, also did not abandon religious habits until long after they began to share radical ideas (Reginald E. Zelnik, ed. and trans., *A Radical Worker in Tsarist Russia: The Autobiography of Semen Ivanovich Kanatchikov* [Stanford, 1986], p. 34).

[20] *Istoriia ekaterinoslavskoi*, p. xviii.

Social Democratic propaganda the movement seemed unsystematic or episodic and why Social Democrats in the Donbass–Dnepr Bend never led a mass action during the 1890s.[21]

Some of the working-class recruits in Ekaterinoslav's Social Democratic movement made the job of the political police easy by naively failing to keep their involvement in the radical underground secret. While many recruits to kruzhki considered the risk of arrest great and were appropriately conspiratorial, other novice members dismissed the veterans' obsession with the need for precautions. One of the skilled steelworkers in the Briansk kruzhok recalled in his memoirs that he and his young friends scoffed at the warnings of their more experienced leaders and allowed the composition of the Social Democratic kruzhok to become widely known among the work force at the Briansk mill. Throwing all caution to the wind, they freely engaged in political discussions and often openly agitated at the factory. Smirnov recalled feeling proud, not compromised or worried, when workers he had never met before openly approached him at the factory with requests for radical literature.[22]

Workers were more likely to fall into the clutches of the secret police than their *intelligent* leaders. In the 1895 police sweep, almost all the workers in the Briansk kruzhki were arrested and exiled for three years to eastern Siberia, while most of the *intelligenty* managed to escape.[23]

The 1895 arrests created a sensation among Ekaterinoslav's workers. The response to the arrests reflects just how little workers still understood about the Social Democrats and their goals. According to one of the arrested workers, news of the roundup left workers at the factory mystified:

> Workers had no idea why we had been arrested; to them we were just "good old boys." They asked in amazement, "How is it they got involved in such bad business?" Some said that books were the cause of our arrest. Based on this, it was rumored that we had been taken away for falsifying the books in the factory payroll office. The comrades who escaped arrest were not able to explain the true cause of our arrest because of the danger of revealing their association with us.[24]

Indeed, those workers who had had some involvement in Social Democratic circles and escaped arrest were seized by a "terrible panic."[25] Even so, within a few years Ekaterinoslav again became a center of Social Democratic worker activism. In fact, at various times during the second half of the 1890s, no other Russian city had a Social Democratic organization

[21] Wildman, *Making of a Workers' Revolution*, p. 103.
[22] *Istoriia ekaterinoslavskoi*, pp. 16, 22.
[23] Ibid., pp. 16, 29.
[24] Belkin, "Vospominaniia briantsa," p. 29.
[25] *Rabochee delo*, no. 1 (April 1, 1899): 84.

with as many working-class participants as Ekaterinoslav.[26] When the Russian Social Democratic party held its founding First Congress in 1898, just five local organizations were represented. Ekaterinoslav was one of them.

The rebirth of the Social Democratic movement in Ekaterinoslav following the 1895 arrests can largely be attributed to the arrival from elsewhere of another wave of political exiles and activists. Many of the country's leading Social Democrats, including workers and artisans previously active in Social Democratic groups elsewhere, flowed into Ekaterinoslav and quickly put their experience to work.[27] By 1898 the new arrivals more than filled the vacuum left by the 1895 arrests. Following the large textile strikes in St. Petersburg in 1896 and 1897, many of the capital's veteran Social Democrats arrived in Ekaterinoslav. One of the St. Petersburg exiles was the worker-revolutionary Ivan Babushkin, who soon headed a group consisting primarily of factory workers. Before long, other exiles managed, through prison contacts, to locate Social Democrats in Ekaterinoslav who had escaped arrest. Isaak Lalaiants joined with two other political exiles, K. A. Petrusevich and M. Orlov, to form kruzhki and lead an organization that was known in Ekaterinoslav as the "*intelligent* group."[28] Jewish activists from the northwest led a third group of Social Democrats in Ekaterinoslav. These three groups all operated independently of one another.

Jews played a large role in the formation of Social Democratic groups in Ekaterinoslav and elsewhere in the Donbass–Dnepr Bend, as they did throughout the Pale of Settlement.[29] Later, the Social Democratic committees at times consisted exclusively of Jews. That Jews were active in the revolutionary underground is hardly surprising, given the autocratic government's anti-Semitism and its discriminatory policies. Even within the Pale, those Jews who managed despite the quotas to acquire a higher secular education found it difficult to practice law, medicine, or other professions, and they were barred from academic and bureaucratic circles.[30]

Most of Ekaterinoslav's leading Jewish activists initially came from the Pale's northwestern provinces, where Social Democracy enjoyed unparalleled success in the 1890s, particularly in Vilna and Minsk. Itching to expand their radical organizing to include industrial workers, increasing numbers of these Jewish activists "crossed over" after 1895 into the Don-

[26] Potolov, *Rabochie Donbassa*, p. 219; Soiuz russkikh sotsial'demokratov, *Rabochee dvizhenie v Ekaterinoslave*, pp. 2–3; B. Eidel'man, ed., "K istorii vozniknoveniia R.S.-D.R.P.," *Proletarskaia revoliutsiia*, no. 1 (1921): 55; *Istoriia ekaterinoslavskoi*, pp. xx–xxi, xxv, 171.

[27] Wildman, *Making of a Workers' Revolution*, p. 44.

[28] Ibid., pp. 103–104.

[29] Naimark, *Terrorists*, pp. 187–188.

[30] High-ranking authorities were not all so blind that they failed to see the political risks in their persecution of Jews. The anti-Semitic minister of internal affairs V. K. Plehve, for example, unsuccessfully sought less-restrictive policies to improve Jewish conditions in "the interests of the state and of a sensible policy" (Rogger, *Jewish Policies*, p. 79).

bass–Dnepr Bend and the Slavic movement because the "proletariat" in northwestern cities consisted almost entirely of Jewish artisans.[31] Jewish activists commonly felt that without support from Russian workers, their dream of creating a mass movement to radically change the Russian empire's political and social system would remain just that, a dream.[32] To these Russified Jewish radicals, eager to enter the mainstream of the revolutionary movement, Ekaterinoslav seemed especially attractive because it was one of the few industrial centers located within the Pale, where they did not need a special "right of residence."[33]

It is important to note that the Donbass–Dnepr Bend revolutionary movement had a thoroughly Great Russian character throughout the period covered by this study, despite the Donbass–Dnepr Bend's location in the Ukraine and the considerable participation of Jews in the revolutionary movement. With few exceptions, leaflets distributed in the Donbass–Dnepr Bend were written in Russian, not Ukrainian or Yiddish. Social Democrats, as well as the intelligentsia generally, viewed Ukrainian as a crude peasant dialect of Russian. It was Russified Ukrainians, just as it was Russified Jews, who became active in the revolutionary movement.

All the Social Democratic groups in Ekaterinoslav busily formed worker kruzhki. But despite the manifest need to educate workers drawn into the movement, dissatisfaction with *kruzhkovshchina*—study circles as the central focus of the movement—was growing in Ekaterinoslav, as it was elsewhere. Critics argued that the working-class recruits in kruzhki were usually artisans or the more skilled of the industrial workers, who commonly did not share the idealism and revolutionary fervor that motivated students and other *intelligenty* to form or enter radical study circles. Artisans especially entered radical kruzhki with the goal of personal betterment, rather than political activism. Leaders complained that the young Jewish artisans active in their kruzhki were interested less in becoming selfless revolutionaries than in improving their Russian and gaining the schooling that would enable them to pass the high school equivalency exam, enter a university,

[31] *Istoriia ekaterinoslavskoi*, p. xx. Social Democrats referred to artisans, who in the Donbass–Dnepr Bend were primarily Jewish and worked and lived in the city center, as *gorodskie*, townsfolk.

[32] Furthermore, such Jewish activists often wanted to leave the traditional Jewish life of the Pale behind. As one historian has explained, since they themselves had abandoned Yiddish and religious orthodoxy, it was natural for them to want "to participate in general political movements" (Mendelsohn, *Class Struggle*, p. 29). Some Jewish revolutionaries denounced Jewishness in the strongest terms. Lev Deutsch stated that to him and his fellow Jewish revolutionaries, "everything that smelled of Jewishness called forth among us a feeling of contempt, if not more" (quoted in Henry J. Tobias, *The Jewish Bund in Russia: From Its Origins to 1905* [Stanford, 1972], p. 18).

[33] A. Vilenskii, "Iz vospominanii partiinogo tipografa ('Soiuz bor'by' i 'Rabochaia gazeta')," *Istoriia ekaterinoslavskoi*, p. 78; Wildman, *Making of a Workers' Revolution*, pp. 40–44.

and leave their fellow artisans behind.[34] Even so, artisans did figure among the Jewish Social Democrats arriving in Ekaterinoslav from the northwest in the second half of the 1890s—proof that circles often did achieve their goal of training worker-activists.

In industrial districts, kruzhki leaders were often afraid to identify themselves as Social Democrats because of factory workers' conservatism and lack of schooling. Wary of their working-class recruits, many kruzhki leaders waited to raise political and economic issues, and then did so quite carefully. Rather than discussing illegal literature and training socialist propagandists, the leaders of Ekaterinoslav's early factory circles often spent their time providing workers with an introduction to such subjects as history, geography, or physics, because recruited factory workers, like artisans, often expressed an enthusiasm for learning and demanded an education.[35] As one activist remembered, kruzhki leaders approached social and political issues "indirectly, by providing information about the situation of the working class in other countries, about the political system in Western Europe, so that a comparison with the system in our country unconsciously rose in their minds."[36] But as in the northwest, many of the artisanal and factory recruits tutored in Ekaterinoslav kruzhki later did play leading roles in Social Democratic activities. From the early years of the Social Democratic movement in Ekaterinoslav, once the artisanal and working-class members won the leaders' trust, kruzhki such as the one at the Briansk factory actively agitated workers. *Intelligent* members composed leaflets in simple language urging workers to fight for their economic interests; the kruzhki workers distributed the leaflets during the wee hours of the morning. They would make a complete sweep of the streets around the city's major factories and railroad workshop, leaving small piles of mimeographed leaflets where workers would see them when they tramped to work. Although most workers were still afraid to touch them (as of the mid-1890s, at least), Social Democratic leaflets were increasingly creating a stir among the mass of workers.[37] With the aid of their worker-recruits' knowledge of workers' grievances, the *intelligenty* could list in their leaflets specific demands and elucidate the connection between their grievances and the tsarist political order.

[34] Other Jewish *intelligenty* exhibited a "condescending, contemptuous attitude" toward the uneducated Jewish workers, whom they considered unworthy of "the teachings of socialism" (Mendelsohn, *Class Struggle*, pp. 45–46).

[35] G. Novopolin, "Iz istorii ekaterinoslavskogo 'Soiuz soiuzov'," *Puti revoliutsii*, no. 4 (1926): 22.

[36] Polonskii, "Iz zhizni," p. 140.

[37] *Istoriia ekaterinoslavskoi*, pp. xxx, 6–7, 13–14; M. Zeikman, "Ekaterinoslavskii Soiuz bor'by za osvobozhdenie rabochego klassa, 1895–98 gg.," *Letopis' revoliutsii*, no. 6 (1924): 171.

In 1897 organizational and tactical disputes hardened the splits in Ekaterinoslav's barely reborn Social Democratic movement. The infighting in Ekaterinoslav was hardly unusual. The radical Russian underground was notorious for disputes over seemingly minor issues. The initial dispute in Ekaterinoslav concerned the desire of the Jewish group from Vilna to transplant to Ekaterinoslav organizing techniques they had employed with success in the northwest. The Jewish activists from Vilna arrived in Ekaterinoslav determined "to recommend the adoption of more energetic tactics—in the jargon of the day, 'to proceed from propaganda to agitation.' "[38] In the major northwestern cities, Social Democrats had organized proto–trade unions known as *kassy* among Jewish artisans. Organized by craft, the kassy were mutual-aid societies to which workers contributed dues of as much as 10 percent of their monthly incomes. The kassy maintained strike funds, provided financial support or loans to their members in the event of illness or accidents, and organized lectures, libraries, "Saturday readings," and "evenings."[39] Ekaterinoslav's Vilna group organized some artisanal kassy, and it was not long before the kassy led a few small artisanal strikes.

The dispute concerned both the need for secrecy and the role of artisans in the movement—the same issues that helped split the Russian Social Democratic party on the national level a few years later. The opposition to the Vilna group, led by I. Kh. Lalaiants and K. A. Petrusevich, argued that forming kassy along craft lines or introducing them in large enterprises could not be done conspiratorially and would inevitably lead to arrests. They also questioned the importance of organizing kassy among artisans—and even the importance of organizing artisans at all, since the Social Democrats still had only minimal contacts inside Ekaterinoslav's factories. When the opponents of the Vilna group argued that the artisan movement should be secondary, they hit upon a touchy subject. This attack particularly stung because the Vilna group itself thought that to organize, agitate, and propagandize in the factories ought to be the priority; after all, the reason these activists had left the northwest for the Donbass–Dnepr Bend was to expand their radical activities beyond artisans to industrial workers. But their aspirations aside, there was no denying that it was among artisans, not industrial workers, that their efforts had enjoyed success in Ekaterinoslav. Of course, as even their critics conceded, there was also no denying that in the mid-1890s Ekaterinoslav's Jewish artisans were much

[38] J. L. H. Keep, *The Rise of Social Democracy in Russia* (Oxford, 1963), p. 45.

[39] Ezra Mendelsohn, "The Jewish Labor Movement in Czarist Russia, from Its Origins to 1905" (Ph.D. diss., Columbia University, 1966), p. 96; Priimenko, *Legal'nye organizatsii*, p. 127.

more receptive to the radical message than the city's factory workers.[40] The denigration of the role artisans could play in the movement proved to be the opening salvo in what would be a long and divisive battle in Ekaterinoslav's Social Democratic movement. The rebuked Vilna group responded by calling themselves the "workers' group," even though they had established few, if any, ties among factory workers.[41]

Ekaterinoslav's small but vigorous Social Democratic groups refused to cooperate with one another for months. Then, in December 1897, influenced by the example of Social Democrats in St. Petersburg, they came together to form a local section of the Soiuz bor'by za osvobozhdenie truda (Union of Struggle for the Emancipation of Labor). The nonviolent work stoppages by almost the entire textile work force in St. Petersburg in 1896 and again in 1897 greatly bolstered Social Democratic spirits throughout the country. The solidarity achieved by the thirty thousand textile workers in the capital seemed to demonstrate that agitation could succeed. In Ekaterinoslav, as in other centers of Social Democratic activity, local leaders hoped that the St. Petersburg strikes indicated that the Russian labor movement was finally making the transition from *stikhiinost'* (spontaneity) to *soznanie* (consciousness), from unorganized, often riotous outbursts of discontent to more disciplined, organized mass actions. Ekaterinoslav's Social Democrats thought that the city's workers might be ready to respond to agitation for such mass actions. The riot at the Briansk mill in 1898, following their largest leaflet campaign ever, disabused them of this notion, at least temporarily. The top priority of the Ekaterinoslav Soiuz bor'by in the months after the Briansk riot became not agitating for mass strikes, but convincing workers of the damage to the labor movement that such a "wild outburst" caused. Social Democratic leaflets held up the nonviolent strikes in St. Petersburg and other Russian cities as an example that Ekaterinoslav's workers should emulate.[42] Workers were discouraged from acting as they thought best. Ekaterinoslav's revolutionary movement sought not to ignite workers, but rather to channel discontent into nonviolent, "conscious" actions. As a historian of the Jewish labor movement

[40] Lalaiants, "O moikh vstrechakh," p. 60. In Odessa at this time, Social Democratic leaders were so afraid of scaring off or antagonizing Russian workers, or of giving the government reason for labeling the SD movement a "Jewish intrigue," that they prohibited activists from recruiting Jewish workers (Weinberg, "Social Democracy," pp. 6–7). That artisans generally proved to be more radical and active than industrial workers has been well documented by historians of European labor and revolutionary movements (E. Mendelsohn, "The Russian Jewish Labor Movement and Others," in *Studies in Modern Jewish Social History*, ed. Joshua A. Fishman [New York, 1972], pp. 91–92).

[41] *Rabochee delo*, no. 1 (April 1, 1899): 85; Wildman, *Making of a Workers' Revolution*, p. 103; *Istoriia ekaterinoslavskoi*, pp. xx–xxi, 174; *Listok rabotnika*, no. 9–10 (November 1898): 15.

[42] Soiuz russkikh sotsial'demokratov, *Rabochee dvizhenie v Ekaterinoslave*, p. 5.

concluded, to the extent that the Social Democrats thought their actions had helped to instigate violent outbursts, in the Donbass–Dnepr Bend and elsewhere, the movement "must have occasionally felt that it had created a Frankenstein monster, a force quite alien to the ideals of the Marxist intelligentsia."[43]

While the Social Democratic party's influence on the mass of workers in Ekaterinoslav remained minimal, between 1898 and 1902 the party did dramatically increase in importance and size and succeeded in organizing street demonstrations.[44] Ekaterinoslav's Social Democrats not only became charter members of the Russian Social Democratic Labor party (RSDRP), they were responsible for proposing the First Party Congress, which met secretly in a simple one-story house in Minsk in 1898.[45] In January 1899, Ekaterinoslav's Social Democrats issued the first leaflet that proudly displayed the new party seal. A year later, Ekaterinoslav superseded Kiev as the most important SD center in southern Russia when a group of Jewish *intelligenty* published the first issue of *Iuzhnyi rabochii* (Southern Worker), which proved to be a serious competitor to *Iskra* (Spark) as the party's leading organ.[46] The political police, a Bund correspondent, and a local SD activist all estimated that by 1903 membership in Ekaterinoslav's Social Democratic party had grown to eight hundred people. Another two hundred members resided in the industrial suburb of Amur.[47]

The success Social Democrats achieved in recruiting both Great Russian industrial workers and Jewish artisans, despite the tensions between them, was partly due to their isolation from one another. The Social Democrats' organizational method and residential patterns in industrial towns kept the two groups separate. The Social Democrats organized propaganda groups by district, so that kruzhki usually did not bring together workers residing in the industrial districts or suburbs with artisans, who generally resided in the center of town. In addition, kruzhki composed of Jewish artisans gen-

[43] Mendelsohn, *Class Struggle*, p. 104.

[44] By the last years of the century, two hundred members participated in a total of twenty-five kruzhki in Ekaterinoslav (*Istoriia ekaterinoslavskoi*, p. xxvi).

[45] Novopolin, "Iz istorii rabochego dvizheniia," p. 23.

[46] Soiuz russkikh sotsial'demokratov, *Rabochee dvizhenie v Ekaterinoslave*, p. xxvii. Lenin was so jealous of *Iskra*'s regional competitor that he ordered his local agents to "penetrate" and "undermine" it. One might even wonder whether it was merely fortuitous that *Iuzhnyi rabochii*'s editors were later arrested after the police followed I. Kh. Lalaiants from Lenin to the *Iuzhnyi rabochii* press since *Iskra*-ites replaced *Iuzhnyi rabochii*'s arrested editors. See Elwood, *Russian Social Democracy*, p. 13; Wildman, *Making of a Workers' Revolution*, pp. 222–240; and *Istoriia ekaterinoslavskoi*, pp. xxvi, xxix.

[47] TsGAOR, DP OO, f. 102, 1905, d. 1800, ch. 2 (Okhrana report, November 11, 1905), p. 5; *Posledniia izvestiia*, no. 249 (September 18, 1905): 9; I. B. Polonskii, "Vospominaniia," *Istoriia ekaterinoslavskoi*, p. 360.

erally met on Saturdays, while industrial workers met on Sundays.[48] Where ethnic intermingling commonly did occur was in Great Russian worker kruzhki led by Jewish *intelligenty*.

Ekaterinoslav Social Democrats helped create Social Democratic groups elsewhere in the Donbass–Dnepr Bend. In the late 1890s, the party organization in Ekaterinoslav, as well as those in Khar'kov and Rostov, began to organize in the Donets Basin. Many party members believed that the time was finally ripe to begin seriously trying to organize the miners and steelworkers outside Ekaterinoslav. Until then, the Social Democratic movement had never secured more than a foothold in the Donets Basin. In contrast to Ekaterinoslav, the radical groups that existed in Donets Basin towns during the 1890s were mainly tiny groups of *intelligenty*—for example, from among the white-collar staffs at the railroad stations—who gathered to discuss theoretical issues and radical literature.[49] Such kruzhki were isolated, with little or no contact with one another or with workers. Occasionally the arrival of an underground newspaper with reports on activities elsewhere lessened somewhat their isolation and fortified their sense of participating in a growing movement. Agitational leaflets usually reached workers only when circulating activists happened to pass through the Donets Basin.

Yet when the call went out in 1898 to spread social-democratic propaganda to the mines and factories of the Donets Basin, activists such as N. Zelikman, a member of the Don committee in Rostov, became wildly optimistic:

> Our hearts and minds were seized with big plans to flood the mines with leaflets and literature and awaken the masses from their somnolence, and then to organize mass meetings and study groups and thereby forge a powerful union of factory workers and miners, creating support for the Petersburg and Moscow labor movements and unifying Donets workers into one powerful, threatening, southern proletarian group, extending from the walls of Rostov to Lugansk and Ekaterinoslav.[50]

Reality quickly deflated such grandiose dreams. Activists soon complained again that "the workers are benighted and move too often from place to place . . . [so that] to establish even a simple organization is inconceivable."[51] As difficult as it was to organize workers in Ekaterinoslav, it proved to be much more difficult in the steel towns and especially in the mining communities of the Donets Basin.

Social Democratic party organizations in the Donets Basin did slowly

[48] *Rabochee dvizhenie v Rossii v XIX veke*, vol. 4, pt. 1:164.
[49] Kharechko, "Sotsial-demokraticheskii soiuz," p. 15.
[50] Ibid., p. 16.
[51] Levus, "Iz istorii," p. 60.

grow after 1898, and by 1901 kruzhki existed in most of the large factory towns and in some of the larger mining communities. Many of these kruzhki considered themselves social democratic, but often that meant little. As in Ekaterinoslav, many kruzhki, such as the one in the mining settlement of Shcherbinovsk, were concerned more with simply educating the miners than with political propaganda.[52] In addition, a particularly acute shortage of leaflets and revolutionary literature in the Donets Basin hindered radicals intent on agitating workers.

Social-democratic groups in the mining settlements generally were smaller and less active than groups in the Donets Basin's steel towns. Most mining settlements suffered chronically from the absence of a radical intelligentsia, although some radical engineers and doctors and some student interns from the St. Petersburg Mining Institute provided leadership and wrote leaflets. But even the few experienced organizers active in the Donets Basin generally found it extraordinarily difficult to make inroads among workers in pit villages. A. Shestakov, an enthusiastic young veteran of the underground, managed to get hired as a clerk at the Chulkovskii mine outside Iuzovka. But despite the seemingly intolerable conditions there, his determined efforts succeeded in establishing only one good contact with a miner. A mining accident could temporarily arouse the miners' ire, but Shestakov discovered the Chulkovskii work force to be a hard-drinking lot with no interest in reading or politics. Shestakov could chat politics with Nikita, his sole contact, and the friends that often accompanied Nikita, but Shestakov always found it necessary "to hold back. To hand out literature in such conditions was ticklish. It was necessary to come up with some other way."[53] Before long, Shestakov conceded defeat and returned to Iuzovka. There he enjoyed success organizing Jewish artisans, who were more literate and politically aware.

In Iuzovka and Lugansk, Social Democratic kruzhki began distributing leaflets in 1901, and formal party organizations were set up in both of these steel towns in 1902. As in the case of Ekaterinoslav, the activism in Iuzovka and Lugansk can be explained largely by the sizable Jewish and artisanal populations and the greater number of *intelligenty* present there. In Iuzovka, the Social Democratic party organization at first consisted "almost entirely of Jews," according to the memoirs of T. Kharechko.[54] Factory workers were more active in Lugansk, but the hostility between Ukrainian and Great Russian workers posed an especially serious obstacle for Social Democrats trying to recruit Ukrainian workers. One Soviet historian, I. Berkhin, acknowledged that "the well-known estrangement be-

[52] Kharechko, "Sotsial-demokraticheskii soiuz," pp. 19–20.

[53] Shestakov, "Na zare," p. 160.

[54] "Sotsial-demokraticheskii soiuz," p. 19. See also Shestakov, "Na zare," p. 159.

tween migrant and local workers, which the factory administrations and police authorities did their best to inflame, hampered the unification of workers and created difficult conditions for underground work . . . especially since the first propagandists and agitators and the most active participants in circles were visiting Russian workers."[55]

Undeterred, in January 1902 the party committees in Iuzovka and Lugansk, with support from Ekaterinoslav and Rostov, organized an umbrella organization to unite all the Social Democratic groups active in the Donets Basin. During 1903 the Social Democratic Mining and Metal Workers Union changed its name to the Donets Union of the Russian Social Democratic Labor Party and established connections with local groups in almost every sizable industrial town in the Donets Basin, to include a total of thirty circles and five hundred *intelligent* and worker-*intelligent* members.[56] By the standards of provincial SD organizations elsewhere in Russia, the Donets Union was "an unusually successful undertaking."[57] The Donets Union tried to overcome the isolation of the pit villages by giving individual activists in Iuzovka and Lugansk personal responsibility for some mines.[58] During the first one and a half years of its existence, members of the Donets Union distributed in nighttime "excursions" a large amount of radical literature to workers in the Donets Basin: 63,000 copies of thirteen leaflets that the Union itself had composed and printed; 3,000 leaflets by member organizations; and 15,500 leaflets from the Ekaterinoslav and Rostov party organizations. The "letters," as the miners called the leaflets, often created a stir, but the Social Democrats repeatedly complained that miners completely misunderstood their message. Just as had happened earlier in 1898 when the Social Democrats in Ekaterinoslav first began distributing leaflets on a large scale, workers in the Donets Basin interpreted the leaflets as calls to riot, even after the Donets Union issued a special leaflet explaining the futility of rioting and the harm to the labor movement caused by earlier Donbass–Dnepr Bend riots.[59] But in contrast to the situation in Ekaterinoslav in 1898, when the Briansk *bunt* followed the first mass distribution of the leaflets, no major disturbance erupted following the beginning of the SD's propaganda and agitation campaign in the Donets Basin.

[55] *Luganskaia bol'shevistskaia organizatsiia*, p. 14.

[56] *Iskra*, no. 45 (August 1, 1903): 8; Kirzner, *Gornorabochie*, pp. 20–21; I. Moshinskii, "K voprosu o s.-d. (Donetskom) soiuze gornozavodskikh rabochikh," *Proletarskaia revoliutsiia*, no. 65 (1927): 233.

[57] Wildman, *Making of a Workers' Revolution*, p. 222.

[58] Elwood, *Russian Social Democracy*, p. 47.

[59] Kirzner, *Gornorabochie*, p. 20; Keep, *Rise of Social Democracy*, p. 110; *Iskra*, no. 45 (August 1, 1903): 8; Kharechko, "Sotsial-demokraticheskii soiuz," p. 26.

Revolutionaries in the Donbass–Dnepr Bend, as throughout Russia, continually failed to practice the unity they preached to workers. Squabbles within Social Democratic organizations repeatedly absorbed the activists' attention and undermined their ability to lead the labor movement. Disputes over party democracy were at the root of the internal dissension and bickering. The gulf that separated educated society from the Russian masses contributed to the inbred distrust politically active skilled workers felt toward students and other *intelligenty* active in radical circles.[60]

In 1900 the first issue of the Social Democrats' newspaper *Iskra* had called for "a firm division of labor in the various aspects of our work."[61] Social Democrats in the Donbass–Dnepr Bend, as elsewhere, set up local party organizations in a three-tiered structure.[62] At the top of each of these pyramids was a small "committee," with "centers" in the middle and "cells" at the bottom. The committee members decided all the important tactical questions, although the centers and cells had the right to vote on everything from changes in the party program to when to distribute leaflets. While artisans and industrial workers might occasionally sit on the committee, the half dozen to dozen members occupying these positions were almost always *intelligenty*, and they were reluctant to keep workers informed on internal party politics.[63]

Workers in the Donets Union proved more successful than workers in Ekaterinoslav and elsewhere in gaining positions of responsibility because of the relative shortage of party *intelligenty* in the Donets Basin. In its report to the Social Democrats' Second Party Congress, the Donets Union asserted that it was "one of just a few organizations in Russia in which the workers themselves play a predominant and highly influential role."[64] On the other hand, the shortage of SD *intelligenty* leaders in the Donets Basin helps account for the Donets Union's comparative inability to organize

[60] Here is how one worker-activist in another region of the empire put it: "Don't believe in their radicalism; it won't last long. As long as you're a student, you sing forbidden songs, tell funny anecdotes about the royal family, put on high boots, and go around unkempt, with long hair. But once he finishes the university and gets a good position, the student will become a hard taskmaster or a tsarist flunky, the kind who sits on our necks just like the ones we're fighting now. . . . All I'm saying is not to put too much faith in the intelligentsia—it will deceive you" (Zelnik, *Radical Worker*, pp. 142–143).

[61] *Iskra*, no. 1 (December 1900), quoted in Leopold Haimson, *The Russian Marxists and the Origins of Bolshevism* (Boston, 1955), p. 119.

[62] Kharechko, "Sotsial-demokraticheskii soiuz," p. 19.

[63] *Istoriia ekaterinoslavskoi*, pp. xxxi–xxxvii; V. O. Levitskii [V. Tsederbaum], *Za chetvert' veka: Revoliutsionnye vospominaniia, 1892–1917* (Moscow-Leningrad, 1927), vol. 1, pt. 2:134; TsGAOR, DP OO, f. 102, 1898, d. 5, ch. 8, l. I (Okhrana report, March 23, 1903), pp. 4–5. Within the Social Democrats' hierarchical, secretive organizational structure, local central committees themselves were subservient to the *intelligenty* in the top central committee, which operated from abroad.

[64] *Vtoroi s"ezd RSDRP: Protokoly*, p. 550.

general strikes in 1903 and during the 1905 Revolution, when their own workers failed to issue leaflets and maintain ties among factories and cities. Conversely, in Ekaterinoslav, *intelligent* domination of the party organization led to serious problems within party ranks.

From the inception of Ekaterinoslav's SD organization, worker unhappiness with the *intelligent* leaders' condescension and with their monopoly on power led to infighting. Worker-activists long remembered how, in Ivan Babushkin's words, the local *intelligenty* "had acted wrongly and even criminally towards the workers" when they decided to send one of their own to the First Party Congress, without even bothering to inform the rank and file.[65] Workers' discontent with what the *intelligent* leaders called the "natural division of labor" became endemic in the Social Democratic movement.[66] Later, around 1903, many disaffected working-class Social Democrats defected when the Socialist Revolutionary party and Anarchist groups started to become established in Ekaterinoslav and the option to switch to a different revolutionary party became available.

Radical workers' attitudes toward party *intelligenty* were often much more ambivalent than their complaints indicated. *Intelligent* condescension only reinforced workers' own insecurity about their oratorical and writing ability. Babushkin recalled that SD artisans and workers felt "orphaned" after the arrest of the party's intellectuals.[67] Following such a wave of arrests in Ekaterinoslav in 1900, local artisans formed a new committee, but they welcomed guidance from veteran Social Democrats when they arrived.[68]

The new Ekaterinoslav committee provoked the first brouhaha when in 1901 it abandoned any pretense of adhering to the "elective principle." Obviously influenced by Lenin's *Iskra* platform, the newly arrived *intelligenty* on the Ekaterinoslav committee announced that the committee would henceforth appoint or "co-opt" all new members of the centers and cells, as well as members of the committee. To justify its conspiratorial, nondemocratic character, the committee cited the security risks elections posed.[69] The committee also argued—not unreasonably—that besides the

[65] *Pervyi s"ezd R.S.D.R.P., mart 1898 g.: Dokumenty i materialy* (Moscow, 1958), p. 184, quoted in Keep, *Rise of Social Democracy*, p. 54.

[66] It is notable that much of the worker-*intelligent* discord Allan Wildman cited in his seminal study *The Making of a Workers' Revolution* comes from Ekaterinoslav's Social Democratic party organization.

[67] *Recollections*, p. 111.

[68] Evgeniia Adamovich, who brought to Ekaterinoslav significant experience in the SD movement in various cities around Russia, was elected head of the new committee. Even the bookbinder Fishel Shteinberg ("Samuil"), who in 1902 helped lead the "Workers' Opposition" in Ekaterinoslav, initially supported the outside *intelligenty* (*Istoriia ekaterinoslavskoi*, pp. xxxi–xxxii).

[69] Security concerns were legitimate; the reports in the archives of the Okhrana (the political

security risks, the problem with elections was that they often deprived the local committee of the best, most experienced leaders in the Social Democratic movement. In an attempt to stay one step ahead of the police and to be where the movement was most active, many of the party's leading *intelligenty* inside the country continually moved from city to city. Ekaterinoslav's committee wanted to be able to "co-opt" these "professional revolutionaries" immediately upon their arrival in Ekaterinoslav, instead of forcing them to execute minor functions until they won the respect of the rank and file and could be elected. For their part, local artisan and factory-worker activists, who generally could not afford the luxury of moving on when the revolutionary movement experienced a lull or flared up elsewhere, resented the ability of the *intelligenty* to fly into town and expect a leadership position.[70]

In short, workers in the Ekaterinoslav SD party organization understandably resented the notion that they should be at the beck and call of a committee within which they enjoyed little influence. Members of the centers and cells strongly objected to the committee's decision to exclude them from positions of power and the decision-making process. "For workers to agree to these reforms would mean they would lose any influence in party affairs and would become just a tool in the hands of the *intelligenty*."[71] Of course, this was not new. Even before this dispute, members of the lower bodies perceived the committee as elitist and little inclined to solicit workers' input on important matters. But now the inner group operated in such secrecy and cloaked itself in such mystery that working-class party members, including members of the center, were allowed to know the identity of only one or two members of the committee.[72] The directive stipulating that members of the committee should not risk arrest by participating in the demonstrations they organized also rankled members of the lower bodies.

After a year of discord that almost split the Ekaterinoslav Social Democratic party, and despite some concessions guaranteeing members of the opposition a voice in committee decisions, a so-called Workers' Opposi-

---

police) make clear that even without elections, the secret police gained such inside information as the identities of party members. Of course, it could also be argued that the elections did not matter if the Okhrana was able to identify party leaders anyway. Regardless, workers commonly thought the conspiratorial precautions of the *intelligenty* reflected a lack of trust in workers.

[70] TsGAOR, DP OO, f. 102, 1898, d. 5, ch. 8, l. I (Okhrana report, March 23, 1903), p. 5. It should be noted, however, that many worker-activists, increasingly "afraid of their own shadow," were quick to leave the movement when they felt threatened by the prospect of arrest (Babushkin, *Recollections*, pp. 116, 137).

[71] TsGAOR, DP OO, f. 102, 1905, d. 1800, ch. 2 (Okhrana report, November 11, 1905), p. 6.

[72] Polonskii, "Iz zhizni," p. 135.

tion formed in the summer of 1902 to mobilize the resentment of the workers against the committee. The Workers' Opposition clearly enjoyed the support of a large percentage of the party's workers, even though it was led by a student, the former tailor David Braginskii. In the spring of 1903, relations reached the breaking point, and the Workers Opposition proclaimed itself the "Ekaterinoslav Workers' Committee" and adopted *Rabochee Delo*'s more democratic platform. In an embarrassing exchange of public recriminations, both the old and the new committees issued leaflets denouncing the other as an imposter.[73]

The two sides did manage to cooperate during Ekaterinoslav's general strike in August 1903, when the two Social Democratic factions formed a single strike commission consisting of three representatives each from the pro-*Iskra* and the pro-*Rabochee Delo* committees. Nonetheless, the split continued until December 1903, when the two factions formed a composite committee. Of course, after Lenin's intransigent insistence at the Second Party Congress in 1903 that the party be directed from abroad and membership limited to professional revolutionaries, the divisions among Ekaterinoslav's Social Democrats became institutionalized. When Ekaterinoslav's Social Democrats formally divided late in 1904 into Bolshevik and Menshevik factions, the Workers Opposition came to constitute the Mensheviks. Entering the revolutionary upsurge that followed, the Mensheviks were the larger of the two SD factions in Ekaterinoslav and in almost all the other centers of revolutionary activity in the Donbass–Dnepr Bend, although many of Ekaterinoslav's Worker Oppositionists left the SDs to join the Socialist Revolutionaries when the Mensheviks proved to be hardly more democratic than the Bolsheviks.[74]

The Mensheviks would dominate the Social Democratic movement in the Donbass–Dnepr Bend throughout the course of the 1905 Revolution.[75] They owed their predominance largely to the overwhelming support they received from Jewish artisans. Industrial workers divided their

[73] TsGAOR, DP OO, f. 102, 1905, d. 1800, ch. 2 (Okhrana report, November 11, 1905), pp. 5–6; TsGAOR, DP OO, f. 102, 1898, d. 5, ch. 8 (Okhrana reports, March 30, 1903 and April 10, 1903), pp. 17, 21; *Istoriia ekaterinoslavskoi*, pp. xxxvii, 337, 362–363; Wildman, *Making of a Workers' Revolution*, pp. 220, 242–244; Levitskii, *Za chetvert' veka*, p. 135. Similar anti-*Iskra* groups formed in the Donets Basin (Lane, *Roots*, p. 162).

[74] TsGAOR, DP OO, f. 102, 1898, d. 5, ch. 8, l. I (*Prestupnaia propaganda sredi rabochikh i rasprostranenie sredi nikh prestupnykh vozvanii*), p. 163; TsGAOR, DP OO, f. 102, 1905, d. 1800, ch. 2 (Okhrana report, November 11, 1905), p. 8; Wildman, *Making of a Workers' Revolution*, p. 252.

[75] TsGAOR, DP OO, f. 102, 1905, d. 1800, ch. 2 (Okhrana report, November 11, 1905), p. 8; Zaitsev, "Bol'sheviki Iuzovki," p. 161. Representatives of both the Ekaterinoslav organization and the Donets Union voted with the Mensheviks at all the SD party congresses until 1909 (Elwood, *Russian Social Democracy*, p. 80).

allegiance more evenly.[76] The ethnic composition of the Menshevik leadership reflected the composition of the party's membership, as Jewish *intelligenty* generally filled the majority of Menshevik leadership positions.[77]

It is important to note that these labels often meant nothing to worker-activists. In out-of-the-way mining towns, the schism for some time remained just a rumor. Even after separate factions formed, activists could see little difference between the Bolsheviks and Mensheviks and often worked simultaneously in both organizations.[78] One such worker informed a Bolshevik leader in Ekaterinoslav, "Apparently we, the workers, are considered Mensheviks simply because Mensheviks came here. If the intelligentsia here were Bolsheviks we would be Bolsheviks."[79] While many *intelligenty* in Ekaterinoslav became engrossed in the intraparty dispute between Mensheviks and Bolsheviks, becoming "factionalists to the point of fanatics,"[80] workers predictably became disenchanted with the leaders of the labor movement when they devoted their time to squabbles far removed from workers' concerns. The delegate from Ekaterinoslav complained to the Third Party Congress that the SDs' factional dispute had led many workers to think of the Bolsheviks as a "small group of intellectuals who are all talk and no action."[81]

Workers were in no position to participate in the doctrinal disputes that so concerned the *intelligent* leadership of the two Social Democratic factions, even if they had wanted to. Even worker-activists only vaguely understood Marxist doctrine and the political goals of the revolutionary movement.[82] The Social Democrats, and the Socialist Revolutionaries as well, would learn later that the liberal goals of the revolutionary movement, which they all grudgingly supported in 1905, were not what workers thought they had been fighting and dying for. As we will see, when workers saw revolutionaries rejoicing at the announcement of the October Manifesto, many would feel they had been duped by the revolutionary intelligentsia.

[76] Lane, *Roots*, p. 163.

[77] This difference between the ethnic composition of the Mensheviks and Bolsheviks holds true for the émigré leadership of the two factions. Of the nine top Menshevik leaders through 1905, four were Jewish and two were Georgian. The Bolsheviks' top leaders, whose ethnicity is more difficult to identify, may all have been Great Russians (Lane, *Roots*, p. 32).

[78] P. A. Moiseenko, *Vospominaniia, 1873–1923* (Moscow, 1924), p. 150.

[79] "Perepiska ekaterinoslavskoi i luganskoi organizatsii s N. Leninym i N. K. Krupskoi," *Proletarskaia revoliutsiia*, no. 51 (1926): 23.

[80] Diadia Vania, "Russko-Iaponskaia voina," *Materialy po istorii ekaterinoslavskoi sotsial-demokraticheskoi organizatsii bol'shevikov i revoliutsionnykh sobytii 1904–1905–1906 gg.* (Ekaterinoslav, 1926), quoted in Lane, *Roots*, p. 164.

[81] Letter no. 9 (May 30, 1905), *Proletarskaia revoliutsiia*, no. 51 (1926): 18.

[82] The tsarist censors, for their part, did not consider Marxism particularly dangerous, sanctioning the publication of abstract and theoretical works by Marx and Engels and by such leading Russian Social Democrats as Plekhanov, Lenin, and Martov.

During the 1905 Revolution, Ekaterinoslav's Social Democrats found they were unprepared to lead a revolutionary movement at least partly because of their undemocratic party organization. In mid-1905 the Social Democrats wrote that their underground activities and secretive, centralized organizational structure left them ill equipped to lead a mass movement:

> The conscious workers became too accustomed to relying on the top of our organization, on our committee . . . believing that most of the work will be implemented without their knowledge. . . . In order for our organization to adjust to the present mass movement, we need to distribute responsibility for important functions to the widest circle of workers. In order for the lower groups and organized cells to achieve the greatest possible independence, we need to put widely into practice the elective principle.[83]

But despite defections and internal problems, the Social Democrats in Ekaterinoslav still possessed considerable strength on the eve of the 1905 Revolution, compared with Social Democratic party organizations elsewhere in the empire. Comparisons of party strength between cities are difficult, partly because arrests subjected local parties to dramatic ups and downs in membership. But one indication of the strength of the Social Democrats in Ekaterinoslav in 1905 is that the Menshevik leader Iulii Martov, in a 1909 study of the socialist movement, considered Ekaterinoslav one of the three largest Social Democratic strongholds during the 1905 Revolution. Including both Mensheviks and Bolsheviks, Martov estimated that the Social Democratic parties in St. Petersburg, Odessa, and Ekaterinoslav each had about one thousand members early in 1905, with a slightly smaller number in Moscow.[84] The success achieved by the Social Democrats in Ekaterinoslav is, of course, particularly striking considering the small size of the city compared to the capitals and Odessa. Social Democratic parties grew considerably during 1905 and 1906. Ralph Elwood estimates Social Democratic membership in Ekaterinoslav to have been 2,000 in 1905–6. The party organization in Lugansk could claim 1,000 members, while membership in the Donets Union reached 4,500.[85]

Activists of all ideological hues enjoyed success among workers in the Donbass–Dnepr Bend. While the Socialist Revolutionaries never threatened the Social Democrats' dominance of Ekaterinoslav's revolutionary movement, they did become serious rivals, as did the Anarchists to a much lesser extent. The Socialist Revolutionary party, as distinct from earlier Populist groups, began organizing in Ekaterinoslav and elsewhere in the Donbass–

[83] *Sotsial'demokrat*, no. 12 (August 18, 1905): 11.

[84] L. Martov, "Sotsialdemokratiia 1905–1907 gg.," in Martov, Maslov, and Potresov, *Obshchestvennoe dvizhenie*, 572.

[85] Elwood, *Russian Social Democracy*, pp. 19, 38.

Dnepr Bend in 1902, soon after the founding of the national party. Ekaterinoslav's Socialist Revolutionaries (SRs) acquired a press almost immediately after the formation of their party and began distributing thousands of copies of their leaflets. In Ekaterinoslav, as in other centers of SR activity, the less-doctrinaire SRs built their party on a base that initially consisted largely of disaffected Social Democrats. As the local party organization grew, activists from elsewhere, including many Jewish *intelligenty*, were drawn to Ekaterinoslav. The Socialist Revolutionaries developed support among Russian workers and Jewish artisans in numerous factories and workshops in the city and industrial suburbs. Support for the SRs was especially strong at the railroad workshops and the Briansk mill, which employed a large number of migrants from the countryside. In addition, the SRs enjoyed some support among peasants in the neighboring villages.[86]

Socialist Revolutionary and Anarchist organizations benefited from a wave of popular support for terrorism beginning in 1904. Many worker-activists had long had trouble grasping why Social Democrats were unequivocally opposed to the use of terror. They felt that "to pass out proclamations and leaflets is useless . . . it is better to throw bombs."[87] One Social Democrat who had been active in Ekaterinoslav recalled how his "propaganda work coincided with the growth of Socialist Revolutionary terror. The working masses were aroused by these terrorist acts and definitely sympathized with them. The committee issued a directive for party members to struggle against this terrorist mood. I remember whole evenings spent in passionate and fiery debate."[88] The differences over terrorism provide yet another case in which the SDs had to struggle against many of the workers they sought to lead. But within the Social Democratic movement, it was not just workers who expressed support for what was called "organized revenge." The Donets Union conceded that even some

[86] I. Zakharenko, "O moei rabote v partii (za 1904–1905)," *Materialy po istorii* (Ekaterinoslav), p. 128; *Revoliutsionnaia Rossiia*, no. 34 (October 15, 1903): 21 and no. 12 (October 1902): 19, 28; Maureen Perrie, *The Agrarian Policy of the Russian Socialist-Revolutionary Party, from Its Origins through the Revolution of 1905–1907* (Cambridge, England, 1976), p. 71; TsGAOR, DP OO, f. 102, 1905, d. 1800, ch. 2 (Okhrana report, November 11, 1905), p. 18; Christopher Rice, *Russian Workers and the Socialist-Revolutionary Party through the Revolution of 1905–1907* (Basingstoke, England, 1988), pp. 19, 37, 49; *Vtoroi s"ezd RSDRP: Protokoly*, pp. 546–547; Haimson, *Russian Marxists*, p. 60; Lane, *Roots*, pp. 165, 210; Michael Melancon, "The Socialist Revolutionaries from 1902 to 1907: Peasant and Workers' Party," *Russian History* 12, no. 1 (Spring 1985): 16, 18.

[87] A. Smirnov, "Vospominanie o I s.-d. rabochem kruzhke Ekaterinoslava v 1894 g.," *Istoriia ekaterinoslavskoi*, p. 16. It was a Marxist principle that revolution became possible only with the growth of workers' class consciousness and participation in mass actions. Assassinations, Marxists argued, would lead worker-activists to believe that the hard work of organizing the mass of their fellows was unnecessary.

[88] Leonov [Vilenskii], "Vospominaniia (delegata II-go s"ezda ot Ekaterinoslava)," *Istoriia ekaterinoslavskoi*, pp. 339–340.

of its *intelligent* leaders displayed "platonic sympathy" for assassination attempts.[89]

The empirewide influx into Socialist Revolutionary organizations occurred after the party's "battle detachments" embarked on a terrorism campaign in 1904 that culminated in the assassination of the unpopular minister of internal affairs, V. K. Plehve. On the local level, Ekaterinoslav's Socialist Revolutionaries distributed leaflets that explained how terror could contribute to the overthrow of the autocracy.[90] Putting theory into practice, Ekaterinoslav's Socialist Revolutionary "people's battle detachment" made an unsuccessful attempt on the life of the city's police chief. In addition, they made plans to assassinate the governor, as well as other local government officials. According to an exaggerated Ekaterinoslav secret-police report, in early 1905 "almost all the people in the organization were armed with revolvers and daggers; some of them had poisoned bullets that had been bored and filled with strychnine."[91]

Initially, in 1903 and 1904, relations between the Socialist Revolutionary and Social Democratic parties were fairly civil. On the eve of the 1903 general strike, Ekaterinoslav's Social Democrats cooperated to some extent with the Socialist Revolutionaries, as the chance to organize a general strike overcame some of the party fighting that plagued the revolutionary movement. The two parties jointly sponsored illegal rallies outside town and agreed to select jointly the day on which to begin the general strike. But the Social Democrats flatly rejected the Socialist Revolutionaries' proposal to form a single strike commission.[92]

As the dispute over terrorism demonstrated, the Social Democrats and Socialist Revolutionaries did have tactical differences. The Socialist Revolutionaries also responded far more militantly when the police and Cossacks forcibly dispersed prestrike rallies. During the 1903 general strike, the Socialist Revolutionaries, unlike the Social Democrats, encouraged those who came to their rallies armed with iron rods and other crude weapons. At one rally, two Socialist Revolutionary orators, who themselves brandished new Browning revolvers, called on the crowd to offer armed resistance if the police tried to break up the rally. The crowd roared its approval of this militant rhetoric.[93]

Before long, Ekaterinoslav's Socialist Revolutionary party experienced

[89] *Vtoroi s"ezd RSDRP: Protokoly*, p. 547.

[90] A. Beliavskii, "Vospominaniia," *Istoriia ekaterinoslavskoi*, p. 334; *Materialy po istorii* (Ekaterinoslav), p. 3.

[91] TsGAOR, DP OO, f. 102, 1905, d. 1800, ch. 2 (Okhrana report, November 11, 1905), pp. 18–19.

[92] *Iskra*, no. 47 (September 1, 1903): 7; I. Shevchenko, "Moi vospominaniia," *Istoriia ekaterinoslavskoi*, p. 61; *Revoliutsionnaia Rossiia*, no. 31 (September 1, 1903): 17 and no. 33 (October 1, 1903): 13.

[93] TsGAOR, DP, 7-e d-vo, f. 102, 1903, d. 2, ch. 15, p. 36; *Iskra*, no. 52 (Prilozhenie, November 7, 1903); Ia. Kravchenko, "Vospominaniia," *Istoriia ekaterinoslavskoi*, p. 349.

the same infighting and divisiveness that had plagued the Social Democratic party. Intelligentsia haughtiness toward artisans and workers within the organization provoked serious discord in this party as well. The party's national paper, *Revoliutsionnaia Rossiia*, reported worker unhappiness in Ekaterinoslav with the "*intelligent* committee" because "nothing gets done, there isn't even enough literature."[94] Obviously, as in the Social Democratic party, the workers' sense of the intelligentsia's ineptitude undercut the latter's claim to leadership positions and greatly increased worker frustrations. Just as the Socialist Revolutionaries lured disgruntled activists away from the Social Democrats, defectors from the SDs and SRs were crucial to the growth of the Anarchist movement.

Numerical estimates of the size of the Anarchist party in Ekaterinoslav early in 1905 are unavailable, but Ekaterinoslav appears to have been the second major center of Russian Anarchism after Belostok.[95] Even so, the Anarchists remained a quite small group until the revolutionary events of 1905 produced both a great expansion in the size of the revolutionary movement and increased worker discontent with the SD and SR leadership.[96] For defectors from the SDs and SRs, a large part of the Anarchists' initial appeal was their principled opposition to hierarchical forms of organization. In contrast to the Social Democrats and Socialist Revolutionaries, the smaller Anarchist movement appears to have been free of serious internal tension between *intelligenty* and workers. Anarchists enjoyed complete freedom from the restraints of party discipline, as they tried to implement in each local group the anarchist ideal of freedom. But while their hostility to any form of authority or imposed discipline insured against monopolization of leadership positions by the *intelligenty*, it also undercut attempts to coordinate organizational activity among Anarchist groups. Anarchist groups were impervious to centralized control at the national and regional level, as well as at the local level. Only loose federational ties linked the various local groups.

The Anarchists engaged in many of the same day-to-day propaganda and agitational activities as the other revolutionary parties. As with the SDs and SRs before them, the Anarchists' first objective was to enroll workers in Anarchist kruzhki. And as in the Social Democratic and Socialist Revolutionary party organizations, a large percentage of the Anarchist party activists consisted of young Jews. The Anarchists achieved in addition

[94] *Revoliutsionnaia Rossiia*, no. 42 (March 1, 1904): 18. The Ekaterinoslav committee suffered from a chronic shortage of funds (Rice, *Russian Workers*, pp. 37–38).

[95] B. I. Gorev [B. I. Gol'dman], *Anarkhizm v Rossii: Ot Bakunina do Makhno* (Moscow, 1930), p. 62; Paul Avrich, *The Russian Anarchists* (New York, 1978).

[96] Ekaterinoslav's Anarchists themselves conceded that until 1905 "the working masses did not even know of their existence" (*Prilozhenie k Burevestniku*, no. 6–7 [September–October, 1907]: 4).

unusual success among the city's unemployed, according to one of the local Bolshevik leaders.[97]

The Anarchists continually strove to incite the working class to pursue militant tactics. The leaflet entitled "To Arms!" urged workers to arm themselves and outlined a very simple method for assembling a bomb. Such eye-catching leaflets conveyed the Anarchists' support for violent methods. This support for terrorism went beyond the rhetorical; the Anarchists committed more acts of terrorist violence in Ekaterinoslav during the 1905 Revolution than the Socialist Revolutionaries. And while the Socialist Revolutionaries in Ekaterinoslav were the first SRs associated with the notion of "factory terror," Anarchist terrorists actually made factory owners and managers a prime target.[98]

Interparty strife was yet another source of divisiveness in the Donbass–Dnepr Bend working class, along with ethnic and regional animosities. Factionalism and competition among parties was characteristic of the Russian left, but the strength of the various revolutionary parties in Ekaterinoslav meant factionalism there eventually proved particularly intense. The revolutionary parties did occasionally cooperate during such surges in the revolutionary movement as the 1903–5 general strikes, but these instances were exceptions. Relations between the Anarchists and the Social Democrats illustrate the extremes to which interparty rivalry and hostility could go and indicate that at least some workers came to share the partisan spirit of party leaders. A worker at the Chadoir factory remembered fights frequently breaking out inside the factory during the workday between Social Democrat and Anarchist workers.[99] The Anarchists frequently accused the Social Democrats of sabotaging their efforts. According to the Anarchists, the SDs destroyed Anarchist leaflets or attempted to prevent Anarchists from distributing them.[100] The Anarchists also accused the Social Democrats of spreading rumors that the Anarchists were responsible when a wave of thievery swept through Ekaterinoslav. They even accused the SDs of trying to frame them with the police.[101]

Ekaterinoslav's Social Democrats also had tense relations with the Bund.

[97] E. Iaroslavskii, "Posle stokgol'mskogo s"ezda v Ekaterinoslave," *Letopis' revoliutsii*, no. 3–4 (1926): 143–149. Even fringe groups enjoyed relatively strong support in Ekaterinoslav. Makhaevism, the militantly anti-intelligentsia movement, competed with the Anarchists for support among the city's unskilled and unemployed workers after one of Russia's leading Makhaevists, a former Social Democrat named Vera Gurari, arrived in Ekaterinoslav in 1903 (Marshall S. Shatz, "The Makhaevists and the Russian Revolutionary Movement," *International Review of Social History* 15 [1970]: 254–255; TsGAOR, DP OO, f. 102, 1905, d. 1800, ch. 2 [Okhrana report, November 11, 1905], pp. 16–17).

[98] *Khleb i volia*, no. 24 (November 1905): 4; Rice, *Russian Workers*, p. 31.

[99] P. A. Arshinov, *Dva pobeda (iz vospominanii anarkhista, 1906–9 gg.)* (Paris, 1929), p. 34.

[100] *Khleb i volia*, no. 23 (October 1905): 7.

[101] *Listki Khleb i volia*, no. 1 (October 30, 1906): 11.

In 1897 Jewish Social Democrats in the northwestern Pale had organized the General Union of Jewish Workers in Russia and Poland, popularly known as the Bund after the Yiddish word for union.[102] The Russified *intelligenty* primarily responsible for organizing the Bund did so because of their attention to the particular problems and needs of the Jewish working class and their recognition that Russian workers "could not always be relied upon to live up to the principles of international proletarian solidarity."[103] The Bund claimed to be "the sole representative of the Jewish working class." In 1903 it sought to expand into the Ukraine and organize the Jewish artisans there by forming a local organization in Ekaterinoslav.

Relations between the Social Democrats and the Bund were tense because the Bund was determined to maintain its independence within the RSDRP. Relations quickly proved to be unusually hostile in Ekaterinoslav. It was the dispute over the Bund's role in Ekaterinoslav that provoked the bitter fight between national leaders that preceded the Second Party Congress.[104] The Bund had criticized Ekaterinoslav's Social Democrats for a leaflet the SDs directed at the city's Jewish workers; the leaflet argued that anti-Semitism was an exclusively bourgeois phenomenon to which workers were immune.[105] The Bund pointed out that the recent pogrom in Czestochowa and "the boasts of Christian workers who replaced striking workers that they would massacre the Jews" provided indisputable proof of workers' susceptibility to violent anti-Semitism.[106] *Iskra* vehemently denounced this public attack and the Bund's "infantile view that anti-Semitism has taken root in the working masses."[107] This was the opening salvo in Lenin's attempt to stop the Bund from broadening its activities outside the northwest.

Lenin initially insisted that workers' participation in pogroms was of little significance. "If they [the Bund] had given it a little more thought, they might have realized that the social character of anti-Semitism today is not changed by the fact that dozens or even hundreds of unorganized workers, nine-tenths of whom are still quite ignorant, take part in a pogrom."[108] Lenin proceeded to belittle the Jewish labor movement, stating that the leaders of the Bund were "so accustomed to dealing with large strikes involving five or ten workers that the behavior of twelve ignorant

[102] "Lithuania" was added to the party's official name later.

[103] Keep, *Rise of Social Democracy*, p. 44. All the same, the Bund shared the mainstream SD belief that with the revolution, the "Jewish problem" would disappear (A. L. Patkin, *The Origins of the Russian-Jewish Labour Movement* [Melbourne, 1947], p. 219).

[104] The Social Democratic party condemned the Bund program at its Second Party Congress, and the Bundists stormed out of the hall in protest.

[105] Tobias, *Jewish Bund*, p. 192; *Posledniia izvestiia*, no. 105 (January 28, 1903): 1–2.

[106] *Posledniia izvestiia*, no. 112 (March 14, 1903): 2–3.

[107] Tobias, *Jewish Bund*, pp. 192–193.

[108] *Iskra*, no. 34 (February 15, 1903): 2.

Zhitomir workers is dragged out as evidence of the link between international anti-Semitism and one 'section' or another 'of the population.' "[109] In other statements elaborating on his opposition to the Bund and to the "principle" of the separateness of parties or a "federation" of parties, Lenin conceded that such working-class ethnic animosity hurt the revolutionary cause. "The accursed history of tsarism has left us a legacy of tremendous estrangement between the working classes of the various nationalities which are oppressed by tsarism. This estrangement is a very great evil, a very great obstacle in the struggle against tsarism."[110]

The Bund's portrayal of the workers' anti-Semitic and pogromist proclivities proved to be deadly accurate and already by the middle of 1904, Ekaterinoslav's Bund had enlisted around one hundred artisans and many *intelligenty* members. During 1905, when all the revolutionary parties enjoyed a surge in membership, Bund membership soared to over five hundred, according to a Bolshevik active in Ekaterinoslav.[111]

Despite this success, many past or potential Bundists joined the Labor Zionists (*Poialei Tsion*). The Bund's argument that the Social Democrats ignored the special problems facing Jews increased the appeal of the Labor Zionists, who, unlike the Bund, were not affiliated with the Social Democrats. The Labor Zionists were basically social democratic in their political orientation but included in their program a belief in the necessity of a Jewish homeland in Palestine.[112] In 1903 the news that Russian workers had perpetrated the pogroms in Kishinev and elsewhere drew many Jews away from the Bund and toward the separatist Jewish nationalism of the Labor Zionists.[113] In their competition with the Bund, Ekaterinoslav's Labor Zionists continually proclaimed that they were "the only true representative of the Jewish proletariat."[114] The conflict within the Jewish left became so acrimonious that during 1905 "armed clashes" erupted inside Ekaterinoslav's main synagogue between Bundists and Labor Zionists, to the horror of the synagogue elders.[115]

Much of the Labor Zionists' work concentrated on preparing to defend

[109] Ibid., quoted in Tobias, *Jewish Bund*, p. 193.

[110] Patkin, *Origins*, pp. 185–186.

[111] Lane, *Roots*, p. 167. Nationally, Bund membership far outstripped the combined membership of the Mensheviks and Bolsheviks. On the eve of the 1905 Revolution, when the Bund numbered twenty-three thousand members, the entire SD party could claim only eight thousand members (Leonard Schapiro, "The Role of the Jews in the Russian Revolutionary Movement," *Slavonic and East European Review* 40, no. 94 [December 1961]: 160).

[112] TsGAOR, DP OO, f. 102, 1905, d. 1800, ch. 2 (Okhrana report, November 11, 1905), p. 13; Ekaterinoslavskaia sots.-dem. organizatsiia "Bund," "Ko vsem rabochim i rabotnits. g. Ekaterinoslava," April 1905.

[113] Tobias, *Jewish Bund*, p. 249.

[114] Ekaterinoslavskii Bund, "Letuchii listok," June 1905.

[115] *Khleb i volia*, no. 21–22 (August–September, 1905): 6.

Jews in the event of a pogrom. They were determined that Jews, unlike during earlier pogroms, would not be so thoroughly terrorized that they failed to fight back. The police reported that as of early 1905, when the other parties had just begun to organize self-defense units, the Labor Zionists "appear to be the heart and soul of self-defense in the city. A large number of this organization's members are armed with revolvers."[116] The police failed to infiltrate the Labor Zionist organization, but thought the party enjoyed considerable support.

The majority of Ekaterinoslav's Jewish activists, however, chose not to join the Bund or Labor Zionists and worked within the non-Jewish parties because they believed only the broader movement could hope to bring about the political changes necessary to improve the condition of both Jews and workers. Judging by arrests, Jews continued to account for a large percentage of the activists in the city's largest revolutionary party, the Social Democrats. Police raids on the Social Democrats sometimes netted an almost exclusively Jewish catch.[117] With Jews assuming prominent positions nationally as well as locally in the Social Democratic party, workers and others had reason to identify the revolutionary movement largely with Jews.[118]

Liberals—moderates unwilling to enter one of the revolutionary parties—often engaged in legal SD activities in the Donbass–Dnepr Bend before they became prominent as a group in their own right in the opposition movement. Liberal well-wishers from professional and other educated groups had provided the revolutionary parties with financial support, false addresses for mail, and temporary hiding places for activists and illegal literature. In 1904, liberals began to organize during the "political spring" that followed Nicholas's appointment of Prince Sviatopolk-Mirskii as minister of internal affairs to replace the assassinated Plehve. Developments in the capitals quickly reverberated in the Donbass–Dnepr Bend, with the formation in Ekaterinoslav of a local branch of the Union of Liberation (Soiuz osvobozhdeniia)—a loose confederation of white-collar and professional groups, teachers, students, zemstvo activists, and liberal landowners. On November 28, 1904, Ekaterinoslav became one of thirty-eight Russian

[116] TsGAOR, DP OO, f. 102, 1905, d. 1800, ch. 2 (Okhrana report, November 11, 1905), p. 14.

[117] Of the fifty-two Social Democrats arrested in February 1905 in Ekaterinoslav, for example, forty-nine were Jews (TsGAOR, DP OO, f. 102, 1905, d. 4, ch. 17 [*O volneniiakh i stachkakh sredi rabochikh po Ekaterinoslavskoi gub.*], p. 97).

[118] Among the SDs, such prominent leaders as Leon Trotsky, Pavel Akselrod, Lev Deutsch, Iulii Martov, and Arkadii Kremer were all Jewish. In fact, almost half of the delegates—twenty-five of the fifty-five—to the Social Democrats' Second Congress in 1903 were Jewish. Jews also assumed prominent positions in the Socialist Revolutionary party. Michael Gotz, Grigorii Gershuni, and other Jews helped to found the SR party (Joseph Nedava, *Trotsky and the Jews* [Philadelphia, 1972], pp. 142–144).

towns to hold a political banquet to demand a constituent assembly and political reforms.[119] Although the liberals were not as strong in the Donbass–Dnepr Bend as elsewhere in Russia, their attempt to serve as an intermediary between the revolutionary labor movement and the government, while building support within educated society, sufficiently impressed Ekaterinoslav's Mensheviks that they decided to ignore central-party instructions and work with the Union of Liberation. The SRs followed suit.[120]

The liberal movement helped to galvanize support for the 1905 Revolution in the Donbass–Dnepr Bend and elsewhere, but liberals did not try to compete with the revolutionary parties for working-class support until the October Manifesto made it legal to address mass rallies. The liberal movement was especially weak in industrial cities and towns in the Donets Basin, where professionals and other *intelligenty* were in short supply. While a few members of the white-collar staffs employed by factories and mines "viewed the revolutionary movement sympathetically,"[121] many more supported liberal political and social critiques. Others were more conservative. The prospect of working-class violence scared away many potential liberals in the Donbass–Dnepr Bend. *Iskra* conceded that the weakness of the liberal movement in Iuzovka, for example, was due to the "liberals' inability to forget the cholera *bunt* of 1892."[122]

The Ukrainian national movement—which supported liberal goals and, like the liberals, lacked working-class support—made little headway in the Donbass–Dnepr Bend. The movement was of little or no consequence during the 1905 Revolution there, although the Kiev-centered Ukrainian Social Democratic Union (the Spilka), which began organizing Ukrainian-speaking workers in December 1904, came to enjoy a smattering of support in the Donbass–Dnepr Bend during the revolutionary year. Spilka shared the Marxist belief that socialism's victory would automatically make "national problems" a thing of the past.[123]

[119] A. Egorov, "Zarozhdenie politicheskikh partii i ikh deiatel'nosti," in Martov, Maslov, and Potresov, *Obshchestvennoe dvizhenie*, 396; Terence Emmons, *The Formation of Political Parties and the First National Elections in Russia* (Cambridge, Mass., 1983), pp. 31–32 and "Russia's Banquet Campaign," *California Slavic Studies* 10 (1977): 84.

[120] Novopolin, "Iz istorii ekaterinoslavskogo," pp. 67–69.

[121] Shevchenko, "Moi vospominaniia," p. 60.

[122] *Iskra*, no. 79 (December 1, 1904): 10. It was not until October 1905 that liberals formally organized the Constitutional Democratic party, known as the Kadet party after its Russian initials. Ekaterinoslav's Kadets elected a doctor, Innokentii Andreev-Butakov, as president and held meetings at the English Club (TsGAOR, DP OO, f. 102, 1906, d. 7, ch. 34, p. 11). A month later, in November 1905, conservatives formed the Union of October 17, known as the Octobrist party.

[123] Oleh Semenovych Pidhainy, *The Formation of the Ukrainian Republic* (Toronto, 1966), p. 27.

Unlike the liberals and Ukrainian nationalists, the government finally began to try seriously to woo workers away from the revolutionary movement after the turn of the century. The government-sponsored Independent Workers' party—the brainchild of the chief of the Moscow secret-police department, Sergei V. Zubatov—was an attempt by the ministry of internal affairs to provide workers with a legal alternative to the revolutionary parties. By offering workers an opportunity to better their lives legally, as long as they avoided politics, the Zubatovites evoked interest from many of Ekaterinoslav's artisans. Zubatovites overcame workers' distrust of the authorities by playing upon workers' distrust of radical *intelligenty*.[124] The Zubatovites supported such practical working-class organizations as a kassa for printers—the Printers' Mutual Aid Society, which enrolled around one hundred members, supported demands for higher wages and shorter hours, and organized lectures and discussion sessions that anyone could attend.

Ekaterinoslav's Social Democrats distributed leaflets attacking "police socialism" and engaged in "legal work" to reach workers attracted to the Zubatovites.[125] But the demise of "police socialism" in Ekaterinoslav, as elsewhere, owed little to Social Democratic opposition. The closing of Ekaterinoslav's "societies" followed the abrupt breach between Zubatov and Minister of Internal Affairs Plehve that came on the heels of the 1903 general strikes in the south, which had been sparked in part by strikes in Odessa the Zubatovite organization there supported. The Zubatovite attempt to support workers against employers while preventing economic discontent from coming into conflict with the interests of the tsarist state was abandoned as a failure.

The autocracy was also associated with the reactionary effort to organize workers by the so-called Black Hundreds, which is how liberals and revolutionaries labeled anti-Semitic, extremist right-wing groups. Although they were reported to be relatively strong in the Donbass–Dnepr Bend, their actual strength is difficult to measure because of the amorphous nature of the Black Hundreds before the 1905 Revolution. It was only in response to the revolutionary upsurge that Black Hundreds became more organized.[126] In the spring and summer of 1905, groups formed in Eka-

[124] Jeremiah Schneiderman, *Sergei Zubatov and Revolutionary Marxism: The Struggle for the Working Class in Tsarist Russia* (Ithaca, N.Y., 1970), p. 233; *Istoriia ekaterinoslavskoi*, p. xxxii; *Krasnoe znamia*, no. 2 (December 1902): 17; G. Novopolin, "Zubatovshchina v Ekaterinoslave," *Istoriia proletariata SSSR*, no. 2 (1930): 233–249; Tobias, *Jewish Bund*, p. 144.

[125] The Social Democrats, for example, established legal libraries. Social Democrats also joined liberals and others in forming educational kruzhki to teach workers to read and write (Beliavskii, "Vospominaniia," p. 333; TsGAOR, DP OO, f. 102, 1905, d. 1800, ch. 2 [Okhrana report, November 11, 1905], p. 5).

[126] In 1901, *Iskra* expressed its concern with reactionaries, who *Iskra* reported were calling

terinoslav and other Donbass–Dnepr Bend towns with names such as the Brotherhood of the Struggle against Sedition (Bratstvo bor'by s kramoloi) and the Union of True Russians (Soiuz istinno-russkikh liudei). After the announcement of the October Manifesto in the Donbass–Dnepr Bend, Black Hundreds staged rallies, called "patriotic demonstrations," that attacked revolutionaries and liberals and helped to instigate pogroms. A couple of weeks later, on November 8, 1905, the radical right formed a nationwide reactionary party, the Union of Russian People (Soiuz russkogo naroda). The Union of Russian People, whose leadership in Ekaterinoslav and elsewhere came from a small group of reactionary bureaucrats, *intelligenty*, landlords, and clergy, called for violent retribution against Jews and revolutionaries and for government reforms to improve conditions for workers and peasants. Contrary to a popular misconception, the Union of Russian People was not created by the government, although it did enjoy government subsidies and the blessing of Nicholas II.[127]

By 1905 the Donbass–Dnepr Bend revolutionary movement had expanded dramatically since the middle of the 1890s, when it consisted of a handful of isolated study circles. But the growth in the size of the revolutionary parties following the influx of radical *intelligenty* with the education and skills necessary to tap workers' discontent and build a mass movement can be considered truly impressive only in comparison with other regions. While it would be a mistake to belittle the growing strength of the revolutionary underground, as reflected in the parties' ability to recruit students, artisans, and skilled workers into their ranks and organize the demonstrations in Ekaterinoslav in 1901 and 1902, in absolute terms the revolutionary movement in the Donbass–Dnepr Bend remained weak.

The small size of the revolutionary movement was at least partly due to the strife within and among the parties. The lack of internal democracy hurt parties when the long-awaited opportunity to lead a mass movement finally arrived. In addition, while workers from different parties sometimes attacked one another, adding yet another source of divisiveness in the working class, most worker-activists grew increasingly angry with the factional divisions splitting the revolutionary movement. The factionalism, the highly charged ideological disputes among the parties, and the sabo-

on workers "to direct their enmity against fellow workers who are, for example, Polish or Jewish, under slogans such as 'Russia for Russians' " (*Iskra*, no. 2 [February 1901], p. 2).

[127] Howard D. Mehlinger and John M. Thompson, *Count Witte and the Tsarist Government in the 1905 Revolution* (Bloomington, Ind., 1972), p. 57; Ascher, *Revolution of 1905*, p. 239; Levitskii, *Za chetvert' veka*, p. 394; Rogger, *Jewish Policies*, p. 32; Lane, *Roots*, p. 165; Steven J. Zipperstein, "Old Ghosts: Pogroms in the Jewish Mind," *Tikhun* 6, no. 3 (1991): 51.

taging of one another's efforts, all of which so debilitated the movement, seemed senseless and fantastically petty to most working-class militants. During strikes, workers often told party agitators to stop their incessant quarreling among themselves, citing the need "to unite against our common enemy."[128]

The strength the Donbass–Dnepr Bend revolutionary movement possessed was also highly concentrated. Working-class participation in the revolutionary parties was restricted primarily to artisans and skilled workers in the three largest steel towns—Ekaterinoslav, Lugansk, and Iuzovka. Radical activists still hardly existed in Donbass–Dnepr Bend mining communities. The revolutionary parties could not count on the mass of workers to follow them. Even in the large steel towns, revolutionaries did not play a role in directing labor unrest before the beginning of the twentieth century. Revolutionary agitation articulated worker grievances, but it did not lead the mass of workers to take political action. In Ekaterinoslav, crowds of students and Jewish artisans demonstrated in 1901 and 1902, but mass labor unrest continued to pursue nonpolitical goals and showed no sign of planning by outside revolutionaries. The leaders of the Donbass–Dnepr Bend revolutionary movement, many of whom were Jewish, were quite simply estranged from the worker constituency they courted. The mass of workers remained out of their reach. That changed dramatically in 1903.

[128] Zakharenko, "O moei rabote," p. 133.

6

The Revolutionary Surge: 1903 to October 1905

The history of the Russian general strike is the history of the Russian revolution [of 1905].
(*Rosa Luxemburg*)

FOLLOWING the rise in labor unrest and socialist agitation during the 1890s and three years of recession at the beginning of the twentieth century, the Donbass–Dnepr Bend labor movement burst onto the national scene in the summer of 1903 with an impressive display of revolutionary collective action. The revolutionary upsurge was concentrated in Ekaterinoslav, where, seemingly overnight, labor made the transition from a movement characterized by spontaneous, uncoordinated, nonpolitical disturbances to a movement able to coordinate a general strike. From the first general strike in Ekaterinoslav in 1903 until 1905, when general strikes recurred in January, June, October, and December, workers greeted calls to strike with mass work stoppages and mass participation in rallies and demonstrations. Revolutionary-party commentators thought that during the 1905 Revolution, "perhaps the most important center of the Russian labor movement after St. Petersburg was Ekaterinoslav. At every stage, the movement proceeded here almost as brilliantly as in the capital."[1] Outside Ekaterinoslav, where the revolutionary parties were weaker, workers in Kamenskoe, Iuzovka, and Lugansk supported en masse some of the calls to strike. Miners contributed to the dramatic increase in Donbass–Dnepr Bend labor unrest during 1905, although the rural isolation of most mines made it difficult for miners to engage in strikes that included workers other than those employed in a single enterprise.

Mass working-class support for general strikes was what supplied the Russian revolutionary movement with its power during the 1903–5 pe-

[1] *Posledniia izvestiia*, no. 249 (September 18, 1905): 9. That correspondent report was published before the dramatic events at the end of 1905. But other, more authoritative accounts, including the history of the 1905 Revolution by the Menshevik Cherevanin, correctly place Ekaterinoslav "in the first ranks of the October movement" (Cherevanin [F. A. Lipkin], *Proletariat v revoliutsii*, vol. 2, *Bor'ba obshchestvennykh sil v russkoi revoliutsii* [Moscow, 1907], p. 54). Chapter 8 will demonstrate the Donbass–Dnepr Bend's leading role in the December armed uprisings.

riod. The general strike was a tactic that had been much discussed in Western European syndicalist and social-democratic circles, but it was in Russia that it received its first and widest use. The strategy of "direct action" allowed workers and radicals to exert a power that far exceeded their numbers. By walking off their jobs citywide, workers could paralyze a city. And when railroad and telegraph workers struck, an entire region's transportation and communication system could be affected. Donbass–Dnepr Bend general strikes and the large, illegal rallies and demonstrations that accompanied them presented a direct challenge to the autocracy's monopoly over political power. The government responded to the mass unrest by alternating concessions and naked force. The concessions, always too late, had a radicalizing effect, since they encouraged the belief that strikes would bring more concessions. When the government again stiffened, demonstrators repeatedly paid with their lives as they stood their ground in the face of officers who ordered them to disperse.

The course of events during the revolutionary upsurge—as labor became politically more conscious, realized its power, and exercised it with increasing effect—has been described well in other studies.[2] To document a similar trajectory, emphasizing the significant contribution to the national movement by workers in the Donbass–Dnepr Bend, is not the main point here. Instead, this chapter and the following one are devoted to a dissecting of labor involvement in mass actions—first in general strikes and then in pogroms. Historians have not dealt thoroughly with the ambiguity of Russian labor discontent, an ambiguity that is revealed by a close study of the connection between general strikes and pogroms in the Donbass–Dnepr Bend. Even though the Donbass–Dnepr Bend labor movement was able repeatedly to bring industry to a stop, support for general strikes was ambiguous. In addition to the workers who needed to be coerced to walk off the job, many among the mass of unskilled and semiskilled workers who were initially exhilarated by the power the labor movement exerted during general strikes were repeatedly disappointed and disillusioned by the outcome of general strikes. In chapter 7, we will see how this frustration led to pogroms.

When Ekaterinoslav's workers responded to the revolutionaries' appeals and struck en masse in 1903, they were joining the wave of labor unrest that swept across the empire's southern region that summer. As many as a quarter of a million southern workers struck in what was Russia's largest

[2] See particularly Engelstein, *Moscow, 1905*; Reichman, *Railwaymen and Revolution*; Surh, *1905 in St. Petersburg*; and Weinberg, "Worker Organizations."

display of labor unrest yet. General strikes engulfed one city after another in the Ukraine and Caucasus, from the beginning of the strike wave early in July in Baku until its end in the middle of August in Ekaterinoslav. In between, workers struck in such major southern industrial centers as Tiflis, Odessa, Nikolaev, and Kiev. Of these strikes, Ekaterinoslav's proved to be the most organized.[3]

In the weeks preceding the 1903 general strike, skilled workers appeared among the students and Jewish artisans at the rallies organized by Ekaterinoslav's revolutionary parties. The Social Democrats and the Socialist Revolutionaries joined together to form a united strike committee, which organized open-air rallies outside the city. The crowds that gathered on an island in the middle of the Dnepr River and in the woods near a local monastery usually numbered in the hundreds.[4] Some opposition to the plans for a general strike was raised at these rallies, but on the whole, according to a report in the SRs' national newspaper, "workers hearing of the strikes elsewhere in the south were eager to strike. . . . This offered an unusually favorable circumstance to prepare [the general strike] and lead the workers from the beginning in an organized and planned manner."[5]

Ekaterinoslav's Social Democrats and Socialist Revolutionaries distributed a large number of leaflets, which explained the purpose of a simultaneous strike by a city's entire work force. The Social Democrats' leaflet tried to convey with drama the power a general strike possessed:

> When darkness reigns on the streets because there is no one to light the streetlights, when there is no food in the city, when goods worth millions of rubles spoil and rot at the railroad stations and docks, when all transportation and production is stopped, and finally, when during the course of several days enterprise losses reach the tens of millions of rubles—then everyone will have felt how all of life depends on workers, and it will seem possible to meet all of the workers' demands.[6]

Despite the apparent militance of such leaflets, the Social Democrats approached the general strike gingerly. Both the Social Democrats' and Socialist Revolutionaries' prestrike leaflets concentrated on demands for such

[3] *Narodnoe delo*, no. 5 (1904): 139. The beginning of the revolutionary upsurge could be dated back a little earlier, to the Rostov-on-Don general strike in November 1902 (Henry Reichman, "The Rostov General Strike of 1902," *Russian History* 9, pt. 1 [1982]: 1).

[4] *Obvinitel'nyi akt*, reprinted in *Iskra*, no. 81 (December 23, 1904): 2; TsGAOR, M. Iu., f. 124, 1903, op. 12, d. 1450 (Okhrana report, August 11, 1903), p. 61; I. Shevchenko, "Moi vospominaniia," *Istoriia ekaterinoslavskoi*, p. 61. According to the secret police, many of the participants at a rally on July 27 came armed with metal poles. Two of the orators brandished new Browning revolvers (TsGAOR, DP OO, f. 102, 7-delo, 1903, d. 2, ch. 7, p. 36).

[5] *Revoliutsionnaia Rossiia*, no. 33 (October 1, 1903): 12.

[6] *Pod"em revoliutsionnogo dvizheniia na Ukraine nakanune pervoi russkoi revoliutsii (1901–1904 gg.)*, ed. F.E. Los' (Kiev, 1955), p. 370.

economic changes as an eight-hour day and wage increases. Although the revolutionary parties did demand the right to strike and to form unions, as well as basic freedoms of speech, the press, and religion, they deemphasized political demands. On the eve of the strike, some Social Democrats even questioned whether to proceed at all. This was not just last-minute jitters. After the workers' destruction and looting of the 1890s, the Social Democrats had good reason to fear that the mass of workers might riot. They also argued that early August was not a propitious time to call for a general strike because troops assembled in Ekaterinoslav then for their summer maneuvers.[7]

Cooperation between the Social Democrats and Socialist Revolutionaries broke down on the eve of the 1903 general strike when the Social Democrats decided at the last minute to postpone the beginning of the strike for three days, even though it was too late to inform many activists of their decision and thousands of workers walked off the job the next day.[8] The prestrike fiasco meant that police informers were well aware of the revolutionaries' plans, and the element of surprise was missing when the strike began.[9]

Bright and early August 7, troops were stationed at the gates of Ekaterinoslav's railway workshops and other large employers, as well as on the bridge across the Dnepr that connected the two factory districts. But troop barriers did not prevent the general strike. When the railroad workshop whistle signaled the beginning of the strike, workers shouted, "Stop working!"—and Ekaterinoslav's 1903 general strike was under way. Workers who wanted to continue working were prevented from doing so, and nearly the entire work force—all twenty-five hundred workers—eventually streamed out of the railroad workshops.[10]

[7] *Iskra*, no. 52 (Prilozhenie, November 7, 1903).

[8] On August 1, Ekaterinoslav's Socialist Revolutionaries had distributed thousands of leaflets announcing that the SR and SD strike commissions had agreed to begin the strike August 4. But on the eve of the fourth, the Social Democrats abruptly postponed the strike until Thursday because they had not yet prepared their final leaflet and proclamation, thereby cutting the ground out from under the three thousand artisans and bakers who could not be informed of the change in plans and walked off the job on the fourth. The Socialist Revolutionaries felt they had no choice but to go along with the postponing of the strike (I. Bender, "K stachechnomu dvizheniiu na Iuge Rossii v 1903 godu," *Arkhiv istorii truda v Rossii*, no. 6–7 [1923]: 185; TsGAOR, DP OO, f. 102, 1898, op. 1, d. 4, ch. 18, p. 7; *Obvinitel'nyi akt*, in *Iskra*, no. 81 [December 23, 1904]: 2; TsGAOR, DP OO, f. 102, 1898, op. 1, d. 4, ch. 18, l. D [*O volneniiakh i stachkakh sredi rabochikh: Bezporiadki v g. Ekaterinoslave*, gendarme report, August 8, 1903], p. 60; *Revoliutsionnaia Rossiia*, no. 31 [September 1, 1903]: 17–18; Melancon, "Socialist Revolutionaries," p. 17).

[9] TsGAOR, DP OO, f. 102, 1903, d. 1473 (Okhrana report, August 7, 1903), p. 2 and Ekaterinoslav governor's report, September 16, 1903, p. 99.

[10] TsGAOR, DP OO, f. 102, 1898, op. 1, d. 4, ch. 18, l. D (Gendarme report, August 15, 1903), pp. 76–77; *Pod"em revoliutsionnogo dvizheniia*, p. 369.

The manner in which Ekaterinoslav's general strike spread from the railroad workshops to other factories in August 1903 presaged the manner in which general strikes spread in 1905. It was a standard feature of general strikes for groups of strikers and their supporters to go from factory to factory shouting and recruiting. Strike supporters ran into factories yelling, "Stop working!" Given the general excitement, the authorities' apparent acquiescence, and the threat of violence from the strikers, it was often sufficient for a crowd of strikers to appear at a factory for the workers there to put down their tools and walk out, even if many wished to continue to work. Factories in Ekaterinoslav closed one after another, as some workers joined the crowd and others dispersed homeward. After the general strike began in 1903, crowds of strikers numbering in the hundreds set off from the railroad workshops to close factories and call on workers to attend a rally at the Briansk mill. Almost all of the factories in Ekaterinoslav's industrial quarter were soon closed. This was a dramatic show of worker militance even though it was achieved partly through the strikers' use of intimidation and force against resistant workers.

Many non–factory workers were conspicuous among those who assembled at the large Briansk factory courtyard. The crowd included people who "did not have any relation to the factories," in the words of the indictment, which identified the outsiders as radical activists, striking artisans, and "the simply curious" from the city's center. A large contingent consisted of young Jewish artisans and salesclerks, including many women, who had set off from the center of the city that morning to join the striking workers in the industrial suburb. On the way, while throwing rocks in the windows of workshops, stores, and factories, they distributed leaflets and shouted, "Stop working now!" Although many refused, most artisans and workers in the center did stop working—including the tram workers, who brought the city's streetcar system to a stop; and the printers, who closed the city's daily newspapers. Police estimated that two to six thousand workers assembled in the Briansk factory courtyard. The Socialist Revolutionaries and Social Democrats claimed the number of demonstrators during the general strike totaled around fifteen thousand.[11]

The predominantly working-class crowd in the Briansk factory courtyard had all the hallmarks of a revolutionary force. Activists waved red flags and banners and shouted, "Down with the autocracy!" Jews in the crowd shouted at the police chief, "Give Russia freedom!" Apparently the crowd

[11] TsGAOR, DP OO, f. 102, 1898, op. 1, d. 4, ch. 18, l. D (Gendarme report, August 8, 1903), p. 60; TsGAOR, DP OO, f. 102, 1903, d. 1473 (Ekaterinoslav governor's report, August 11, 1903), p. 2; TsGAOR, M. Iu., f. 124, 1903, op. 12, d. 1450 (Okhrana report, August 11, 1903), p. 62 and (*Obvinitel'nyi akt*), p. 106; TsGIA, f. 23, op. 30, d. 47, p. 228; *Iskra*, no. 80 (December 15, 1904): 6; Bender, "K stachechnomu dvizheniiu," p. 186; *Revoliutsionnaia Rossiia*, no. 31 (September 1, 1903): 18.

initially responded to an SD orator who sought to control the crowd and keep it calm: "We will stand peacefully and not permit ourselves any violence against the person and property of others."[12] But later the crowd's mood shifted, and shouts of "Hurrah!" greeted the Socialist Revolutionaries' more fiery and radical appeals. Workers responded with "We understand, we see it clearly" when an SR agitator asked, "Comrades, do you understand that the government and tsar act as one with the capitalist exploiters?"[13] The Social Democrats justified their more moderate tactics by noting that at this rally, as well as at most of the other rallies during the general strike, a large percentage of the crowd consisted of "unconscious" workers swept up in the enthusiasm of the moment, rather than workers with some previous initiation into left-wing politics. Numerous sources agreed that crowds such as the one that gathered this day in the Briansk mill included a high number of unskilled and semiskilled workers. It would be evident later that the Social Democrats were right to skirt political issues, to question the depth of the "unconscious" workers' enthusiasm, and to fear their running amuck.[14] The authorities also noted the lack of political consciousness among workers but gave it a different and somewhat mistaken interpretation. The governor reported to the ministry of internal affairs that "the workers themselves did not understand the revolutionary proclamations . . . a large percentage of them . . . were carried away by the deceit and smooth-tongued promises of revolutionary leaders. The enormous crowd of workers acted as if it were hypnotized. They unconsciously went wherever the revolutionaries told them to go."[15]

In fact, workers were neither under the spell of revolutionary leaders nor entirely lacking in class consciousness, even though, in the first mass action by industrial workers that they had managed to instigate, Ekaterinoslav's revolutionary activists knew they could not depend on the mass support the strike seemed to be enjoying. For example, the fortitude of the strikers had appeared to waver soon after the closing of the railroad workshops, with the arrival there of the director, the police chief, and the vice-governor. This threesome, accustomed to workers' obsequiousness in the face of authority, was encouraged by the sight of many workers deferentially removing their caps and ignoring those in the crowd shouting, "Don't take them off!" The authorities ordered the strikers to return to work.[16] But although the crowd appeared submissive, it stood firm. They hooted at the director's transparent attempt to defuse the strike by promising to explore

[12] *Iskra*, no. 47 (September 1, 1903): 7; no. 52 (Prilozhenie, November 7, 1903).

[13] Quoted in Rice, *Russian Workers*, p. 50.

[14] *Iskra*, no. 52 (Prilozhenie, November 7, 1903); no. 81 (December 23, 1904): 3.

[15] TsGAOR, DP OO, f. 102, d. 4, ch. 18, p. 99.

[16] TsGAOR, M. Iu., f. 124, 1903, op. 12, d. 1450 (Okhrana report, August 11, 1903), p. 62.

the possibility of improving working conditions. However, they dispersed when the vice-governor ordered the workers to leave the courtyard. Later that day, an attempt was made on the life of the workshop director.[17]

Troops fired into crowds often during Donbass–Dnepr Bend general strikes, although the troops always claimed to have provided plenty of warning first, including the firing of warning volleys.[18] In 1903, blood flowed in the Briansk courtyard on August 7 soon after the increasingly agitated crowd ignored the Social Democrats and decided to march into the city.[19] The crowd also ignored the commander's order to disperse and started toward the main gate, which soldiers and troops blocked. Some in the crowd threw rocks, seriously injuring one policeman and a soldier. While some members of the crowd taunted the soldiers, others called on their "brothers" to mutiny and join them. At the front of the crowd stood young men such as Semen Gukov, a single, twenty-four-year-old steelworker from Orel who was not a member of any of the revolutionary parties. According to the police, Gukov was "a wild character" who often found himself in trouble at work, "but as far as we knew he had never shown any political awareness."[20] The leader of the crowd during the confrontation with the troops and mounted police was Nikolai Solenyi. Just twenty years old, this member of Ekaterinoslav's Socialist Revolutionary committee was a clerk for the railroad and a native son of Ekaterinoslav. Solenyi and others cursed and taunted the officers and repeatedly shouted to those around them, "Comrades, have no fear, they would never shoot; they do not have the right," or "They have only blank cartridges."[21] As would so often be true during the course of general strikes, this belief on the part of leaders of crowds—that soldiers would not fire into the crowd—proved to be dead wrong. After a number of warnings had no effect, and with the crowd about to break through the army ranks, the troops fired two volleys at the workers, leaving thirteen dead and fourteen seriously injured. Shocked and terrified, the strikers rushed back in a panic and scattered, although some later gathered in various places around the city. The governor justified the massacre by stating that the crowd "would have carried out disorders on an unprecedented scale" if permitted to march into the city.[22]

[17] *Iskra*, no. 81 (December 23, 1904): 2.

[18] The law stipulated that commanders must provide at least three trumpet or drum warnings before giving the order to fire (Robbins, *The Tsar's Viceroys*, p. 197).

[19] *Iskra*, no. 47 (September 1, 1903): 7; no. 81 (December 23, 1904): 2, 4.

[20] TsGAOR, DP OO, f. 102, 7-delo, 1903, d. 1473 (Gendarme report, August 8, 1903), p. 60.

[21] TsGAOR, M. Iu., f. 124, 1903, op. 12, d. 1450 (*Obvinitel'nyi akt*), pp. 107, 155. In their search of Solenyi's room the secret police found a large quantity of SR, SD, and Anarchist literature.

[22] TsGAOR, DP OO, f. 102, 1898, op. 1, d. 4, ch. 18, l. D (Reports of Okhrana, gen-

The government's willingness to use force to suppress workers opened many workers' eyes, confirming what the revolutionaries had been preaching about the need to engage in a political struggle. Support for the general strike continued to grow the following day, August 8, despite the casualties. Strikers closed all but a few of Ekaterinoslav's smaller workshops and stores. Trams remained in their barns and schools closed. Workers must have been impressed by this demonstration of their power. They had shut down the city.

Crowds consisting primarily of workers and artisans, and with a few exceptions free of drunks, gathered for large rallies in a mood police described as "hostile." Three thousand people at the Briansk factory in the Chechelevka district and sixteen hundred across the river in the suburbs of Amur and Nizhnedneprovsk listened for hours to orators on makeshift platforms denounce labor's plight and explain that the general strike would lead to economic and political change. The Briansk rally again ended with a call to march into the center of the city. The authorities, in contrast, changed their tactics and eschewed a repeat of the bloodshed of the day before. After an orator announced that "we will go quietly, peacefully singing, without chanting and shouting," the authorities, who had posted Cossacks, an infantry division, and a hundred mounted artillery soldiers around the city, allowed the demonstrators to begin their march. The crowd, according to some accounts, doubled in size along the way.[23]

The sight of such a large working-class crowd struck fear in the hearts of many city residents. Even the artisans, with their memories of previous worker rampages, must have been uneasy. Rumors of an impending riot or pogrom spread through the city. Frightened residents locked up their houses and shops at the sight of the demonstration, prompting strikers to shout, "Don't be afraid of us, there's no need to lock your gates and your stores, we will not touch you; we are not going to loot and beat, we are fighting for a just cause."[24] The troops and Cossacks prevented the bulk of

darme, and Ekaterinoslav governor, August 8–16, 1903), pp. 48, 61, 87, 99. Some detailed information about the composition of this crowd can be gleaned from secret-police data on those killed and wounded on August 7. Of the twenty-seven casualties, two were Jewish artisans, eighteen were factory workers, three were women—wives and a sister of steelworkers—and four were young, unemployed, working-class males. The median age of the casualties was twenty-four, and all but seven were single. A number of the casualties were characterized by the investigators as of good character but given to drunkenness. Only one of them, Petr Morokhon'ko, a seventeen-year-old worker with three years of experience at the Briansk mill, had been arrested previously for revolutionary activity (TsGAOR, DP OO, f. 102, 1903, d. 1473 [Gendarme report, August 8, 1903], pp. 60–64).

[23] TsGAOR, DP OO, f. 102, 1898, d. 4, ch. 18, l. D, p. 71; TsGAOR, DP OO, f. 102, 1903, d. 1473 (Ekaterinoslav governor's report, August 11, 1903), pp. 3–4; TsGAOR, M. Iu., f. 124, 1903, op. 12, d. 1450 (Okhrana report, August 11, 1903), pp. 54, 65.

[24] *Iskra*, no. 47 (September 1, 1903): 7.

the crowd from reaching the central boulevard, and the strikers dispersed for the night.

Almost all of Ekaterinoslav's workers remained out on strike the next day, August 9. While a crowd of more than two thousand gathered in Amur, troops prevented the strikers from gathering in central Ekaterinoslav.[25] The failure to hold a large rally in the city center seemed to discourage the strikers, and by the end of the day it was evident that support for the general strike was declining. Some factories began to reopen the following day, August 10. By the afternoon of the eleventh, almost all of Ekaterinoslav's factories had resumed production. Having regained control, vice-governor V. Kniazev issued a proclamation August 12 that threatened to dismiss and expel from the city all workers who had not returned to work by the next day. Even so, some militants threatened those who did return. At the Ekaterinoslav railway workshops, strikers beat three skilled workers who had opposed the strike. The governor's office issued another proclamation announcing that anyone caught trying to prevent workers from returning to work would be arrested. On August 13, most of Ekaterinoslav's workers went back to work. Smoke once again spewed forth from the city's smokestacks, and managers at the bigger factories and workshops reported that except for the presence of the military, everything had returned to normal.[26]

The Social Democrats deemed the 1903 general strike a success because it showed how far the working masses had evolved since the spontaneous riot at the Briansk factory in 1898. *Iskra* proudly reported that several factory directors and the factory inspector had stated that workers conducted themselves "correctly" during the strike.[27] It also reported that residents congratulated the SD committee for reeducating "this horde."[28]

The mass support the strike elicited did impressively display the labor movement's growing strength and the shift from the nonpolitical unrest of the late nineteenth century. Many of the working-class leaders of the Ekaterinoslav strike were the educated, skilled workers active in the revolutionary parties. They demonstrated that they could lead the working class and shut the city down. But after the strike, many of these revolutionary activists questioned whether it had been a success. Discontent with the strike

[25] TsGAOR, DP OO, f. 102, 1898, op. 1, d. 4, ch. 18, l. D (Ekaterinoslav governor's report, August 19, 1903), p. 91.

[26] TsGAOR, M. Iu., f. 124, 1903, op. 12, d. 1450 (Okhrana report, August 11, 1903), pp. 6, 8, 59; TsGAOR, DP OO, f. 102, 1898, op. 1, d. 4, ch. 18, l. D (Report of the chief [*nachal'nik*] of Ekaterinin railroad, August 12, 1903), pp. 58–59.

[27] *Iskra*, no. 80 (December 15, 1904): 6.

[28] *Iskra* conceded that after the 1898 *bunt*, Ekaterinoslav residents "had some basis in reason" for viewing the working class as a "wild horde" (*Iskra*, no. 52 [Prilozhenie, November 7, 1903]).

was widespread among workers, who felt disappointed with the outcome. They complained that they had lost wages and exposed themselves to soldiers' bullets without achieving any concrete improvements. Ekaterinoslav's Social Democrats felt compelled to recognize as much at the party's Third Congress in 1905 in London. After reporting that "the wave of summer strikes and demonstrations [during 1903] undoubtedly greatly revolutionized the most conscious elements among the factory workers," the delegates' report went on to state that "as for the gray masses, the massacre of demonstrators, in which many were wounded and killed, left most of them feeling depressed. The strike had not resulted in any improvements in their living conditions, and for some time bitter disillusionment and the consciousness that their humble sacrifices had been in vain prevailed among the gray masses."[29] To make matters worse, hundreds of the young, skilled workers sympathetic to the revolutionary movement were fired or arrested after the strike, depriving the parties of important factory contacts and reinforcing the dangerous consequences of going on strike.[30]

The next major Donbass–Dnepr Bend strike wave did not occur until a year and a half after the 1903 general strike. For a variety of reasons, many workers expressed their opposition "to any strikes and disorders."[31] First among these reasons was the general strike's failure to lead to increased wages after the three years of high unemployment and pay cuts that Donbass–Dnepr Bend workers suffered between 1900 and 1903. In addition, workers were swept up in the patriotic mood that engulfed Russian cities following the outbreak of the Russo-Japanese War on January 27, 1904.

Whether or not Russia entered the war in order to "distract the attention of the masses from political concerns," as some have believed, the war at first did have that effect. In the Donbass–Dnepr Bend, as elsewhere, workers shouting "Long live the autocracy!" marched in the patriotic parades organized by local rightists, and they donated money to the war effort.[32] But when Russian fortunes in the war soured and one bloody humiliating defeat followed another at the hands of the "little short-tailed monkeys," as the press called the Japanese, the patriotic fervor quickly dissipated. Even those workers who had just recently marched in patriotic demonstrations now were cursing the government and appeared to be swinging back toward supporting the revolutionary movement.[33]

Liberals, whose disenchantment with the autocracy was aggravated by

[29] *Tretii s"ezd RSDRP: Protokoly*, April–May 1905 (Moscow, 1959), p. 623.

[30] Ibid.; *Iskra*, no. 52 (Prilozhenie, November 7, 1903).

[31] TsGAOR, DP OO, f. 102, 1904, d. 4, ch. 17 (Okhrana report, May 10, 1904), p. 2.

[32] *Iskra*, no. 64 (April 18, 1904): 6; *Gorno-zavodskii listok*, February 28, 1904, p. 6670; *Ekaterinoslavskii listok*, May 11, 1904, p. 3.

[33] *Iskra*, no. 64 (April 18, 1904): 6; Lincoln, *In War's Dark Shadow*, p. 243.

the government's conduct of the Russo-Japanese War, were emboldened by the autocracy's adoption of a more conciliatory posture following the assassination of Plehve in July. This disenchantment came to the fore in the last months of 1904. The liberal banquet campaign that ushered in the 1905 Revolution duly reached Ekaterinoslav. The local branch of the Union of Liberation held a banquet in November at which, as elsewhere, professional men met to demand not only the immediate end of the war, but more significantly the summoning of a constituent assembly.[34] Ekaterinoslav's liberals were in a radical and uncompromising mood. The movement's organ, *Osvobozhdenie* (Liberation), proclaimed that the Union of Liberation was no longer open to "any intermediary point between absolutism and constitutionalism."[35]

Against this background of a military debacle and liberal agitation, the lull in the upsurge of the revolutionary movement ended on January 9, 1905 in St. Petersburg, when troops opened point-blank fire on crowds of unarmed workers and their families, killing and wounding about one thousand of the demonstrators and onlookers. The dramatic events on this bitterly cold and snowy day were the result of a demonstration led not by the opposition movement, but by a charismatic priest with police connections. The crowds of workers, which totaled somewhere between fifty thousand and two hundred thousand, had peacefully come in their Sunday best, carrying crosses, religious banners and icons—even portraits of the tsar—and singing such hymns as "Save, O Lord, Thy People" and the imperial anthem, "God Save the Tsar," to present the tsar with a petition of their grievances. The news that troops, whose commanders had been ordered by the tsar to deal forcefully with the demonstrators, had fired directly into unarmed crowds of men, women, and children outraged seemingly all of Russian society and ignited the 1905 Revolution.

Bloody Sunday, as the massacre was immediately dubbed, sparked mass action throughout the empire and marked the beginning of a year of extraordinary turmoil. Within a few days, representatives of the Social Democrats, Socialist Revolutionaries, and Anarchists in Ekaterinoslav feverishly began to prepare another general strike.[36] Activists distributed fresh leaflets around the city informing workers about events in the capital and inciting them to take action locally. Ekaterinoslav's two Social Democratic factions called for a general political strike: "The time to act has arrived. . . . Long live the great solidarity of the working class!"[37]

The mood was electric as news of strikes elsewhere increased workers' sense of their own power. Despite the earlier disappointment with the out-

[34] Emmons, *Formation of Political Parties*, p. 32; Ascher, *Revolution of 1905*, p. 59.

[35] Haimson, *Russian Marxists*, p. 199.

[36] I. Shevchenko, "O revoliutsii 1905 g.," *Materialy po istorii* (Ekaterinoslav), pp. 130–133.

[37] V. I. Nevskii, *Rabochee dvizhenie v ianvarskie dni 1905 goda* (Moscow, 1930), p. 347.

come of the 1903 general strike, work stoppages began on January 17 in Ekaterinoslav, Kamenskoe, and Iuzovka. In Ekaterinoslav, workers at the railroad workshop once again struck first. Over half of the workers there quit working immediately, but many others—in fact, whole departments—refused at first to strike. Some violent brawls resulted, as the striking workers were determined to bring all work to a halt. The following day, nineteen other factories joined the strike. By January 20, the city's printers, as well as workers at many additional factories and workshops, followed suit; and although workers' support for the strike was beginning to waver, the stopping of the tramway on January 21 made Ekaterinoslav's general strike seem complete.[38]

In January 1905, Ekaterinoslav's workers indicated again that they were able and willing to withstand the hardships of a general strike. The manner in which the strike spread and its citywide scope followed a pattern similar to that of the 1903 general strike. The major difference was that the January strike lacked the coordination and political agenda of the 1903 strike, as workers responded on their own to the events of Bloody Sunday and pressed for improvements at their places of work. In January 1905, management capitulated to many of the workers' demands and made significant concessions, which encouraged more workers to go out on strike just as others were already returning to work. Most factories were able to resume production after three to five days. Workers at the Briansk factory returned to work after three days, only to stop work again later that same day.[39] Despite the lack of synchronization, Ekaterinoslav's governor thought the strike impressive and reported in his request for additional troops that more than twenty thousand workers had struck. By January 24, the strike wave clearly was subsiding. By the twenty-seventh, the authorities could pronounce the strike over, even though a few enterprises still remained closed.[40]

Ekaterinoslav's workers demonstrated a greater capacity for independent and organized action in the January 1905 strike than in the 1903 strike. The revolutionary parties did not dominate the January strike; it was notable for its relative absence of radical politics, even though Mensheviks, Bolsheviks, Socialist Revolutionaries, and Anarchists were active, competing for working-class allegiance and addressing the rallies. Striking workers

[38] TsGIA, f. 23, op. 16, d. 3, p. 36; *Pridneprovskii krai*, January 25, 1905, p. 5; *Ekaterinoslavshchina v revoliutsii 1905–1907 gg: Dokumenty i materialy*, ed. A. Ia. Pashchenko et al. (Dnepropetrovsk, 1975), pp. 41, 52–57.

[39] *Pridneprovskii krai*, January 25, 1905, p. 6.

[40] *Ekaterinoslavshchina*, pp. 48–49; V. Nevskii, "Ianvarskie dni 1905 goda v Ekaterinoslave i Donetskom basseine," *Letopis' revoliutsii* no. 10 (January–February 1925): 170, 173–175; TsGAOR, M. Iu., f. 124, 1905, d. 1293, pp. 5–6. In the capitals, labor unrest subsided within a week of Bloody Sunday (Tobias, *Jewish Bund*, p. 299).

at the major factories and the railroad workshop elected their own representative organizations, since workers were no longer afraid to send delegates to present their demands to their employers. At the Briansk factory, of the eight worker delegates, only two were affiliated with a revolutionary party, the Social Democrats. At the railroad workshops, the elected council quickly established a patrol to protect orators and maintain order at the rallies. I. Shevchenko, a Social Democratic activist, later recalled that the Briansk council's efforts were largely devoted to "holding the masses back from 'excesses' " and "keeping the revolutionary waves from overflowing the shores." In addition to the danger of worker rioting, Shevchenko had in mind the "undesirable elements," who wheelbarrowed foremen out of the factory during the strike and engaged in other acts he called "terroristic deviations."[41] Wheelbarrowing was an increasingly popular form of working-class protest, which workers considered extremely "insulting" and therefore very effective. They would throw a sack over the head of a foreman or antistrike worker, wheelbarrow him outside the factory gates, and dump him.

Factory delegations consisting of skilled workers, some of whom were aligned with one or another of the revolutionary parties and received input from party *intelligenty*, drew up long lists of demands for their factories or workshops, in contrast to the less-coordinated work stoppages of the late nineteenth century. The demands often numbered twenty-five or more. The factory activists and revolutionary parties hoped these exclusively economic demands would rally the city's industrial workers, who, unlike the more radical artisans (especially the printers), displayed little enthusiasm for the revolutionary parties' political goals. Even at the few rallies revolutionaries organized during the strike, the thrust of most of the speeches was more economic than political. In the Donbass–Dnepr Bend generally, when orators began to speak about "the political struggle," workers often shouted their disapproval—"We don't need politics!"[42] Some of the revolutionary parties' leaflets did address the need to rid Russia of a government guilty of shooting down peaceful workers and the importance of such democratic rights as freedom of speech and freedom of the press, but most leaflets were devoted to presenting individual factories' demands. As an organizer wrote years later, Donbass–Dnepr Bend workers, especially outside Ekaterinoslav, still hoped to improve their economic position "without politics."[43]

The two main demands factory delegations raised during the January strike were the familiar ones of higher wages (30 percent higher was the

[41] "O revoliutsii 1905 g.," pp. 130–131.

[42] *Iskra*, no. 101 (*Prilozhenie*, June 1, 1905): 3.

[43] T. Kharechko, *1905 god v Donbasse* (Leningrad, 1926), p. 49.

figure most often specified) and the eight-hour day. Demands also invariably included the right to be addressed respectfully, improvements in working conditions, availability of worker insurance, greater machine safety, improvement of medical aid, prohibition of extra hours and night work (except in the unusual case of the railroad workers, whose overtime pay doubled), strike immunity, an end to fines, protection for workers under sixteen years old, elected inspectors, improvements in the factory baths, and the lighting and heating of the workplaces. The list for each striking factory or workshop also usually included demands specific to that enterprise—such as the dismissal of a particularly harsh foreman or a foreign foreman who barely spoke Russian, the building of a cafeteria, or the addition of a female ward to the factory hospital. In the January strikes, while management usually refused to satisfy the majority of workers' demands, many of their particular demands were met, despite management's well-founded fear that granting concessions under pressure would increase demands in the future.[44] The Briansk workers' council also managed to convince its factory director to reverse his decision to fire twenty-three workers for their participation in a wheelbarrowing incident—to the horror of the factory's foremen and staff.[45] Donbass–Dnepr Bend administrators were often reluctant to take a hard line against the strike. Even though they opposed the workers' economic goals, many supported the liberal and revolutionary movement's political goal of replacing the autocracy with a more democratic government.

After the January general strike ended, Ekaterinoslav's workers remained unsatisfied, and new strikes flared up in early February. During this epidemic of strikes in early 1905, workers who had never before entertained thoughts of striking walked off the job. Even domestic servants, who were lucky if they earned ten rubles a month, went on strike. They demanded that their hours and wages be regulated. These female workers, many of them the wives and daughters of steelworkers, also demanded that they be addressed and treated with respect. They argued, for example, that if they should have to submit to medical exams, so should their bosses, "since among them there can be people with infectious diseases."[46]

[44] *Dnepropetrovsku*, pp. 77–79; *Ekaterinoslavshchina*, pp. 55–57; TsGIA USSR, f. 1597, d. 84 (Okhrana report, May 9, 1905), p. 56; Nevskii, "Ianvarskie dni," pp. 180–183, 186; S. Meksina, "Pervye stachki ekaterinoslavskikh metallistov v 1905 g.," *Materialy po istorii professional'nogo dvizheniia v SSSR*, bk. 5 (Moscow, 1927), p. 216; TsGAOR, DP OO, f. 102, 1905, d. 4, ch. 17 (Okhrana reports, February 1905), pp. 71, 83, 107; *Pridneprovskii krai*, January 25, 1905, p. 6; TsGIA, f. 23, op. 30, d. 47 (Factory inspectorate report, February 10, 1905), pp. 260–266.

[45] Meksina, "Pervye stachki," p. 216. After the strike, workers returned to work angry. In the railroad workshops, workers threw nuts and bolts at foremen unsympathetic to the strike (*Ekaterinoslavshchina*, p. 62).

[46] *Pridneprovskii krai*, February 10, 1905, p. 3.

News of the strikes and rallies in Ekaterinoslav spread out into the Donets Basin. During January and February, workers throughout the Donbass–Dnepr Bend mining and metallurgical region went on strike with economic demands similar to those presented earlier in Ekaterinoslav.[47] Although the movement spread in an uncoordinated manner, production stopped at a total of forty-five different factories and mines in the Donets Basin, and the strikes included approximately eighty thousand workers.[48]

Workers struck in parts of the Donbass–Dnepr Bend where, in the words of one Social Democratic correspondent, "everyone had been in a deep sleep"[49] and, in the the words of another, the work force still consisted "for the most part of rather benighted [*temnye*] migrants who only yesterday left the plough behind."[50] The amazed *Iskra* correspondent in Enakievo reported that "life has absolutely changed."[51] Factory concessions to worker demands dramatically increased worker participation in revolutionary-party organizations at enterprises such as the Hartmann factory in Lugansk, where the Social Democrats did not have two dozen members before 1905.[52]

The Donbass–Dnepr Bend strikes in February continued to lack simultaneity, but they possessed considerable power nonetheless. The authorities, greatly concerned, were continually forced to send troops throughout the region to restore order and end the strikes; they felt they were on the verge of being overwhelmed. The governor reported to the ministry of internal affairs, "The vastness of the region does not permit troops to be everywhere simultaneously . . . in the event of simultaneous disorders in many places, the number of troops undoubtedly would prove to be insufficient."[53] Outside the cities, the appearance of troops was usually enough to bring workers back into line, except at a few mines where troops fired and inflicted casualties to suppress small-scale rioting and pogroms. The three thousand miners at the Rykov mines, after going on strike on February 19, began to sack stores. In the face-off that followed the miners' attempt to destroy mine property, Cossacks answered rock throwing with a volley of gunfire, killing one miner. In similar disorders at the Shcherbinov mine, three miners were shot dead. At the Auerbakh mine, Cossacks killed three more, with many suffering serious wounds.[54]

[47] Lane, *Roots*, p. 169.

[48] TsGIA, f. 23, op. 16, d. 3, p. 36; Nevskii, *Rabochee dvizhenie*, p. 352.

[49] *Iskra*, no. 107 (July 29, 1905): 7.

[50] *Iskra*, no. 92 (March 10, 1905): 5.

[51] *Iskra*, no. 96 (April 5, 1905): 5.

[52] Nikolaenko, *Revoliutsionnoe dvizhenie*, p. 14.

[53] TsGAOR, DP OO, f. 102, 1905, d. 4, ch. 17, vol. 2 (*O volneniiakh i stachkakh sredi rabochikh po Ekaterinoslavskoi gub.*), p. 6.

[54] Nevskii, "Ianvarskie dni," pp. 178–179.

Most of the Donbass–Dnepr Bend's February strikes did not last long. The strikes in the major industrial cities were notable exceptions. In Iuzovka, when a small percentage of the steelworkers at the Hugheses' New Russia Company went on strike and presented economic demands on January 17, the factory administration satisfied many of their demands almost immediately. The strikers returned to work the next day. But on February 22, the entire work force—all ten thousand employees—stopped working, and the next day miners at the firm's nearby mines also struck. Simultaneously, printers and other artisans in Iuzovka quit working. The city's streets filled with strikers; they were generally peaceful and returned to work after a few days when troops arrived from Ekaterinoslav.[55] In Kamenskoe, the work force of almost ten thousand at the Dneprovsk factory struck in an attempt to achieve the higher wages and shorter hours they had demanded weeks earlier. The Dneprovsk workers had struck on January 17, concurrently with the first strikes in Ekaterinoslav, only to return to work on January 19. The sixteen-day strike that began February 3 became the longest strike in the Donbass–Dnepr Bend during the January–February strike wave. Management never did grant the workers' demands.[56]

In Lugansk, where strikers had achieved a general work stoppage on January 18, another strike began on February 16 at the Hartmann factory and quickly spread to the railroad workshops and nearby factories.[57] The strike became citywide on February 18 as artisans, salesclerks, and others in mostly Jewish professions stopped work, closing workshops and stores. The strike ended victoriously for the Hartmann workers on February 22, after the administration of the factory announced the establishment of a nine-hour day, higher wages, the removal of workshop (*tsekh*) guards, expansion of the factory school, and the creation of a library. Other city workers and artisans also won higher wages and improvements in working conditions.[58]

Throughout 1905, as earlier, Donbass–Dnepr Bend companies claimed to be shocked at worker discontent. The Association of Southern Coal and Steel Producers refused to accept that factory and mine conditions bore responsibility for the strikes.[59] In late February, the Association reported to the ministry of internal affairs that "unrest among workers in the mining and metallurgical region of southern Russia assumed a dangerous charac-

[55] *Gorno-zavodskii listok*, March 5/12, 1905, p. 7612.

[56] TsGAOR, DP OO, f. 102, op. 5, d. 975, vol. 1, p. 42; TsGAOR, DP OO, f. 102, 1905, d. 4, ch. 17 (Ekaterinoslav governor's report, February 15, 1905), p. 91.

[57] Nevskii, *Rabochee dvizhenie*, p. 356.

[58] Voroshilov, *Rasskazy o zhizni*, p. 170; Berkhin, *Luganskaia bol'shevistskaia organizatsiia*, p. 44.

[59] TsGIA, f. 37, op. 59, d. 211, p. 251; TsGIA, f. 37, op. 58, d. 306 (Report of the Association of Southern Coal and Steel Producers, February 21, 1905), p. 118.

ter after the St. Petersburg strikes, despite the fact that these workers are more secure than workers in the north and center of the empire, as they receive significantly higher wages. . . . In general, the entire workers' movement in southern Russia is undoubtedly the result of political agitation."[60]

The government often disagreed with this assessment, noting that employers "did not even want to implement [workers'] just demands."[61] Government representatives often pressured firms to make concessions to their workers to restore order. At the Petrovsk factory in Enakievo, after the vice-governor arrived and consulted with worker deputies as well as the factory administration, he recommended that improvements in worker housing be made and that wages be raised, with a daily minimum of ninety kopecks for unskilled workers.[62] The administration reluctantly agreed, but such government pressure angered industrialists. Mine operators began to complain to the central government that local authorities compelled them to increase workers' pay to such an extent that operation of the mines might become impossible.[63]

The Association of Southern Coal and Steel Producers felt that increased force was needed, not concessions. It pleaded with the central government to send additional troops to the region. The Association's leadership, the industrialists N. S. Avdakov, F. E. Enakiev, and A. Auerbakh, believed that the Donbass–Dnepr Bend strikes threatened to become violent.[64] With this the local authorities agreed.

In February, almost a month after the first strikes began, the governor wrote to the ministry of internal affairs: "Despite the nonviolent character of the strikes occurring in the province, the workers' mood is strongly elevated . . . persistent rumors circulate, particularly in Ekaterinoslav, about a general strike with demonstrations, violence, and armed resistance on February 19 and 20. The city is alarmed."[65] Many revolutionary-party activists also thought the strike movement was reaching revolutionary proportions. One Ekaterinoslav activist, writing to a friend in Moscow in mid-February, captures the exhilaration many felt:

[60] TsGAOR, DP OO, f. 102, 1905, d. 2609 (Report of the Association of Southern Coal and Steel Producers, February 23, 1905), p. 38.

[61] TsGAOR, DP OO, f. 102, op. 5, d. 975, vol. 1, p. 40.

[62] TsGIA, f. 37, op. 59, d. 211 (Report of the chief [*nachal'nik*] of State Mining Administration, February 24, 1905), p. 248.

[63] Ibid., p. 175.

[64] TsGAOR, DP OO, f. 102, 1905, d. 2609, p. 36.

[65] TsGAOR, DP OO, f. 102, 1905, d. 4, ch. 17 (Ekaterinoslav governor's report, February 16, 1905), p. 125. The governor reported on March 3, after a show of force on February 19 and 20 maintained order, that it had been widely rumored that the street disorders would be pogromist in character (*Ekaterinoslavshchina*, pp. 64–65).

> The workers and laboring people generally are stirring again. Clerks and domestic servants have struck. Life is boiling over. Forces long held in check have broken out into the open, and soon the gigantic pyramid consisting of the bourgeoisie, police, priests, and ministers, with the tsar and crown at the top, which has for centuries weighed down on working people, will collapse with a terrible crash. Many lives, very many, will be buried in the crash, but it is better to immediately die in the wreckage than to die slowly supporting the pyramid.[66]

As elsewhere in Russia, Donbass–Dnepr Bend revolutionaries were not ready to lead any such assault against the government. Ekaterinoslav's Social Democratic leaders conceded that the revolutionary surge at the beginning of 1905 caught them unprepared. "Having been reared in the underground, it was difficult [for us] to immediately move into the open. The long underground existence had left its imprint on our movement. . . . Arming the masses, organizing the masses, leading mass action . . . [the *komitet*] was not able to respond to such tasks."[67] In addition, for doctrinal reasons, neither of the two Social Democratic factions nor the Socialist Revolutionaries entertained any thoughts of directly challenging the power of the local government or seizing control of factories, at least not before the end of the year. At both the Menshevik and Bolshevik congresses, convened abroad simultaneously in April, delegates gave lip service to the need to prepare for an armed uprising. But before the October Manifesto, all the revolutionary parties except the Anarchists continued to fight nonviolently for liberal rather than socialist goals. According to the Social Democrats' program minimum, 1905 was to be a "bourgeois-democratic" revolution—since according to a Marxian analysis of Russian conditions, a democratic republic was a necessary step on the path to socialism.[68]

Since Donbass–Dnepr Bend revolutionaries were unprepared or unwilling to exploit the opportunities the "revolutionary situation" presented, the revolutionary movement lost momentum. The liberal movement came to the fore as the alarmed tsar appeared to reverse course in response to the January and February strikes and protests. To quell political unrest, Nich-

[66] TsGIA USSR, f. 1597, op. 1, d. 84 (Letter sent February 14, 1905, intercepted by the Okhrana), p. 52.

[67] *Sotsial'demokrat*, August 18, 1905, p. 11.

[68] As noted above, the Mensheviks, the stronger of the two Social Democratic organizations in the Donbass–Dnepr Bend, even wanted, along with the SRs, to work with the growing liberal movement to take advantage of "this extraordinarily important moment." The liberals, for their part, argued that they had "no enemies on the left." The Bolsheviks bucked these efforts to unify the opposition movement, even though they agreed that Russia was not ready for a socialist revolution. They adamantly opposed working with the liberals. One Bolshevik activist wrote, "Taken unawares, stunned by the unprecedented movement in the liberal world, we workers need not delude ourselves. This deafening verbiage will dissipate like smoke in the face of the first light breeze . . . the sole fighters and leaders of the revolution will be the working class" (Nevskii, "Ianvarskie dni," p. 185).

olas directed the new minister of internal affairs, A. G. Bulygin, to draft a plan to "attract most deserving persons, vested with public confidence and elected by the people, to undertake the preliminary examination and consideration of legislative projects."[69] The discussions that followed the call for elections and popular participation in the preparation of legislation emboldened those demanding that the autocracy be replaced by a parliamentary monarchy along Western European lines.

The lull in labor unrest after February did not necessarily signify working-class satisfaction or even a decline in discontent. To quell labor unrest, the tsar set up a special commission to investigate workers' problems and propose ways to improve working conditions. The tsar's conciliatory gesture may have pacified workers, if only temporarily.[70] More likely, with the approach of the Easter holidays, workers did not want to lose any more workdays to strikes.[71] Furthermore, plans for a large May Day demonstration were abandoned in response to rumors about coming pogroms in Ekaterinoslav and throughout Russia.[72] During the spring lull, many revolutionaries tried to accumulate weapons. By the middle of 1905, conversations among radicals increasingly revolved around guns and the difficulty of acquiring them. The *Iskra* correspondent reported that in Ekaterinoslav, "everyone dreams about acquiring a revolver. But the [SD] organization is of almost no help and almost no one has the money necessary for their purchase."[73]

Although the revolutionary movement experienced declines in activity during 1905 and radicals occasionally suffered arrest during searches of their homes, by the middle of the year the clear weakening of government control greatly emboldened the revolutionary parties. Following May Day, an "exchange" (*birzha*) was established on Ekaterinoslav's central boulevard. Every evening at the end of the workday, dozens, if not hundreds, of members of all the revolutionary parties used the central *birzha* to exchange news, propagandize, and recruit. Although the police were aware of this illegal activity, they generally did not interfere.[74] Nor did the authorities do much to dam the flow of illegal literature into the Donbass–Dnepr Bend from abroad.[75]

[69] V. I. Gurko, *Features and Figures of the Past: Government and Opinion in the Reign of Nicholas II*, trans. Laura Matveev (New York, 1939), p. 371.

[70] The strike movement died down just as outbreaks of peasant attacks on noble estates began in the surrounding countryside.

[71] TsGIA, f. 23, op. 16, d. 3, p. 43.

[72] TsGIA USSR, f. 1597, op. 1, d. 84 (Okhrana report), p. 89; Kharechko, *1905 god*, p. 49.

[73] *Iskra*, no. 106 (July 18, 1905): 3.

[74] S. I. Gopner, "Bol'sheviki Ekaterinoslava v 1905 godu: Iz vospominanii," *Voprosy istorii*, no. 3 (1955): 29; *Posledniia izvestiia*, no. 249 (September 18, 1905): 9.

[75] For the year ending in April 1905, the SDs alone distributed ten tons of underground material from abroad, much of it to local organizations in the Donbass–Dnepr Bend. But

In 1905 the Donbass–Dnepr Bend revolutionary movement unfolded within the larger context of national economic and political changes, and in late spring it was events outside the region that once again spurred local workers into action. Ekaterinoslav's revolutionary movement displayed renewed vigor when news arrived June 16 of the strikes, street fighting, and naval mutinies convulsing Odessa. The joint strike committee of the local Social Democrats, which consisted of three Mensheviks and three Bolsheviks, quickly convened. After hearing from working-class militants who wanted to strike, the committee decided to call a sympathy strike. Once again, as in 1903, general strikes erupted in the major industrial centers throughout southern Russia while the capitals remained relatively quiet.[76]

Ekaterinoslav was tense on the eve of the planned general strike. The daily newspaper *Pridneprovskii krai* reported that "all day yesterday [June 19], the city was in an anxious mood. Any rumor was sufficient to set off public panic. Beginning in the morning, rumors circulated about disorders at the Ozernyi market, about killings and pillage, even though everything was quiet. . . . In the city there were large military patrols."[77] Everyone waited to see whether the workers at the city's largest factory would strike.[78] When, on June 20, the Briansk factory workers responded to the revolutionaries' call to strike, their example spread quickly. Within hours, production stopped at most, if not all, of the factories in the city's industrial district and suburbs. Downtown, the strike wave quickly spread to include artisans and other nonindustrial workers. Stores in the city again closed.[79]

Intimidation overcame divisions in the workers' ranks. The following

---

revolutionaries there felt that the émigré leaders slighted their organizations in favor of the capitals. The secretary of the Ekaterinoslav Bolshevik faction conveyed this at the end of May in an angry letter to the émigré central committee: "Please direct your attention to us! Many times we have asserted that Ekaterinoslav is a large industrial region consisting not only of itself but of the mines, Lugansk, and other places. From all sides they are turning to us for literature. . . . Sixty percent of the city is organized. Write!" (Ralph C. Elwood, "The RSDRP in the Underground: A Study of the Russian Social Democratic Labor Party in the Ukraine, 1907–1914" [Ph.D. diss., Columbia University, 1969], p. 63, quoted in McCaffray, "New Work," p. 170; Elwood, *Russian Social Democracy*, p. 138).

[76] Donbass–Dnepr Bend workers outside Ekaterinoslav failed to support the June general strike, except for a one-day strike in Kamenskoe. Only brief, isolated strikes occurred in Donets Basin factories and mines throughout the summer of 1905 (TsGAOR, DP OO, f. 102, 1905, op. 5, d. 975, vol. 3, p. 78; *Iuzhnaia zaria*, March 21, 1907; I. Shmyrov, "Iz istorii revoliutsionnogo dvizheniia v Luganske," *Letopis' revoliutsii*, no. 3 [1924]: 93).

[77] June 20, 1905, p. 4.

[78] *Iskra*, no. 106 (July 18, 1905): 1.

[79] Ibid.; *Pridneprovskii krai*, June 24, 1905, p. 5; *Gorno-zavodskii listok*, July 2, 1905, pp. 7901, 7904; *Khleb i volia*, no. 21–22 (August–September 1905): 5. The bakers' strike attracted the most attention, as the price of bread rose dramatically before it disappeared from the shelves (*Pridneprovskii krai*, June 20, 1905, p. 4).

morning, June 21, a major setback almost occurred when most of the workers at the city's railroad workshop returned to work. However, after the factory whistle sounded, militants once again brought work to a stop. Elsewhere, a crowd of strikers in the industrial district descended on still-open factories and the railroad office, inducing workers at these enterprises to join the strike. Another crowd went through Ekaterinoslav's center, closing artisanal shops and retail stores. Although fights broke out between strikers and those opposed to the strike, by the afternoon the tram lines, the railroad, and all telegraph and telephone communications were closed. The labor movement had once again brought normal urban life in Ekaterinoslav to a halt.[80]

Unlike the strikes in January and February, the June general strike was dominated by radical leaders. Despite worker appeals, strike leaders often did not present economic demands to employers.[81] Most workers simply went home after walking off the job, generally ignoring the radicals at the factory gates, who were shouting "Down with the autocracy!" and "Down with the war!" and calling on them to attend rallies. Many workers even voiced their opposition to the Social Democrats and liberals, who were shouting "Long live a constituent assembly!" and "Long live equality for all citizens!"[82]

Crowds did gather at four different locations in the city the next day, June 22. Under the noses of Cossacks, troops, and police, several hundred Jewish youths held a demonstration in the center of town, complete with red flags and the singing of revolutionary songs. They tried to merge with a crowd of factory workers, but the workers rebuffed them, apparently because they were Jewish.[83] Later that day, a crowd numbering perhaps in the thousands assembled for a rally at a central square in the city. Orators denounced employers' exploitation of workers and emphasized the importance of showing solidarity with the workers in Odessa, as well as acquiring such freedoms as the right to strike, assemble, and vote.[84]

Radical sectarianism marred the summer strike as fighting among the various parties worsened during June. The Mensheviks and Bolsheviks issued separate leaflets, and, unlike in the earlier strike waves, Social Democrats and Socialist Revolutionaries did not try to mask their hostility toward one another. Social Democratic, Socialist Revolutionary, Anarchist, and Zionist orators commonly attacked one another in their speeches.[85]

[80] *Revoliutsionnaia Rossiia*, no. 72 (August 1, 1905): 19; *Ekaterinoslavshchina*, pp. 122–123.

[81] TsGAOR, M. Iu., f. 124, 1905, op. 43, d. 1305 (Gendarme report, June 24, 1905), p. 3; *Pridneprovskii krai*, June 24, 1905, p. 5; Shklovskii, "Vospominaniia," p. 190.

[82] *Khleb i volia*, no. 23 (October 1905): 6.

[83] *Iskra*, no. 106 (July 18, 1905): 2.

[84] *Gorno-zavodskii listok*, July 9, 1905, p. 7914; *Iskra*, no. 106 (July 18, 1905): 2.

[85] *Revoliutsionnaia Rossiia*, no. 72 (August 1, 1905): 18.

The final speech of the rally on June 22 was by an SR. He lambasted the SDs for being out of touch with the masses: "Russian *intelligenty* who wear yellow shoes, hats costing 2.50 rubles, and other expensive things, and yet still attempt to lead the movement, call themselves SDs. They do not even notice that peasants go barefoot and wear cheap caps."[86]

In some cases during the summer strike, radicals tried to initiate violence against the Cossacks. Before the SR orator finished, someone from the crowd threw a bomb (which failed to explode). Others fired revolvers at nearby Cossacks. The enraged Cossacks charged the crowd. Cossack gunfire seriously wounded four, and one worker was hacked to death with a saber.[87] A rally in the industrial district also ended in bloodshed. The crowd dispersed when Cossacks approached the Briansk square, but a group of about thirty radicals, armed with revolvers, remained behind to fire at the Cossacks. They managed to wound a couple of Cossacks and some policemen before Cossack gunfire wounded fourteen workers, three fatally.[88]

Ekaterinoslav's general strikes lacked able leadership and clear direction after workers hit the streets. As one Social Democrat account admitted, the worker-activists did not know what to do once the strike began. "They expected instructions from above; when these did not come, the organized workers were confused and embarrassed. The working masses, not receiving from the advanced workers what they had a right to expect, dispersed home disillusioned and disappointed."[89] By June 22, the third day of the strike, there was no mistaking the strikers' low spirits. Workers began to return to work June 23. To most workers, it seemed as if the strike had achieved nothing.

Some returning workers had to brave a gauntlet of thrown rocks and threats by revolver-waving teenagers. This last bit of bravado soon disappeared when, in what must have come as quite a shock to many workers, the management at the railroad workshop and some factories where workers had begun presenting economic demands decided to "teach the workers a lesson." The railroad administration locked its workers out and threatened to eliminate legal and religious holidays when the workshop did reopen. Workers soon demanded nothing more than to be allowed to return to work.[90]

The Social Democrats tried to put a brave face on the outcome of the

[86] *Iskra*, no. 106 (July 18, 1905): 2.

[87] *Khleb i volia*, no. 21–22 (August–September 1905): 6; *Revoliutsionnaia Rossiia*, no. 72 (August 1, 1905): 19; *Ekaterinoslavshchina*, pp. 122, 128.

[88] *Posledniia izvestiia*, no. 249 (September 18, 1905): 10.

[89] *Sotsial'demokrat*, no. 12 (August 18, 1905): 10; *Posledniia izvestiia*, no. 249 (September 5/18, 1905): 10.

[90] *Iskra*, no. 106 (July 18, 1905): 3.

June strike. As the workers returned to work, they issued a leaflet entitled "To Conscious Workers" that congratulated workers for their willingness during these "portentous days" to concentrate on political change and forgo incremental economic improvements in their lives. "The strike that engulfed our city carried a truly political character. We did not raise any nongeneral demands, but acted only out of a sense of solidarity with the Odessa proletariat and a desire to struggle against the existing order."[91] The local Socialist Revolutionaries and Anarchists correctly believed the SDs were deluding themselves.

The Socialist Revolutionaries had expressed dissatisfaction with the general-strike tactic as early as 1903. Following the June general strike, the Socialist Revolutionaries openly challenged the Social Democrats to explain how the strike had been successful, arguing that its failure to achieve any political, social, or economic change left many workers disgruntled with the revolutionary movement.[92] Anarchist unhappiness with general strikes also surfaced in June 1905. To a large extent, their dissatisfaction focused on how the other parties handled the strikes. Strong proponents of the general-strike tactic, the Anarchists blamed the Social Democrats for enervating the strikes after setting them in motion. The Anarchists argued that the Social Democrats pursued a moderate course partly because they were terrified that the general strike might move too far to the left and include attacks on the bourgeoisie.[93]

Many workers shared the Anarchists' frustration over the insipid denouements of the general strikes. As will be discussed in the following chapter, once the euphoria accompanying the workers' initial realization of their power passed, workers inevitably began to question the long-term value of general strikes.[94]

If general strikes were to wrest political concessions from the autocracy, it was increasingly apparent that they could not be geographically isolated. Of course, to some extent, leaders in Ekaterinoslav's radical movement had always realized this. The Social Democrats and Socialist Revolutionaries in Ekaterinoslav never initiated a general strike. All of the city's general strikes were in response to similar actions elsewhere in Russia, usually in southern Russia. When the call for a general strike emanated from the center in October, the workers of Ekaterinoslav responded more enthusiasti-

[91] *Sotsial'demokrat*, no. 12 (August 18, 1905): 10.

[92] *Revoliutsionnaia Rossiia*, no. 72 (August 1, 1905): 19.

[93] *Khleb i volia*, no. 21–22 (August–September 1905): 6.

[94] Of course, an important reason the general strikes had done little to improve workers' lot was the weakness of the economy in 1905. As the threat of lockouts in June dramatically suggested, for workers to close factories might have been almost a favor to the owners in many cases (Meksina, "Pervye stachki," p. 221).

cally than ever before, as if doubts concerning the tactic's effectiveness had been dispelled.

Some worker disenchantment with the general-strike tactic centered on the Social Democrats' insistence that the strikes be nonviolent. In the June general strike, attempts to rally the activists among the artisans and workers often met responses such as "Where are the arms? Do you really think it's possible to go out on the street with empty hands? . . . Without bombs we won't go to rallies to be shot at and whipped."[95] When the authorities gained the upper hand on the third day of the June strike, "the mass of the proletariat looked with hostile eyes at the 'organizers.' [Workers were heard exclaiming,] 'They called it, they began it, but they did nothing. Where were their arms, their bombs?—Those frauds.' "[96] Stung by such criticism, Menshevik, Bolshevik, and Bundist leaders in Ekaterinoslav came together in July and agreed to coordinate their activities, jointly collect weapons, and plan an armed insurrection.[97]

Strike waves and general strikes during the revolutionary upsurge proved to be extremely complex events. The drama and power of these strikes have obscured this complexity—particularly the ambivalence of many general-strike participants, the sputtering way in which general strikes unfolded, and the reactionary backlashes they provoked. Especially complex was the October general strike, the most dramatically successful of the 1905 Revolution's general strikes.

The nationwide October general strike wrested from the tsar the promise of a parliament and civil freedoms, including the right to form trade unions. This wave of unrest began to gather momentum in the second half of September, when printers, tobacco workers, trolley workers, and bakers walked off the job in Moscow. Strikes then engulfed St. Petersburg before spreading out into the provinces. In the capital, revolutionary orators spoke in university lecture halls before tightly packed crowds of students, workers, and many others. Similarly, mass meetings in the open air and in various auditoriums resumed in Ekaterinoslav in the fall.[98] On September 28, a funeral march carrying the body of a Jew killed during the latest disorders sparked the organization of a large antigovernment rally at the Mining Institute.[99] On October 6, a crowd of five hundred youths assembled on the central boulevard. Rallies, which to the authorities seemed to

[95] *Iskra*, no. 106 (July 18, 1905): 2.

[96] Ibid.

[97] Lane, *Roots*, p. 167.

[98] *Novaia zhizn'*, no. 7 (1905): 6.

[99] TsGAOR, DP OO, f. 102, 1905, op. 5, d. 975, vol. 3, p. 200.

be occurring everywhere, featured bold, inflammatory speeches and often included calls to raise money for arms.[100]

The growing antigovernment movement included increasingly broad support from the local population. Throughout the empire, as in Ekaterinoslav, students boycotted classes and became enthralled by the drama of the unfolding revolution. Vladimir Voitinskii spoke for many when he recalled his experiences:

> I had not been converted by any particular book or propagandist, and I was not obsessed by blind hatred of the tsarist regime. What brought me to the revolution was the revolution itself. I believed that a violent clash between the people and the government was approaching, and I felt the urge, if not the moral obligation, to be with the people in the decisive hour, and thought that only by joining a revolutionary group would I be able to play my part.[101]

Ekaterinoslav's liberals began meeting more and more often at the English Club and at the Mining Institute to discuss politics. Sizable contingents of students and members of the city's middle class attended rallies in the city center and the factory district.[102] But tension between radical workers and liberals was often evident. I. Shevchenko recounted a confrontation that occurred early in October:

> I remember at one of the rallies at the Mining Institute, we workers arrived in large number; we were met at the stairs by students who refused to allow us to enter. They spoke about how the room was already overcrowded and might collapse. Of course, we knew that the strength of the floor was not the problem, but simply that the Kadets didn't want to have such a crowd of workers in their audience. We stormed the line and broke through the barrier on the stairs and entered the hall. . . . The mood clearly changed with our appearance: the "pure public" of professors and others left the hall.[103]

Despite such tension, the October general strike brought the entire opposition movement together and was the most dramatic display yet of the strength of the working class—although the strike's power and popularity, as indeed its success, took all participants by surprise. The local leaders of the revolutionary parties played no role in the planning for the general strike. In fact, when word of events in Moscow reached the Donbass–

[100] TsGAOR, DP OO, f. 102, 1906, op. 234, d. 7, ch. 34 (*Otchety o revoliutsionnom dvizhenii, Ekaterinoslavskaia gub.*), p. 1.

[101] W. S. Woytinsky, *Stormy Passage: A Personal History through Two Russian Revolutions to Democracy and Freedom, 1905–1960* (New York, 1961), p. 15.

[102] V. Dal'man, "Oktiabr'skie dni v Ekaterinoslave," *Serp*, collection 1 (1907): 202; L. M. Ivanov, "Oktiabr'skaia politicheskaia stachka 1905 g. na Ukraine," *Istoricheskie zapiski* 54 (1955): 60.

[103] "O revoliutsii 1905 g.," p. 134.

Dnepr Bend, many questioned whether Ekaterinoslav's workers would heed the Central Bureau of the All-Russian Railroad Union, which had organized the strike to bring the country's entire economy to a stop and thereby extort major liberal reforms from the autocratic government.[104] One of the Social Democrats in Ekaterinoslav, V. Dal'man, later recalled, "As the revolutionary wave rose, we in Ekaterinoslav debated the mood of the '*briantsy*,' trying to surmise whether or not they would support the city actions and demonstrations. This debate unfailingly created splits in our revolutionary circles, as the skeptics and those of little faith recommended that we wait to act until we see the mood of the '*briantsy*,' that is, the factory workers in the suburbs."[105]

Yet in Ekaterinoslav, as in nearly every major urban center, workers responded to calls to strike. On October 11, Ekaterinoslav's workers quickly brought most, if not all, of the business of the city to a halt and seized control of the city's telegraph and telephone system, as well as all rail traffic.[106] Regular rail service stopped as strikers outfitted trains with red flags and carried large numbers of workers back and forth between Ekaterinoslav and the suburbs of Amur and Nizhnedneprovsk. In the city center, crowds of students went from one educational institution to another demanding an end to all classes. In the early evening, a crowd of thousands, drawn from both the factory district and the center of the city, listened to hours of fiery speeches at the railroad terminal before troops dispersed them. Another large rally was held in the center of the city at the Mining Institute.[107]

The two most significant developments of the Ekaterinoslav October general strike were the extensive violence involved in confrontations between armed troops and demonstrators on the streets and the emergence of a soviet during the last day of the strike.

During the October genral strike, more demonstrators died in Ekaterinoslav than in any other city in the empire.[108] Unlike the revolutionary parties, the government was prepared for a militant display. When Ekaterinoslav's governor sent the minister of internal affairs a telegram that ended on an ominous note—"Expect disorders tomorrow"[109]—General

[104] For a discussion of the role of the railroad union in 1905, see Walter Sablinsky, "The All-Russian Railroad Union and the Beginning of the General Strike in October, 1905," in *Revolution and Politics in Russia*, ed. Alexander and Janet Rabinowitch (Bloomington, Ind., 1973); and Reichman, *Railwaymen and Revolution*, pp. 159–223.

[105] "Oktiabr'skie dni," pp. 206–207.

[106] TsGIA, f. 23, op. 30, d. 47 (Factory inspectorate report, October 18, 1905), p. 283; *Iuzhnyi krai*, October 24, 1905, p. 5.

[107] *Vserossiiskaia politicheskaia stachka v oktiabre 1905 goda*, ed. L. M. Ivanov (Moscow-Leningrad, 1955), pp. 98, 104–105; *Ekaterinoslavshchina*, pp. 168, 181–185.

[108] See, for example, Ascher, *Revolution of 1905*, p. 219.

[109] *Ekaterinoslavshchina*, p. 167.

D. F. Trepov responded with his notorious demand for ruthlessness. Trepov telegraphed back orders instructing the governor to use "the most resolute measures to suppress the disorders. Do not hesitate before using armed force."[110] In addition to stationing police and Cossacks at "assembly points" around the city on the morning of October 11, the authorities had three infantry companies at the ready in the barracks of the city garrison.[111]

The revolutionary disorders the governor had predicted occurred in Ekaterinoslav all day long on October 11. Early in the morning, nervous troops and a large crowd faced off on the streets of the city, not long after the first commandeered "workers' train" arrived in Ekaterinoslav from Nizhnedneprovsk at 6 A.M.[112] Already by eight o'clock, a crowd of over one thousand workers had gathered at the Ekaterinoslav depot; there were also many "outsiders," among whom were women with children and some "fine ladies" [*baryshni*].[113] The crowd defiantly ignored the commanding officer when he threatened to fire if they did not disperse. Then, when someone in the crowd allegedly fired a shot, the officer ordered his troops to shoot two volleys into the dense mass of protesters. Most of the troops aimed over people's heads, but one of the wounded—Fedor Popka, a depot worker—died.[114] This confrontation succeeded only in shifting the urban battlefield elsewhere, since, as was soon to be demonstrated, the militant spirits of October were not easily dampened.

Three thousand people gathered in the city center. Teenagers repeating revolutionary slogans were the most vociferous participants, but the crowd was notable for its heterogeneous character.[115]

> The crowd filling the sidewalks and boulevard wore a lively assortment of coats. Boys and girls from the gymnasiums mixed with civil servants [*chinovniki*] and all sorts of "fathers of families" of the middle estate . . . intelligentsia and non-intelligentsia bourgeoisie merged with a stream of salesclerks, Jewish artisans, . . . muscular millers covered with flour from head to foot, factory workers, and artels of carpenters and joiners.[116]

Throughout the day, militant crowds refused to yield the streets to the authorities. If dispersed at one location, crowds regrouped at another.[117] They shouted, "The *briantsy* are acting! The *briantsy* are acting! There will be a colossal demonstration!" Relatively few industrial workers were to be

[110] Ibid., p. 170.
[111] Ibid., pp. 164–166.
[112] *Iuzhnyi krai*, October 24, 1905, p. 5; *Nachalo*, no. 10 (November 25, 1905): 6.
[113] *Vserossiiskaia*, p. 105.
[114] *Ekaterinoslavshchina*, p. 168.
[115] Dal'man, "Oktiabr'skie dni," pp. 202–203.
[116] Ibid., p. 205.
[117] *Novaia zhizn'*, no. 7 (1905): 6; *Vserossiiskaia*, pp. 105–106.

found in the city center, though, if for no other reason than that the troops had cordoned off the working-class district and suburbs from the inner city.

On a side street near the center of the city, a crowd of students organized a rally. While speakers attacked conditions in the schools, students hastily constructed an impromptu barricade before Cossacks and troops appeared. Soldiers soon formed a military line in front of the barricade, while Cossacks advanced from behind. The troops answered thrown rocks and a few revolver shots with three volleys. After the smoke cleared, clusters of youths lay on the ground. Five to eight of the demonstrators were killed and a large number wounded.[118]

At about this time, at the other end of the city, the biggest demonstration of the day began to form near the market square outside Chechelevka before moving into the factory district. The crowd had grown from around five thousand people to well over ten thousand by the time it reached the Briansk factory.[119] They then decided to march into the center of the city. The peaceful, though agitated, demonstrators carried a multitude of red banners, sang the "Marseillaise," and listened to orators demanding political freedom. When they ran into a troop blockade, they refused repeated orders to disperse. The troops fired a warning shot, but instead of dispersing, the crowd screamed abuses and, led by some railroad engineers, actually began to advance on the soldiers. Once again, the order to fire was given. The number killed and wounded here is unclear.[120] One newspaper counted seven fatalities and eighteen seriously wounded.[121]

Still more blood flowed on the streets that day in Ekaterinoslav's main working-class district, where revolutionaries had quickly built six barricades by chopping down telephone, telegraph, and tramway poles and covering them with boards, stones, rails, bricks, and dirt. They topped the barricades with barbed wire and red banners inscribed with militant political slogans.[122] Unlike in confrontations in the center of the city, troops as well as demonstrators suffered casualties in Chechelevka, as some workers outside the control of the Social Democrats decided to meet force with force. Military units had quickly formed opposite the barricade on the street bordering the Briansk square. The large crowd behind the barricade greeted the soldiers with shouts of "Down with the autocracy!" and with

[118] *Novaia zhizn'*, no. 7 (1905): 6; *Vestnik Iuga*, October 18, 1905, p. 3; *Iuzhnyi krai*, October 24, 1905, p. 5; TsGAOR, DP OO, f. 102, 1906, op. 234, d. 7, ch. 34 (*Otchety o revoliutsionnom dvizhenii, Ekaterinoslavskaia gub.*), p. 2.

[119] *Ekaterinoslavshchina*, p. 171; *Vserossiiskaia*, pp. 105–106. An Anarchist correspondent estimated the crowd to be closer to twenty thousand (*Khleb i volia*, no. 24 [November 1905]: 6.

[120] *Ekaterinoslavshchina*, pp. 171, 176; *Vserossiiskaia*, pp. 106–107.

[121] *Iuzhnyi krai*, October 24, 1905, p. 5.

[122] *Vserossiiskaia*, p. 107.

entreaties to throw down their arms and join the strikers. When the troops and Cossacks began to move toward the barricade, the militants again stood their ground. Armed radicals opened fire. The troops responded with a series of volleys, scattering the rebels onto nearby side streets. Then, as the soldiers began to dismantle the barricade, a bomb thrown from a rooftop landed in their midst. It instantly killed two soldiers and seriously injured eight to eleven more. A Cossack sharpshooter promptly killed the bomb thrower, an Anarchist. But from behind a nearby fence, a second bomb was thrown; it exploded and was followed by a dud. The second bomb injured nine more soldiers, six Cossacks, and four horses.[123] The bombs exploded with such force that they blew out the windows of the school across the street. Panic momentarily seized the soldiers. Fearing more bombs and the revolver fire now coming from behind nearby fences and from open windows and rooftops, they temporarily retreated.[124] With eight of the rebels dead and four seriously wounded (additional wounded were carried away to avoid arrest), casualties had fallen on both sides of the barricade.[125] The narrow streets of Chechelevka left the troops open to potshots, and they moved slowly to clear the streets. It took three and a half hours, almost until nightfall, before the military had cleared away the last of the barricades. A number of other skirmishes occurred around the city as night approached. Patrols remained on the dark streets through the night and were the target of isolated sniper shots, none of which found its mark.[126]

Troops continued to patrol the city on October 12, while all commercial and industrial enterprises remained closed. The governor's office issued the following proclamation: "In light of the progression of events in Ekaterinoslav and the necessity of calling armed troops into action, inhabitants of the city are requested not to leave their houses for other than an extreme emergency."[127] In defiance of this proclamation, crowds of strikers and demonstrators gathered on the streets of the city, though in smaller numbers than the day before. According to one journalist, however, revolutionary-party activists led "grandiose" rallies in the factory district of Chechelevka. Workers continued to travel about in locomotives draped with red flags and revolutionary banners.[128]

Sniper fire persisted on October 13, but the major event of that day was

[123] *Ekaterinoslavshchina*, pp. 171, 183; *Vserossiiskaia*, p. 107; *Iuzhnyi krai*, October 24, 1905, p. 5; *Vestnik Iuga*, October 18, 1905, p. 3; TsGAOR, DP OO, f. 102, 1906, op. 234, d. 7, ch. 34 (*Otchety o revoliutsionnom dvizhenii, Ekaterinoslavskaia gub.*), p. 2.

[124] *Vserossiiskaia*, p. 107; *Khleb i volia*, no. 24 (November 25, 1905): 6.

[125] *Proletarii*, no. 24 (October 25, 1908): 2; *Burevestnik*, no. 6–7 (September–October 1907): 5.

[126] *Nachalo*, no. 2 (November 15, 1905): 5; *Vserossiiskaia*, p. 108.

[127] *Ekaterinoslavshchina*, p. 170.

[128] Journalist's account quoted in Lane, *Roots*, p. 170; *Vserossiiskaia*, p. 108; *Iuzhnyi krai*, October 24, 1905, p. 5.

a funeral procession for the twenty-eight protesters killed on the eleventh. The funeral procession again brought together, temporarily, the entire opposition movement, including liberals. It was transformed into a mass demonstration as thousands, if not tens of thousands, marched to the cemeteries. Liberals from the Union of Unions, along with some deputies from the railroad union, had secured a guarantee from the governor that the marchers would not be attacked. The governor, A. B. Neidgart, decided some concession was necessary to relieve the tension in the city. He promised that the procession would not be obstructed by Cossacks, soldiers, or police.[129]

The governor kept his promise for the remainder of the strike, and no major bloody confrontations occurred after October 11. Revolutionary activists organized antigovernment rallies in various parts of the city every day, in which Jewish teenagers carrying red flags were often at the forefront.[130] By October 17, when some workers in light industry returned to work, the general strike had clearly subsided. But though the mood of the revolutionaries began to deflate, all the large factories and railroad workshops remained closed, and rallies continued to take place in the factory district. Clashes with the troops and police did not recur, but the city remained an armed camp until the news of the announcement of the October Manifesto reached Ekaterinoslav on October 18.[131]

Ekaterinoslav's workers proved in October that they could be among the most militant in the empire. Before the October Manifesto, mass militance and violent resistance were at a far higher level in Ekaterinoslav than in Russia's capitals, where mass confrontations with troops did not occur in October.[132] But other than in Ekaterinoslav, strike activity in the Donbass–Dnepr Bend was generally limited to the railroad stations, where miners from neighboring mines often attended rallies.[133] Although workers did strike in Aleksandrovsk and Kamenskoe in October, workers in most Donbass–Dnepr Bend cities did not.[134] With the trains not running and the newspapers not being printed, residents in Donbass–Dnepr Bend towns

[129] *Novaia zhizn'*, no. 7 (1905): 6; Dal'man, "Oktiabr'skie dni," p. 212.

[130] Most of these Jewish youths were said to be in their late teens, but more than a few reportedly were even younger (*Iuzhnaia zaria*, October 20, 1907, p. 3).

[131] *Novaia zhizn'*, no. 7 (1905): 6; TsGAOR, DP OO, f. 102, 1905, d. 4, ch. 17, vol. 4 (*O volneniiakh i stachkakh sredi rabochikh po Ekaterinoslavskoi gub.*), p. 82; TsGAOR, DP OO, f. 102, 1906, op. 234, d. 7, ch. 34 (*Otchety o revoliutsionnom dvizhenii, Ekaterinoslavskaia gub.*), p. 4.

[132] Comparable activity erupted only in Odessa and Khar'kov.

[133] Ivanov, "Oktiabr'skaia politicheskaia stachka," p. 61.

[134] Nikolaenko, *Revoliutsionnoe dvizhenie*, p. 24; Shabel'nikov, "Dekabr' 1905 goda v Aleksandrovske (Zaporozh'i) (Iz vospominanii uchastnika vosstaniia)," *Puti revoliutsii*, no. 3 (1925): 72.

such as Lugansk knew little, if anything, about what was occurring in Ekaterinoslav and the capitals.[135]

Employees at Donbass–Dnepr Bend railroad stations supported the October general strike, but at some points along the railroad lines, the heterogeneity of the work force created serious tensions. In Dolinsk and elsewhere, manual laborers demonstrated considerable hostility toward the office employees (*sluzhashchie*) who called the general strike. To avoid "unpleasantness," revolutionary activists closed liquor stores.[136] Khersontsev, one of the leaders of the strike in Dolinsk, recalled that "most of the workers at the depot were hostile toward us; there were even rumors that they were coming with hammers to attack the telegraphists' dormitory. . . . At the time, none of us was able to explain why workers were so hostile."[137]

The evolution of working-class militance and political consciousness was demonstrated not only in battles with troops, but also in the creation, on October 17, of a representative body to lead and organize the strike. During the last days of the October general strike, revolutionary activists and workers in Ekaterinoslav formed an Assembly of Workers' Deputies—a citywide working-class council, or soviet. The origin of Ekaterinoslav's new radical institution is undoubtedly traceable to the example provided by workers in St. Petersburg when they formed a Soviet of Workers' Deputies on October 13. The St. Petersburg soviet became the symbolic headquarters of the October general strike and popularized the idea of the soviet for the entire empire.[138]

Recognition of St. Petersburg's leading role should not obscure the facts that Ekaterinoslav's soviet was the product of independent action and that it was formed too soon after the capital's soviet for St. Petersburg to have offered much more than a vague example. The strike had cut communication lines in the country—newspapers, the telegraph, and railroad lines rarely operated. In Ekaterinoslav, as throughout the country, the city's strike leadership was in virtual isolation from the leadership in other cities. The strongest similarity between the Ekaterinoslav and St. Petersburg soviets was their grass-roots evolution. As in St. Petersburg, councils of elected worker representatives first appeared in Ekaterinoslav when work-

[135] TsGAOR, DP OO, f. 102, 1905, op. 5, d. 975, vol. 3, pp. 263–264; *Donetskii kolokol*, no. 1 (October 17, 1906): 1.

[136] *Materialy po istorii revoliutsionnykh sobytii 1905 goda na territorii, nyne vkhodiashchei v Artemovskom okruge (k 20-ti letnemy iubileiu revoliutsii 1905 g.)* (Artemovsk, 1925), p. 31.

[137] Khersontsev, "V poiskakh puti," *Puti revoliutsii*, no. 3 (1925): 87–88.

[138] Although St. Petersburg was late in joining the October general strike, the city's role in the October events assumed great significance when the St. Petersburg soviet first met on October 13. Moscow, in contrast, played the leading role in the strike but was late in forming a nonpartisan revolutionary council to represent all workers. A soviet was not formed in Moscow until late November (Anweiler, *Soviets*, pp. 46–47; Engelstein, *Moscow, 1905*, p. 162).

ers elected delegates in individual factories to negotiate with management during the strikes early in 1905.[139] Many of the city's factories that had yet to elect deputies did so during the first days of the October general strike.[140]

In Ekaterinoslav, more than one hundred delegates, representing all the large industrial enterprises in the city, participated in the soviet's inaugural meeting on October 17.[141] The largest delegation was from the Briansk plant, the city's largest factory.[142] Despite the predominance of the Social Democrats among the workers who were members of a revolutionary party, workers belonging to the Socialist Revolutionary, Zionist, and Anarchist parties made their presence felt. The consensus among delegates was that the Assembly should transcend the divisions within the radical movement and be nonpartisan. By secret ballot, Ekaterinoslav's soviet elected a seven-person executive committee.[143] The soviet quickly began to wield an influence in the city that the parties individually did not possess.

Along the railroad lines crisscrossing the Donbass–Dnepr Bend, railroad workers were also electing representatives. Occasionally, unskilled workers—political novices—were among those elected at the smaller stations. One employee later recalled, "Only yesterday a drunken Makar Mikhailovich was chasing the plump buffet girl around the station demanding 'more vodka on credit'; today he is a delegate to the Liubotin railroad congress, a top-notch speaker, and the first to sing the Marseillaise."[144] How profound such conversions were remained to be seen.

The first meeting of the Assembly of Ekaterinin Railroad Workers' Deputies provides a sense of what Mikhailovich and his fellow delegates thought was the goal of the general strike. The assembly passed a resolution calling for the establishment of the "kingdom of socialism," under which "all land, factories, and establishments of art and science will belong to the people. In the kingdom of socialism there will be neither rich nor poor, oppressed nor oppressors; all will labor equally and everyone will have everything necessary for the satisfaction of their physical and spiritual needs."[145] Ironically, much of the first meeting of the Ekaterinoslav soviet

[139] P. M. Shmorgun, "Sovety rabochikh deputatov na Ukraine v 1905 godu," *Istoricheskie zapiski* 49 (1954): 4.

[140] *Nachalo*, no. 13 (November 29, 1905): 4; N. N. Demochkin, *Sovety 1905 goda* (Moscow, 1963), p. 43; Shmorgun, "Sovety," p. 26.

[141] *Pridneprovskii krai*, October 18, 1905, p. 3.

[142] Shmorgun, *Sovety*, p. 26.

[143] *Nachalo*, no. 13 (November 29, 1905): 4.

[144] *1905 vo vospominaniiakh ego uchastnikov* (Rostov-on-Don, 1925), pp. 69–70, quoted in Reichman, *Railwaymen and Revolution*, p. 231.

[145] *Vysshii pod"em revoliutsii 1905–1907 gg.: Vooruzhennye vosstaniia, noiabr'–dekabr' 1905 god*, ed. A. L. Sidorov (Moscow-Leningrad, 1955), vol. 3, pt. 1: 33, quoted in Reichman, *Railwaymen and Revolution*, p. 233.

was devoted to the question of whether to end the general strike, which had shown clear signs of weakening. Unaware that the tsarist government was just then announcing the October Manifesto, the soviet resolved, after a discussion of the workers' mood and the shortage of basic goods in the city, to end the political strike in Ekaterinoslav, although workers at individual factories intent on achieving economic concessions could continue to wage their own private battles.[146]

The next day, October 18, news arrived in Ekaterinoslav that Nicholas II, who less than a year earlier had dismissed calls for a constitution as "an unthinkable illusion," had signed a manifesto transforming Russia (however imperfectly) into a constitutional monarchy. In response, in the words of one radical newspaper, "the people seized the streets."[147] The revolutionary movement, despite having conceded defeat the day before, appeared triumphant.

Ekaterinoslav's workers had shown themselves to be militantly revolutionary in October, and they deserved credit for helping push the tsar into making major political concessions to the opposition movement in the hope of restoring order. The tsar's pledge to establish a legislative assembly, the Duma, and guarantee full civil liberties appeared to mark the end of the Romanov dynasty's nearly three hundred years of unlimited power.

In the October general strike, Ekaterinoslav's workers had once again shut down the city's economy. Activists in their midst had built barricades and taken up arms against the military, although they were neither sufficiently prepared nor adequately armed to engage in serious combat. Ekaterinoslav's revolutionary parties, while they neither called nor directed the strike, also had reason to be proud of their role. Years of education and propaganda by the revolutionary parties had led to the emergence of a worker elite committed to radical change. Working-class militants affiliated with the parties played the leading role in establishing a militant representative body that enjoyed widespread support among the city's workers. But these revolutionary triumphs obscured the deep tensions just beneath the surface. These tensions, building since the first general strike in 1903, exploded after the October 1905 general strike in a particularly vicious backlash.

[146] *Pridneprovskii krai*, October 18, 1905, p. 3; *Vserossiiskaia*, p. 100.

[147] *Burevestnik*, no. 6–7 (September–October 1907): 5.

7

The Reactionary Backlash: 1903 to October 1905

> Peasants and workers, listen to our speech. Why are you, the great Russian people (*narod*), going against humanity? Like cruel beasts you attack the Jewish poor, devastating and putting to death Jews, those you call *zhids*. Why do you spill the innocent blood of Jewish children? . . . [The families you victimize] are your brothers in poverty, your brothers in labor.
>
> (*Ekaterinoslav SD leaflet, October 1905*)

> We become cruel to ourselves and to others, because they teach us to be haters of mankind. Not knowing in our darkness what we should do to save ourselves, in blind despair we commit unheard of atrocities which horrify the whole world. We have pogroms, we burn people and animals, we create martyrs the like of which have not yet been seen on the earth.
>
> (*A. I. Svirskii,* Notes of a Worker)

WORKING-CLASS UNREST in the Donbass–Dnepr Bend during the revolutionary surge was not limited to general strikes, radical demonstrations, and confrontations with government troops. Since 1903, and even earlier, demonstrations and strikes had provoked reactionary ferment among workers and violent backlashes. In the wake of radical labor demonstrations, workers temporarily reversed their support for the revolutionary movement and engaged en masse in looting and violent attacks on Jews and radical *intelligenty*. The worst pogrom occurred at the pinnacle of the 1905 Revolution, during the "Days of Freedom" that followed the October Manifesto. Workers' proclivity to engage in pogroms provides insight into their "working-class consciousness" and shows how this consciousness could be dissipated by frustrations with the revolutionary movement, frustrations that in turn could bring to the surface long-term hostilities. In their rampages, Russian and Ukrainian working-class pogromists disregarded any community of interest based on class or economic status they might have shared with Jewish workers.

During the late nineteenth and early twentieth centuries, revolutionary leaders continually found themselves in the ironic position of having to curb the labor movement for fear of provoking a pogrom. Activists were forced to recognize that even though growing labor discontent offered propitious opportunities for the revolutionary movement, appeals to workers to demonstrate were dangerous. Revolutionaries were well aware that their ties with factory workers and miners remained tenuous during the revolutionary upsurge. When combined with most workers' lack of political sophistication, this meant that any street protest could easily assume the character of a riot, if not a pogrom. One early Soviet historian, V. Nevskii, conceded that during a wave of strikes, such as that in January 1905, the "easily inflammable" Donbass–Dnepr Bend working class was a tinderbox, ready to explode in response to pogromist appeals. The possibility that Donbass–Dnepr Bend workers might "succumb to Black Hundred scum . . . was well understood by the underground organization."[1] Ethnic antagonism, the prevalence of violence in working-class culture, and the workers' eagerness to use violence to express their frustration with the outcome of general strikes help explain why the Social Democrats, the largest and most influential party in the Donbass–Dnepr Bend, often favored cautious tactics during the revolutionary surge.

May Day 1899 in Ekaterinoslav had taught this lesson early and in dramatic fashion. On the eve of May Day, Social Democrats distributed thousands of leaflets around Ekaterinoslav's factories and artisanal workshops calling for a public demonstration on the city's main boulevard in support of working-class solidarity. The radicals' plan backfired. As workers read the leaflets, rumors began spreading through the factory districts that May Day would be the occasion for a pogrom in Ekaterinoslav, similar to the one that had recently erupted not far away on the streets of Nikolaev. May Day coincided with the Easter-Passover season, when the tension between the Jewish and Christian communities was always heightened. As the pogromist mood spread, it became obvious that the celebration of working-class solidarity by Jewish artisans, along with their radical supporters, was to be the target of a mass assault by the factory workers they sought as allies. The threat was thought to be so serious that on May Day—no doubt much to the relief of the revolutionary leadership—nearly all the factories were surrounded by troops, police, and Cossacks, who cordoned off the industrial suburbs from the center of the city and thus prevented a pogrom.[2]

[1] Nevskii, "Ianvarskie dni," p. 184.

[2] *Iuzhnyi rabochii*, no. 1 (January 1900), reprinted in *Istoriia ekaterinoslavskoi.*

The bloodshed and destruction Russia's Jews suffered in the wave of pogroms that erupted between 1903 and 1905 in the Pale far exceeded the horrors of the pogroms in the early 1880s. The 1903–1905 pogroms in the Donbass–Dnepr Bend were part of the wave that began with the ghastly pogrom in Kishinev in April 1903.[3] Though not unprecedented, this brutal attack by workers and other members of the lower classes in Kishinev caught the public by surprise.[4] Inside Russia, and worldwide, denunciations and outrage greeted news of the Kishinev pogrom. No such outrage was felt by the mass of Donbass–Dnepr Bend workers—quite the contrary. Plans for a May Day demonstration in 1903 again provoked pogromist ferment among workers in the Donets Basin.

Social Democratic agitators in the towns and mining settlements of the Donets Basin had been active for months in early 1903. The SDs' Donets Union distributed eighteen thousand leaflets at fifteen factories and nineteen mines in preparation for May Day strikes and demonstrations they planned to call across the Donbass–Dnepr Bend in 1903. But instead, on the eve of May Day, the campaign was again abruptly canceled. When news of the Kishinev pogrom arrived, the Donets Union abandoned all plans for May Day, as rumors spread that pogroms on an unprecedented scale would erupt in factories and mines across the Donbass–Dnepr Bend on May Day. The Social Democrats decided that to organize a demonstration at that time was far too risky "in view of the miners' extreme lack of culture." "Persistent rumors of a pogrom circulated everywhere, including Mariupol', Iuzovka, and Lugansk. . . . The white-collar employees at many mines did their best to be as far from the mines as possible [on May Day]; everyone prepared for an unprecedented riot."[5]

In the following year, when mobilization for the Russo-Japanese War quickly proved unpopular, many Social Democrats began to agitate the seventy-seven thousand urban and rural youths the government assembled and trained in Ekaterinoslav, Lugansk, and other Donbass–Dnepr Bend

[3] The rabidly anti-Semitic daily newspaper in Kishinev, *Bessarabets*, incited the pogrom by reporting that the Jews of Kishinev had murdered a Christian boy to use his blood to knead their Passover bread. The pogromists murdered forty-five Jews, injured six hundred more, and looted and vandalized over thirteen hundred homes and shops. International investigators reported the most gruesome violence—pogromists reputedly not only gang-raped women and girls, they drove nails into the head of one still-alive victim and castrated and then trampled to death an artisan who attempted to stop one gang rape (Lincoln, *In War's Dark Shadow*, pp. 220–221).

[4] Kishinev's mayor identified the pogromists as "the frequenters of the cafes and the workingmen who are hostile to the Jews" (Lambroza, "Pogram Movement," p. 70).

[5] *Iskra*, no. 45 (August 1, 1903): 8. The Social Democrats in Ekaterinoslav did manage to hold a rally, which 250 people attended, to denounce the Kishinev pogrom (*Iskra*, no. 44 [July 15, 1903]).

cities, of whom a large percentage were workers.[6] Again, the threat of provoking a pogrom persuaded them to desist. In the words of an Okhrana agent, the desire of many of Ekaterinoslav's Social Democrats to incite the mobilized youths to engage in acts of insubordination provoked a serious debate within the city's party organization. "The more sober-minded of the antigovernment activists opposed disorders, contending that they could be turned into Jewish pogroms, while others were not troubled by this issue and continued to insist on distributing militant propaganda among the draftees."[7] In fact, although copies of "To All Ekaterinoslav's Reservists" and other such leaflets were distributed, Ekaterinoslav's Social Democrats concentrated during the autumn on conducting antipogrom agitation among the city's factory workers. In the face of the growing pogromist threat, planned demonstrations were canceled. The SD committee even organized rudimentary self-defense units. "During the days when the city was flooded with thousands of reservists, the SD committee stationed detachments at various points around the city of more or less armed and organized workers (Jews and Christians), who agitated against a pogrom among the gray mass of migrant peasants and workers."[8] Despite such precautionary actions, a limited pogrom occurred in Ekaterinoslav on September 3–4, 1904.[9]

In Ekaterinoslav and the towns of the Donets Basin, May Day 1905 recalled the events of May Day 1903. In Iuzovka and Lugansk, rumors were flying on the eve of May Day about plans to beat Jews and students and other intellectuals. In Lugansk, the SD leaders and dozens of party members clandestinely met outside the city to discuss how to respond to the pogromist threat. They resolved to oppose the pogromists and organize some defensive measures "if the attempt to direct the movement into the desired channel, that is, to follow the slogan 'Beat the police,' failed."[10] For the overwrought Jewish residents, haunted by fear of pogroms, every rumor inspired panic. Before May Day, many of the city's Jewish residents (those who could afford it), and many others as well, fled the city.[11] Ekaterinoslav's Bolshevik committee distributed a leaflet on the eve of May Day appealing to workers to renounce their desire to attack Jews:

[6] Of the reserves called up on August 24, 12,400 were Donets Basin coal miners and 1,100 were Krivoi Rog iron miners (Iu. I. Kir'ianov, *Perekhod k massovoi politicheskoi bor'be: Rabochii klass nakanune pervoi rossiiskoi revoliutsii* [Moscow, 1987], p. 152). See also TsGAOR, DP OO, f. 102, 1905, d. 1885 (Okhrana report, December 7, 1904), p. 130.

[7] Ibid.

[8] *Tretii s"ezd RSDRP: Sbornik dokumentov i materialov* (Moscow, 1905), p. 660.

[9] TsGIA, f. 23, d. 47 (Report of Ekaterinoslav's senior factory inspector, S. Evtushevskii, September 7, 1905), p. 251.

[10] Berkhin, *Luganskaia bol'shevistskaia organizatsiia*, p. 48.

[11] TsGAOR, DP OO, f. 102, 1905, op. 5, d. 975, vol. 2, p. 242; *Iskra*, no. 99 (May 1, 1905): 4.

> Comrade Workers! Down with enmity between workers of different nationalities and religions. Such enmity benefits only the thieves and tyrants who thrive on the ignorance and divisiveness among the proletariat. Jews and Christians, Armenians and Tatars, Poles and Russians . . . everyone come together under the common banner of socialism. All workers are brothers.[12]

The Socialist Revolutionaries made similar appeals. During the 1903 general strike, an SR orator identified as a worker spoke about the necessity of overcoming ethnic animosities within the labor movement. The SRs distributed a leaflet that called on workers "to go arm in arm, whether Russian, Jewish, Polish, or foreign, to struggle against the capitalist enemy. Comrades, if anyone speaks to you about national hatred—know he is an enemy of the workers' cause. The interests of all workers are one."[13] But as the Okhrana reported: "In view of the significant quantity of unemployed people and assorted riffraff in Ekaterinoslav, who in large number arrive daily on the rafts they float on the Dnepr, once a pogrom begins it would be able to assume serious dimensions, especially considering that *the majority of the factory workers are Christian and have bitter animosity toward Jews*."[14] The Social Democrats awaited the day with trepidation: "Once again new victims, the spilling of blood, mounted troops, piles of mutilated bodies, and thousands of orphaned families."[15] The Bund and Labor Zionists intensified their efforts to form self-defense units, but they possessed few weapons, as was true of radicals generally until the second half of 1905.[16]

In response to the rumors, the government took decisive steps. Governor Neidgart posted a warning throughout Ekaterinoslav and the neighboring villages, which announced that any disorders would be immediately crushed. On May Day itself, police and Cossacks patrolled the streets and quickly quashed the few disturbances that broke out, mostly drunk teenagers throwing rocks at Jewish stores and workshops. In Lugansk, the police issued a declaration advising residents not to gather in a crowd and informing them that military force would be applied immediately to halt violence against persons and property.[17] As a result of these measures, and because revolutionaries canceled the mass actions they had planned, May Day 1905 passed largely without disorders in Ekaterinoslav and throughout the Donbass–Dnepr Bend. Radical activities were essentially restricted

[12] *Letopis' revoliutsii*, no. 4 (1925): 278.

[13] *Revoliutsionnaia Rossiia*, no. 33 (October 1, 1903): 18.

[14] TsGAOR, DP OO, f. 102, 1905, op. 5, d. 4, ch. 17, vol. 2, p. 56 (emphasis in the original).

[15] *Iskra*, no. 99 (May 1, 1905): 6.

[16] *Posledniia izvestiia*, no. 236 (June 16, 1905): 6.

[17] *Pridneprovskii krai*, May 4, 1905, p. 4.

to small gatherings of students, workers, and artisans—the party faithful.[18] While Donbass–Dnepr Bend revolutionaries could mobilize mass worker support for general strikes, attempts to elicit mass worker support for May Day demonstrations repeatedly proved to be failures, if not disasters.

During the revolutionary upsurge, Donbass–Dnepr Bend revolutionaries constantly worried that any mass action might lead to, or be transformed into, a pogrom. As one historian has noted in this context, "the international solidarity of the proletariat had to be seen quite literally as a matter of life or death."[19] Clearly concerned that the February 1905 strike in Lugansk would lead to pogroms, the Social Democratic Donets Union concluded the leaflet they distributed at the Hartmann factory with a plea: "During the strike, conduct yourself peacefully, don't smash machines and other factory property, don't loot stores, don't attack Jews—in a word, conduct yourself as workers in other cities have conducted themselves."[20]

The threat of a pogrom followed each of the four general strikes or strike waves that occurred in the Donbass–Dnepr Bend between 1903 and October 1905. Such threats took the form of rumors, which spread like wildfire. In June 1905, rumors that worker frustration with the general strike in Ekaterinoslav would erupt into a pogrom hovered in the air throughout the strike. On June 21, the second day of the general strike, workers attacked and beat several Jews so badly that one of them died. But this time, the fears were not realized, and a full-blown pogrom did not occur. In his memoirs, the Social Democratic worker-activist I. Shevchenko claimed that Black Hundreds members of the Union of True Russians, along with members of the police, had disguised themselves as workers and were responsible for the anti-Semitic attacks.[21] But by going on to state that "agitational means" did not stop the "national persecution," Shevchenko seemed to concede that genuine workers played some part, at least, in the pogromist activity.[22] There was no doubt about worker support for anti-Semitic attacks in Kamenskoe during a one-day sympathy strike there in June. When the six thousand workers at the Dneprovsk steel mill struck on June 23 to demonstrate their solidarity with workers in Ekaterinoslav, Odessa, and elsewhere, the strike almost provoked a pogrom there, too. A large number of workers did not want to join the strikers, and some of them openly supported one of the factory administrators recruiting workers to attack all the "yids and democrats."[23]

[18] *Ekaterinoslavshchina*, pp. 107–108; *Iskra*, no. 99 (May 1, 1905): 4; *Vestnik Iuga*, May 8, 1905, p. 2 and May 3, 1905, p. 3; Kharechko, *1905 god*, p. 49.

[19] Frankel, *Prophecy and Politics*, p. 145.

[20] Nevskii, "Ianvarskie dni," p. 184.

[21] I. Shevchenko, "O revoliutsii 1905 g.," *Materialy po istorii* (Ekaterinoslav), p. 132.

[22] Ibid., p. 131.

[23] *Iskra*, no. 107 (July 29, 1905): 7; *Vestnik Iuga*, July 15, 1905, p. 3; TsGAOR, DP OO, f. 102, 1905, op. 5, d. 975, vol. 1, p. 134.

A few weeks later, a limited pogrom broke out in Ekaterinoslav. According to the police, Jews had perpetrated a number of recent attacks on members of the police and troops, which "extraordinarily irritated local workers, who indignantly repeated over and over that Jews needed to be taught a lesson for their impudence."[24] Early in the evening of July 21, on Ekaterinoslav's central boulevard, a group of young Jews and a group of drunken workers crossed paths. The workers began to taunt the Jews for their revolutionary activities: "You Jews, who take it into your heads to attack the autocracy."[25] One of the drunken workers, Nikifor Zaika, pulled out a knife and began to make threats. The confrontation soon turned into a brawl, during which one of the Jews wrested Zaika's knife from him and stabbed him in the neck. This wound ended the brawl, as Zaika was taken to the hospital and the crowd dispersed. But the rumor that some Jews had cold-bloodedly murdered a Russian quickly spread through the city. Crowds of workers shouting "Beat the yids!" soon gathered on many streets. They were joined by "hooligans," who poured out of some of Ekaterinoslav's seedy dives.[26] The crowd threw rocks at residential buildings known to be occupied by Jews and attacked a few Jewish stores and some Jewish passersby, especially those they considered *demokraty*.[27]

Self-defense played a significant role in containing the disorders.[28] Some Jews, members of a Social Democratic self-defense unit, fired revolvers at the mob from the windows of buildings under attack.[29] Others stood guard at the synagogue.[30] Cossacks were called in, and according to one local newspaper, troops and police energetically patrolled the city.[31] According to the other newspaper, the police and Cossacks stood by passively during pogromist attacks.[32] In any case, before long the disorders stopped. One Jewish student lay dead, four were injured. The pogromists were not unscathed, either; self-defense units had succeeded in injuring three Russians.[33]

A resident's letter intercepted by the Okhrana captures the dispirited mood that pervaded much of Ekaterinoslav's Jewish community in mid-

[24] TsGAOR, DP OO, f. 102, 1905, op. 5, d. 975, vol. 3, p. 55.

[25] Ibid., pp. 55–56.

[26] *Sotsial'demokrat*, no. 11 (August 4, 1905): 12.

[27] "Perepiska s N. Leninym i N. K. Krupskoi," p. 19.

[28] *Pravo*, no. 30 (August 2, 1905): 2475.

[29] TsGAOR, DP OO, f. 102, 1905, op. 5, d. 975, vol. 3, pp. 56, 121; TsGIA USSR, f. 1597, op. 1, d. 86 (Okhrana report, July 21, 1905), pp. 87, 94; *Sotsial'demokrat*, no. 11 (August 4, 1905): 12.

[30] *Pravo*, no. 30 (August 2, 1905): 2475.

[31] *Pridneprovskii krai*, July 22, 1905, p. 4.

[32] *Vestnik Iuga*, July 24, 1905, p. 3.

[33] TsGAOR, DP OO, f. 102, 1905, op. 5, d. 975, vol. 3, p. 56; Mebel', ed., "1905 god na Ukraine: Khronika i materialy," p. 328.

1905 following the rumors, threats, and this pogrom. Safir Shapiro, a Ekaterinoslav midwife, wrote on July 25 to a friend in Kiev: "Yesterday your friend's husband spent the entire day, until 11 P.M., in self-defense because of terrifying rumors. . . . Basically everything here is foul. . . . I don't know what will happen."[34] Conditions remained tense, and a large number of Cossacks continued to patrol Ekaterinoslav's streets throughout the summer—as much because of the danger of pogroms as of revolutionary mass actions.[35]

Many worker-activists in the city center expressed their outrage with the July pogrom in letters to the local newspapers.[36] One of these letters placed the entire blame for the pogrom on "hooligans, that scum of society that holds nothing sacred." This letter, which was signed by about sixty printers at the city's biggest press, went on to state, "Comrades, it's time to put an end to this infamy. Jews are our brothers. . . . We have honor—workers' honor. We not only have not defamed ourselves through participation in this infamous persecution, but now with this declaration we show that Russian workers are not on the side of the hooligans and other dark forces."[37] The formation of self-defense units and the procurement of arms became the order of the day in revolutionary and Zionist circles during the late summer and early fall of 1905.

Representatives of the radical parties met with a group of Ekaterinoslav's Jewish "bourgeoisie" and retail clerks on July 25 to organize and prepare to fight future pogroms. The meeting resulted in the formation of a "neutral committee" consisting of local representatives of the Bolsheviks, Mensheviks, and Bund and in an agreement to collect money jointly to purchase firearms to combat pogromists.[38] This news from Menshevik-dominated Ekaterinoslav heartened Lenin:

> We read that in Ekaterinoslav an agreement was concluded between the Bolsheviks, the Mensheviks, and the Bund in anticipation of violence (a pogrom by the Black Hundreds was expected! Is there a city or village in Russia today that is not expecting something of the kind?). . . . What kind of plan this was is evi-

[34] TsGIA USSR, f. 1597, op. 1, d. 84, pp. 306–308.

[35] *British Documents*, vol. 3 (1983): 223.

[36] *Vestnik Iuga*, July 28, 1905, p. 3, July 31, 1905, p. 3.

[37] *Pridneprovskii krai*, July 30, 1905, p. 4.

[38] M. I. Mebel', "1905 god na Ukraine," p. 332; "Perepiska s N. Leninym i N. K. Krupskoi," p. 19. Representatives of the Labor Zionists may also have sat on the committee, despite the verbal attacks hurled at them by representatives of the three Social Democratic groups. Reason to doubt the success of such a cooperative effort surfaced quickly. On July 28, hundreds of people, mostly young Jews, gathered in the Jewish cemetery beside the grave of the Jewish student killed during the July pogrom. The victim had been a member of the Labor Zionists. The graveside speeches provoked a heated dispute between the Bundists and the Labor Zionists assembled there that ended when a Labor Zionist fired gunshots into the air (TsGIA USSR, f. 1597, op. 1, d. 86, p. 106).

denced by the fact that at the Briansk Works, for instance, the Social Democrats, at a meeting of five hundred workers, called for the organization of resistance. "Then in the evening the organized workers of the Briansk Works were quartered in various houses; patrols were stationed, a headquarters was appointed, etc.—in short we were in complete fighting trim." . . . Social Democrats all over Russia must and will follow on an ever wider scale the example set by the comrades of Ekaterinoslav.[39]

The strengthening of self-defense squads in the Donbass–Dnepr Bend changed the character of pogroms. By mid-1905, Donbass–Dnepr Bend pogroms had more in common with internecine working-class brawls than with earlier pogroms, in which neither Jewish nor other residents typically offered much resistance to the pogromists. Pogroms in the second half of 1905 began like brawls in the sense that both the self-defense squad members and the pogromists consisted predominantly of young workers. The self-defense squads were formed primarily by the Jewish parties and the Social Democrats. Radical Jewish artisans and Russian skilled workers participated in them, along with students and intellectuals of both nationalities. Although they were poorly organized, self-defense squad members were typically much better armed than the pogromists. The pogromists attacked with knives, daggers, axes, and other "cold" weapons, whereas the self-defense units had by now stockpiled a small cache of revolvers, which they were quick to fire.[40] In some cities, the self-defense units could fight the far more numerous pogromists on even terms until the arrival of the troops summoned to stop the disorders, who kept the self-defense units at bay.[41] During the October 1905 pogrom in Ekaterinoslav, the self-defense squads' greatest success was to deny entrance into the central city to many workers eager to join the anti-Semitic rampage. Self-defense units' gunfire also dispersed pogromist activity and a patriotic demonstration in the factory district of Chechelevka.[42]

On other occasions, the self-defense units were utterly impotent in their attempts to stave off the working-class pogromists. L. Shklovskii, an SD activist in the steel town of Enakievo, later recalled the helplessness he and his comrades felt when they began to hear that the "black wave" crashing down on nearby cities and towns was also forming in their town: "The darkest masses usually were unable to resist the temptation to riot and thus

[39] *Proletarii*, no. 4 (August 29, 1905), quoted in V. I. Lenin, *Collected Works* (Moscow, 1960–63), 9:203.

[40] *Obvinitel'nyi akt*, reprinted in *Iuzhnaia zaria*, October 24, 1907, p. 4.

[41] *Syn otechestva*, November 19, 1905, p. 2; Dal'man, "Oktiabr'skie dni," pp. 227–230; Lambroza, "Pogrom Movement," p. 220.

[42] *Materialy po istorii* (Ekaterinoslav) (Report to Okhrana, October 25, 1905), pp. 332–334; TsGAOR, DP OO, f. 102, 1906, op. 234, d. 7, ch. 34 (*Otchety o revoliutsionnom dvizhenii, Ekaterinoslavskaia gub.*), p. 6; *Syn otechestva*, October 31, 1905, p. 2.

in rather significant numbers were drawn into pogroms. Carried away by savage men from the Okhrana, the dark crowd turned into wild beasts. These pogroms for the most part began suddenly, making it impossible to organize resistance."[43] When self-defense units fired on the pogromists and soldiers, their gunfire only aggravated the situation. The actions of self-defense units more often enraged than deterred crowds of rioters.[44]

Not all revolutionaries supported the tactic of armed resistance to pogroms. Ekaterinoslav's Anarchists opposed the organization of self-defense units because these groups were committed to defending rich as well as poor Jews. "What business is it of workers to protect capitalists, Jewish or otherwise? Are there really not enough troops and gendarmes to serve them? Do you really think that we revolutionaries should be defending property and shooting at the gray masses being led by hooligans and police provocateurs?"[45] Likewise, in their newspaper, *Revoliutsionnaia Rossiia*, the Socialist Revolutionaries opposed taking up arms against workers to protect Jewish property. The SRs asked, "How can we align ourselves against the pogromists? After all, the main mass of the pogrom-makers will consist of those same destitute toilers whose interests socialists are pledged to defend. . . . Is it really to be expected that we, the socialists, should go forth and beat up our admittedly blinded brothers, but brothers all the same, hand in hand with the police? Or, at best, hand in hand with the Jewish bourgeoisie armed in defense of its property?"[46] But despite many revolutionaries' opposition to the self-defense units and their disagreement about the targets of pogroms, none of the revolutionary parties expressed the slightest support for the pogroms, in contrast to revolutionaries during the wave of pogroms in 1881–83.[47]

Nor, for that matter, did any other element of society defend Jews against the pogromists. Ekaterinoslav's relatively liberal daily newspaper, *Ekaterinoslavskii listok*, published articles immediately following the pogrom that tried to determine why the pogrom had not been prevented or stopped. Citing a few accounts in which pogromists heeded protests when residents proffered them, the newspaper blasted educated society in Ekaterinoslav for its passivity, arguing that the middle and upper classes' fail-

[43] "Vospominaniia," p. 201.

[44] Nikolaenko, *Revoliutsionnoe dvizhenie*, pp. 28–29; A. Gambarov, "Ocherk po istorii revoliutsionnogo dvizheniia v Luganske, 1901–1922 gg.," *Letopis' revoliutsii*, no. 4 (1923): 67.

[45] *Khleb i volia*, no. 23 (October 1905): 5.

[46] *Revoliutsionnaia Rossiia*, no. 46 (May 5, 1904), quoted in Leonard Schapiro, *Russian Studies*, ed. Ellen Dahrendorf (New York, 1987), p. 274.

[47] There are isolated reports of revolutionary-party participation, usually by Anarchists, in 1906 pogroms in some cities outside the Donbass–Dnepr Bend. In defense of such participation, the Anarchists claimed they "looted but did not kill" (Zosa Szajkowski, "The Impact of the Russian Revolution of 1905 on American Jewish Life," *YIVO Annual of Jewish Social Science* 7 [1978]: 74).

ure to act made them the pogromists' accomplice.[48] All of Russian society, from the government to the zemstvos to the populists, argued that the root cause of the pogroms was Jewish exploitation of the Russian masses in trade and commerce.[49]

Working-class participation in pogroms posed uncomfortable questions for the revolutionaries and put them in an awkward position, as had been the case throughout the history of the Donbass–Dnepr Bend labor movement. During the 1883 pogrom in Ekaterinoslav, Populist radicals failed to defend the Jews or even discourage the pogromists. This should not have been surprising. Russian Populist ranks, from the bottom to the top, had long harbored anti-Semites. In his seminal work on Russian Populism, Franco Venturi wrote that "anti-Semitism was violent among the workers" in Populist study circles. He noted that Ukrainian workers protested when Jews first entered the Workers' Union of South Russia, saying that "they had crucified Christ."[50] Many national leaders of the Populist movement evidently shared the workers' anti-Semitism. Mikhail Bakunin, for example, was known to make occasional anti-Jewish remarks. He—and Karl Marx, for that matter—portrayed Jews as agents of capitalism, guilty of exploiting the poor.

The upsurge in violent anti-Semitism in the 1880s, as well as the problems it created for revolutionaries, was not restricted to Russia. In central Europe, Karl Kautsky wrote to Friedrich Engels: "The workers here have powerful petty-bourgeois instincts, since for the most part they grew up within the framework of petit-bourgeois ideas; so that our leaders have had great difficulty in preventing the masses from going over to the anti-Semites."[51] Although troubled by workers' anti-Semitism, Kautsky did not think the radical movement ought to oppose workers on this score, for he assumed, as did other European Marxists, that pogroms promised to ignite the awaited social revolution. "This Jew baiting will and must be repeated in increasing intensity, and in the end will include not only Jews but all propertied people."[52]

Kautsky too

Likewise, Russian Populists sympathized with the pogroms in the early 1880s primarily for tactical reasons rather than because of explicit anti-Semitism. Narodnaia Volia agitated in support of the anti-Semitic ram-

[48] S. Ettinger, "The Jews in Russia at the Outbreak of the Revolution," *The Jews in Soviet Russia*, ed. Lionel Kochan (London, 1970), p. 17.

[49] Frankel, *Prophecy and Politics*, p. 58.

[50] Franco Venturi, *Roots of Revolution: A History of the Populist and Socialist Movements in Nineteenth Century Russia*, trans. Francis Haskell (New York, 1960), p. 520.

[51] Letter from Kautsky to Engels, December 22, 1884, quoted in Robert S. Wistrich, *Socialism and the Jews: The Dilemmas of Assimilation in Germany and Austria-Hungary* (New Brunswick, N.J., 1982), p. 228.

[52] Ibid., p. 229.

pages in the hope that they were the first stage of the revolution. While the liberal press and the Russian literati remained silent, Narodnaia Volia claimed that pogroms were acts of popular violence that, like the Pugachevshchina a century earlier, reflected the innately revolutionary character of the Russian masses.[53] This is how the executive committee of Narodnaia Volia concluded an appeal addressed "to the Ukrainian people" at the end of August 1881: "Workers, arise! Wreak your vengeance on the landowners; pillage the Jews; kill the officials!"[54] Many members of Narodnaia Volia opposed the party's support for the pogroms,[55] but they generally stifled their criticism in accord with the advice of Populist leaders such as Petr Lavrov. He argued that attacking the masses for their anti-Semitism and participation in pogroms would be an enormous tactical mistake "in view of popular passions and the need of Russian socialists to have the people on their side whenever possible."[56]

Alexander III and members of the Committee of Ministers opposed and feared the pogroms generally for the same reason Populists welcomed and even supported them. While expressing no sympathy for Jews, the state comptroller, D. M. Sol'skii, exclaimed, "Everyone must be defended from illegal attacks. Today they are harassing and robbing the Jews. Tomorrow it will be the so-called *kulaks*. . . . Then it may be the turn of merchants and landowners. In a word, if the authorities stand by passively, we can expect the development in the near future of the most terrible socialism."[57]

Even the small number of Jews active in the Populist movement initially refused to speak out against the pogromists. They had generally tried to

[53] All but one of the major populist papers supported the pogroms (Abraham Ascher, *Pavel Axelrod and the Development of Menshevism* [Cambridge, Mass., 1972], p. 70).

[54] Dubnov, *History of the Jews*, p. 531. In their leaflet, Narodnaia Volia argued, "The people in the Ukraine suffer worst of all from the Jews. Who takes the land, the woods, the taverns from out of your hands? The Jews. . . . The Jew curses you, cheats you, drinks your blood. . . . You have begun to rebel against the Jews. You have done well" (quoted in Frankel, *Prophecy and Politics*, p. 98).

[55] So, finally, did the editors of *Narodnaia Volia*, in 1884, after the pogromist wave had receded.

[56] Quoted by Ascher, *Pavel Axelrod*, p. 76. See also Naimark, *Terrorists*, pp. 26, 202; and Baron, *The Russian Jew*, p. 375.

[57] E. A. Peretts, *Dnevnik E. A. Perettsa (1880–1883)* (Moscow, 1927), p. 133, quoted in Rogger, *Jewish Policies*, pp. 61–62. Alexander III expressed alarm that the riots were "a red speck on the horizon" and ordered the provincial governors to do whatever was necessary to suppress the violence and protect the Jews (Patricia Herlihy, *Odessa: A History, 1794–1914* (Cambridge, Mass., 1986), p. 302. The following denunciation in *Narodnaia Volia*, from an article published in 1883, refers *not* to the pogromists, but to the government's use of force to end the rampage: "In Ekaterinoslav the people's blood was shed. This fact is disturbing both in its cruelty and its injustice" (V. Ia. Bogucharskii, *Literatura partii Narodnoi Voli* [Moscow, 1907], p. 311, quoted in Stephen M. Berk, *Year of Crisis, Year of Hope: Russian Jewry and the Pogroms of 1881–1882* [Westport, Conn., 1985], p. 89).

conceal their identities in order to work among the Russian masses, and during the pogroms they, too, thought that denouncing the pogromists would amount to political suicide. Jewish radicals active in the Populist movement feared that criticizing the pogroms would consign them to participating in an exclusively Jewish movement.

Later, during the pogroms of the 1903–5 period, Donbass–Dnepr Bend revolutionaries were still reluctant to confront publicly the violent anti-Semitism of the bulk of their lower-class constituency. Although they distributed leaflets pleading with workers to stop engaging in pogroms and organized self-defense squads, progressives of all stripes commonly chose to blame the autocracy and capitalism for the pogroms, rather than popular anti-Semitism. "Who is guilty? . . . don't speak about the ignorance, about the barbarous instincts of the dark masses. The initiative for pogroms never comes from here."[58] Even so, pogroms did try the faith in the Russian working class and peasantry of the starry-eyed among the leftist Russian intelligentsia, be they Marxist or Populist.[59] And many liberals no doubt remained liberal, rather than revolutionary, partly out of fear of workers' propensity for violent rampages. As we saw, liberals in Iuzovka never were able to forget the workers' 1892 riot and pogrom—the so-called cholera riot.[60]

Among Jews, the Bund and Labor Zionists gained strength as a result of the pogroms, since even in the face of working-class pogroms, most Social Democratic and Socialist Revolutionary ideologues steadfastly argued that anti-Semitism was a bourgeois phenomenon of little direct or long-term concern, destined to disappear with capitalism.[61] *Iskra*'s editors specifically lectured Ekaterinoslav's Bundists about how, regardless of the connection between benighted workers and pogroms, they "should understand that anti-Semitism is connected with the interests of the bourgeoisie, not the working stratum of the population."[62]

Below party polemics, Donbass–Dnepr Bend rank-and-file radicals did

[58] *Syn otechestva*, October 25, 1905, p. 1.

[59] Some were "perplexed" (Gambarov, "Ocherk," p. 67).

[60] *Iskra*, no. 79 (December 1, 1904): 10.

[61] Working-class anti-Semitism did not, of course, disappear after the revolution. Trotsky, for one, conceded this: "All serious and honest observers, especially those who have lived among the toiling masses, bear witness to the existence of anti-Semitism, not only of the old and hereditary, but also of the new, 'Soviet' variety" (quoted in Nedava, *Trotsky and the Jews*, p. 173).

[62] *Iskra*, no. 34 (February 15, 1903): 2. Trotsky argued in the fight against the Bund at the SD's Second Congress in 1903 that "there really was no need to fight anti-Semitism specifically. Anti-Semitism, as is well known, was nothing but the result of the general unconsciousness of the wide masses. It was therefore necessary to make them conscious and then they would anyhow cast anti-Semitism away. To talk with them specifically about Jews was superfluous" (quoted in Nedava, *Trotsky and the Jews*, p. 91).

recognize and try to counter working-class anti-Semitism with propaganda. Numerous leaflets preached the brotherhood of all the oppressed, regardless of ethnicity, but to no apparent avail. Once the pogroms were under way, the worst fury of the pogromist mobs was directed against the very poorest of the Jews. Merchants had their shops looted and often destroyed, but artisans and their families were left homeless, if not also beaten, raped, or killed.[63] The Social Democrats' and Socialist Revolutionaries' formation of self-defense units speaks, of course, to their commitment to oppose any worker participation in pogroms. Nonetheless, anti-Semitism and intraparty ethnic tensions remained rife within revolutionary-party ranks. After the 1905 Revolution, at the SDs' Fourth Party Congress, a Bolshevik, Grigorii A. Aleksinskii, described the Mensheviks as the "Jewish faction" and the Bolsheviks as the "true-Russian faction." He went on to suggest, apparently in jest, that it might not be a bad idea for the Bolsheviks "to conduct a pogrom in the party." Joseph Stalin later recounted the episode approvingly.[64]

The worst pogroms ever to besiege imperial Russia followed the October 1905 general strike and the promulgation of the October Manifesto. In the Donbass–Dnepr Bend, a huge number of workers joined other members of the lower classes in the drunken looting, battery, rape, and murder characteristic of pogroms. Wildly destructive and violent pogromists ravaged nearly every Donbass–Dnepr Bend city and town, including Ekaterinoslav, Lugansk, Iuzovka, Kamenskoe, Aleksandrovsk, Bakhmut, and Mariupol', as well as the mining settlements of Gorlovka, Almaznaia, Lisichansk, Krivoi Rog, and Makeevka. Jews were the main target of the pogromists' fury, but students and others thought to be sympathetic to revolution also were attacked.

Massive and unrestrained antigovernment celebrations, the so-called Days of Freedom, followed the announcement of the October Manifesto. Ecstatic at the apparent victory over the autocracy and their attainment of political and civic freedoms, the revolutionary parties in the Donbass–Dnepr Bend organized the largest antigovernment rallies ever in the days between October 18 and 20. The October Manifesto seemed to offer the revolutionaries a golden opportunity to reach a wider audience. The

[63] I. Nikolaenko, "Revoliutsionnaia rabota v luganskikh zh.-d. masterskikh (iz vospominanii)," *Letopis' revoliutsii*, no. 5 (1926): 31; D. Rapoport, "1905 god na st. Dolgintsevo i Krivom Roge," *Puti revoliutsii*, no. 3 (1925): 96.

[64] Robert C. Tucker, *Stalin as Revolutionary, 1879–1929: A Study in History and Personality* (New York, 1973), pp. 139–140, 143.

newly-founded Kadet party joined in the street celebrations and, with the authorities' permission, organized rallies.[65]

Workers present at Donbass–Dnepr Bend post-manifesto rallies often became indignant at the orators' mocking of Nicholas II, although at the time they generally kept their anger at the "damned *demokraty*" to themselves.[66] With no police or troops to be seen, Jewish youths had been especially defiant during the victory celebrations that greeted news of the manifesto and preceded the pogroms.[67] At rallies in Ekaterinoslav during the Days of Freedom, radicals said to be Jewish solicited donations "for Nicholas II's coffin."[68] Without identifying those responsible for such appeals, beyond noting that they were teenagers, the Social Democratic worker-activist I. Shevchenko remembered that "to us such a collection seemed strange, but in the general excitement it didn't attract our attention."[69] V. Dal'man recalled that to his experienced eyes, the "exaggerated *revoliutsionnost'*" of those soliciting donations marked them as clearly not revolutionary types.[70] Many of the workers present at these demonstrations were outraged at the audacity of the radicals, especially those they thought to be Jewish. In addition, a stubborn rumor spread through the city that Jews had also mocked the Orthodox faith, hung crosses around the necks of dogs, and fired at Orthodox churches.[71] In Lugansk, a crowd composed of "Jewish youths," according to the Okhrana, forced the closure of stores in the city during the Days of Freedom.[72] Those few workers who expressed their anger during the rallies were sometimes attacked.[73] This is how one unskilled worker explained his participation in Ekaterinoslav's pogrom in October 1905:

[65] Shmyrov, "Iz istorii," p. 94; Gambarov, "Ocherk," p. 65; *Donetskii kolokol*, no. 1 (October 17, 1906): 1.

[66] TsGAOR, DP OO, f. 102, 1906, op. 234, d. 7, ch. 34 (*Otchety o revoliutsionnom dvizhenii, Ekaterinoslavskaia gub.*), p. 5.

[67] The troops and police "did nothing to maintain order" (TsGAOR, DP OO, f. 102, 1907, d. 18, ch. 10 [Article from *Russkaia zemlia*, October 31, 1907], p. 160). Already by October 15, demoralized police began to refuse assignments or simply stopped coming to work (*Ekaterinoslavshchina*, p. 184; *Obvinitel'nyi akt*, reprinted in *Iuzhnaia zaria*, October 20, 1907, p. 3).

[68] TsGAOR, DP OO, f. 102, 1906, op. 234, d. 7, ch. 34 (*Otchety o revoliutsionnom dvizhenii, Ekaterinoslavskaia gub.*), pp. 4–5; *Obvinitel'nyi akt*, reprinted in *Iuzhnaia zaria*, October 20, 1907, p. 3; TsGAOR, DP OO, f. 102, 1905, op. 5, d. 4, ch. 17, vol. 4 (Gendarme report, October 26, 1905), p. 117; TsGAOR, DP OO, f. 102, op. 5, d. 975, vol. 3, p. 264.

[69] "O revoliutsii 1905 g.," p. 137.

[70] "Oktiabr'skie dni," p. 220.

[71] *Obvinitel'nyi akt*, reprinted in *Iuzhnaia zaria*, October 20, 1907, p. 3.

[72] TsGAOR, DP OO, f. 102, op. 5, d. 975, vol. 3, pp. 263–264.

[73] TsGAOR, DP OO, f. 102, 1906, op. 234, d. 7, ch. 34 (*Otchety o revoliutsionnom dvizhenii, Ekaterinoslavskaia gub.*), pp. 3, 5.

> For a long time, I had been unable to find work because of the strikes that everywhere were organized by Jews, so I was then already angry with them. . . . Then at the rally in Nizhnedneprovsk, Jews addressed the crowd, insulting the tsar and religion, and then they beat me and took my jacket, and I felt toward them still more hatred. . . . Then I saw how they beat a solitary Russian and generally insulted the Russian *narod*.[74]

Reactionary violence cut short the celebration of the October Manifesto in Ekaterinoslav and other Donbass–Dnepr Bend cities. In Aleksandrovsk, a brawl between workers and Jewish radicals at a rally began that city's pogrom.[75] Across the Donbass–Dnepr Bend, parading patriotic demonstrators began to compete for dominance of the streets with the opposition movement. Marchers carried portraits of the tsar, waved the national flag, and sang "God Save the Tsar." True to form, this reaction assumed a largely anti-Semitic character as the counterrevolutionary mood spread. Agitators told crowds of workers that Jews had mocked the Orthodox faith and had bragged that they would rid Russia of the tsar and take power for themselves. Rumors spread that immunity from arrest for looting of Jewish shops had been assured by the local police, who had gone on strike and vanished from the streets.[76]

Black Hundred rallies and marches, called "patriotic demonstrations," were the organized events that triggered most of the pogroms in October. In Ekaterinoslav, opponents dispersed the first patriotic demonstration, a small and poorly organized procession down Ekaterininskii Prospekt on October 20.[77] The counterpogromists' success was not to be repeated when support for pogroms snowballed. Earlier that day, it had already become clear that support for the radicals was disappearing. At the rallies in the working-class districts of Ekaterinoslav, workers no longer hesitated to make known how their mood had changed. They demanded that orators stop attacking the tsar, avoid political issues altogether, and instead concentrate exclusively on how to improve workers' economic position. More ominously, workers rebuffed Jews at one rally when they arrived to request help from the "organized" workers against the growing threat of a pogrom in the center of the city.[78] Similarly, in Iuzovka, the Days of Freedom

[74] *Obvinitel'nyi akt*, reprinted in *Iuzhnaia zaria*, October 21, 1907, p. 4.

[75] TsGAOR, DP OO, f. 102, 1905, op. 5, d. 4, ch. 17, vol. 4 (Gendarme report, October 26, 1905), p. 118.

[76] Nikolaenko, *Revoliutsionnoe dvizhenie*, pp. 26–28; Gambarov, "Ocherk," p. 66; Dal'man, "Oktiabr'skie dni," p. 219; *Materialy po istorii* (Report to Okhrana, October 25, 1905), p. 333.

[77] TsGAOR, DP OO, f. 102, 1906, op. 234, d. 7, ch. 34 (*Otchety o revoliutsionnom dvizhenii, Ekaterinoslavskaia gub.*), p. 5.

[78] Ibid.

ended October 20 after participants in a political demonstration set off toward the steel factory to call on workers to close the factory and join their ranks. Instead, the steelworkers attacked the demonstrators—a crowd consisting primarily of five hundred Jews—beat many of them, and then set off to loot Jewish stores.[79]

The following day, October 21, was an Orthodox high feast day. On such holidays, as has been noted, the chance of drunken lower-class violence was already high. That day, in what still seemed to many revolutionaries "like a bolt from the blue," pogromists in Ekaterinoslav seized the streets.[80] More self-defense detachments tried to form, but Ekaterinoslav's soviet, and the revolutionary parties generally, were caught off guard by the reactionary violence that erupted so quickly on the heels of their triumph. In the industrial suburbs of Amur and Nizhnedneprovsk, many strikes had not yet even ended when the pogrom began.

Pogromists met little, if any, resistance from the police; by October 21, violence had gripped the region. Jews throughout the Donbass–Dnepr Bend became the targets of intoxicated mobs. Pogromists stormed down Jewish streets and into homes known to be inhabited by Jews, breaking down doors and windows and savagely assaulting all the hapless Jews they could get their hands on. Of the hundreds of pogroms that occurred throughout the empire between October 1905 and January 1906, forty-one occurred in Ekaterinoslav province, which encompassed most of the Donbass–Dnepr Bend.[81] This pogromist wave was among the most deadly and destructive in the empire: 285 people died, an incalculable number were injured, and the 13.2 million rubles' worth of damage exceeded the losses in any other province.[82] The worst pogrom in the province occurred October 21–23 in Ekaterinoslav. Witnesses provide details of the most horrifying violence. In the words of a local newspaper, "Ekaterinoslav suffered all the horrors of the Dark Ages, as people had their eyes gouged out

[79] TsGAOR, DP OO, f. 102, 4-delo, 1905, op. 5, d. 2454, p. 85. A counterrevolutionary demonstration by workers in Lugansk culminated in a pogromist rampage (TsGAOR, DP 00, f. 102, op. 5, d. 975, vol. 3, p. 264). In Taganrog, thousands of steelworkers and railroad workers attacked a smaller number of young radicals and beat them until they were "half dead" (Kharechko, *1905 god*, p. 67).

[80] *Burevestnik*, no. 6–7 (September–October 1907): 5. One of the pogromists' first victims was a Jewish worker, Gershel Svidskii, who just three hours before his death disagreed with his comrades who feared that a pogrom was imminent (Dal'man, "Oktiabr'skie dni," p. 224).

[81] Lambroza counted 657 pogroms in Russia from October to January ("Pogrom Movement," p. 114). Bushnell counted 150 in October (*Mutiny amid Repression*, p. 79).

[82] Lambroza, "Pogrom Movement," p. 165. The single most deadly and destructive pogrom in the empire occurred in Odessa, where the police estimated pogromists killed more than 400 Jews, seriously injured approximately 300, and damaged 1,632 Jewish houses, apartments, and stores (Robert Weinberg, "Workers, Pogroms, and the 1905 Revolution in Odessa," *Russian Review* 46, no. 1 [1987]: 53).

and were cut to pieces."[83] Those raped included young girls and pregnant women.[84] Children were thrown out the windows of multistory buildings.[85] By the end of Ekaterinoslav's three-day pogrom, nothing thought to be of any value was left behind, as pogromists pillaged 311 business establishments, 40 apartment buildings, and 5 houses. Many buildings were set afire and burned to the ground. Ekaterinoslav's pogrom left 95 dead, 245 seriously wounded, and thousands homeless and destitute.[86] In Iuzovka, pogromists did almost a million rubles' worth of damage as they looted and destroyed 84 stores and more than 100 residences. Iuzovka's pogromists killed 10 Jews and wounded 38, not including countless rape victims, during their rampage.[87]

Here, as in other pogroms in the Pale, many better-off Jews generally managed to escape the October violence by bribing the authorities, hiring protection, or moving to safety. What protection troops provided was often restricted to the parts of town where the wealthier Jews lived or owned shops and other businesses. Troops left the poor and their property defenseless. In Lugansk, the larger Jewish businesses emerged unscathed. Pogromists managed to ransack only artisanal workshops and small stores.[88]

Ekaterinoslav's pogrom began on October 21 after the "patriotic procession" on its way to the Briansk factory passed a Jewish apartment building.[89] In a last-ditch attempt to prevent a pogrom, members of a Jewish self-defense unit suddenly, from inside residential buildings and from around street corners, fired at the counterrevolutionary demonstrators and the soldiers marching behind the procession. The self-defense unit later viewed its decision to shoot first as a serious mistake.[90] The soldiers returned the fire. Being fired upon and seeing one of their fellows fall dead agitated the crowd terribly. With a vengeance they rushed into the neighboring residences, as well as nearby shops and stores, which they smashed and looted. Members of the crowd sacking shops often shouted, "This is for collecting money for the coffin of the tsar and for shouting 'Down with the autocracy'."[91] A thousand people broke off from the crowd and ran to the Ozernyi marketplace and the streets nearby, where they proceeded to sack almost all the small shops. Throughout the day, soldiers and self-de-

[83] *Vestnik Iuga*, November 1, 1905, p. 3.

[84] Their shame prevented many from being counted.

[85] Rapoport, "1905 god," p. 96.

[86] *Iuzhnyi krai*, November 3, 1905, p. 4.

[87] Kharechko, *1905 god*, p. 67; TsGAOR, DP OO, f. 102, 1905, op. 5, d. 2454, p. 85; *Syn otechestva*, October 23, 1905, p. 4.

[88] Nikolaenko, "Revoliutsionnaia rabota," p. 31. See also Rapoport, "1905 god," p. 96; and Tobias, *Jewish Bund*, pp. 223, 227–228.

[89] *Materialy po istorii* (Ekaterinoslav) (Report to Okhrana, October 25, 1905), p. 332.

[90] Dal'man, "Oktiabr'skie dni," pp. 224–226.

[91] *Iuzhnaia zaria*, October 20, 1907, p. 3.

fense units continued to fire at each other.[92] At the same time, soldiers were ordered, at least once, to fire on a crowd of looters in Ekaterinoslav. The platoon refused, and the crowd carried the pogrom down the street.[93] It was clear that by October 1905 soldiers, and in particular the Cossacks, generally sympathized with the pogromists.[94] While military forces did not actually take part in the looting, their reluctance to deter the rioters, especially after pogromists had been fired upon by Jewish and revolutionary self-defense groups, overcame inhibitions within the crowds and made restoring order extremely difficult.[95] The worst pogroms occurred when the pogromists sensed the troops' reluctance to defend Jews by firing on their Russian and Ukrainian attackers.

Rumors that they could profit and give vent to their pent-up hostilities spurred the pogromists on.[96] Policemen in uniform had disappeared from the streets, although at least one policeman in civilian clothes played a leadership role in Ekaterinoslav's pogrom. Nikifor Kuznetsov, a policeman of peasant origin, was later tried for approaching a crowd of peasants who had come to the city to join the pogrom. After telling them that Jews opposed the tsar and Christianity and had sacked the local convent and hung crosses around the necks of dogs, Kuznetsov urged them on. "Why are you standing there? Go beat the yids. The tsar and governor have authorized it." When the crowd said the yids were difficult to beat because they were armed with revolvers, Kuznetsov replied, "If you are afraid, give me a cap and jacket and I will go with you to beat the yids."[97]

Rumors on October 21 that young Jews had beaten and often killed individual Russian passersby carrying stolen property added more fuel to Ekaterinoslav's pogrom.[98] Some of these rumors were true. The resistance was much better armed than the pogromists, and Zionist and radical self-defense groups continued to fire on pogromists throughout the course of the pogrom.[99] Self-defense units were no doubt responsible for most of

[92] *Obvinitel'nyi akt*, reprinted in *Iuzhnaia zaria*, October 20, 1907, p. 3.

[93] *Vestnik Iuga*, November 2, 1905, p. 2.

[94] TsGAOR, DP OO, f. 102, 1906, op. 234, d. 7, ch. 34 (*Otchety o revoliutsionnom dvizhenii, Ekaterinoslavskaia gub.*), p. 6.

[95] *Novaia zhizn'*, no. 18 (1905): 70.

[96] *Iuzhnaia zaria*, October 24, 1907, p. 3.

[97] *Iuzhnaia zaria*, October 20, 1907, p. 3. Although Black Hundred groups organized political parties in Ekaterinoslav in 1905, parties that included workers in their ranks, and although "patriotic" demonstrations were responsible for helping to stir up anti-Semitic sentiment, there is no evidence that right-wing groups played a significant role in directly inciting workers to participate in pogroms, despite instances such as this of individual policemen or agitators egging workers on after a pogrom was already under way.

[98] TsGAOR, DP OO, f. 102, 1906, op. 234, d. 7, ch. 34 (*Otchety o revoliutsionnom dvizhenii, Ekaterinoslavskaia gub.*), p. 6; *Materialy po istorii* (Ekaterinoslav) (Report to Okhrana, October 25, 1905), p. 333.

[99] *Iuzhnaia zaria*, October 20, 1907, p. 3.

the twenty-five Russians killed and the eighty-five seriously wounded during Ekaterinoslav's pogrom.[100] The city doctor, who examined approximately ninety corpses after the pogrom, testified at the 1907 trial that Jews died mainly from attacks with knives, daggers, hammers, axes, crowbars, and other "cold" weapons, while Russians and Ukrainians died of wounds from firearms.[101]

Workers were not solely responsible for pogromist attacks. In addition to some disguised police and firefighters, sources repeatedly speak of "hooligans" and the "scum" (*otbrosy*) of the working class. Such terms occasionally were defined. One crowd of "hooligans" in Ekaterinoslav was said to consist predominantly of millers, dock workers, and vagabonds (*bosiaki*).[102] Another crowd labeled as "hooligan" was said to consist primarily of pickpockets.[103]

Donbass–Dnepr Bend urban pogroms also received outside reinforcements when news of the pogrom reached neighboring miners, railroad workers, and peasants.[104] Miners were especially quick to respond to the opportunity to "beat yids and loot."[105] At some railway stations, large mobs of miners commandeered trains, threatening to destroy the station if a train did not immediately transport them to a nearby city or town. At each railroad station along the way, the train stopped, the whistle sounded, and the support of those nearby was elicited. In this manner, the pogromist throng riding the rails toward the town of Krivoi Rog swelled.[106] During pogroms, anything of value that pogromists did not destroy or take with them was thrown out into the street, where it was picked through by peasant women labeled "beasts of prey" by the local newspapers.[107] All that remained was "down, feathers, torn wool and cotton, shattered glass, and broken and scattered kitchen utensils."[108]

The October pogromists assaulted others besides Jews. Students and workers thought to be revolutionaries and defenders of Jews were brutally beaten when caught alone on the streets. Others were attacked solely because they were of the educated class or were mistaken for Jews. On Oc-

[100] *Iuzhnyi krai*, November 3, 1905, p. 4. The official casualty count provided later was higher than these figures, which are what was reported at the time in the local press (Dal'man, "Oktiabr'skie dni," p. 241).

[101] *Iuzhnaia zaria*, October 24, 1907, p. 4.

[102] Dal'man, "Oktiabr'skie dni," p. 227.

[103] *Vestnik Iuga*, November 4, 1905, p. 2. Radical commentators were quick to exaggerate the role of these criminal elements.

[104] Nikolaenko, *Revoliutsionnoe dvizhenie*, p. 26.

[105] Rapoport, "1905 god," p. 96.

[106] TsGIA, f. 37, op. 58, d. 305 (Report of assistant district engineer, Ekaterinoslav mining district, October 31, 1905), p. 298; *Gorno-zavodskii listok*, December 10/31, 1905, p. 8268.

[107] *Vestnik Iuga*, November 2, 1905, p. 2.

[108] Shklovskii, "Vospominaniia," p. 203.

tober 23, the third and final day of the pogrom in Ekaterinoslav, when the pogromist crowd passed the Mining Institute, voices switched from shouting "Beat the yids!" to "Beat the students!" Throughout the Donbass–Dnepr Bend, the outbreak of the pogroms threw industrialists into a panic, as they, too, feared the pogromists. The president of the Association of Southern Coal and Steel Producers, N. S. Avdakov, telegraphed the governors of Ekaterinoslav and Kherson provinces, as well as prime minister Sergei Witte, requesting that more troops be immediately dispatched to Donbass–Dnepr Bend factories and mines to avert the serious dangers facing Russian industry. During the pogromist wave, miners at some mines pillaged residences in the "colony," attacked liberal members of management, and threatened to destroy the mines if their economic demands were not met and certain administrators were not fired.[109] At the Bodovsk mines, miners subjected the director to a three-hour trial, during which they continually threatened to beat him for his "antitsarist agitation."[110] Away from the mines, rampaging miners joined blue-collar railroad employees in looting Jewish shops and in attacking Jews and the white-collar employees at railroad stations. They assaulted people with "soft hands and starched collars"—those they blamed for the October general strike.[111]

Pogroms sometimes began in a manner strikingly similar to the way general strikes began. With the inversion of the workers' mood following the October Manifesto, the demonstrations initiated by local rightists often spread by including factories or mines in their itinerary en route to Jewish quarters.[112] Sometimes the amassed marchers made the link with general strikes explicit by adopting the labels and symbols of both the reactionary and revolutionary movements or by calling themselves strikers. When the pogrom began in Lugansk, pogromists carrying both the red flags of the revolutionary movement and portraits of the tsar shouted, "We are going to our brother workers; together with them we will defend our motherland from our enemies."[113] Troops finally managed to stop Ekaterinoslav's po-

[109] *Gorno-zavodskii listok*, November 12, 1905, p. 8200; TsGAOR, DP OO, f. 102, 1905, op. 5, d. 4, ch. 17, vol. 4 (Report of mine operators, October 23, 1905), p. 98; Kharechko, *1905 god*, p. 69; Kirzner, *Gornorabochie*, p. 70; TsGIA, f. 37, op. 58, d. 305 (Report of assistant district engineer, Ekaterinoslav mining district, October 31, 1905), p. 297.

[110] Kirzner, *Gornorabochie*, p. 67.

[111] TsGIA, f. 37, op. 58, d. 305 (Report of assistant district engineer, Ekaterinoslav mining district, October 31, 1905), p. 297; Khersontsev, "V poiskakh puti," pp. 87–88.

[112] *Materialy po istorii* (Ekaterinoslav) (Report to Okhrana, October 25, 1905), p. 332; *Novaia zhizn'*, no. 18 (1905): 70; TsGIA, f. 37, op. 58, d. 305 (Report of assistant district engineer, Ekaterinoslav mining district, October 31, 1905), p. 297.

[113] Nikolaenko, *Revoliutsionnoe dvizhenie*, pp. 28, 31. This Soviet account asserts that workers responded negatively to this appeal, "excepting of course all sorts of scum, possibly even workers by birth, who were guided by their lust for gain." In an earlier Soviet account of the pogrom in Lugansk, Gambarov states that "since the factories were closed during these days

grom just as they prevented strikes from spreading, by cordoning off the city's working-class districts and the Nizhnedneprovsk suburb from the center of the city.[114] Pogromist crowds sometimes went from factory to factory, or mine to mine, to gather support. Donets Basin miners were especially fond of simultaneously adopting the symbols of both the patriotic and revolutionary movements. Miners sometimes even referred to pogroms as strikes. They often attacked the administrators and staff at mines and railroad stations as well as local Jews.[115] Clearly, the Donbass–Dnepr Bend workers who participated in pogroms exhibited a consciousness unlike what Soviet and Western historians have led one to expect. Many radical commentators themselves did not know how to classify these working-class actions. The Anarchists rhetorically asked, following the pogrom in Ekaterinoslav, "What was this phenomenon? Was this riot of the downtrodden—a revolution?"[116]

After the pogroms in the cities ended, most on October 23, pogroms continued to erupt in small mining towns and villages. On October 29, forty Jewish families in the village of Veselo Terny lost all they owned when miners from the Briansk mine attacked.[117] Miners returned to the mines with all the loot they could carry.[118]

Other motivations in addition to the prospect of loot and violent excess explain the participation of the Donbass–Dnepr Bend working class in the 1903–5 pogroms. Nor can the pogroms in the Donbass–Dnepr Bend during these years be attributed simply to anti-Semitism or government intrigue, as has generally been believed. Pogroms were a basic part of the dynamic of the 1905 Revolution, inextricably linked with revolutionary events. It is significant that the revolutionary general strikes and confrontations with troops that triggered the pogroms of the 1905 period in the Donbass–Dnepr Bend produced frustration all over Russia, not only within the Pale. Laura Engelstein writes, for example, that during the Days of Freedom in Moscow, "workers everywhere, even among those sympathetic to the strike movements, were generally hostile to intelligentsia ac-

on account of the holiday, it was impossible [for the SDs] to take any measures to stave off the pogrom" ("Ocherk," p. 67). The secret police reported that a crowd of Russian workers began the Lugansk pogrom after witnessing red-flag-waving Jews demonstrating on the streets (TsGAOR, DP OO, f. 102, d. 975, vol. 3, p. 264).

[114] TsGAOR, DP OO, f. 102, 1906, op. 234, d. 7, ch. 34 (*Otchety o revoliutsionnom dvizhenii, Ekaterinoslavskaia gub.*), p. 6; *Materialy po istorii* (Ekaterinoslav) (Report to Okhrana, October 25, 1905), p. 333.

[115] Kharechko, *1905 god*, pp. 68–69; *Novaia zhizn'*, no. 18 (1905): 70.

[116] *Khleb i volia*, no. 24 (November 1905), p. 6.

[117] TsGAOR, DP OO, f. 102, 1905, op. 5, d. 4, ch. 17, vol. 4 (Gendarme telegram to Witte, October 29, 1905), p. 132.

[118] TsGIA, f. 37, op. 58, d. 305 (Report of assistant district engineer, Ekaterinoslav mining district, October 31, 1905), pp. 297–300.

tivists who brought the political message."[119] Students, teachers, lawyers, salaried railroad and zemstvo employees, and anyone else suspected of revolutionary sympathies—including even fellow workers, as well as members of racial or ethnic minorities—were subject to violent attack following the general strikes in cities such as Tomsk, Tula, Tver', and Tiflis. In Baku, Russian and Tatar "patriots" joined together to attack Armenians as well as Jews.[120] Elsewhere, including in the capitals, pogroms did not erupt, although groups of Black Hundreds did roam the streets and assault students, Jews, and others on such a scale that they provoked mass panic.[121] The significance of anti-Semitism is that in cities where large populations of unskilled workers and Jews were brought together, anti-Semitism gave the backlash a particular fierceness and a far larger scale.

Widespread dissatisfaction with the general-strike tactic was evident among Donbass–Dnepr Bend workers following the very first general strike in 1903. This dissatisfaction can be attributed largely to the emotional roller coaster, invariably ending in frustration, that workers experienced during the course of a general strike. At the outset, the display of working-class strength would raise workers' hopes sky-high. The successful closing of factories and workshops and the authorities' failure to disperse enormous rallies were heady experiences for the mass of workers involved. But feelings of euphoria usually proved short-lived.

The nature of revolutionary mass actions helped turn discontent with industrialists and the government into violence against traditional ethnic enemies. The Social Democratic party issued a leaflet after the end of the 1903 general strike in Ekaterinoslav in which it conceded that it was not just "the bourgeoisie," but also "a significant part of the worker masses" that were saying that "workers achieved nothing, the strike was a complete defeat."[122] But while it might be true that this attitude reflected workers' inability "to see beyond the end of their noses," as the leaflet characterized workers' failure to appreciate the political significance of the strike, it is also true that employers were not forced to grant any major concessions as a result of the general strike. Only the wave of strikes in January–February 1905 achieved significant economic improvements.

Workers' deep-seated anger at the inequities of life in tsarist Russia and

[119] Engelstein, *Moscow, 1905*, p. 161.

[120] *Vserossiiskaia*, vol. 2, pt. 2:273.

[121] Sidney Harcave, *The Russian Revolution of 1905* (London, 1970), pp. 204–205; Keep, *Rise of Social Democracy*, p. 227; Ascher, *Revolution of 1905*, p. 255; Surh, *1905 in St. Petersburg*, pp. 353–354. A Soviet historian recently estimated that throughout the empire, Black Hundred mobs killed up to four thousand people and injured over ten thousand during the Days of Freedom (L. T. Senchakova, *Boevaia rat' revoliutsii: Ocherk o boevykh organizatsiiakh RSDRP i rabochikh druzhinakh, 1905–1907 gg.* [Moscow, 1975], p. 113).

[122] *Pod"em revoliutsionnogo dvizheniia*, p. 382.

the feeling of power they derived from general strikes, as well as the minor concessions sometimes obtained from employers, help explain why workers repeatedly responded to the call for general strikes in the Donbass–Dnepr Bend and elsewhere throughout Russia, even though they generally felt so misused afterwards. To be sure, in the years following 1905, calls for general strikes went unheeded.

From the point of view of many Donbass–Dnepr Bend workers, general strikes all ended in failure. The absence of wage hikes or other tangible improvements in working-class conditions left workers feeling frustrated, abused, and confused about who was to blame for their failure.[123] Economic demands typically were not even presented to the factories during a general strike.[124] Workers, as a result, were prone to feel deceived by those they held responsible for calling the strike. In his study of railroad workers, Henry Reichman noted that the outcome of the October general strike "left a deep reservoir of resentment" across the country, which railroad authorities attributed to "the skill with which agitators managed to use the uneducated masses in the struggle for political goals, seducing them with simultaneous promises of immediate and decisive improvements in the material position of the majority."[125]

At the mass rallies that were a central feature of general strikes, revolutionaries were often misled by shouts of "Down with the autocracy!" from their audience. As the *Iskra* correspondent noted in regard to the 1903 general strike in Ekaterinoslav, "such enthusiasm was extremely superficial."[126] And if the government's criminal indictments are to be believed, most of the orators were Jewish, and it was the Jewish artisans and nonworkers in the crowds who were largely responsible for enthusiastically responding to calls for political freedom. The industrial workers' shouts usually reflected economic concerns.[127] Whatever the validity of such attempts to blame Jews for Donbass–Dnepr Bend mass radicalism, it is true that beyond the shouting of slogans, orators aroused mass working-class enthusiasm during rallies only by first attacking economic conditions.[128]

[123] See, for example, the Okhrana and *Iskra* reports regarding the 1903 general strike in Ekaterinoslav (TsGAOR, DP OO, f. 102, 1898, op. 1, d. 4, ch. 18, l. D [*O volneniiakh i stachkakh sredi rabochikh: Bezporiadki v g. Ekaterinoslave*, gendarme report, August 8, 1903], p. 83; *Iskra*, no. 52 [Prilozhenie, November 7, 1903]).

[124] TsGAOR, M. Iu., f. 124, 1903, op. 12, d. 1450, p. 56.

[125] Reichman argues that administrators failed to appreciate that while the mass of workers were not interested in liberal reform, they were interested in reversing power relations at the local level. The general strike gave workers the sense that "yesterday we were slaves, but today masters" (Reichman, *Railwaymen and Revolution*, pp. 230–231).

[126] *Iskra*, no. 52 (Prilozhenie, November 7, 1903).

[127] Excerpts from the *Obvinitel'nyi akt* for the 1903 general strike, reprinted in *Iskra*, no. 81 (December 23, 1904): 3.

[128] TsGIA, f. 23, op. 30, d. 47, p. 228.

During general strikes, radical orators sometimes skirted political issues altogether when they found themselves confronted with large crowds of workers uninitiated into radical politics.

The disappointment and hardship associated with general strikes led to widespread grumbling among workers. In addition to the risk of arrest and the possibility of death, the shutdown of all stores and public services and the loss of wages imposed severe hardships on workers, especially the mass of poorly paid unskilled workers. A great many of the workers forced off the job wanted to vent their frustration on those they deemed responsible for the difficulties resulting from the strike.

At the first rallies during a general strike, the excitement typically intimidated workers who opposed militant revolutionary appeals. But later, even among those workers who had been the first to join the strike, voices repeatedly expressed discontent with the political purpose of the strikes and the neglect of economic demands. Workers complained that political freedom was needed only for socialists and "the well-educated"; workers ought to think only about satisfying their own economic needs. Workers shouted, "We don't need politics!" or "For what do we need a constitution?"[129] Following the announcement of the October Manifesto, administrators along the Ekaterinin railroad line reported that "the strike was declared over, since the leaders were satisfied, but the masses, uninterested in politics and seeking only to improve their material welfare, were secretly disappointed."[130] As the attacks of pogromists on the railroad's white-collar strike leaders would soon demonstrate, workers' disappointment did not remain secret for long. Open hostility toward the "organizers," who were said to be using workers for their own ends, followed strikes and demonstrations all over the Donbass–Dnepr Bend.[131] Thus, what have long been taken as signs of the "maturity" of the labor movement in 1905—its going beyond economic issues to embrace political issues and its mass support for general strikes—were seen by workers in the Donbass–Dnepr Bend as failure.

Given their ideology and general attitude toward the other revolutionary parties, it is not surprising that Ekaterinoslav's Anarchists were alone

[129] *Khleb i volia*, no. 23 (October 1905): 6; *Iskra*, no. 101 (Prilozhenie, June 1, 1905), p. 3; TsGAOR, DP OO, f. 102, 1906, op. 234, d. 7, ch. 34 (*Otchety o revoliutsionnom dvizhenii, Ekaterinoslavskaia gub.*), p. 5. Anti-politics sentiment was part of general strikes throughout Russia. See, for example, Reichman on Russia's first general strike ("Rostov General Strike," pp. 79–80).

[130] Quoted in Reichman, *Railwaymen and Revolution*, p. 230.

[131] This was especially true among coal miners. In October many coal miners were thrown out of work because of the coal reserves accumulated during the railroad general strike. In the mining districts, white-collar employees at railroad stations, as well as radical workers and engineers, became the targets of miners' rage (*Novaia zhizn'*, no. 18 [1905], cited in Kirzner, *Gornorabochie*, p. 70).

among the revolutionaries in blaming the revolutionary movement itself for the pogroms. The Anarchists argued that the liberal political goals of the revolutionary movement offered the pogromists nothing and angered them as well, particularly the lumpenproletarian component. Ekaterinoslav's Anarchists reported that "the ragged and hungry" pogromists "cursed 'pure' society, all those 'satisfied and content *demokraty*' wanting to direct the *narod*."[132] Even the most political workers in the various revolutionary parties called for a tactical retreat. They argued that the divisive political fight should wait until the workers' faith in the movement had been fortified by such victories as the attainment of a shorter workday and increased wages.[133]

Some of workers' hostility to general strikes and their Jewish leaders stemmed from the manner in which the strikes spread. As workers moved from factory to factory recruiting strikers, the general enthusiasm, the threat of violence, and the lack of any deterrence from either the factory or the police were often sufficient to convince workers to put down their tools without protest, even if the majority wished to continue to work. Some of these workers joined the growing crowd, while many simply headed for home.[134] But a great many workers opposed the general strikes from the beginning and refused to stop work willingly. Bitterness and resentment among workers forced off the job by revolutionary activists during general strikes contributed to a violent mood. Even at such relatively militant strongholds as Ekaterinoslav's railroad workshop or the Briansk steel mill, where general strikes usually began in that city, at least one-quarter of the work force might refuse the initial call to strike.[135]

The strikers' success at closing down factories during general strikes can in many cases be attributed to their willingness to resort to threats and violence. Strikers arriving at a factory sometimes met stiff resistance, even when many of them came armed with everything from rocks to brass

[132] *Khleb i volia*, no. 24 (November 1905): 7.

[133] *Iskra*, no. 52 (Prilozhenie, November 7, 1903).

[134] TsGAOR, DP OO, f. 102, 1898, op. 1, d. 4, ch. 18, l. D (Reports of Okhrana and gendarme, August 9, 1905), pp. 54, 71; TsGAOR, DP OO, f. 102, 1903, d. 1473, p. 3; TsGAOR, M. Iu., f. 124, 1903, op. 12, d. 1450, p. 124; *Revoliutsionnaia Rossiia*, no. 31 (September 1, 1903): 18.

[135] Workers who did not want to strike were often identified as Black Hundreds. The authorities maintained that the majority of workers usually did not want to strike. The court investigation of the 1903 strike stated that "it was obvious that the great majority of workers wanted to continue working, but feared violence or revenge from strikers" (TsGAOR, M. Iu., f. 124, 1903, d. 1450, p. 146). The factory inspector reported that when he asked separate groups of workers why they had stopped working, he always received the same answer—"We want to work but are afraid to" (TsGIA, f. 23, d. 47, p. 229). Such answers need to be viewed with skepticism, of course, since the workers might have genuinely supported the strike but not wanted to risk punishment.

knuckles, iron rods, or even revolvers.[136] In an often repeated scene, workers opposed to closing their factory would throw nuts and bolts at the oncoming crowd or temporarily drive them back with axes and whatever else was at hand.[137] In June 1905, when a crowd of strike supporters burst into some workshops at the Briansk factory, they were met by workers wielding crowbars. The strikers were not to be deterred and also resorted to violence, including even the firing of revolvers.[138] In such instances, full-scale brawls might break out. In Iuzovka in October 1905, such a factory brawl, rather than ending with the closing of the factory, ignited a riot and pogrom. The suddenly bloodthirsty mob at the New Russia Company mill managed to hurl some of the Jewish activists they cornered into a blast furnace and on the following day went on a pogromist rampage.[139]

Workers bitterly antagonistic to revolution were joined in pogroms by workers who had supported the general strikes. Many strikers were upset with the nonviolent tactics party activists adopted. In the 1903 and 1905 general strikes, workers were often more combative than those in leadership positions. Although Anarchists and even many Socialist Revolutionaries rhetorically called for armed demonstrations or even an armed uprising in connection with the general strikes, for most of the leading activists, especially the Social Democrats, to have workers strike and attend rallies was an end in itself. Given the past connection between labor unrest and pogroms, fear of provoking or unleashing a pogrom helps explain why radical leaders continually found themselves in the ironic position of trying to curb the labor movement. Party activists by and large were intent on imbuing the agitated crowds that gathered with a peaceful spirit. This was never easy. Many workers came to demonstrations armed with rocks or metal poles. To many, an insurrection seemed to be the logical outcome of a general strike, although even they must have realized that workers had little hope of winning such a confrontation. When speakers and leaflets counseled workers that the strike was to be nonviolent, workers could be

[136] TsGAOR, M. Iu., f. 124, 1903, d. 1450, p. 62.

[137] TsGAOR, DP OO, f. 102, 1898, op. 1, d. 4, ch. 18, l. D, pp. 48, 54.

[138] TsGAOR, M. Iu., f. 124, 1905, op. 43, d. 1305 (Ekaterinoslav procurator's report, June 24, 1905), p. 2; *Materialy po istorii* (Ekaterinoslav), p. 131.

[139] Shklovskii, "Vospominaniia," p. 201; TsGAOR, DP 00, f. 102, 1907, ch. 9, p. 16. See also TsGAOR, DP OO, f. 102, 1905, op. 5, d. 2454; and Kharechko, *1905 god*, p. 67. The accounts of violent discord so common at the beginning of strikes are not meant to suggest that at some factories, or parts of factories, the arrival of the crowd of strikers and the closing down of operations did not proceed in a relatively orderly manner. At the Briansk factory, despite the fighting occurring elsewhere in the factory, when the director asked the blast-furnace workers to remove the cast iron in the open-hearth furnace before they walked off the job, they did so, in order to prevent the enormous damage that otherwise would have resulted. Even some of the arriving demonstrators helped, so that the revolutionary movement would not be held responsible for worker layoffs later (Ia. Kravchenko, "Vospominaniia," *Istoriia ekaterinoslavskoi*, p. 350; *Iskra*, no. 80 [December 15, 1904]: 6; *Dnepropetrovsku*, pp. 77–79).

heard answering, "What should we do when we're attacked?" Consequently, following rallies or marches in which workers were killed or wounded, many workers felt bewildered, disillusioned, and indignant about what they took to be a lack of direction, not to mention protection and support, from their Social Democratic and Socialist Revolutionary leaders.[140]

Frustration and bitterness in the wake of general strikes and the fact that Donbass–Dnepr Bend workers were at best only superficially influenced by revolutionary propaganda meant that incendiary rumors fell on fertile soil and gave rise to pogroms.[141] Reactionary agitators in the Donbass–Dnepr Bend mobilized working-class support for pogroms by adroitly exploiting popular prejudices. Revolutionary parties competed with right-wing organizers who distributed at factories anti-Semitic newspapers in which Jews were portrayed as the culprits responsible for the failures of the general strikes. For many workers, it was a short step—however despicable—to turn their frustration with revolutionaries against the Jews.[142]

Jews did play a prominent role in the Donbass–Dnepr Bend revolutionary movement. The local Social Democratic party leadership—its rank-and-file orators—was largely Jewish, especially in the dominant Menshevik faction. Workers also wrongly identified many non-Jewish revolutionaries as Jews simply because they were intellectuals or wore glasses. Young Jewish artisans shouting revolutionary slogans and carrying banners were conspicuously more militant politically than the Russian factory workers during general strikes.[143] Antirevolutionary and anti-Semitic ferment tended to be especially strong when workers had been killed during a general strike. In the last days of the 1903 general strike, for example, the workers' mood was so bitter that the Social Democratic committee was compelled to heed the advice of its "organized workers" to adopt a low profile and refrain from issuing any more leaflets, since they were only adding to the animosity welling up against the socialists. In this atmosphere, reactionary instigators set rumors afloat blaming the "yids" for everything. It was rumored that after inciting Russian workers, Jews went into hiding. Jews were said to have incited workers to strike in 1903 in order to make them the targets of the soldiers' volleys, as revenge for the Kishinev pogrom.[144] The police made it known that all but two of the twenty-seven fatalities from Cossack volleys in the 1903 general strike were non-Jewish.[145] A rumor also circulated following the general strike that Jewish soldiers had

[140] *Iskra*, no. 81 (December 23, 1904): 4 and no. 106 (July 18, 1905): 2.

[141] *Revoliutsionnaia Rossiia*, no. 31 (September 1, 1903): 19.

[142] *Iskra*, no. 107 (July 29, 1905): 7.

[143] *Iskra*, no. 87 (February 10, 1905): 4.

[144] Governor's report, reprinted in *Istoriia ekaterinoslavskoi*, p. 396.

[145] Such accounts failed to mention that of the 287 arrested during the 1903 general strike, 96 were Jewish (TsGAOR, M. Iu., f. 124, 1903, op. 12, d. 1450, p. 65).

been responsible for firing into the crowd of workers. Russian soldiers were said to have fired over their heads.[146] Many workers concluded, more generally, that the *intelligent* leaders of the revolutionary parties cynically used the mass of workers as the cannon fodder of the revolution.

The pogromist proclivity of Donbass–Dnepr Bend workers was not suddenly revealed for the first time during the 1903–5 period, as we saw in chapter 4. Donbass–Dnepr Bend workers had been prone to engage intermittently in pogromist actions as well as factory riots or strikes, beginning with the first outbreaks of labor discontent there. What changed in 1903–5 was the nature of the events that triggered pogroms, as well as the scope and political significance of pogroms. In the politicized atmosphere during the revolutionary upsurge, pogroms largely took the form of a mass backlash, a somewhat-organized reaction against the failure of the general strikes and of the revolutionary movement to fulfill the expectations of many Donbass–Dnepr Bend workers. Jews became the scapegoat for workers' dissatisfaction with the revolutionary movement.

The 1905 Revolution in the Donbass–Dnepr Bend was a seesaw battle between revolution and reaction. The reactionary backlashes reveal how the success of the radical intelligentsia and the "conscious" workers in leading the working masses—a success to which the impressive Donbass–Dnepr Bend strikes repeatedly testified—could be reversed literally overnight. Pogromist activity did not develop independently of the general-strike movement, but rather in conjunction with the radicalization of labor. It has long been known that general strikes in areas within the Pale tended to be followed by pogroms. But historians' concentration on radical elements within the working class has made them miss the link that exists between these two forms of mass action. In the post–general strike pogromist waves, workers filled the ranks in the army of reaction against their own revolutionary action, along with peasants, drifters, and petty criminals. When the pogromist wave peaked in October 1905, workers from nearly every Donbass–Dnepr Bend factory and mine either rioted or threatened to do so.[147] Even where it is not clear that the workers who joined the strikes were the same ones who turned on the Jews, it is clear that the events themselves were closely related. Pogroms did not follow strikes by accident. They were produced by worker frustration and anger over the outcome of general strikes, frustration and anger that inflamed long-standing ethnic hostility in a region where violent behavior was central to working-class culture.

[146] *Iskra*, no. 52 (Prilozhenie, November 7, 1903); *Obvinitel'nyi akt*, reprinted in *Materialy po istorii* (Ekaterinoslav), p. 24; TsGAOR, M. Iu., f. 124, 1903, op. 12, d. 1450, p. 141.

[147] *Gorno-zavodskii listok*, November 12, 1905, p. 8200; Kharechko, *1905 god*, pp. 68–69.

8

The Bid for Power: December 1905

> The fight against the Black Hundreds is an excellent type of military action, which will *train* the soldiers of the revolutionary army, give them their baptism of fire, and at the same time be of tremendous benefit to the revolution.
>
> (*Lenin, late October 1905*)

THE OCTOBER POGROMS left the opposition movement depressed and discouraged and its ranks depleted. Ekaterinoslav's Anarchists wrote immediately afterward, "One is able to say with certainty that for a long time any organized work will be suspended. The revolutionary forces are paralyzed."[1] The casualties suffered during the October strike and pogrom, and the arrests that followed, gave the revolutionary movement in the Donbass–Dnepr Bend good reason to retreat and lick its wounds. Yet that is not what happened. Instead, a militant movement quickly reemerged in the Donbass–Dnepr Bend to keep the revolution alive during the last months of 1905. Unrest resumed on a mass scale, prompted by local government's weakness following the October Manifesto, an outbreak of military mutinies, and a growing perception of the autocracy's intention to renege on the promises of October.

During the December general strike, the Donbass–Dnepr Bend revolutionary movement once again proved to be among the most combative in the empire. Only the Moscow uprising overshadowed the battle along the Ekaterinin railroad line between armed troops and thousands of armed insurgents in Gorlovka. In Ekaterinoslav, a Fighting Strike Committee (*Boevoi stachechnyi komitet*) brought together all the various strands in the revolutionary movement and operated as the city's de facto government during the December general strike. In contrast, the revolutionary movement in St. Petersburg and elsewhere in December never advanced beyond a state of "quiet disturbance."[2]

The buoyancy of the Donbass–Dnepr Bend revolutionary movement

[1] *Khleb i volia*, no. 24 (November 1905): 7.

[2] Harcave, *Russian Revolution*, p. 236.

during the course of 1905 was remarkable. Peculiar as it may seem, workers' resentment and disappointment with the outcomes of previous strikes did not prevent many of them from supporting one more call to strike. By December the reactionary mood had largely passed, and although mixed feelings surely remained, the aversion many workers felt toward revolutionary *intelligenty* appears to have largely evaporated. Donbass–Dnepr Bend workers' abiding hostility to the social and economic order, as well as the need they perceived for leadership if they were to achieve economic concessions from management, overcame reluctance and past disappointments, leaving many workers receptive to calls to strike. During November, the newly won freedom to organize legally helped the most determined activists buoy up drooping spirits in their midst. In December, as throughout the 1905 Revolution, workers once again responded to revolutionary agitators and leaflets. The optimists in revolutionary circles could once more argue that factory workers appeared to be "infected" with the revolutionary mood.[3]

The tensions within the labor movement, however, did not vanish. Following the October pogroms, the reactionary mood remained strong in certain sectors of the Donbass–Dnepr Bend working class. Miners particularly continued to pose a pogromist threat in November and December 1905. In addition, the strike along the railroad lines had to contend with the tension at railroad stations between liberal and revolutionary white-collar employees, who played a leading role in December, and the mass of workers, even those who were politically active. This tension came to the fore even before the beginning of the December strike. Blue-collar workers in the Ekaterinin railroad assembly responded with scorn to an invitation by white-collar employees to organize a union local. "We workers . . . have nothing in common with the engineers and higher employees. . . . [They] don't have to listen to the cries of hungry children. . . . They are not our comrades. They are prepared to struggle with us only to better their own position."[4]

Despite such working-class sentiments, the Donbass–Dnepr Bend revolutionary movement became more organized than ever during November. Workers and radicals formed soviets and trade unions, to which they elected delegates—prompting the secret police to report that an "epidemic of *delegatstvo*" was occurring throughout the region.[5] Two soviets in Ekaterinoslav, the Assembly of Workers' Deputies and the Assembly of Ekaterinin Railroad Workers' Deputies, enjoyed widespread support and held large, open meetings. The industries and factories that had been slow to

[3] Dal'man, "Oktiabr'skie dni," p. 206.

[4] *Vysshii pod"em*, vol. 3, pt. 1:34, quoted in Reichman, *Railwaymen and Revolution*, p. 247.

[5] TsGAOR, M. Iu., f. 124, 1905, op. 44, d. 1310 (Ministry of Justice court report, May 12, 1906), p. 54.

act in October elected delegates in November to Ekaterinoslav's soviet, while the movement toward unionization, which had begun earlier in the year, also took off.[6] Almost every conceivable group of workers and white-collar employees formed a trade union in November. Such professional groups as academics, teachers, engineers, and accountants joined what one historian has called "the rush to organize" that followed the October Manifesto.[7] A total of forty-seven different trade unions, professional organizations, and political parties entered Ekaterinoslav's Union of Unions (Soiuz soiuzov).[8] Later, during the general strike, assemblies of workers' deputies and strike committees formed in other major Donbass–Dnepr Bend working-class cities—Iuzovka, Lugansk, and Kamenskoe—as well as in numerous railroad and mining towns.[9]

The upsurge in the labor movement was also evident in less-organized forms. Following the October general strike and pogroms, a multitude of government and industry reports announced that what had passed for order and worker discipline at Donbass–Dnepr Bend factories, mines, and railroad stations was quickly disappearing.[10] When a railroad inspector arrived in Ekaterinoslav in late November to investigate conditions on the Ekaterinin railroad line, he found "total disorder and anarchy. . . . The situation on the road is such that the director and higher officials are isolated from power and besieged by all kinds of delegations, which demand everything and request nothing."[11] The industrialists' newspaper *Gorno-zavodskii listok* reported that anarchic conditions prevailed in Ekaterinoslav's steel factories in November: "The spirit of willfulness and violence completely rules the working masses, and they consider themselves the absolute rulers of the country. Order and discipline are history, and worker demands on factory administrations grow literally from day to day."[12] Despite the possibility of hyperbole in these reports, there is no question that labor discipline in the Donbass–Dnepr Bend fell well below its normally low level and that workers were asserting themselves inside the workplace as never before. All over the Donbass–Dnepr Bend, the promulgation of the October Manifesto emboldened workers and unnerved authorities. The manifesto gave workers new confidence in the justice of their grievances, while it put employers as well as government officials on the defensive. No one

[6] Shmorgun, *Sovety*, p. 27.

[7] Reichman, *Railwaymen and Revolution*, pp. 224–258.

[8] Novopolin, "Iz istorii rabochego dvizheniia," p. 70.

[9] Kharechko, *1905 god*, p. 74.

[10] TsGAOR, M. Iu., f. 124, 1905, op. 44, d. 1310 (Ministry of Justice court reports, May 12, 1906 and August 4, 1906), pp. 54, 117.

[11] TsGIA, f. 273, d. 350, pp. 340–342, quoted in Reichman, *Railwaymen and Revolution*, pp. 225–226.

[12] *Gorno-zavodskii listok*, December 10/31, 1905, p. 8269.

seemed to know what was permissible. Workers, quick to exploit the confusion, commonly stopped demanding changes and took matters into their own hands. In November 1905, Ekaterinoslav's railroad workers, "without preliminary permission," began to end their workday an hour early and thereby introduced "in a revolutionary manner" the eight-hour day.[13] After having had to endure haughty and foulmouthed foremen, many workers reveled in the opportunity to turn the tables and swear at members of management. If rebuked, workers threatened to "wheelbarrow."

Their dwindling authority and control led some foremen and administrators to quit abruptly and leave the Donbass–Dnepr Bend. Others fought back. In what would become an increasingly common tactic, made more palatable by the deteriorating economy, enterprises tried to reassert their control in November by locking out their work forces and suspending operations. During 1906, the lockout eventually proved to be an effective counterweapon against worker unrest. But in the last months of 1905, even this desperate measure could not always achieve the desired result. Management of the Nizhnedneprovsk factory in Ekaterinoslav's suburb ended its lockout and resumed production in November upon receiving the assurance of the factory's worker delegates that workers would observe "factory discipline." The delegates evidently were in no position to make such assurances. Production had barely resumed when "mob rule," in the words of the industry newspaper, led to the wheelbarrowing of one of the factory's foremen. Almost all the management personnel walked off the job in protest, and the factory closed down again.[14]

Students were also unruly during November. In Ekaterinoslav and elsewhere in the Donbass–Dnepr Bend, students demanded that they be freed from attending classes to participate in the rallies and meetings occurring almost daily. Attempts by school authorities to quell student ferment proved futile. A high absentee rate became the rule even among elementary-school students.[15]

During November and December, Donbass–Dnepr Bend unrest was not limited to cities and towns. In contrast to the earlier strike waves, labor and agrarian unrest occurred simultaneously. With troops in short supply, peasants attacked landlords and their property all over the countryside. In the Ekaterinoslav district of Verkhnedneprovsk, peasants plundered sixty-six estates. By Christmas, agrarian unrest in Ekaterinoslav province had

[13] TsGAOR, M. Iu., f. 124, 1905, op. 44, d. 1310 (Ministry of Justice court report, May 12, 1906), p. 54. Workers in the capital also engaged in this campaign to institute the eight-hour day through direct action (Engelstein, *Moscow, 1905*, p. 167; Surh, *1905 in St. Petersburg*, pp. 347–348). Southern railroad workers won the nine-hour day in February 1905.

[14] *Gorno-zavodskii listok*, December 10/31, 1905, p. 8269.

[15] TsGIA USSR, f. 1597, op. 1, d. 86 (Okhrana report, November 19, 1905), p. 324.

taken at least fifty lives and resulted in over 1.5 million rubles' worth of damage.[16]

Workers' pogromist rampages in October and their increased unruliness on the job in November, as well as student unrest and peasant rampages, help explain why the sympathy, or even support, the revolutionary movement had enjoyed in some white-collar quarters dwindled following the promulgation of the October Manifesto. Of course, the manifesto itself cost the revolutionary movement support. White-collar personnel were no longer so willing to tolerate disorders simply because of their opposition to the autocracy. Now that the manifesto had largely met their more limited objectives, the better-off sectors of the population in the Donbass–Dnepr Bend, as throughout the empire, craved order above all else.[17] Yet while the revolutionary movement lost liberal support because of workers' pogromist rampages and unruliness on the job and because of the autocracy's newfound willingness to make concessions, it is also true that the concessions the autocracy granted in the October Manifesto emboldened liberals to work openly for political and social reforms in a way they never had before. In the Donbass–Dnepr Bend and elsewhere in the empire, liberals reached out for mass support now that it finally was legal.[18]

Locally, as well as nationally, liberals found themselves in a difficult situation during November. They sought to keep pressure on the autocracy to ensure implementation of the manifesto while at the same time moderating the revolutionary movement. Most liberals wanted, above all else, to prevent another confrontation between the government and the left. Liberal leaders correctly feared that another general strike "would push the autocracy to outright reaction," while the October pogroms confirmed their fears of the danger of unleashing the mob.[19] In the Donbass–Dnepr

[16] *Nasha mysl'*, no. 5 (February 17, 1906), cited in Shmorgun, *Sovety*, p. 37; *Ekaterinoslavshchina*, pp. 206–207, 210, 222, 234, 238; *Vysshii pod"em*, vol. 3, pt. 1:165–180.

[17] However, even those liberals most inclined to be satisfied with the manifesto must have been alarmed when they learned in early December that the tsar had given his blessing to the Black Hundreds when he welcomed a delegation from the recently formed Black Hundred party, the Union of Russian People. Nicholas II not only embraced the Black Hundreds, he accepted badges of membership in the party for himself and the tsarevich Aleksei (Surh, *1905 in St. Petersburg*, p. 509).

[18] TsGIA USSR, f. 346, op. 1, d. 11 (*Obvinitel'nyi akt*), p. 13.

[19] Emmons, *Formation of Political Parties*, p. 49. The leaders of the local Union of Liberation and Union of Zemstvo Constitutionalists, who had led the liberal movement since the banquet campaign of late 1904, merged and joined the newly formed Constitutional Democratic party (the Kadet party), which was formed nationally in October 1905. Ekaterinoslav province's more conservative constitutionalists joined with M. V. Rodzianko, the chairman of the provincial zemstvo and future leader of the party, to form the National Party of October 17, known as the Octobrist party (ibid., p. 211; Ivanov, "Oktiabr'skaia politicheskaia stachka," p. 70).

Bend, as in other trouble spots, many liberals shared Kiev professor E. N. Trubetskoi's fearful view of the consequences of an armed uprising:

> The wave of anarchy that is advancing from all sides, and that at the present time threatens the legal government, would quickly sweep away any revolutionary government: the embittered masses would then turn against the real or presumed culprits; they would subject to destruction the *entire intelligentsia*; the masses would begin indiscriminately to slaughter all who wear German clothes [i.e., the well-dressed]—conservatives, liberals, revolutionaries. Our unruly hordes will roam all over Russia, plundering and burning everything in their path.[20]

Despite such pronounced fears, Donbass–Dnepr Bend liberals were reluctant to abandon the policy of "no enemies on the left" and attack the revolutionary parties directly. In cities such as Lugansk, the liberal intelligentsia—which consisted primarily of zemstvo members, doctors, teachers, and agronomists—organized "unification conferences" that "curious" leaders of the SD party agreed to attend.[21] As elsewhere in the empire, Donbass–Dnepr Bend liberals' attempt to moderate the mass movement in December failed.

The immediate cause of the post-October resumption of mass labor unrest was the government's decision not to extend to public employees the right to form legal trade unions. Donbass–Dnepr Bend telegraph workers supported their national union's response to the firing of three of the union's organizers in Moscow by beginning a protest strike on November 15. Local postal workers followed suit and struck on the seventeenth. The Union of Postal-Telegraph Employees presented demands regarding wages and working conditions, but the main thrust of the strike by this basically white-collar segment of the work force was political. The union demanded the immediate release of members of the Peasant Union arrested in St. Petersburg; the removal from office of the minister of internal affairs and the national director of the postal-telegraph service; and most important, the right to form a union. The postal-telegraph strike occurred in two short waves and seemed to end in failure. The "all-Russian strike" initially lasted only a few days; it resumed on the twenty-seventh to protest wholesale arrests by the postal administration. The second postal-telegraph strike lasted until December 2, when the union was forced to concede de-

[20] E. N. Trubetskoi, "Dve diktatury," *Russkie vedomosti*, November 16, 1905, p. 2, quoted in Ascher, *Revolution of 1905*, pp. 296–297. Trubetskoi, one of the empire's liberal leaders, withdrew from the Kadet party early in 1906 because the party was too "revolutionist" (Emmons, *Formation of Political Parties*, p. 73).

[21] Shklovskii, "Vospominaniia," pp. 204–205.

feat because of the government's success in recruiting strikebreakers and arresting strikers.[22]

The central government's decision to arrest 223 members of the St. Petersburg soviet on December 3 indicated its determination to reassert control and its willingness to risk provoking a showdown with the revolutionary movement. These arrests galvanized the revolutionary movement in the Donbass–Dnepr Bend, as elsewhere in the empire, although discussion of another general strike had begun in earnest in Ekaterinoslav on November 17, well before the St. Petersburg soviet resolved "to prepare for armed insurrection" (a threat it took no steps to implement).[23] The Assembly of Ekaterinin Railroad Workers' Deputies had held a meeting November 17 at Ekaterinoslav's English Club, attended by some seven hundred railroad employees and workers. The assembly's president, Vasilii Nauman, announced that the assembly needed to prepare to strike again to combat the government's lack of good faith, despite his own misgivings about calling such a strike at that time.[24]

Nauman was right to think that December 1905 was hardly the optimum time for a general strike—not because of labor quiescence, but because of the reemergence of the pogromist threat. Already by the middle of November, one newspaper had reported in Ekaterinoslav that "all of Ekaterinoslav society expects violent attacks on the intelligentsia. This means a new pogrom."[25] Panicked Social Democrats responded with leaflets that announced, "The government has begun new pogroms. They are preparing a pogrom in Ekaterinoslav. The garrison committee calls on all conscious comrades to respond to the first alarm with arms in hand to quell any attempt at a pogrom. The struggle with the Black Hundreds is a struggle for freedom, for land and freedom."[26] Outside Ekaterinoslav, rumors of another pogromist wave flew up and down the Donbass–Dnepr Bend in November just as talk of another general strike began. The danger was thought to be greatest at the railroad stations in the mining districts.[27]

Miners—whom contemporary reports now commonly referred to simply as "hooligans" or "Black Hundreds"—were believed to be ready to sack

[22] TsGAOR, DP OO, f. 102, 1905, d. 2100 (Okhrana reports, November 19–30, 1905), pp. 112, 170, 241; Reichman, *Railwaymen and Revolution*, p. 262.

[23] Engelstein, *Moscow, 1905*, p. 187.

[24] *Ekaterinoslavshchina*, p. 263; TsGIA USSR, f. 346, op. 1, d. 11 (*Obvinitel'nyi akt*), p. 17; Kirzner, *Gornorabochie*, p. 27. Leaders of the movement elsewhere in the empire also thought that the government sought to provoke a confrontation when support from the masses was uncertain.

[25] *Syn otechestva*, November 16, 1905, p. 5.

[26] *Vysshii pod"em*, vol. 3, pt. 1:45–46.

[27] TsGAOR, M. Iu., f. 124, 1905, op. 44, d. 1310 (Ministry of Justice court report, August 4, 1906), p. 117.

the railroad stations and adjacent towns once again.[28] Reports such as the one on November 12 in *Gorno-zavodskii listok* concerning a wave of unrest in the Bokovskii mining district a couple of weeks earlier hardly encouraged those who hoped miners' reactionary sentiments had subsided. What began as a strike for economic improvements at the Kol'berg mine had spread to a number of neighboring mines to include a few thousand miners. In addition to their economic grievances, a good part of the miners were also evidently still seething over the October general strike. Perhaps because no Jews resided in this part of the Donets Basin, which was located outside the Pale, the miners focused their anger on administrative staff members, whom they accused of being against the tsar. On November 2, around five hundred miners stormed the office of the Bokovskii mine. With coal dust still in their pores, these "half-baked patriots," in the words of the newspaper account, seized two mine managers as well as a clerk and a skilled worker. The "Black Hundreds" accused them of distributing SD leaflets and inciting workers to oppose the tsar. The miners released the managers and others, but during the next few days, before Cossacks arrived and restored order, rampaging miners destroyed mine property and assaulted other administrators and white-collar employees.[29]

The danger of a pogrom weighed on the minds of the railroad representatives when they met in Ekaterinoslav on November 17 to discuss another general strike. One after another, speakers and voices from the audience addressed the working-class threat and urged caution in using the strike weapon. Speakers devoted little thought to whether the government, the target of the proposed strike, might respond to the strike with force. To the railroad representatives, the threat from below was of much greater concern than the threat from above. Speakers argued that if coal were not transported during another general strike, mines would suspend operations, leaving miners without work and wages and in a mood to seek revenge.[30]

Donbass–Dnepr Bend miners' jobs were in jeopardy because enormous coal reserves had already piled up on the loading platforms during the October general strike. Mines cut back on production during November; some closed down. The New Russia Company, for example, shut down operations at its mine outside Iuzovka and summarily released all 2,782 miners.[31] Many steel mills were also operating well below capacity and threatened their workers with layoffs. A few factories, such as the steel mill

[28] *Burevestnik*, no. 6–7 (September–October 1907): 6.

[29] *Gorno-zavodskii listok*, November 12, 1905, pp. 8206-8208; Kirzner, *Gornorabochie*, pp. 66–67.

[30] TsGIA USSR, f. 346, op. 1, d. 11 (*Obvinitel'nyi akt*), pp. 14, 23.

[31] Kharechko, *1905 god*, p. 77; S. S. Anisimov, *Vosstanie v Donetskom basseine* (Moscow, 1929), p. 52.

in Makeevka, actually closed.[32] To call another general strike in the Donbass–Dnepr Bend under these conditions would cost thousands more jobs, which many thought was almost certain to invite a pogromist wave from miners and other unskilled workers. A pogromist wave, no one doubted, would have dreadful consequences.[33]

It was clear that the tensions that had been evident within the labor movement throughout 1905 did not vanish following the October pogroms. But in the Donbass–Dnepr Bend, as elsewhere in the empire, it was the threat of a backlash by elements in the working class that ironically served to push the revolutionary movement to take more concerted, militant action as December approached.[34] The widespread belief in the need to defend against attacks by miners and other workers who shared their discontent and were itching for another pogrom led the revolutionary movement in the Donbass–Dnepr Bend to intensify efforts to form "battle detachments" (*boevye druzhini*) and obtain arms.[35] The emergence of battle detachments was one of the most significant developments of late 1905 because it was the battle detachments that made possible the militance displayed by the Donbass–Dnepr Bend revolutionary movement in December. Thus, the pogroms of October had as large a role in producing an armed uprising in December as discontent with tsarism.

Battle detachments evolved out of the self-defense units organized during the course of the 1905 Revolution to battle pogromists. The number of self-defense units multiplied greatly in November, especially out in the smaller towns where none had existed before the October pogroms. Along the railroad lines, self-defense units mainly consisted of Jewish residents, particularly artisans, skilled Russian workers, and radical white-collar railroad employees. Self-defense units screened applicants and more or less limited membership according to the number of guns a unit possessed. In addition, self-defense units commonly denied admittance to those under seventeen years of age.[36] Even so, some of the bigger units included hundreds of members.

When pogroms did not erupt during November, self-defense units at the railroad stations and the neighboring towns began to serve as a shadow

[32] K. Ershov, "Dekabr'skoe vooruzhennoe vosstanie v Donbasse," part 1, *Katorga i ssylka*, no. 8–9 (1930): 8; Kharechko, *1905 god*, p. 77. Some factories—such as the mill in Iuzovka, where workers had been locked out in November—won workers' cooperation during the December strike by guaranteeing them their jobs despite the downturn in economic conditions (TsGAOR, DP OO, f. 102, 1907, op. 116, d. 18, ch. 9, p. 16). Despite its guarantee, after the end of the unrest, the factory laid off eight hundred workers (*Gorno-zavodskii listok*, January 14, 1906, p. 8300).

[33] TsGIA USSR, f. 346, op. 1, d. 11 (*Obvinitel'nyi akt*), pp. 14, 23.

[34] Surh, *1905 in St. Petersburg*, pp. 459–460, 495.

[35] Cherevanin, *Bor'ba obshchestvennykh sil*, p. 87.

[36] TsGIA USSR, f. 346, op. 1, d. 11 (*Obvinitel'nyi akt*), p. 45.

police force.[37] The main actions of the self-defense units before the December strike consisted of breaking up minor disturbances of the peace and "arresting drunks, rowdies, suspicious-looking people, and thieves."[38] Relations between the self-defense units and the local police and city dumas were strained, as one might suspect, but the authorities in the Donbass–Dnepr Bend generally did little to stop the self-defense units from patrolling neighborhoods and guarding stations and freight cars.[39] In Lugansk, where the revolutionary movement possessed few weapons and the reactionary sympathies of many workers were evident, the city government even considered supplying self-defense units with arms in response to demands from the revolutionary movement. At two council meetings, in front of a packed auditorium, members of the revolutionary parties and duma called for the city government to fund a "people's militia." When the mayor finally announced that he lacked the "legal grounds" to do so, even though "anarchy and another Pugachevshchina" threatened Lugansk and the entire Donbass–Dnepr Bend, an angry protest from the crowd ensued.[40]

In the crisis atmosphere, self-defense units across the Donbass–Dnepr Bend enjoyed considerable support beyond radical circles. Local merchants and shopkeepers, white-collar industrial and railroad employees, and even some factory and mine directors contributed money toward arming the self-defense units. Factory managers allegedly donated thousands of rubles.[41] Many of these middle- and upper-class contributors apparently appreciated the protection self-defense units could offer against mob violence.[42] They were, nonetheless, quite wary of the self-defense units. Most contributors did not share the political goals of the radical members of the self-defense units, and many expressed misgivings about how the units might be used in the future. Their skepticism proved to be well-founded. Although activists had reassured them that self-defense units were established solely to protect people and property from "hooligans and Black Hundreds," during the general strike revolutionaries transformed units

[37] Ibid., p. 46; Sergei Anisimov, *Delo o vosstanii na Ekaterininskoi zh. d.* (Moscow-Leningrad, 1926), p. 14; *Materialy po istorii* (Artemovsk), p. 3.

[38] TsGAOR, M. Iu., f. 124, 1905 op. 44, d. 1310 (Ministry of Justice court report, August 4, 1906), p. 118.

[39] *Materialy po istorii* (Artemovsk), p. 163.

[40] Berkhin, *Luganskaia bol'shevistskaia organizatsiia*, pp. 79, 81; Shklovskii, "Vospominaniia," pp. 207–208. Similarly unsuccessful requests for city-government funding of a "people's militia" occurred outside the Donbass–Dnepr Bend as well. See, for example, Engelstein, *Moscow, 1905*, p. 146.

[41] Anisimov, *Vosstanie v Donetskom basseine*, p. 58; *Vysshii pod"em*, vol. 3, pt. 1:147.

[42] Elsewhere as well, industrialists funded the arming of battle detachments. For Moscow, see Joseph L. Sanders, *The Moscow Uprising of 1905: A Background Study* (New York, 1987), p. 427.

originally formed for defense against pogromists into detachments ready to do battle with government troops.[43]

The extent to which Donbass–Dnepr Bend revolutionaries had planned all along to transform the self-defense units into battle detachments is uncertain. They clearly created them to counter the pogromist threat, yet by the same token the revolutionaries quickly put the battle detachments to use as guards at meetings and rallies. Local party leaders certainly knew that their various party congresses had adopted resolutions supporting an armed insurrection. For months, Lenin had been calling for the formation of "revolutionary" combat detachments, whose task would be "to proclaim the insurrection, to give the masses military leadership . . . if only at first in a small part of the country."[44] The Menshevik and SR national leadership also supported the notion of an armed insurrection, although they assumed it would arise more spontaneously.[45]

The December general strike in the Donbass–Dnepr Bend began after Ekaterinoslav's Railroad Union received a telegram from Moscow on December 7 announcing that the Conference of Twenty-nine Railroad Lines, the Central Bureau of the All-Russian Railroad Union, and the St. Petersburg and Moscow soviets of workers' deputies had declared a "general political strike."[46] Although the mood was tempestuous at the Ekaterinoslav station after the telegram was received, the crowd displayed a new sense of the importance of disciplined organization. No further action was taken until the railroad workers' representatives could meet and formally decide whether to support the general strike.

Early the next morning, December 8, the railroad workers' soviet convened. The meeting opened with delegates vying to outdo one another with the torrents of indignation they directed at the autocracy. The noise and confusion of the meeting made a poor setting for serious discussion, and the orators failed to discuss the pros and cons of calling on workers to once again support a general strike—which presumably was the purpose of having speeches precede the formal vote. Fifty-one of the fifty-four delegates voted to call a general strike.[47] After this voice tally, the three opponents of the strike reversed their votes and the formal resolution declared

[43] TsGAOR, M. Iu., f. 124, 1905, op. 44, d. 1310 (Ministry of Justice court report, August 4, 1906), p. 117; *Gorno-zavodskii listok*, November 19, 1905, p. 8227.

[44] Quoted in Sanders, *Moscow Uprising*, pp. 60–61.

[45] Ibid., p. 71.

[46] Anisimov, *Vosstanie v Donetskom basseine*, pp. 25–26.

[47] Ibid., p. 27.

unanimous support.[48] The Assembly of Workers' Deputies also met that morning and unanimously supported the general strike.

Following the vote, the Assembly of Ekaterinin Railroad Workers' Deputies dispatched a telegram to all the stations along the Ekaterinin line announcing, "Today at 10 o'clock, a general strike of all railroad lines and workers was declared."[49] Fifty to sixty armed Russian and Jewish revolutionary activists marched into the Ekaterinoslav train station's office and announced the station's takeover by the "provisional government."[50] After the Ekaterinoslav and Nizhnedneprovsk stations were secured, one of the Socialist Revolutionary party leaders, Leontii Radchenko, organized a train to go down the line disarming police.[51] Later that day, members of Ekaterinoslav's Fighting Strike Committee went down the railroad line to Grishino to learn how the strike was faring out in the Donets Basin.

Ekaterinoslav's workers once again struck en masse after armed strikers sounded factory whistles and went from factory to factory. How much enthusiasm there was for the strike is uncertain. According to a secret police agent, "workers, even the organized workers, overstrained by a whole series of general strikes, strongly opposed this strike. . . . I have information that all local revolutionary committees spoke out in principle against this strike, since such a strike unproductively wastes the energy of workers."[52] Accounts in the revolutionary press, in contrast, suggested that Ekaterinoslav's workers were once again ready for mass action. There is little question that when the railroad workers received news of the strike, they quickly gathered and displayed the sort of enthusiasm evident during the first days of the October general strike.

In Ekaterinoslav and in other Donbass–Dnepr Bend cities, the mass movement in December proved to be more organized than ever, thanks to the formation of soviet-style committees. After the beginning of the general strike on December 8, the leaders of Ekaterinoslav's revolutionary and labor movements, disregarding the continued existence and operation of the secret police, came up from the underground to quickly create a new administrative body, the Fighting Strike Committee (FSC), which publicly announced that the goal of the general strike was political—"to secure the convocation of a constitutional assembly elected by all the people without regard to gender and nationality through a general, equal, direct, and secret ballot."[53] The FSC was entrusted with the power to coordinate the

[48] P. Gorin, *Ocherki po istorii sovetov rabochikh deputatov v 1905 g.* (Moscow, 1925), p. 274.

[49] Anisimov, *Vosstanie v Donetskom basseine*, p. 26.

[50] TsGAOR, M. Iu., f. 124, 1905, op. 44, d. 1310 (Ministry of Justice court report, May 12, 1906), p. 59.

[51] TsGAOR, DP OO, f. 102, 1906, op. 234, d. 7, ch. 34, p. 8.

[52] TsGAOR, DP OO, f. 102, 1905, op. 5, d. 4, ch. 17, vol. 4, p. 154.

[53] B. Krugliakov, "Revoliutsionnoe dvizhenie sredi zheleznodorozhnikov v 1905 g.," *Proletarskaia revoliutsiia*, no. 11 (1925): 107.

strike movement. The power it attained reflected the new sophistication and spirit of cooperation in Ekaterinoslav's revolutionary and labor movements.

The revolutionary parties organized the FSC in Ekaterinoslav in a nonpartisan spirit, together with the railroad workers' assembly, the assembly of workers' deputies, and the strike committee of the postal-telegraph employees. Though interparty squabbling continued, through the FSC the various components of Ekaterinoslav's revolutionary movement appeared, for the first time, to have put most of their differences aside in order to work together. The members of the Fighting Strike Committee elected a president and generally cooperated with one another during the December general strike. The individual members of the FSC cosigned all the decrees the executive body issued.[54] To the best of the Okhrana's knowledge, the members of Ekaterinoslav's FSC consisted, by party affiliation, of eight Social Democrats from the "united Committee of the Social Democratic Party," six Socialist Revolutionaries, two Anarchist-Communists, and three unaffiliated members of the Assembly of Ekaterinin Railroad Workers' Deputies.[55] This report failed to mention the Bund, which was also represented.[56] The FSC rejected the Labor Zionists' bid to gain representation on the committee, claiming the Labor Zionists "lacked enough influence among the Jewish proletariat to make the presence of their representatives necessary."[57]

As a result of the quick formation of the FSC, the December strike movement in Ekaterinoslav proceeded in a more deliberate manner than had been possible in October. After striking workers once again brought the city's economy and trams to a stop on December 8, the FSC proclaimed itself the executive branch of Ekaterinoslav's "provisional government." Amid the chaos inevitable during such a turbulent time, the FSC was acting as if it were indeed a revolutionary government. During the first week, it assumed control of many governmental functions in the city and along the Ekaterinin railroad line.[58]

[54] Bulletin nos. 1–8 of the Ekaterinoslav Fighting Strike Committee, reprinted in *Vysshii pod"em*, vol. 3, pt. 1.

[55] TsGAOR, DP OO, f. 102, 1905, d. 106, ch. 13 (Okhrana court report, December 26, 1905), pp. 41–46; Anisimov, *Vosstanie v Donetskom basseine*, p. 26.

[56] *Ekaterinoslavshchina*, p. 349.

[57] *Vysshii pod"em*, vol. 3, pt. 1 (FSC Bulletin no. 1): 58. In protest, some one hundred Jewish activists, largely artisans and clerks, formed a "Jewish soviet" (Shmorgun, *Sovety*, p. 32). Of course, while the Labor Zionists were not especially strong, they may have been denied representation because the FSC did not want to send the "wrong" message to its anti-Semitic working-class constituency. Regardless, in the second *Bulletin* the FSC reaffirmed its position, but agreed to coordinate its actions with the Labor Zionists (*Ekaterinoslavshchina*, p. 219).

[58] Initially, in an attempt to avoid facilitating or provoking a military crackdown, the FSC declared that unarmed troops were to be given transportation on the trains along the Ekate-

The FSC promulgated its directives through eight issues of the *Bulletin of Ekaterinoslav's Fighting Strike Committee*, which striking printers printed on the presses of *Vestnik Iuga*. Supporters openly distributed twenty thousand copies of each of the bulletins. For many Donbass–Dnepr Bend residents, the *Bulletin* provided the only information available on the course of the strike in Ekaterinoslav, as well as elsewhere in the region and around Russia.[59] The *Bulletin*, while trying to dispel rumors, also reported such local developments as the meeting of "hooligans" at Ekaterinoslav's tavern the "Volga," where plans were "apparently" laid for a pogrom.[60]

That socially diverse elements of the population submitted petitions to the FSC requesting special exemptions from the general strike attests to the popular recognition of the committee. An edited collection of some of the decrees printed in the *Bulletin* indicates the sort of power the FSC tried to exert. "The Fighting Strike Committee has decided":

> **1.** To discontinue the supply of electric current to theaters and to stop all performances.
>
> **2.** To permit the distribution of food and other basic necessities such as lamp oil, coal, and matches at the Ekaterinoslav station.
>
> **3.** In answer to the merchants' proposal that they will contribute 20 percent of their proceeds to the Fighting Strike Committee if the latter permits them to continue their trade: the request is rejected.
>
> **4.** To stop the departure and arrival of trains, in view of the occupation of the Ekaterinoslav station by government forces.
>
> **5.** In answer to a request from a group of workers at the government printing press for permission to resume work, in view of special circumstances: during a general all-Russian strike, all workers must take part in the strike; consequently the request is rejected.
>
> **6.** In answer to the question of some private bankers dated December 10, 1905, the Fighting Strike Committee confirms its decision of December 9 to the effect that all official and unofficial establishments, except the State Bank and the savings bank, must remain closed.
>
> **7.** In answer to an enquiry on the part of the comrades of the press and of the daily *Pridneprovskii krai* whether the publication of newspapers during a general political strike may be permitted: during a general political strike, no publication may be permitted to appear except those of the Fighting Strike Committee and of the revolutionary organizations; consequently newspapers may not be permitted to appear.[61]

---

rinin line, which strikers controlled (F. E. Los', "Dekabr'skoe vooruzhennoe vosstanie na Ukraine," *Istoricheskie zapiski* 49 [1954]: 55).

[59] TsGAOR, DP OO, f. 102, 1905, d. 5, ch. 6 (Okhrana report, December 14, 1905), p. 353.

[60] *Ekaterinoslavshchina*, p. 214; see also *Vysshii pod"em*, vol. 3, pt. 1:72.

[61] M. N. Pokrovskii, *A Brief History of Russia*, vol. 2, trans. D. S. Mirsky (New York, 1933), p. 190. Point 6 ordering strikers not to close the state and private savings banks was intended

The FSC also organized free cafeterias and free medical aid in the "Chechelevka Republic." It controlled the bakeries and waterworks and ordered workers to withhold taxes.[62] Stores that sold basic groceries were ordered to reopen. On December 13, the FSC ordered residents to stop paying rent.[63]

Ekaterinoslav's Fighting Strike Committee appeared to enjoy a surprising amount of support from members of the city's upper classes, even though the October Manifesto, here as elsewhere, split moderate supporters of the opposition movement off from the revolutionary movement. During the course of the December general strike, Ekaterinoslav's FSC organized a fund-raising commission consisting of liberal members of the city's elite. The commission's directors were A. M. Terpigorev, a professor at the city's Mining Institute; I. N. Fedorenko, a manager at the Briansk factory; and G. I. Kupianskii, a medical doctor.[64] Directors of local factories donated considerable sums to the commission: the Briansk factory contributed 4,000 rubles, the Trubnyi factory 2,000 rubles, and the Esau factory 300 rubles. In addition, during the general strike the Briansk factory gave workers one ruble of credit per day at the factory store and provided free meals at the factory cafeteria.[65] How much of the support for the strike was contributed under duress is impossible to determine, but to the extent that support for the FSC was genuine, it reflected a judgment on the part of the city's elite that the FSC represented the best hope for maintaining some semblance of order during the general strike. In the absence of governmental power—the available police and soldiers felt disoriented and overwhelmed—the armed patrols of the FSC could be seen as the only viable force standing in the way of a working-class rampage in Ekaterinoslav. In Ekaterinoslav, as throughout the Donbass–Dnepr Bend, the revolutionary movement sought to police the mass of workers milling around on the streets. One of the strikers' first actions in Ekaterinoslav was

---

to lend support to the St. Petersburg soviet's financial manifesto. The St. Petersburg plan was for bank employees to continue to work so that citizens could convert their deposits into gold. The soviet believed that a mass conversion of savings into gold would drive the government into quick bankruptcy. To contrast the level of activity of the soviets in Ekaterinoslav and St. Petersburg, it is interesting to note that, according to Engelstein, "the financial manifesto of December 2 constituted the single concrete measure undertaken by the St. Petersburg body before its own existence was abruptly terminated on December 3" (Laura Engelstein, "Moscow in the 1905 Revolution: A Study in Class Conflict and Political Organization" [Ph.D. diss., Stanford University, 1976], p. 319). Nonetheless, the threat apparently was the main reason the government decided to reassert its authority and quash the St. Petersburg soviet (Ascher, *Revolution of 1905*, p. 300).

[62] Lane, *Roots*, p. 174.

[63] *Ekaterinoslavshchina*, p. 216; *Vysshii pod"em*, vol. 3, pt. 1:70.

[64] TsGAOR, DP OO, f. 102, 1906, op. 234, d. 7, ch. 34, p. 8.

[65] TsGAOR, DP OO, f. 102, 1905, d. 2555, vol. 8 (Okhrana report, December 14, 1905), p. 113; *Gorno-zavodskii listok*, January 14, 1906, p. 8301.

to prohibit the sale of vodka and to close liquor stores.[66] Orators and leaflets admonished workers to not get drunk or riot.[67]

The power the FSC wielded largely reflected the government's weakness and passivity during the first ten days of the December general strike. Governmental authorities did little to stop the spread of the strike and the actions of such bodies as the FSC.[68] When the strike began, Ekaterinoslav's governor, A. B. Neidgart, felt he lacked a sufficient number of reliable troops to take forceful action against the strike. Most of the troops in the province had been dispatched in mid-November to Sevastopol' to contain the mutiny in the Black Sea fleet and to suppress disorders elsewhere.[69] Among the remaining troops, mutinies on November 18 and December 1 involved all three of the infantry regiments and the one Cossack regiment garrisoned in Ekaterinoslav.[70] The leaflets the Social Democrats and other parties distributed among garrison recruits apparently enjoyed some success. Regiments refused to carry out orders and individual soldiers attended radical meetings and rallies.[71] The government, lacking confidence in the troops at its disposal, made no attempt to penetrate the industrial district and arrest the strike's leadership, the FSC. Nor did the government attempt to disperse rallies or demonstrations; it did not even stop raids on weapons storehouses. The military did, however, recapture the Ekaterinoslav train station on December 11 following an exchange of gunfire in which as many as fifteen rebels lost their lives and twenty suffered serious wounds. The secret police described conditions in Ekaterinoslav on December 12 as follows: "The lack of reliable troops makes itself felt. Attacks on police, in which they are disarmed, occur almost daily. The bulletin of revolutionary events is sold openly and the population believes in the success of the revolution."[72] Unlike in October, revolutionaries in Ekaterinoslav had almost a free hand during the December general strike—until the governor's increasingly desperate pleas for military reinforcements finally were answered on December 18 and the authorities regained power in the city center.

The FSC, despite its best efforts, lacked the means to control many of its supporters and ensure order. People purporting to be revolutionaries "kept the whole city in fear," according to the secret police.[73] While many

[66] *Materialy po istorii* (Artemovsk), p. 163; TsGIA USSR, f. 419, d. 4393 (Okhrana court report, December 13, 1906), p. 7; *Vysshii pod"em*, vol. 3, pt. 1:70.

[67] *Iuzhnaia zaria*, April 10, 1908, p. 3; *Ekaterinoslavshchina*, pp. 218, 252.

[68] A. M. Pankratova, "Dekabr'skie dni v Donbasse v 1905 g.," *Krasnyi arkhiv*, no. 73 (1935): 95.

[69] Ershov, "Dekabr'skoe vooruzhennoe vosstanie," part 1, p. 24.

[70] Bushnell, *Mutiny amid Repression*, p. 107.

[71] *Ekaterinoslavshchina*, pp. 219, 227–229.

[72] Quoted in Los', "Dekabr'skoe vooruzhennoe vosstanie," p. 56.

[73] TsGAOR, DP OO, f. 102, 1906, op. 234, d. 7, ch. 34, p. 10.

of the students and workers in battle detachments collecting money door-to-door and from train passengers did not rely on overt coercion during the December general strike, the revolutionaries confessed that others were not so "correct." Battle detachments and groups consisting of dozens of teenage radicals not only did not hesitate to use force to close commercial and industrial enterprises that tried to reopen, they forced their way into private apartments to disarm police or extort money from residents. One crowd of armed workers from the Briansk factory burst into the apartment of a police officer and shot him dead.[74] "Gangs of thieves" calling themselves "anarchist-communists" and "black ravens" reportedly committed numerous armed robberies, or "expropriations."[75] Black Hundreds, for their part, distributed inflammatory leaflets.[76] The terror gripping the center of the city during December's revolutionary upsurge made any organized, mass displays there too dangerous for the FSC to contemplate. Because of the danger of sparking another pogromist rampage, the FSC restricted rallies to the industrial districts. One Social Democrat wrote not long afterward that after the strike began, "rumors of a Jewish pogrom circulated without interruption. The population vividly remembered the savagely brutal pogrom of October 20. The terrible nightmare of a pogrom hung over the city during the entire strike, paralyzing any aggressive actions."[77]

Elsewhere in the Donbass–Dnepr Bend, the situation was similar to that in Ekaterinoslav in many respects. The revolutionary movement enjoyed success along the Ekaterinin line as well as in Ekaterinoslav. The December 8 appeal to strike from the Assembly of Ekaterinin Railroad Workers' Deputies in Ekaterinoslav elicited immediate support along the Ekaterinin line, particularly from the railroad's white-collar employees. In what the military described as "an extremely threatening situation," rebels seized control of every station along the 1,850-mile-long railroad line crisscrossing the Donbass–Dnepr Bend. Patrols of armed workers guarded the stations. In almost every Donbass–Dnepr Bend railroad town, including the steel cities of Iuzovka, Lugansk, Enakievo, and Kamenskoe, soviet-style organizations followed Ekaterinoslav's example and formed strike committees they also dubbed "fighting committees."[78] The uprising did not, however, enjoy

[74] Anisimov, *Delo*, pp. 13–14; TsGAOR, DP OO, f. 102, 1906, op. 234, d. 7, ch. 34, pp. 9–10; Gorin, *Ocherki*, p. 275; *Ekaterinoslavshchina*, p. 215.

[75] *Iuzhnaia zaria*, June 29, 1906, p. 3.

[76] Los', "Dekabr'skoe vooruzhennoe vosstanie," pp. 58–59.

[77] Cherevanin, *Bor'ba obshchestvennykh sil*, p. 86.

[78] TsGIA USSR, f. 346, op. 1, d. 11 (*Obvinitel'nyi akt*), p. 34; TsGAOR, M. Iu., f. 124, 1905, op. 44, d. 1310 (Ministry of Justice court report, August 4, 1906), p. 124; Kharechko, *1905 god*, p. 74; *Ekaterinoslavshchina*, pp. 221, 230; Shmorgun, *Sovety*, p. 29; E. D. Chermenskii, "Dekabr'skoe vooruzhennoe vosstanie 1905 goda," in *Pervaia russkaia revoliutsiia, 1905–1907 gg.*, ed. A. M. Pankratova (Moscow, 1955), p. 224.

universal support among the workers at the railroad stations. Workers at some railroad workshops, such as the one in Lugansk, opposed the strike and, as noted above, lent an ear to the growing number of counterrevolutionary agitators in their midst.[79]

Yet the call for a general strike received considerable support from industrial workers in the Donets Basin. Individual factories and mines supported the call for a three-day strike, December 9–11.[80] Miners joined steelworkers in supporting the strike in Gorlovka, Berovka, Zhilovsk, and Kadeevka, towns that were all located in the vicinity of steel mills. Local leaders of the revolutionary movement decided that to call on these workers to support a longer strike was impossible, as growing unemployment and the approach of the Christmas holidays meant workers particularly needed their wages.[81] That workers struck at all was impressive considering the deteriorating Donbass–Dnepr Bend economy.

During December, rallies at railroad stations and factories attracted large crowds of workers and miners. Rallies continued to attract large crowds even after workers returned to work on the twelfth, because organizers held the rallies in the evenings after the day shift finished work. The largest rallies in the Donets Basin occurred in Gorlovka, where crowds numbering in the thousands gathered almost daily.[82] In addition to its position as a major railroad junction, Gorlovka was also the site of a large machine-building plant and one of the largest mines in the Donets Basin, the French-owned South Russian Mine.

Relatively small rallies occurred in Grishino, but this railroad junction proved to be in many ways the true center of the Donbass–Dnepr Bend revolutionary movement in December. The strike committee at the Grishino train station took the lead in trying to coordinate the activity at the various stations in the basin. The self-defense units in Grishino were among the first to transform themselves into battle detachments and disarm small groups of troops and Cossacks passing through its station. On December 11, the Grishino committee encouraged others to do the same with a telegram sent to other railroad stations calling for "the organization of battle detachments and the disarming of troops and police, which will guarantee our victory."[83] On December 13, a battle detachment in Grishino disarmed its biggest catch—a dozen soldiers, whom it proudly kept

[79] Berkhin, *Luganskaia bol'shevistskaia organizatsiia*, p. 82.

[80] Ershov, "Dekabr'skoe vooruzhennoe vosstanie," part 1, p. 8; Kharechko, *1905 god*, p. 90. Wherever "work did not stop, it did not proceed normally," according to the *Obvinitel'nyi akt*; quoted in Los', "Dekabr'skoe vooruzhennoe vosstanie," p. 79.

[81] TsGAOR, M. Iu., f. 124, 1905, op. 44, d. 1310 (Ministry of Justice court report, July 21, 1906), p. 96.

[82] TsGIA USSR, f. 346, op. 1, d. 11 (*Obvinitel'nyi akt*), p. 30.

[83] Ershov, "Dekabr'skoe vooruzhennoe vosstanie," part 1, pp. 11, 15.

on display.[84] The battle detachment met no armed resistance in that or the other instances in which it disarmed troops and police.[85]

Strikers used armed force to disarm troops in a few other places, most notably in Iasinovataia on December 13. Iasinovataia's battle detachment surrounded and disarmed a large number of soldiers after the company commander refused to surrender peacefully. In the gunfire, the commander was killed and two of his troops suffered serious wounds.[86] Coupled with rumors that mutinies were occurring across Russia, the success of battle detachments in disarming soldiers made quite an impression, boosting confidence and bolstering spirits throughout the Donbass–Dnepr Bend revolutionary movement. Orators began to talk of seizing mines and factories and the necessity of an armed struggle with the government. Battle detachments built barricades in preparation for a confrontation with troops.[87]

Their ability to disarm troops inflated the battle detachments' sense of their own power, but because of the pogromist threat fellow workers posed, few revolutionary leaders believed that the December movement might end in success. According to one early Soviet account of December in the region, "everyone expected a repeat of the pogromist experience of the October days."[88] While the FSC in Ekaterinoslav posted battle detachments at various points around the city in the hope of preventing any pogromist activity, the danger of a pogrom appeared to be greatest in the mining districts, even though some mines had joined the strike wave.[89] For, as had been predicted, the December railroad strike threw ten thousand coal miners out of work.

From the first days of the December railroad strike, rumors spread of unemployed miners converging on railroad stations intent on wreaking havoc and looting. The tension grew with each day, as many believed miners were preparing for a second "cholera *bunt*." A few drunk miners getting into a fight often was sufficient to spark wild rumors of violence.[90] Panic gripped Avdeevka when a rumor spread that "hooligans" had surrounded the town. Residents "pleaded with Father Krasnopol'skii to open the

[84] Anisimov, *Vosstanie v Donetskom basseine*, p. 37.

[85] A similar coup occurred in Debal'tsevo, where members of the soviet captured the police's stockpile of thirty-five rifles (Shmorgun, *Sovety*, p. 43).

[86] K. Ershov, "Dekabr'skoe vooruzhennoe vosstanie v Donbasse," part 2, *Katorga i ssylka*, no. 10 (1930): 45; *Vysshii pod"em*, vol. 3, pt. 1:92.

[87] Ershov, "Dekabr'skoe vooruzhennoe vosstanie," part 1, p. 16; Anisimov, *Vosstanie v Donetskom basseine*, p. 42.

[88] Sergei Anisimov, *Gorlovskoe delo: Ocherk vosstaniia na linii Ekaterininskoi zheleznoi dorogi v 1905 godu* (Khar'kov, 1926), p. 10.

[89] *Ekaterinoslavshchina*, p. 218.

[90] Anisimov, *Gorlovskoe delo*, p. 10.

church in order to save our children from the miners."[91] Similar alarms were sounded elsewhere. The strike often cut communication between railroad stations, encouraging the spread of rumors and making it impossible to dispel them. After a few days of this, many Jews and mine and factory managers, as well as railroad employees and other residents, left the Donets Basin.[92]

To counter the pogromist threat, the Donbass–Dnepr Bend revolutionary movement concentrated on eliciting miners' participation in the large rallies radicals organized during November and throughout the December strike. Revolutionary activists even organized special trains to bring miners to and from the rallies. Revolutionaries hoped that the rallies would be able to defuse miners' anger at the strike.[93] Their efforts had mixed results.

Revolutionary orators tried hard not to offend miners' sensibilities at these mass meetings. In addition to demanding such economic improvements as higher wages and shorter workdays, orators commonly emphasized the goal of land and freedom rather than the overthrow of the autocracy when a large number of miners, other "backward" workers, and peasants from neighboring villages were present. Aware that unhappiness with the strike had strengthened monarchist sentiments, orators not only avoided attacking the tsar, they dropped the standard rallying cry of "Down with the autocracy!" The revolutionary speakers instead focused their rhetorical attacks on the tsar's ministers and the bureaucracy, themes to which even reactionaries could respond enthusiastically. The Socialist Revolutionaries dominated many of the station strike committees, and their populist speeches calling for the confiscation and redistribution of noble, church, and state lands to those who worked them, as well as the confiscation of mines and factories from their "parasitical" owners, were warmly received by the crowds of steel and railroad workers, miners, and peasants.[94] Such workers continued to share a worldview nicely characterized back in the 1890s by Semen Kanatchikov, a St. Petersburg metalworker and revolutionary worker-activist. Kanatchikov noted in his memoirs that workers "despised with an equal intensity factory management, police, and priests but tolerated no criticism of the tsar and God; their attitude was 'break the cup but don't touch the samovar.' "[95]

Revolutionaries in the Krivoi Rog used gross deceit in their attempt to defuse the threat to the strike posed by iron miners there. Revolutionary

[91] TsGIA USSR, f. 346, op. 1, d. 11 (*Obvinitel'nyi akt*), pp. 23, 38.

[92] Kharechko, *1905 god*, pp. 77–78.

[93] *Vysshii pod"em*, vol. 3, pt. 1:120.

[94] TsGIA USSR, f. 346, op. 1, d. 11 (*Obvinitel'nyi akt*), pp. 27–30; TsGAOR, M. Iu., f. 124, 1905, op. 44, d. 1310 (Ministry of Justice court report, August 4, 1906), pp. 115–116; Ershov, "Dekabr'skoe vooruzhennoe vosstanie," part 1, p. 21.

[95] Quoted in Brower, "Labor Violence," p. 428.

delegates from some stations organized rallies at Krivoi Rog mines in order to encourage workers to return to their home villages by telling them that the mines would be closed until spring. Throughout the Donbass–Dnepr Bend, unemployed workers could travel for free on the trains during the December railroad strike. Strike representatives even claimed that the long-awaited repartition of the land had begun. A massive exodus from Krivoi Rog mines began. After receiving their pay, thousands of Krivoi Rog miners returned to their native villages during the December general strike, as did other workers throughout the Donbass–Dnepr Bend.[96]

Reactionary sentiment came to the fore at many rallies despite the efforts of revolutionary orators. Angry workers could be heard demanding that the Jews present at rallies be compelled to leave.[97] The more loudmouthed among these workers, aware that the revolutionaries were evading the political issues, commonly challenged the orators. They yelled out, "What will happen to the tsar?" One of the most charismatic orators during December responded, "We need the tsar since we are little educated, but if the tsar doesn't like the new order, then he, perhaps, will have to go."[98] Such answers often failed to appease disgruntled workers. Fights erupted at some rallies where the speakers were more forthright. When an orator at the Iur'evsk factory ended a speech on December 11 by leading the crowd in the customary shout of "Down with the autocracy!" a fight broke out among the workers present. When another orator, the engineer Vasilii Kharchenko, tried to play peacemaker by stressing that it was not the tsar but his ministers, the police, and other bosses whose oppression of the *narod* needed to be stopped, one of the workers, Akin Tokar, yelled "Long live Tsar Nicholas II!" This started another scuffle as other workers denounced Tokar as a provocateur. The rally ended with competing renditions of "God Save the Tsar" and the "Marseillaise."[99] Here was a particularly graphic example of the seemingly bizarre juxtapositions that were a part of the Donbass–Dnepr Bend labor movement during the 1905 Revolution.

In the end, miners did not attack the railroad stations or embark on another pogromist rampage during the December strike. All the rumors of stations being ambushed proved to be unsubstantiated. The threat, none-

[96] *Gorno-zavodskii listok*, January 7, 1906, p. 8287; *Materialy po istorii* (Artemovsk), p. 164. Some instances of misinformation may not have been intentionally deceptive. Following the severing of communications with the capitals, wild rumors circulated that exaggerated the success achieved by the revolutionary movement elsewhere and may have been believed by some revolutionary activists (*Byloe*, no. 8 [1908]: 145).

[97] TsGAOR, M. Iu., f. 124, 1905, op. 44, d. 1310 (Ministry of Justice court report, August 4, 1906), pp. 116, 122.

[98] Ibid., p. 30.

[99] Ibid., p. 20; TsGIA USSR, f. 346, op. 1, d. 11 (*Obvinitel'nyi akt*), p. 38.

theless, did have a profound effect on the outcome of the strike. Rather than acting as a brake on the revolutionary movement, as had earlier threats of reactionary violence, the threat the miners posed had the opposite effect in December. It accelerated the militarization of the Donbass–Dnepr Bend labor movement.

The threat of a reactionary backlash largely accounts for the armed uprising in the Donbass–Dnepr Bend. Even though the miners, contrary to expectations, did not respond with violent hostility to the December strike, their anger with the general strike and generally violent proclivities, not to mention their role in the October pogroms, encouraged the Donbass–Dnepr Bend revolutionary movement to arm itself. Eyewitnesses across the political spectrum, from government officials to revolutionaries, agreed that the armed uprising in the Donbass–Dnepr Bend during December could be traced to the widespread creation of armed battle detachments that evolved out of the self-defense units formed in response to the earlier pogroms. There had been talk about forming battle detachments from the beginning of the 1905 Revolution, but it took the October pogroms and the November–December rumors to bring them into existence on a large scale.[100]

As in Ekaterinoslav, radicals in the Donets Basin raised money for arms in a variety of ways. Local administrators, fearful of pogroms and rioting, sometimes donated considerable sums. For example, at Gorlovka the station doctor donated 609 rubles for arms, while the station manager donated 300 rubles.[101] In addition to collecting money at meetings and from railroad passengers, the Gorlovka strike committee and others stole hundreds of rubles from station safes. In Popasnaia, the committee "taxed" each foreman and white-collar worker eighty kopecks. By taxing local merchants and landlords as well, the battle detachment there raised eighteen hundred rubles.[102] Members of the Enakievo soviet ordered the collection of fifty kopecks from each of the town residents.[103]

With these funds, battle detachments across the Donbass–Dnepr Bend, from Ekaterinoslav to small railroad stations, accumulated a stockpile of weapons probably unmatched in the empire. The detachments in towns such as Grishino and Avdeevka were among the best armed outside Ekaterinoslav, as an inventory of their weapons shows. The Grishino battle detachment possessed twenty-three rifles, forty shotguns, over fifty revolvers, some homemade bombs, and a considerable quantity of explosives obtained from nearby mines. The Avdeevka detachment had fifty-eight rifles, an unspecified number of shotguns, one hundred revolvers, and some dy-

[100] Kharechko, *1905 god*, p. 81.

[101] TsGIA USSR, f. 346, op. 1, d. 11 (*Obvinitel'nyi akt*), p. 2.

[102] Ershov, "Dekabr'skoe vooruzhennoe vosstanie," part 1, p. 17.

[103] Shmorgun, *Sovety*, p. 35.

namite. At the other extreme, however, many detachments were armed with nothing more than metal poles, which workers forged in their workshops and intended to use as if they were spears. Also, many of the firearms were of dubious quality; and the *druzhinniki*, as the members of the detachments were called, often had no experience shooting guns—although during the general strike, some detachments hurriedly organized weekend target practice.[104]

The armed uprising, when it did come, was less a sign of socialist or revolutionary consciousness than a product of the complex and variegated working-class consciousness that had been developing in the Donbass–Dnepr Bend over the decades. Terrible conditions, the prevalence of violence, deep social animosities, and the sense of power provided by arms and recent events led workers to rise up and assault government power directly. In earlier general strikes, Donbass–Dnepr Bend workers—including many whose seemingly enthusiastic support for the revolutionary movement was, in fact, shaky and could abruptly flip-flop—had pushed the revolutionary leadership to take more militant action. Workers had continually expressed their desire to confront troops and Cossacks with arms in hand. Numerous confrontations finally did occur in December throughout the region. None was as large or violent as that at the Donets Basin mining and factory town of Gorlovka, where a full-scale armed showdown with government troops occurred on December 17. One miner, N. S. Lialikov, later recalled, "I still didn't understand anything about politics. I had heard a lot about the manifesto and the Duma, but the essence of what was going on I understood only when workers were called to fight dragoons and Cossacks at Gorlovka . . . I hadn't figured out whether the tsar was a swine or not, but I knew it was necessary to help my fellow workers."[105]

Workers in Gorlovka had been particularly agitated even before the beginning of the railroad strike. Because of the state of the economy during November, the workers at the town's machine-building plant had agreed to reduce their workday from ten to six hours, with a corresponding cut in wages. But even before the general strike, at the beginning of December, these workers struck and demanded a return to longer shifts. Orators had encouraged the workers, telling them that the factory director had no right

[104] Anisimov, *Vosstanie v Donetskom basseine*, p. 59; Ershov, "Dekabr'skoe vooruzhennoe vosstanie," part 1, pp. 18–19; Berkhin, *Luganskaia bol'shevistskaia organizatsiia*, p. 83. When the mining engineer Aleksandr Fenin arrived at Debal'tsevo station, "the passengers' lounge was almost devoid of furniture, the buffet had been removed, and there was a large crowd of people armed with the most incredible weapons—home-made pikes, shotguns, even scythes, which gave the gathering the appearance of one of Pugachev's bands" (Aleksandr I. Fenin, *Coal and Politics in Late Imperial Russia: Memoirs of a Russian Mining Engineer*, trans. Alexandre Fediaevsky, ed. Susan P. McCaffray [De Kalb, Ill., 1990], pp. 158–159).

[105] Ershov, "Dekabr'skoe vooruzhennoe vosstanie," part 1, p. 13.

to reduce their hours after the company had made millions of rubles off workers' labor over the years.[106] The confrontation began during the December strike wave when the government regained its nerve and its confidence in troop reliability and set out to suppress the strike and restore order in the Donbass–Dnepr Bend. Gorlovka was its first target. Troops arrived on December 16. The Gorlovka strikers responded by sending a telegram to other centers of revolutionary activity in the Donbass–Dnepr Bend pleading for armed assistance. To the most militant revolutionaries, it appeared that the moment of truth—the long-talked-about armed uprising—had arrived.

The next day, December 17, saw one of the largest and bloodiest battles between government and radical forces to take place anywhere in the empire. Early that morning, eight commandeered trains carrying armed battle detachments from all over the Donets Basin (primarily Avdeevka, Debal'tsevo, Grishino, Iasinovataia, Iuzovka, and Enakievo), together with thousands of lightly armed supporters, braved a snowstorm and converged on Gorlovka. The size of the armed revolutionary forces that gathered at Gorlovka far exceeded the total number of *druzhinniki* who battled troops in Moscow, the focal point nationally of the December uprising.[107] However, most of the over four thousand insurgents were brandishing nothing more than such "cold" arms as the metal spears described above. Only about one hundred of the insurgents possessed rifles, while another five hundred members of the better-armed battle detachments arrived with revolvers.[108]

The military showdown in Gorlovka proved to be a tragic rout, as government troops easily made up in effectiveness what they lacked in numbers. The four to five thousand unorganized rebels were no match for a better-armed and better-trained force of three hundred Cossacks and soldiers. The insurgents lacked any real leadership. They did not even attempt a surprise attack. In the gunfire that continued for six hours, the battle detachments failed to use ten thousand of their bullets and the dynamite they had accumulated. Individual radicals in positions of leadership realized afterward that they had given little, if any, thought to how to actually wage an armed attack on government troops. Many battle-detachment

[106] TsGIA USSR, f. 346, op. 1, d. 11 (*Obvinitel'nyi akt*), pp. 26–27.

[107] "The most generous estimate, including replacements and substitutes, still does not exceed 2,000 squad members for the entire course of the [Moscow] insurrection" (Engelstein, *Moscow, 1905*, p. 201). However, because the military responded to the uprising in Moscow by brutally assaulting working-class districts in a barrage of artillery fire, injuring or killing thousands of noncombatants over the course of several days, the overall scale of the military confrontation in Moscow was much larger than in Gorlovka.

[108] Senchakova, *Boevaia rat'*, p. 144; TsGAOR, M. Iu., f. 124, 1905, op. 44, d. 1310 (Ministry of Justice court report, March 14, 1906), p. 34.

leaders simply assumed others could provide tactical guidance when it came time to do battle.[109]

Estimates of the number of casualties the insurgents suffered range from the tens to the hundreds. The government reported killing or wounding three hundred insurgents at Gorlovka. *Gorno-zavodskii listok* reported that thirty to thirty-five insurgents died, while a zemstvo doctor afterward counted only twenty-one bodies. These lower figures seem to be much closer to the mark, even if, as the government asserted, the rebels carried away many of their dead and wounded.[110] Three soldiers were killed and twenty wounded. The troops managed to arrest about five hundred of the rebels.[111]

The Gorlovka debacle demoralized the Donbass–Dnepr Bend revolutionary movement. No other major armed confrontations occurred as troops, dispelling any doubts about whether they would remain loyal to the autocracy, went down the railroad line dodging bullets, restoring order, and carrying out mass arrests. By December 21, the government had firmly reestablished control at most of the stations along the Ekaterinin line.

In Ekaterinoslav, troops and workers avoided an armed confrontation on the scale of the one in Gorlovka when the crack Simferopol regiment returned to the city on December 18, although insurgents initially did offer resistance when the authorities placed Ekaterinoslav under martial law and began to clear the streets.[112] Rebels fired on the soldiers from around street corners and threw thirty bombs. But they failed to deter the troops, even though from three to five hundred of the three thousand *druzhinniki* in Ekaterinoslav possessed arms.[113]

Even before the imposition of martial law, the lack of worker enthusiasm for continuing the strike—which had already lasted well over a week—was obvious. Some artisanal workshops had resumed production on December 17. Although factories did not reopen, the overwhelming majority of fac-

[109] TsGIA USSR, f. 346, op. 1, d. 11 (*Obvinitel'nyi akt*), pp. 14, 46; Ershov, "Dekabr'skoe vooruzhennoe vosstanie," part 2, pp. 48, 62; TsGAOR, M. Iu., f. 124, 1905, op. 44, d. 1310 (Ministry of Justice court report, December 21, 1905), p. 2; *Vysshii pod"em*, vol. 3, pt. 1:112.

[110] *Gorno-zavodskii listok*, January 7, 1906, p. 8286; Ershov, "Dekabr'skoe vooruzhennoe vosstanie," part 2, p. 61; TsGAOR, M. Iu., f. 124, 1905, op. 44, d. 1310 (Ministry of Justice court report, March 14, 1906), p. 36.

[111] TsGAOR, M. Iu., f. 124, 1905, op. 44, d. 1310 (Ministry of Justice court reports, December 21, 1905 and March 14, 1906), pp. 2, 36; *Materialy po istorii* (Artemovsk), p. 48. Eighty-four of the arrested were tried in 1908 and sentenced to hard labor; eight were given the death sentence and executed (Shmorgun, *Sovety*, p. 46n).

[112] *Ekaterinoslavshchina* (Police report, December 23, 1905), pp. 232–233. The authorities had already regained control over key points in the center of Ekaterinoslav on December 14.

[113] The *druzhinniki* death toll reached fifty, with another two hundred wounded (Los', "Dekabr'skoe vooruzhennoe vosstanie," p. 76).

tory workers clearly opposed continuation of the strike. The next day, December 18, clerks began to reopen stores and tram workers returned to work. By December 20, Ekaterinoslav's strike could be considered over.[114]

The leaders of the FSC, as well as all active revolutionaries, had retreated into the factory district when troops began to restore governmental control. Soldiers cordoned off the Chechelevka district on all sides. Describing the situation there as complete anarchy, the Okhrana chief reported that the revolutionary committee's hold over this area, known as the "Chechelevka Republic," could not be broken without additional troops. Some battle detachments still seemed determined to offer armed resistance if the government sent troops into the suburbs.[115]

Throughout the course of the December strike, Donbass–Dnepr Bend radicals had looked to the capitals and anxiously awaited news of the events there. "Everyone expected the outcome of the insurrection to be decided in the centers, in Moscow and St. Petersburg."[116] In Ekaterinoslav, the *Bulletin* of the FSC devoted considerable space to events in Moscow, where troops had brutally extinguished rebel street fighting on December 18. On December 22, word reached Ekaterinoslav that the Moscow strike had ended. Ekaterinoslav's FSC, which had been prepared to resist the entrance of troops into the Chechelevka district, decided to forgo a violent confrontation. There seemed to be little reason to resist, given Ekaterinoslav's isolation. The Assembly of Workers' Deputies convened on December 22 and heard a member of the Social Democratic party in Moscow report on how events had unfolded there. The meeting ended with a formal resolution to end the strike. With bravado, Ekaterinoslav's FSC refused to concede defeat. Its final resolution declared, "We were not alone in the struggle. We fought together and were strong. Ending the strike together, we will remain strong and in that way not disperse our strength. We will preserve our strength for that moment when fire engulfs all Russia. We are not retreating; we are putting our arms in scabbards to await the signal when together with all of Russia we will again go to battle."[117] And it was not until December 28 that troops finally regained control of the Chechelevka district and put an end to the "republic." In the weeks that followed, the government decapitated the revolutionary parties, rounding up dozens of the leaders who had come out into the open and shown their faces after

[114] TsGAOR, DP OO, f. 102, 1905, d. 4, ch. 17, vol. 4 (Okhrana report, December 26, 1905), p. 169; TsGAOR, DP OO, f. 102, 1906, op. 234, d. 7, ch. 34, p. 10.

[115] *Vysshii pod"em*, vol. 3, pt. 1:104; TsGAOR, DP OO, f. 102, 1906, op. 234, d. 7, ch. 34, p. 9; Lane, *Roots*, p. 174.

[116] Ershov, "Dekabr'skoe vooruzhennoe vosstanie," part 2, p. 48.

[117] *Biulleten*, no. 8 (December 25, 1905), quoted in Los', "Dekabr'skoe vooruzhennoe vosstanie," p. 84.

the October Manifesto. Other locally prominent revolutionaries eluded arrest and fled the Donbass–Dnepr Bend.[118]

Between 1903 and December 1905, the revolutionary movement in southern Russia proved to be exceptionally militant. Pressure from the Donbass–Dnepr Bend labor movement helped to radicalize the capitals, just as the revolutionary fervor in St. Petersburg and Moscow encouraged radicals in Ekaterinoslav and elsewhere in the Donbass–Dnepr Bend.[119] But without the continuation of revolutionary pressure in the capitals, revolutionary assaults in a provincial center such as Ekaterinoslav were doomed to fail, even when the revolutionaries could control the city more effectively than was possible in the capitals. Donbass–Dnepr Bend revolutionaries had long realized that they were not in a position to lead the revolution in Russia. With the capitals' failure in December, what was left of the revolutionary movement in Ekaterinoslav lost heart.

The militance of the Donbass–Dnepr Bend revolutionary movement in December owed much to the workers' reactionary potential. In December the tension within the working class between revolution and reaction, which had long been evident, once again became a central dynamic in the revolutionary process in the Donbass–Dnepr Bend. Miners' proven proclivity toward violence in revolutionary situations provoked rumors and fears as the railroad strike threatened to cost miners their jobs. The revolutionary movement armed itself to combat the counterrevolutionary threat of pogroms and attacks on railroad "employees." Strikers throughout the region joined self-defense units that evolved into battle detachments. As the strike unfolded, even many of the miners, whom the workers thought to be most hostile to the goals of the general strike, were once again drawn into the revolutionary movement. Many miners joined the workers who responded to the call to support their fellow workers under siege in Gorlovka in an unexpected display of working-class solidarity.

Following the defeat of the revolutionary movement in Ekaterinoslav and across the Donbass–Dnepr Bend in December, a reactionary mood once again spread among workers, as if on cue. When troops easily crushed the Gorlovka uprising, workers accused revolutionary leaders of cowardice and of betraying workers. Rumors spread from all sides regarding violent reprisals against those thought to be responsible for the failure of the strike and uprising.[120] But any mass reprisal was preempted by government ac-

[118] TsGAOR, DP OO, f. 7, 1906, ch. 34, p. 14; TsGAOR, DP OO, f. 25, 1906, ch. 8, p. 8.

[119] Reichman, *Railwaymen and Revolution*, pp. 308–309.

[120] Kharechko, *1905 god*, pp. 109–110.

tion. Through mass arrests, the government took the lead in the merciless attack on the revolutionary movement that followed the crushing of the December strike throughout Russia. Radicals had come out into the open following the October Manifesto, making it easy for the government to destroy the soviets and gut the revolutionary movement in January 1906. The secret police also enjoyed unprecedented success in its effort to permeate the revolutionary movement with agents provocateurs. Distrust poisoned relations among those who managed to escape arrest, and it threw local organizations into disarray. Employer lockouts and the threat of more pogroms further demoralized radicals; and the Donbass–Dnepr Bend revolutionary movement failed to revive as a mass movement in 1906.[121] When the Social Democrats, now woefully out of touch with the mood of the working class, called for a general strike in July 1906 to protest the autocracy's decision to dissolve the First Duma just months after its convocation, workers failed to respond. Support for battle detachments vanished. Unrest and revolutionary upheaval did not end in December 1905—waves of peasant rebellion, strikes, terrorist assaults and killings, as well as arson and rioting, continued on a significant scale in the Donbass–Dnepr Bend through 1906 and into 1907—but a decade passed before the Donbass–Dnepr Bend labor movement again became a powerful revolutionary force.

For the mass of workers, the first Russian revolution confirmed their distrust of the revolutionaries. Revolutionary *intelligenty* responded in kind. Even some Social Democratic party leaders bluntly expressed their frustration with the working class, as they had before the revolutionary upsurge. At the united SD congress in 1906, the Menshevik leader Pavel Akselrod declared, "I think it is our duty to point out to the workers with complete frankness that they, in the mass, are still very backward and that even their advanced elements are still only in the first stages of their political development."[122]

In local party ranks, mass desertions from the revolutionary underground ensued. In the period following the 1905 Revolution, before the Lena goldfields massacre in 1912 and World War One rejuvenated the movement, the Donbass–Dnepr Bend revolutionary underground all but disappeared. Just a few years after the 1905 Revolution, Ekaterinoslav's SD organization had only one active *intelligent*, while an SD correspondent from Lugansk reported that "there does not remain a single old comrade . . . the intellectuals sleep and wish to do nothing."[123]

[121] Nikolaenko, *Revoliutsionnoe dvizhenie*, pp. 35, 54, 68; *Donetskie novosti*, no. 2 (July 22, 1906): 3.

[122] *Chetvertyi (ob'edinitel'nyi) s"ezd RSDRP: Protokoly* (Moscow, 1959), pp. 320–321, quoted in Ascher, *Pavel Axelrod*, p. 246.

[123] *Golos Sotsial-demokrata*, no. 19–20 (January–February 1910), quoted in Elwood, *Russian Social Democracy*, p. 62.

Conclusion

HISTORIANS of Russia have devoted little attention to the working class's violent, pogromist side. As this study has demonstrated, however, workers in the country's major mining and metallurgical region produced a mixed and volatile labor movement. Workers in the Donbass–Dnepr Bend repeatedly united in revolutionary strikes, rallies, and confrontations with troops. They also engaged in bloody pogroms and counterrevolutionary backlashes, which regularly followed on the heels of mass revolutionary demonstrations. General strikes and pogroms, and the dynamic between them, together reflected the shifting, politically contradictory hostilities and allegiances among Donbass–Dnepr Bend workers during the 1905 Revolution.

The strains of late-nineteenth-century economic and social development in the region were largely responsible for creating this kind of unrest. To be sure, political events and the government's suppression of collective action triggered Donbass–Dnepr Bend workers' revolutionary and reactionary sympathies and actions during the 1903–5 period, but the scope and militance of this mass movement cannot be understood without an appreciation of its economic and social origins.

The migrants recruited to work in the mining and steel industries arrived with troubles brought from their native villages, as the authorities often asserted when trying to explain labor disorders. But the discontent that erupted was primarily the result of conditions in the Donbass–Dnepr Bend. The economic transformation of this coal- and iron-rich region in the late nineteenth century was extremely rapid, even in comparison with the rest of the empire during this period. In the short span of the last three decades of the century, the Donbass–Dnepr Bend became Russia's steel and mining heartland. The telescoped pace of industrialization produced dramatic demographic change in the region. Industrial villages, towns, and cities mushroomed, attracting people with different backgrounds and identities. The Donbass–Dnepr Bend's rapid growth, coupled with its location within the Pale of Settlement, created a work force and environment that was ethnically and regionally more diverse than elsewhere in the Slavic regions of the empire.

Creating a tolerable working and living environment and a productive labor force in such rapidly changing conditions would have been difficult even for a society far better equipped or more committed to meet such challenges than tsarist Russia. The industrialists drawn to the Donbass–Dnepr Bend by the prospect of reaping high profits were forced to create a working class almost from scratch. The overwhelmingly young, male, Russian workers who found unskilled, semiskilled, or skilled employment in the new mines and steel mills worked long, arduous hours. Working conditions were no better for the Jews who left the congested northwestern Pale of Settlement for jobs in the artisanal and retail sectors created by rapid urbanization in the Donbass–Dnepr Bend. Jewish artisans and salesclerks generally worked even longer hours and for less pay than miners and steelworkers.[1] Artisans' discontent grew as handicraft workshops became larger in an increasingly desperate attempt to compete with factory-produced goods and as the chance for apprentices and journeymen ever to own their own shops grew remote.

Donbass–Dnepr Bend workers lived in factory and mining boomtowns notorious for abominable conditions. The seemingly indifferent government did little to ease the problems rapid industrialization and urbanization created. Social and public services were barely funded and in short supply in company towns. The link between material conditions and violent unrest was nowhere as clear as in the Iuzovka "cholera riot" of 1892. Local governmental authorities did little toward providing water supplies and sewage systems, the lack of which caused outbreaks of cholera, typhoid, and other diseases among workers. The cholera epidemic in Iuzovka in 1892 helped provoke one of the most violent and destructive working-class riots Russia saw in the late nineteenth century. Such conditions existed to some degree in other parts of Russia, but medical investigators, as well as visitors to the Donbass–Dnepr Bend, were nearly unanimous in pronouncing the area among the filthiest and municipally least developed in the empire.

The large industrial firms made some effort to compensate for the inadequacy of government programs in the Donbass–Dnepr Bend. Industrialists built worker housing and hospitals, but their efforts hardly began to meet the workers' needs as industrial centers continued to grow rapidly. The improvements in living conditions that company investments achieved by the end of the nineteenth century were usually limited: instead of living crammed together in mud dugouts (*zemlianki*), most miners lived crammed together in earthen-floor company barracks.

The density of the working-class population in the Donbass–Dnepr Bend was higher than elsewhere in Russia. The giant steel mills and mines constructed by foreign capital in the late nineteenth century were large even by international standards. Outside the workplace, workers in Donbass–Dnepr Bend industrial towns and cities lived in an environment more predominantly working-class than in towns and cities elsewhere in Russia.

During their stay in the Donbass–Dnepr Bend, the mass of workers

[1] Artisans' jobs, however, were physically less hazardous than jobs in the mines and mills.

lived apart from the stabilizing influences of home and family. They customarily sought release from intolerable conditions in heavy drinking, brutal fighting, and constant movement from enterprise to enterprise. The mines, which were usually desperate for workers, became notorious for employing the most unsavory characters. This ruffian element within the Donbass–Dnepr Bend working class was also prominent in the steel plants, primarily among the young, single, highly transient, and poorly paid day laborers (*chernorabochie*) and blast-furnace workers. The preponderantly male composition of the population, with its male culture of drinking and gambling—along with the filth of working-class districts, large number of taverns, high rates of violent crime, and distance from families and the central government—gave these districts a wild character.

The masculine, hard-drinking, lawless environment in the industrial towns of the Donbass–Dnepr Bend, combined with deplorable living conditions, workers' belief that they were being exploited by foreign bosses, and animosities created by the rapid influx into factories, mines, and artisanal workshops of so many people from different backgrounds, made violent outbursts of labor unrest likely.[2] Six years after the "cholera riot" in Iuzovka, workers in Ekaterinoslav went on a similar rampage. Time and again, Donbass–Dnepr Bend workers showed a proclivity for violent expression of their discontent. The destruction they wreaked was unmatched in the Russian empire in the last decade of the nineteenth century. While violence often took the form of attacks on factory and governmental authorities and property, ethnic hostility provided a third target, as Slavic workers in the region turned their discontent and propensity for violence against Jews. As elsewhere in Russia and Europe, anti-Semitism was flourishing among workers and other socially and economically frustrated elements of the population. The 1883 pogrom, in which railroad workers ransacked Ekaterinoslav's Jewish community in the early years of industrialization, proved to be a harbinger of things to come. Donbass–Dnepr Bend workers moved from factory and government targets to pogromist targets during the course of the two major riots in the 1890s. They did so repeatedly in 1905.

Terrified by these displays of working-class violence, industrialists and a small number of public-spirited members of the local intelligentsia pinned their hopes for avoiding class and ethno-religious strife on raising the cultural level of the working class. In addition to building and staffing a high percentage of the schools in the Donbass–Dnepr Bend, industrialists opened libraries and reading rooms. Beginning in the 1890s, philanthropic

[2] Drunkenness was hardly the primary cause of labor violence in the Donbass–Dnepr Bend, but there is no denying that heavy drinking helped workers overcome their usual diffidence in the face of authorities and helped unleash their penchant for violence.

organizations as well as industrial enterprises built auditoriums and organized public readings and theatrical presentations. Ekaterinoslav's workers could attend evening and Sunday schools. The city's reformers recognized that unless they moderated mass working-class ignorance and drunkenness, there was little hope that workers would resist future appeals to riot and attack the social order.[3] That such attempts to stave off violent labor unrest failed may have been simply a matter of too little, too late. But it is hard to imagine the mass of Donbass–Dnepr Bend workers voluntarily abandoning drinking, gambling, and fighting for reading and "uplifting" cultural programs.

While there was perhaps more reason for labor discontent in the Donbass–Dnepr Bend than elsewhere in Russia (despite the above-average wages employers paid), outside the city of Ekaterinoslav there were also greater obstacles to the development of a coordinated labor movement. First, the mills and mines around which workers were concentrated were located in isolated towns and villages scattered all over the region, making coordination among them extremely difficult. Second, the working-class composition of Donbass–Dnepr Bend mining and factory towns made it difficult for radical *intelligenty* in these towns to conceal their identity from the authorities and avoid arrest. Third, since almost no industry existed in the region before the 1870s and since the working class was particularly young and transient, the Donbass–Dnepr Bend lacked even the minimum of working-class tradition and solidarity found in central Russia. Management's inability to recruit more than a small percentage of the needed work force from among the Ukrainian peasantry meant most Donbass–Dnepr Bend workers had shallow roots in the region. Developing continuity in the labor movement generally proved extremely difficult. The workers drawn to the Donbass–Dnepr Bend were not the sort from which a disciplined labor movement is easily made. The mass of workers had little interest in running the risks necessary to organize for future, nonviolent change. Among the miners especially, workers viewed their life in the Donbass–Dnepr Bend as a temporary expedient to be abandoned as soon as possible. Throughout the period covered by this study, revolutionaries bemoaned workers' common belief that they were not workers, but transplanted peasants earning some cash in order to improve their lot in the distant villages of central Russia. The ruffian elements within the Donbass–Dnepr Bend working class were no more inclined to view socialism or the radical *intelligenty* as their saviors than they were to respond to the cultural offerings of the industrial and middle-class philanthropists.

[3] This was an empirewide phenomenon. For example, reformers in Moscow likewise thought only a literate, sober worker "would resist the appeals of demagogues of the right and the left" and "avoid class strife" (Joseph Bradley, "Moscow: From Big Village to Metropolis," in Hamm, *The City in Late Imperial Russia*, p. 34).

Western historians, while noting that the more skilled, urbanized workers and artisans in Russia were the most politically active and radical, have often assumed that the mass of peasant-workers, because they were the most uprooted and the most exploited, were prone to follow radicals in a revolutionary situation. Donbass–Dnepr Bend Social Democrats knew otherwise. Revolutionary activists in the region, the Social Democrats particularly, recognized that the especially transient and peasant character of the workers made them politically conservative and prone to riot—the Russian peasant's traditional answer to distress. But while Donbass–Dnepr Bend workers proved difficult to organize and control, they did express their economic discontent in collective actions from the 1870s to 1905. The number of strikes and riots grew with each decade. Skilled workers usually opposed the violent outbursts and acted as a countervailing force to the violent proclivities of the mass of workers in the Donbass–Dnepr Bend labor force. On occasion they succeeded in stopping workers intent on smashing, looting, and burning company property. In 1905, however, when skilled, educated workers came to the fore in the Donbass–Dnepr Bend—as elsewhere in the empire—neither these workers nor *intelligent* party leaders proved capable of subduing the more spontaneous and violent sides of the labor movement.

The Donbass–Dnepr Bend revolutionary and labor movements evolved parallel to one another during the late nineteenth century. It was *intelligenty* exiled to the Donbass–Dnepr Bend from elsewhere who were responsible for forming the revolutionary parties. In comparison with the movement in cities elsewhere, where contacts with workers were generally few, radicalism established a relatively strong foothold in the Donbass–Dnepr Bend, particularly in Ekaterinoslav, from the 1870s on. Although before the twentieth century they made no progress in overcoming the obstacles to leading the mass of workers in the Donbass–Dnepr Bend, virtually every revolutionary party and group enjoyed as much success in Ekaterinoslav as anywhere in the empire. By attracting an increasing number of recruits from among skilled workers—usually Russian steel and railroad workers and Jewish artisans—the Donbass–Dnepr Bend revolutionary movement grew, despite waves of arrests that temporarily decimated the movement.

The importance of the revolutionary parties in the development of the labor movement has been a matter of debate in Russian historiography. In the Donbass–Dnepr Bend, the revolutionary parties did play an important vanguard role; revolutionaries undoubtedly pushed workers in a radical direction. They educated worker-activists, distributed leaflets among the mass of workers, and called general strikes. But revolutionaries were hardly in control. Workers influenced the radical *intelligenty* perhaps as much as the radical *intelligenty* influenced them. The characteristic features of the

Donbass–Dnepr Bend revolutionary movement were largely shaped by the local conditions discussed above and by the revolutionary and reactionary sentiments of Donbass–Dnepr Bend workers.

One problem that plagued revolutionary parties throughout Russia—the tension over the intelligentsia leadership's desire to maintain control and secrecy—was aggravated in the Donbass–Dnepr Bend by ethnic animosity. Revolutionary leaders in the region faced personal hostility from Slavic workers because many of the leaders were Jewish. In addition to having to concern themselves with channeling the workers' virulent anti-Semitism away from pogroms, leaders within the Donbass–Dnepr Bend revolutionary movement often had to face more covert hostility from among the "conscious" workers as well, directed against themselves as Jews.

Workers' proclivity to engage in pogroms made it especially difficult for the revolutionary movement in the Donbass–Dnepr Bend to direct worker discontent toward revolutionary actions. The Social Democrats constantly worried that the radical demonstrations and strikes they organized would degenerate into riots and pogroms. As a result, revolutionaries in the Donbass–Dnepr Bend were often afraid to "unleash" the working class and were sometimes forced to cancel calls for strikes or demonstrations. Because the revolutionary spirit workers exhibited on many occasions evaporated in the face of ethnic animosity and frustrations with the outcome of mass actions, Social Democrats in the Donbass–Dnepr Bend were often placed in an ironic position for revolutionaries: they were compelled to play a moderating role and, once pogroms erupted, to chastise and attack the worker masses they had been courting. All the revolutionary parties, not just the Bund and Labor Zionists, formed self-defense units to combat pogroms.

In addition to ethnic tensions, partisan fighting within and between the revolutionary parties hurt the Donbass–Dnepr Bend revolutionary movement and weakened its authority among the workers. Nonetheless, between 1903 and 1905 the revolutionaries' propaganda and agitation campaigns, combined with discontent over working and living conditions and with the perception that the autocracy was losing its grip, made possible the transition from isolated work stoppages and short-lived, violent outbursts to more coordinated, politically powerful labor actions. Donbass–Dnepr Bend workers—Russian and Ukrainian skilled and unskilled workers, as well as Jewish artisans and clerks—responded to the revolutionaries' calls to strike en masse. These workers proved themselves capable of large-scale revolutionary actions with a militance perhaps unmatched in Russia. From the first general strike in 1903 through the 1905 Revolution, the effects of calls for a general strike were always explosive. Revolutionary confrontations between masses of workers and troops occurred repeatedly.

The strong sense of radical class consciousness that Donbass–Dnepr Bend workers developed was most evident in the armed uprising at Gorlovka in December 1905. However, the political consciousness and militance the Donbass–Dnepr Bend labor movement displayed during 1905 never eradicated workers' willingness to engage in reactionary violence at the same time. There was no linear development of the whole labor movement from "backward" to "class conscious" or from spontaneous to organized. Both aspects of the Donbass–Dnepr Bend labor movement continued to exist throughout the 1905 Revolution.

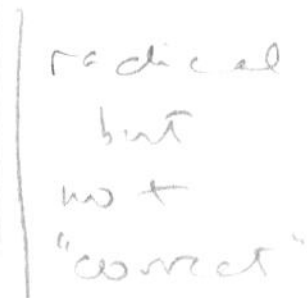

Because the only successful working-class revolution occurred in Russia in 1917, Western labor historians have concentrated on explaining the development there of a revolutionary, working-class consciousness. Much of this discussion shows the influence of E. P. Thompson's seminal work *The Making of the English Working Class*.[4] For example, Diane Koenker argued, following Thompson, that Russian workers' class consciousness did not emerge automatically (in a deterministic sense) from prevailing economic conditions. According to Koenker, the necessary psychological dimension emerged only during class struggle itself as part of the process of the struggle. It was then that wage earners developed a sense of their common identity and truly became a class.[5] But the history of the Donbass–Dnepr Bend labor movement shows that the process by which revolutionary class consciousness developed is only half the story. Working-class solidarity could quickly evaporate. While the labor movement produced radical class consciousness among some workers, it simultaneously spawned a reactionary consciousness, sometimes even among the same workers. In order to understand the Revolution of 1905, one must see these two developments as part of the same process.

Most workers in the Donbass–Dnepr Bend had a strong sense that their interests conflicted sharply with the interests of their employers. The fact that their employers were foreigners facilitated the mining and metallurgical workers' deep sense that their relationship with the management of their enterprises was one of "us" against "them." But the emergence of a radical class consciousness within the Donbass–Dnepr Bend working class had to overcome conflicting internal tensions among workers themselves. While radicalization of the Donbass–Dnepr Bend working class was evident in the success of calls for general strikes, mass actions also intensified the divisions that existed within worker ranks and between workers and *intelligent* activists.

In the Donbass–Dnepr Bend, there were ethnic and regional differences on top of the usual divisions within the working class based on level of

[4] E. P. Thompson, *The Making of the English Working Class* (New York, 1963).

[5] Koenker, *Moscow Workers*, pp. 8–10.

skill, amount of pay, and type of industry. Residential patterns reinforced workers' regional and ethnic identification. Jewish workers lived in the town centers, in their master's workshop or in hovels; migrant Great Russian and Ukrainian workers customarily lived crammed together with fellow workers from the same region, their *zemliaki*, in the industrial suburbs or in the districts around their factory or mine. *Zemliaki* sought each other out in the Donbass–Dnepr Bend, as elsewhere in Russia, and banded together on and off the job. The intensity of *zemliachestvo* was apparent in the brawling that occurred both among Great Russian workers from various regions and between Russian and Ukrainian workers. But these regional divisions within the Donbass–Dnepr Bend working class paled before the demarcation, based on ethnicity, that separated industrial workers from artisans. The virulent hostility that the heterogeneous industrial working class collectively harbored toward Jews was not directed exclusively at well-off Jews, but also included the region's Jewish artisans.

The impact of ethnic and regional diversity in the Russian work force needs to be included in historians' conception of Russian labor history. As in the American South, the heterogeneity of the Donbass–Dnepr Bend working class made class politics difficult and posed a major obstacle to the development of radical class consciousness and organization along class lines. The ruffian, pogromist component of the working class particularly failed to remain class-conscious supporters of the radical cause.

The traditional argument that Bloody Sunday marked a fundamental transformation of the Russian labor movement overlooks continued tensions within the movement. A significant transition did occur during the 1905 Revolution, but the Donbass–Dnepr Bend workers' capacity to effect revolutionary change did not mean that the mass of workers was no longer an extremely volatile group, prone to express discontent in spontaneous, destructive, and reactionary violence. In October 1905, during the worst pogroms to erupt in prerevolutionary Russia, some pogromists made their mixed consciousness explicit when they carried revolutionary flags as well as portraits of the tsar.

It was the grievances workers accumulated during the general strikes—not only the prospect of loot and violent excess—that led to pogroms and attacks on Jewish revolutionaries and artisans. Jewish activism in the revolutionary movement was provocative and disturbing to the mass of workers. In addition, frustration with the goals and tactics pursued by the revolutionary leadership provoked a counterrevolutionary mood among workers as strikes and general strikes wound down. The general strikes' failure to achieve economic advances or other tangible improvements in working-class conditions aroused workers' anger toward the revolutionary movement and its leaders. General strikes involved considerable risks and sacrifices for workers. In addition to the risk of arrest and death in confrontations with troops, general strikes meant the loss of wages, which hit the most poorly paid, unskilled workers the hardest. In spreading the general strike, supporters did not hesitate to use intimidation and force against defiant workers. Many workers bitterly resented being forced to go on strike, while many others must have had mixed feelings. In the aftermath of the October general strike, even many of the more politically radical workers, who had supported the general strike with enthusiasm, felt they had been duped and used by revolutionary leaders. Few workers shared the liberal political goals of the major revolutionary parties in the 1905 Revolution. Unlike general strikes, the looting that was an integral part of the reactionary backlashes satisfied workers' immediate economic needs.

There was considerable overlap in the composition of general-strike and pogromist crowds; the mass of semiskilled and unskilled workers constituted the largest component in the biggest crowds, whether revolutionary or reactionary. Yet in the two forms of mass action, a significant difference can be discerned between the role of skilled workers and that of the mass of semiskilled and unskilled workers. The more skilled, urbanized, and literate artisans and industrial workers were the most enthusiastic supporters of general strikes and often did their best to prevent strikes from degenerating into pogroms. Skilled workers commonly chose to align themselves with Jewish artisans and the revolutionary *intelligenty*. They took up arms in opposition to pogroms and, in effect, against the mass of unskilled workers and miners, who showed a distinct lack of respect for the authority of the revolutionary parties trying to lead the working-class movement. The clash between skilled, radical workers and the mass of workers became so intense that during pogromist rampages, radical *intelligenty* and skilled workers not only found the mass of workers disregarding their advice and guidance, they could even find themselves lumped together with Jews as the targets of the workers' violent rage. The Russian Revolution of 1905 and its ultimate failure cannot be understood without recognizing the contradictions that appeared in particularly extreme forms in the Donbass–Dnepr Bend. Reactionary backlashes were an integral part of the revolutionary process in the Donbass–Dnepr Bend. During the 1905 Revolution, the revolutionaries' repeated success in galvanizing and then channeling working-class hostility coexisted with repeated failure to restrain workers accustomed to expressing anger in destructive violence.

Although the backlash of reactionary violence usually undermined revolutionary aims, the defense organized against the backlash contributed directly to the militarization of the revolutionary movement during the last stage of the 1905 Revolution. The threat of pogromist attacks by miners during the general strike in December intensified the militance of the revolutionary movement. The self-defense units that had formed during the course of 1905 to combat pogromists evolved into battle detachments, armed and ready to combat government troops in December. Rather than serving as a brake on the revolutionary movement, as earlier threats of reactionary violence had, the threat posed by the pogromist miners in December promoted the militarization of the Donbass–Dnepr Bend labor movement.

Radical working-class militance, then, was only one side of the revolutionary coin during the 1905 Revolution. For Donbass–Dnepr Bend workers angry with the revolutionary movement during the 1903–5 revolutionary surge, the Jewish presence in the Donbass–Dnepr Bend provided a scapegoat that local authorities often allowed workers to victimize with impunity. By participating in pogroms, the same class that provided the revolution with its power ultimately undermined the revolutionary movement and made it easier for the government to reassert its control after 1905.

Following the precipitous decline in the tsarist government's authority in the Donbass–Dnepr Bend in November and early December 1905, the government regrouped; by the end of December, loyal military forces had regained the upper hand in Ekaterinoslav and along the railroad lines. In the months that followed, the revolutionary movement disintegrated as mass arrests, government repression, and worker exhaustion prevented another swing in the pendulum toward a revolutionary upsurge. Most of the radical activists who escaped the wave of arrests in early 1906 went into hiding. Others, shocked and disillusioned by the pogroms and the violence the revolution had unleashed, began to drift away from the revolutionary movement, prompting Lenin to conclude ruefully a couple of years later that "the revolution . . . brought out onto the surface so many casuals, so many 'knights for a day,' so many newcomers, that it was quite inevitable that very many of them should lack any kind of integrated outlook on the world."[6] Socialist Revolutionaries and Anarchists continued revolutionary activity, but they abandoned mass politics for individual terror. Their numerous victims, who included foremen, managers, policemen, and Ekaterinoslav's governor, testified to the fact that the revolutionaries had not completely given up hope; but the labor movement was limited to occasional, isolated strikes. Lockouts and layoffs further demoralized workers, and pogrom rumors spread sporadically. By the end of 1906, any lingering hopes that the decapitated revolutionary movement might revive the mass movement soon disappeared. The "dress rehearsal" for the revolution, pogroms, and civil war of 1917–21 was over.

[6] *Proletarii*, no. 13 (November 13, 1908), quoted in Lenin, *Collected Works* 15:289.

In concluding, it is important to note that the failure of revolutionary ideology to penetrate worker attitudes in the Donbass–Dnepr Bend was characteristic of the Russian labor movement as a whole. Throughout Russia during this period, liberal or socialist principles and theories, although embraced by a core of worker-*intelligents*, remained alien to the mass of barely literate workers.

The small size of "educated society" in a provincial region such as the Donbass–Dnepr Bend meant that intelligentsia culture did not exert the influence on the mass movement that it could in the capitals. Even so, the St. Petersburg revolutionary movement, like that in the Donbass–Dnepr Bend, constantly needed to struggle against worker violence. In the early stages, there was a conspicuous difference between the organized, nonviolent 1896 textile workers' strike in St. Petersburg and the 1898 Briansk riot, but activists in St. Petersburg also feared that the workers' low level of consciousness might produce just such a *bunt* as the one that erupted in Ekaterinoslav.[7] When the Soiuz Bor'by began its agitational campaigns in the capital, it continually emphasized the need for workers to forsake violence. Just as in Ekaterinoslav, Soiuz Bor'by leaflets in St. Petersburg implored workers, "Let us prove that the working people can pursue their demands . . calmly and resolutely, without uproar or violence" and "Let's keep calm and show the government that they are not dealing with ruffians, but with conscious and courageous workers."[8] While the number of disciplined, highly literate, and politicized workers was much larger in the capitals, the mass of workers in both regions shared an aversion to "abstract" politics, a frustration with the outcome of general strikes, and a proclivity for violence. At a mass meeting in St. Petersburg after Bloody Sunday, workers jeered an SD orator and shouted, "You pushed us into the abyss! It's necessary to hang you."[9] A Bolshevik activist in Moscow, A. V. Sokolov, recalled that when the "genuine gray masses from the workers' districts" came to mass meetings during the October general strike, they became angry if economic demands did not take precedence. Workers protested when agitators introduced political slogans. "We thought that real business would be discussed here, and once again they're trying to stuff

[7] McDaniel states that "in one St. Petersburg *bunt*' of 1890, for example, the workers almost drowned one engineer in a canal and they got as far as constructing a gallows for the factory director" (*Autocracy, Capitalism, and Revolution*, p. 177).

[8] Quoted in Wildman, *Making of a Workers' Revolution*, p. 65.

[9] S. I. Somov, "Iz istorii sotsialdemokraticheskogo dvizheniia v Peterburge v 1905 godu (lichnye vospominaniia)," *Byloe*, pt. 1, no. 16 (1907): 42, quoted in McDaniel, *Autocracy, Capitalism, and Revolution*, p. 175.

us with politics!"[10] Although they deemphasize it, Gerald Surh and Laura Engelstein note repeated instances of worker violence in their studies of 1905 in St. Petersburg and Moscow. As in the Donbass–Dnepr Bend and elsewhere in the empire, worker threats and violence against those who refused to leave their jobs were a regular feature in strikes in the capitals.[11]

The differences in crowd behavior were due more to the sizable Jewish population and the absence of inhibiting factors in the Donbass–Dnepr Bend than to the presence there of a unique proclivity for violence or some other ruffian quality. In the capitals, with their concentration of liberal professionals and white-collar groups, the 1905 Revolution was much more of an all-class affair. Yet in Moscow, for example, crowds of strike supporters did break windows, damage factory property, and loot during the October general strike, as earlier.[12] Then, during the reactionary backlash that followed—especially after news of the pogromist rampages in other cities reached Moscow—crowds of drunken workers and other "Black Hundreds" ran down streets breaking windows, plundering and destroying private property, shouting "Beat up the Jews!" and assaulting students and others. Dozens were killed, including a veteran Bolshevik activist who was shot and then beaten to death by a worker.[13] In St. Petersburg, Black Hundred sentiment, benefiting from hostility toward the strike organizers, gained considerable working-class support.[14] In addition, similar motives and conditions produced violence, which, in the absence of a significant Jewish scapegoat population, was directed at other targets. As Joan Neuberger shows, hooligans, many of whom were unskilled or casual laborers,

[10] Sokolov, A. V. [Stanislav Vol'skii], "O 1905 gode," in *O 1905 gode: Vospominaniia*, ed. N. Rozhkov and A. Sokolov (Moscow, 1929), pp. 42–43, quoted in Engelstein, *Moscow, 1905*, p. 109. See also McDaniel, *Autocracy, Capitalism, and Revolution*, p. 219.

[11] According to Engelstein, in Moscow "few factories appear to have closed simply on the initiative of their own workers" (*Moscow, 1905*, p. 112; see also p. 77). Surh states in his study of St. Petersburg that "the role of force and the threat of force are mentioned with disturbing regularity in strike reports written by the authorities. The use of force cannot be denied, but neither can it be documented with sufficient accuracy to gauge its overall importance" (*1905 in St. Petersburg*, p. 313). For Kiev, see Michael F. Hamm, "Continuity and Change in Late Imperial Kiev," in Hamm, *The City in Late Imperial Russia*, p. 104.

[12] Ascher, *Revolution of 1905*, p. 218; Engelstein, *Moscow, 1905*, p. 88.

[13] Engelstein, *Moscow, 1905*, pp. 140–147. In a similar manner, in 1917, workers in Moscow's Presnia working-class district—known as "Red Presnia" for its militant resistance to troops in December 1905—turned against the Bolshevik party overnight in the aftermath of the abortive July uprising in Petrograd. Although Bolshevik support for the uprising in the capital had been reluctant—the Bolsheviks felt they had no choice once workers decided to act—in Presnia and elsewhere, angry workers frustrated with the outcome of the uprisings and spurred on by scurrilous rumors attacked Bolsheviks, who were "beaten like Jews" (Koenker, *Moscow Workers*, p. 209). As was true of similar responses in the Donbass–Dnepr Bend during 1905, Moscow workers' reactionary mood in 1917 quickly passed.

[14] Surh, *1905 in St. Petersburg*, pp. 232, 353, 389–390.

struck out at a diverse array of targets in St. Petersburg. Their actions ranged from attacks on policemen to participation in mass rallies and demonstrations, from the destruction of shops, taverns, and brothels in enormous brawls to the frightening but petty public harassment of "respectable" pedestrians on the streets of the capital.[15]

Moving away from the capitals to areas less studied, there is reason to suspect that the combination of strikes and riots, revolutionary upsurges and reactionary backlashes that characterized the Donbass–Dnepr Bend labor movement may have also been a constant and integral part of the labor movement in areas such as the Baltic provinces, Congress Poland, and Transcaucasia.[16] In the periphery, workers' proclivity to lash out in violence when frustrated with the outcome of strikes was not so well masked as in the capitals. While Jews were the favored target in the pogromist bloodletting that followed upsurges in the labor movement—suffering the largest number of casualties in Odessa—minorities of all nationalities, as well as various groups identified with the revolutionary movement, found themselves victimized by the mobs' wrath.[17] The mixed character of the Baku labor movement during the 1905 Revolution has not been examined in detail, but a recent article suggests that Russia's oil capital, which also underwent rapid industrialization and urbanization in the late nineteenth century, experienced ethno-religious tension between Christian and Muslim workers similar to that between Christian and Jewish workers in the Donbass–Dnepr Bend.[18]

The violent, pogromist side of Donbass–Dnepr Bend workers presented here should change our understanding of Russian workers and working-class crowds. Certainly the Donbass–Dnepr Bend was unique within Russia, just as St. Petersburg, Moscow, and other industrial centers possessed

[15] Neuberger, "Crime and Culture" and "Stories of the Street: Hooliganism in the St. Petersburg Popular Press, 1900–1905," *Slavic Review* 48, no. 2 (1989).

[16] See McDaniel, *Autocracy, Capitalism, and Revolution*, pp. 176–178; Harcave, *Russian Revolution*, pp. 107, 181; and Brower, "Labor Violence." More than twelve thousand workers from twenty-eight factories joined in the bloody "Riga riots" of 1899 (Anders Henriksson, "Riga: Growth, Conflict, and the Limitations of Good Government, 1850–1914," in Hamm, *The City in Late Imperial Russia*, p. 198).

[17] Reichman, *Railwaymen and Revolution*, p. 225; McDaniel, *Autocracy, Capitalism, and Revolution*, p. 180; Ascher, *Revolution of 1905*, p. 253. For Odessa, see Weinberg, "Worker Organizations." In Hamm, *The City in Late Imperial Russia*, see Ronald Grigor Suny, "Tiflis: Crucible of Ethnic Politics, 1860–1905"; Stephen D. Corrsin, "Warsaw: Poles and Jews in a Conquered City"; and Hamm, "Continuity and Change." See also the essay-review of the Hamm collection by Joan Neuberger, "Urbanization and the Origins of Ethnic Unrest in Imperial Russia," *Problems of Communism* 38 (July–August 1989): 128–132.

[18] Audrey Alstadt-Mirhadi, "Baku: The Transformation of a Muslim Town," in Hamm, *The City in Late Imperial Russia*. For Baku in 1917–18, see Suny, *The Baku Commune*. During the October pogroms in Baku, mobs killed sixty Armenians (Ascher, *Revolution of 1905*, p. 254).

individual features. All the same, the characteristics of Donbass–Dnepr Bend workers' "backwardness" were evident in some measure among workers throughout the empire. While the Donbass–Dnepr Bend labor movement was largely the product of extreme conditions that provoked extreme responses, reactionary backlashes were nonetheless an empirewide phenomenon during the 1905 Revolution.

Selected Bibliography

Archives

Tsentral'nyi gosudarstvennyi arkhiv Oktiabr'skoi revoliutsii, Moskva (TsGAOR). Fond 102, Departament politsii (DP OO). Fond 124, Vremennaia kantseliariia po proizvodstvu osobykh ugolovnykh del Ministerstva iustitsii. Fond 7952, Gosudarstvennoe izdatel'stvo "Istoriia fabrik i zavodov."

Tsentral'nyi gosudarstvennyi istoricheskii arkhiv, Leningrad (TsGIA). Fond 23, Ministerstvo torgovli i promyshlennosti. Fond 37, Gornyi departament Ministerstva torgovli i promyshlennosti. Fond 1263, Komitet ministrov. Fond 1282, Kantseliariia Ministerstva vnutrennikh del. Fond 1284, Kantseliariia Ministerstva vnutrennikh del, Departament obshchikh del. Fond 1405, Ministerstvo iustitsii.

Tsentral'nyi gosudarstvennyi istoricheskii arkhiv Ukrainskoi SSR, Kiev (TsGIA USSR). Fond 346, Prokuror Odesskogo voenno-okruzhnogo suda. Fond 419, Prokuror Odesskogo sudebnoi palaty. Fond 1597, Ekaterinoslavskoe okhrannoe otdelenie.

Published Statistical Materials and Collections of Government Documents, Memoirs, and Revolutionary Leaflets

Akademiia nauk SSSR. Institut istorii. *Revoliutsiia 1905–1907 gg. v Rossii: Dokumenty i materialy*. 18 vols. Moscow, 1955–65. Individual volumes cited and listed under title.

British Documents on Foreign Affairs: Reports and Papers from the Foreign Office. Part 1, series A, vols. 3–4, *Russia, 1881–1905*. Edited by Domenic Lieven. Frederick, Md., 1982.

Dnepropetrovsku 200 let, 1776–1976: Sbornik dokumentov i materialov. Edited by I. V. Vasil'ev. Kiev, 1976.

Ekaterinoslavshchina v revoliutsii 1905–1907 gg.: Dokumenty i materialy. Edited by A. Ia. Pashchenko et al. Dnepropetrovsk, 1975.

Istoriia ekaterinoslavskoi sotsial-demokraticheskoi organizatsii, 1889–1903. Edited by M. A. Rubach. Ekaterinoslav, 1923.

Materialy po istorii ekaterinoslavskoi sotsial-demokraticheskoi organizatsii bol'shevikov i revoliutsionnykh sobytii 1904–1905–1906 gg. Ekaterinoslav, 1926.

Materialy po istorii revoliutsionnykh sobytii 1905 goda na territorii, nyne vkhodiashchei v Artemovskom okruge (k 20-ti letnemy iubileiu revoliutsii 1905 g.). Artemovsk, 1925.

Pod"em revoliutsionnogo dvizheniia na Ukraine nakanune pervoi russkoi revoliutsii (1901–1904 gg.). Edited by F. E. Los'. Kiev, 1955.

Rabochee dvizhenie v Rossii v XIX veke: Sbornik dokumentov i materialov. Vols. 1–3.

Edited by A. M. Pankratova. Vol. 4. Edited by L. M. Ivanov. Moscow-Leningrad, 1950–63.

Statisticheskii otdel Ekaterinoslavskogo gubernskogo zemstva. *Sbornik statisticheskikh svedenii po Ekaterinoslavskoi gubernii*. Vol. 2, *Bakhmutskii uezd*. Ekaterinoslav, 1886.

Tsentral'nyi statisticheskii komitet Ministerstva vnutrennikh del. *Goroda Rossii v 1904 godu*. St. Petersburg, 1906.

———. *Pervaia vseobshchaia perepis' naseleniia Rossiiskoi imperii, 1897 g*. Vol. 13, *Ekaterinoslavskaia guberniia*. Edited by N. A. Troinitskii. St. Petersburg, 1904.

Ukraine. Arhivnoe upravlenie. *Revoliutsiia 1905–1907 gg. na Ukraine*. Edited by F. E. Los'. Kiev, 1955. Individual volumes cited and listed under title.

Vserossiiskaia politicheskaia stachka v oktiabre 1905 goda. 2 vols. Edited by L. M. Ivanov. Moscow-Leningrad, 1955.

Vysshii pod"em revoliutsii 1905–1907 gg.: Vooruzhennye vosstaniia, noiabr'–dekabr' 1905 god. Edited by A. L. Sidorov. Vol. 3, parts 1–2. Moscow-Leningrad, 1955.

Books, Articles, and Unpublished Works

Akademiia nauk Ukrainskoi SSR. *Istoriia rabochikh Donbassa*. Kiev, 1981.

Algasov, P., and S. Pakentreiger. *Brianskie razboiniki*. Moscow, 1929.

Alstadt-Mirhadi, Audrey. "Baku: The Transformation of a Muslim Town." In *The City in Late Imperial Russia*, edited by Michael F. Hamm. Bloomington, Ind., 1986.

Amal'rik, A. S. "K voprosu o chislennosti i geograficheskom razmeshchenii stachechnikov v Evropeiskoi Rossii v 1905 g." *Istoricheskie zapiski* 52 (1955).

Anisimov, Sergei Sergeevich. *Delo o vosstanii na Ekaterininskoi zh. d.* Moscow-Leningrad, 1926.

———. *Gorlovskoe delo: Ocherk vosstaniia na linii Ekaterininskoi zheleznoi dorogi v 1905 godu*. Khar'kov, 1926.

———. *Vosstanie v Donetskom basseine*. Moscow, 1929.

An-skii, S. "Ocherk kamennougol'noi promyshlennosti." *Russkoe bogatstvo*, no. 2 (1892).

Anweiler, Oskar. *The Soviets: The Russian Workers, Peasants, and Soldiers Councils, 1905–1921*. Translated by Ruth Hein. New York, 1974.

Aronson, I. Michael. "Geographical and Socioeconomic Factors in the 1881 Anti-Jewish Pogroms in Russia." *Russian Review* 39, no. 1 (1980).

Arshinov, P. A. *Dva pobeda (iz vospominanii anarkhista, 1906–9 gg.)*. Paris, 1929.

Ascher, Abraham. *Pavel Axelrod and the Development of Menshevism*. Cambridge, Mass., 1972.

———. *The Revolution of 1905: Russia in Disarray*. Stanford, 1988.

Auerbakh, A. A. "Vospominaniia o nachale razvitiia kamennougol'noi promyshlennosti v Rossii." *Russkaia starina*, 1909 (December).

Avdakov, N. S. *Doklad komissii po voprosu ob uluchshenii byta rabochikh na kamennougol'nykh kopiakh Iuzhnoi Rossii*. Khar'kov, 1900.

———. "O merakh k obezpecheniiu gornykh promyslov rabochimi rukami i ob ucherulirovanii prodazhi vodki v raione gornykh promyslov." In *Doklad komissii XVIII sovet s"ezda*. Khar'kov, 1894.

Avrich, Paul. *The Russian Anarchists*. New York, 1978.

Babushkin, I. V. *Recollections of Ivan Vasilyevich Babushkin, 1893–1900*. Moscow, 1957.

Bakulev, G. D. *Razvitie ugol'noi promyshlennosti Donetskogo basseina*. Moscow, 1955.

Balabanov, M. "Promyshlennost' Rossii v nachale XX veka." In *Obshchestvennoe dvizhenie v Rossii v nachale XX-go veka*, vol. 1, edited by L. Martov, P. Maslov, and A. Potresov. St. Petersburg, 1909.

Baron, Salo W. *The Russian Jew under Tsars and Soviets*. New York, 1964.

Bender, I. "K stachechnomu dvizheniiu na Iuge Rossii v 1903 godu." *Arkhiv istorii truda v Rossii*, no. 6–7 (1923).

Benet, Sula, ed. and trans. *The Village of Viriatino*. New York, 1970.

Berk, Stephen M. *Year of Crisis, Year of Hope: Russian Jewry and the Pogroms of 1881–1882*. Westport, Conn., 1985.

Berkhin, I. *Luganskaia bol'shevistskaia organizatsiia v periode pervoi russkoi revoliutsii*. Leningrad, 1947.

Blackwell, William L. *The Industrialization of Russia*. New York, 1970.

———. "Modernization and Urbanization in Russia: A Comparative View." In *The City in Russian History*, edited by Michael F. Hamm. Lexington, Ky., 1976.

Boikov, I. I. "Otchet o kholernoi epidemii na rudnikakh Rutchenkovskogo gornopromyshlennogo o-va Bakhmutskogo u. VI–X 1910 goda." *Vrachebno-sanitarnaia khronika Ekaterinoslavskoi gubernii*, no. 1 (January 1911).

Bonnell, Victoria E. *Roots of Rebellion: Workers' Politics and Organizations in St. Petersburg and Moscow, 1900–1914*. Berkeley, 1983.

———, ed. *The Russian Worker: Life and Labor under the Tsarist Regime*. Berkeley, 1983.

Bovykin, V. I. "Kontsentratsiia promyshlennogo proizvodstva v Rossii v kontse XIX–nachale XX v." *Istoricheskie zapiski* 110 (1984).

Brower, Daniel R. "Labor Violence in Russia in the Late Nineteenth Century." *Slavic Review* 41, no. 3 (1982).

———. "Urbanization and Autocracy: Russian Urban Development in the First Half of the Nineteenth Century." *Russian Review* 42, no. 4 (1983).

Burstein, Abraham C. "Iron and Steel in Russia, 1861–1913." Ph.D. diss., New School for Social Research, 1963.

Bushnell, John. *Mutiny amid Repression: Russian Soldiers in the Revolution of 1905–1906*. Bloomington, Ind., 1985.

Chaadaev, O., ed. "K istorii vseobshchei stachki na iuge Rossii v 1903." *Krasnyi arkhiv*, no. 88 (1938).

Cheremukhin, N. M. "Kak zhivut i pitaiutsia rabochie Rykovskikh kopei v poselke Iuzovke." *Vrachebno-sanitarnaia khronika Ekaterinoslavskoi gubernii*, no. 1 (January 1910).

Cherevanin [F. A. Lipkin]. *Proletariat v revoliutsii*. Vol. 2, *Bor'ba obshchestvennykh sil v russkoi revoliutsii*. Moscow, 1907.

Chermenskii, E. D. "Dekabr'skoe vooruzhennoe vosstanie 1905 goda." In *Pervaia russkaia revoliutsiia, 1905–1907 gg.*, edited by A. M. Pankratova. Moscow, 1955.

Couvares, Francis G. *The Remaking of Pittsburgh: Class and Culture in an Industrializing City, 1877–1919*. Albany, N.Y., 1984.

Crisp, Olga. "Labour and Industrialization in Russia." In *The Cambridge Economic History of Europe*, edited by Peter Mathias and M. M. Postnan, vol. 7, pt. 2. Cambrdge, England, 1978.

Dal'man, V. "Oktiabr'skie dni v Ekaterinoslave." *Serp*, collection 1 (1907).

Dal'niaia, S. *Pervye shagi (1905 g.)*. Moscow-Leningrad, 1926.

Dan, F. I. *Iz istorii rabochego dvizheniia i sotsial-demokratii v Rossii, 1900–1904 gg*. Rostov-on-Don, n.d.

Decle, Lionel. *The New Russia*. London, 1906.

Demochkin, N. N. *Sovety 1905 goda*. Moscow, 1963.

Dimanshtein, S. "Ocherk revoliutsionnogo dvizheniia sredi evreiskikh mass." In *1905: Istoriia revoliutsionnogo dvizheniia v otdel'nykh ocherkakh*, edited by M. N. Pokrovskii, vol. 3, pt. 1. Moscow-Leningrad, 1927.

Dubnov, Simon. *History of the Jews*. Vol. 4. Translated and revised by Moshe Spiegel. New York, 1973.

Edelman, Robert. *Proletarian Peasants: The Revolution of 1905 in Russia's Southwest*. Ithaca, N.Y., 1987.

Egorov, A. "Zarozhdenie politicheskikh partii i ikh deiatel'nosti." In *Obshchestvennoe dvizhenie v Rossii v nachale XX-go veka*, edited by L. Martov, P. Maslov, and A. Potresov, vol. 1. St. Petersburg, 1909.

Eidel'man, B., ed. "K istorii vozniknoveniia R.S.-D.R.P." *Proletarskaia revoliutsiia*, no. 1 (1921).

Elwood, Ralph Carter. *Russian Social Democracy in the Underground: A Study of the RSDRP in the Ukraine, 1907–1914*. Assen, the Netherlands, 1974.

Emchenko, G. Ia., V. I. Kalashnikov, and P. M. Shmorgun. *Tak nachinalis' bitvy: Bol'sheviki Luganshchiny nakanune i v period pervoi russkoi revoliutsii (1900–1907)*. Khar'kov, 1966.

Emmons, Terence. *The Formation of Political Parties and the First National Elections in Russia*. Cambridge, Mass., 1983.

Engelstein, Laura. "Moscow in the 1905 Revolution: A Study in Class Conflict and Political Organization." Ph.D. diss., Stanford University, 1976.

———. *Moscow, 1905: Working-Class Organization and Political Conflict*. Stanford, 1982.

Ershov, K. "Dekabr'skoe vooruzhennoe vosstanie v Donbasse." Parts 1, 2. *Katorga i ssylka*, no. 8–9 (1930); no. 10 (1930).

Ettinger, S. "The Jews in Russia at the Outbreak of the Revolution." In *The Jews in Soviet Russia*. 2d ed., edited by Lionel Kochan. London, 1970.

Fedor, Thomas Stanley. *Patterns of Urban Growth in the Russian Empire during the Nineteenth Century*. University of Chicago Department of Geography Research Paper, no. 163. Chicago, 1975.

Fenin, A. I. "Neskol'ko slov o polozhenii rabochikh na kamennougol'nykh rudnikakh Iuga Rossii." *Izvestiia obshchestva gornykh inzhenerov* 2 (1896).

———. *Vospominaniia inzhenera: K istorii obshchestvennogo i khoziaistvennogo razvitiia Rossii, 1883–1906*. Prague, 1938.

Fialkovskii, V. P. "Ocherk osennei epidemii kholery v Bakhmutskom uezde v 1908 godu." *Vrachebno-sanitarnaia khronika Ekaterinoslavskoi gubernii*, no. 2 (February 1909).

Frankel, Jonathan. *Prophecy and Politics: Socialism, Nationalism, and the Russian Jews, 1862–1917*. Cambridge, England, 1981.

Frieden, Nancy Mandelker. *Russian Physicians in an Era of Reform and Revolution, 1856–1905*. Princeton, 1981.

Friedgut, Theodore H. *Iuzovka and Revolution*. Vol. 1, *Life and Work in Russia's Donbass, 1869–1924*. Princeton, 1989.

———. "Labor Violence and Regime Brutality in Tsarist Russia." *Slavic Review* 46, no. 2 (1987).

Fuller, William C., Jr. *Civil-Military Conflict in Imperial Russia*. Princeton, 1985.

Galai, Shmuel. *The Liberation Movement in Russia, 1900–1905*. Cambridge, England, 1973.

Gambarov, A. "Ocherk po istorii revoliutsionnogo dvizheniia v Luganske, 1901–1922 gg." *Letopis' revoliutsii*, no. 4 (1923).

Gatrell, Peter. *The Tsarist Economy, 1850–1917*. New York, 1986.

Gessen, Iulii. *Istoriia gornorabochikh SSSR*. Vol. 2, *Vtoraia polovina 19-go veka*. Moscow, 1929.

Glickman, Rose L. *Russian Factory Women: Workplace and Society, 1880–1914*. Berkeley, 1984.

Gopner, S. I. "Bol'sheviki Ekaterinoslava v 1905 godu: Iz vospominanii." *Voprosy istorii*, no. 3 (1955).

Gorev, B. I. [B. I. Gol'dman]. *Anarkhizm v Rossii: Ot Bakunina do Makhno*. Moscow, 1930.

Gorin, P. *Ocherki po istorii sovetov rabochikh deputatov v 1905 g*. Moscow, 1925.

Griffin, Frederick C. "The Formative Years of the Russian Factory Inspectorate, 1882–1885." *Slavic Review* 25, no. 4 (1966).

Haimson, Leopold. "The Problem of Social Stability in Urban Russia, 1905–1917." Parts 1, 2. *Slavic Review* 23, no. 4 (1964): 24, no. 1 (1965).

———. *The Russian Marxists and the Origins of Bolshevism*. Boston, 1955.

Hamm, Michael F. "The Breakdown of Urban Modernization: A Prelude to the Revolutions of 1917." In *The City in Russian History*, edited by Michael F. Hamm. Lexington, Ky., 1976.

———, ed. *The City in Late Imperial Russia*. Bloomington, Ind., 1986.

———, ed. *The City in Russian History*. Lexington, Ky., 1976.

Harcave, Sidney. *The Russian Revolution of 1905*. London, 1970.

Hommaire de Hell, Xavier. *Travels in the Steppes of the Caspian Sea, the Crimea, the Caucasus, &c*. London, n.d.

Iaroslavskii, E. "Posle stokgol'mskogo s"ezda v Ekaterinoslave." *Letopis' revoliutsii*, no. 3–4 (1926).

Ivanov, L. M. "Oktiabr'skaia politicheskaia stachka 1905 g. na Ukraine." *Istoricheskie zapiski* 54 (1955).

———. "Pod"em massovogo dvizheniia gornozavodskikh rabochikh Donbassa letom 1906." In *Iz istorii rabochego klassa i revoliutsionnogo dvizheniia*, edited by V. V. Al'man. Moscow, 1958.

———. "Revoliutsiia 1905–1907 gg. na Ukraine." In *Revoliutsiia 1905–1907 gg. v natsional'nykh raionakh Rossii*. Moscow, 1955.

Johnson, Robert Eugene. *Peasant and Proletarian: The Working Class of Moscow in the Late Nineteenth Century*. New Brunswick, N.J., 1979.

Kavalerov, I. N. "O polozhenii bol'nykh zhenshchin-chlenov semeistv gornorabochikh na rudnikakh, zavodakh i drugikh promyshlennykh predpriiatiiakh, raspolozhennykh v raione Bakhmutskogo uezda Ekaterinoslavskoi gubernii." *Trudy IX pirogovskogo s"ezda* 4 (1905).

Keep, J. L. H. *The Rise of Social Democracy in Russia*. Oxford, 1963.

Kharechko, T. "Sotsial-demokraticheskii soiuz gornozavodskikh rabochikh (iz istorii revoliutsionnogo dvizheniia v Donbasse)." *Letopis' revoliutsii*, no. 3 (1925).

———. *1905 god v Donbasse*. Leningrad, 1926.

Kharlamov, P. *Rozhdenie zavoda (Probnaia glava iz istorii Dnepropetrovskogo metallurgicheskogo zavoda im. Petrovskogo)*. Khar'kov, 1934.

Khersontsev. "V poiskakh puti." *Puti revoliutsii*, no. 3 (1925).

Kir'ianov, Iu. I. *Perekhod k massovoi politicheskoi bor'be: Rabochii klass nakanune pervoi rossiiskoi revoliutsii*. Moscow, 1987.

———. *Rabochie Iuga Rossii, 1914–fevral' 1917 g*. Moscow, 1971.

———. *Zhiznennyi uroven' rabochikh Rossii: Konets XIX–nachalo XX v*. Moscow, 1979.

Kirzner, A. S. *Gornorabochie Donbassa i Krivorozh'ia v pervoi rossiiskoi revoliutsii*. Khar'kov, 1926.

Knyshev, Ivan, V. Pron', and M. Shak. *Zarevo nad Brianskoi*. Dnepropetrovsk, 1970.

Koenker, Diane. *Moscow Workers and the 1917 Revolution*. Princeton, 1981.

Kogan, E. S. "K voprosu o formirovanii proletariata v Donbasse." In *Istoriko-bytovye ekspeditsii, 1951–1953*, edited by A. M. Pankratova. Moscow, 1955.

Kolodub, E. *Trud i zhizn' gornorabochikh na Grushevskikh antratsitnykh rudnikakh*. 2d ed. Moscow, 1907.

Kolpenskii, V. "Kholernyi bunt' v 1892 godu." *Arkhiv truda v Rossii*, no. 3 (1922).

Kol'tsov, D. [V. A. Ginzburg]. "Rabochie v 1890–1904 gg." In *Obshchestvennoe dvizhenie v Rossii v nachale XX-go veka*, edited by L. Martov, P. Maslov, and A. Potresov, vol. 1. St. Petersburg, 1909.

Kondufor, Iu. Iu., ed. *Istoriia rabochikh Donbassa*. Kiev, 1981.

Kononenko, Konstantyn. *Ukraine and Russia: A History of the Economic Relations between Ukraine and Russia, 1654–1917*. Milwaukee, 1958.

Kravchenko, Victor. *I Chose Freedom: The Personal and Political Life of a Soviet Official*. New York, 1946.

Krawchenko, Bohdan. *Social Change and National Consciousness in Twentieth-Century Ukraine*. New York, 1985.

Krugliakov, B. "Revoliutsionnoe dvizhenie sredi zheleznodorozhnikov v 1905 g." *Proletarskaia revoliutsiia*, no. 46 (1925).

Kruze, E. E. *Polozhenie rabochego klassa Rossii v 1900–1914 gg*. Leningrad, 1976.

Kuznetsov, I. "Rabochii klass i alkogol'naia problema." *Gornorabochii*, no. 7–8 (1922).

Lalaiants, I. "O moikh vstrechakh s V. I. Leninym za vremia 1893–1900 gg." *Proletarskaia revoliutsiia*, no. 84 (1929).

Lambroza, Shlomo. "Jewish Responses to Pogroms in Late Imperial Russia." In

Living with Antisemitism: Modern Jewish Responses, edited by Jehuda Reinharz. Hanover, 1987.

———. "The Pogrom Movement in Tsarist Russia, 1903–1906." Ph.D. diss., Rutgers University, 1981.

Lane, David. *The Roots of Russian Communism*. Assen, the Netherlands, 1969.

Lenin, V. I. *Collected Works*. 47 vols. Moscow, 1960–63.

Levitskii, V. O. [V. Tsederbaum]. *Za chetvert' veka: Revoliutsionnye vospominaniia, 1892–1917*. Vol. 1, pt. 2. Moscow-Leningrad, 1927.

Levus. "Iz istorii revoliutsionnogo dvizheniia v Donetskom basseine." *Narodnoe delo*, no. 3 (1909).

Liashchenko, Peter I. *History of the National Economy of Russia to 1917*. Translated by L. M. Herman. New York, 1949.

Lincoln, W. Bruce. *In War's Dark Shadow: The Russians before the Great War*. New York, 1983.

Lisser, I. L. "Gornorabochie na zheleznykh rudnikakh Krivorozhskogo raiona." *Zhurnal Obshchestva russkikh vrachei v pamiat' N. I. Pirogov*, no. 8 (December 1907).

Los', F. E. "Dekabr'skoe vooruzhennoe vosstanie na Ukraine." *Istoricheskie zapiski* 49 (1954).

———. *Formirovanie rabochego klassa na Ukraine i ego revoliutsionnaia bor'ba v kontse XIX i nachale XX stoletiia*. Kiev, 1955.

McCaffray, Susan Purves. "The Association of Southern Coal and Steel Producers and the Problems of Industrial Progress in Tsarist Russia." *Slavic Review* 47, no. 2 (1988).

———. "The New Work and the Old Regime: Workers, Managers and the State in the Coal and Steel Industry of Ekaterinoslav Province, 1905–1914." Ph.D. diss., Duke University, 1983.

McDaniel, Tim. *Autocracy, Capitalism, and Revolution in Russia*. Berkeley, 1988.

McKay, John P. "Elites in Conflict in Tsarist Russia: The Briansk Company." In *The Rich, the Well Born, and the Powerful*, edited by Frederic Cople Jaher. Urbana, Ill., 1973.

———. "Foreign Businessmen, the Tsarist Government, and the Briansk Company." *Journal of European Economic History* 2, no. 2 (1973).

———. *Pioneers for Profit: Foreign Entrepreneurship and Russian Industrialization, 1885–1913*. Chicago, 1970.

Maleev, A. "Aleksandrovskaia organizatsiia RSDRP v 1900–1905 gg." In *Na barrikadakh: 1905 god v Aleksandrovske*, edited by M. L'vovskii. Zaporozhe, 1925.

Martov, L. "Sotsialdemokratiia 1905–1907 gg." In *Obshchestvennoe dvizhenie v Rossii v nachale XX-go veka*, edited by L. Martov, P. Maslov, and A. Potresov, vol. 3. St. Petersburg, 1914.

Martov, L., P. Maslov, and A. Potresov, eds. *Obshchestvennoe dvizhenie v Rossii v nachale XX-go veka*. 3 vols. St. Petersburg, 1909–14.

Mashukov, V. D. *Vospominaniia o gorode Ekaterinoslave, 1887–1910 gg*. Ekaterinoslav, 1910.

Mebel', M. I., ed. *1905 god na Ukraine: Khronika i materialy*. N.p., 1926.

Mehlinger, Howard D., and John M. Thompson. *Count Witte and the Tsarist Government in the 1905 Revolution*. Bloomington, Ind., 1972.

Meksina, S. "Pervye stachki ekaterinoslavskikh metallistov v 1905 g." *Materialy po istorii professional'nogo dvizheniia v SSSR*, bk. 5 (1927).

Melancon, Michael. "The Socialist Revolutionaries from 1902 to 1907: Peasant and Workers' Party." *Russian History* 12, no. 1 (Spring 1985).

Mendelsohn, Ezra. *Class Struggle in the Pale*. Cambridge, England, 1970.

———. "The Jewish Labor Movement in Czarist Russia, from Its Origins to 1905." Ph.D. diss., Columbia University, 1966.

———. "The Russian Jewish Labor Movement and Others." In *Studies in Modern Jewish Social History*, edited by Joshua A. Fishman. New York, 1972.

Modestov, V. V. *Rabochee i profsoiuznoe dvizhenie v Donbasse do velikoi oktiabr'skoi sotsialisticheskoi revoliutsii*. Moscow, 1957.

Moiseenko, P. A. *Vospominaniia, 1873–1923*. Moscow, 1924.

Morachevskii, V. V. "Ekaterinoslav i raskhodiashchiiasia ot nego puti." In *Rossiia: Polnoe geograficheskoe opisanie nashego otechestva*, edited by V. P. Semenov-Tian-Shanskii, vol. 14. St. Petersburg, 1910.

———. "Promysly i zaniatiia naseleniia." In *Rossiia: Polnoe geograficheskoe opisanie nashego otechestva*, edited by V. P. Semenov-Tian-Shanskii, vol. 14. St. Petersburg, 1910.

Moshinskii, I. "K voprosu o s.-d. (Donetskom) soiuze gornozavodskikh rabochikh." *Proletarskaia revoliutsiia*, no. 65 (1927).

Munting, R. "Outside Earnings in the Russian Peasant Farm: The Case of Tula Province, 1900–1917." *Journal of Peasant Studies* 3 (1976).

Nabirkin, N. *Svedeniia ob istoricheskom razvitii g. Ekaterinoslava*. Ekaterinoslav, 1910.

Naimark, Norman M. *Terrorists and Social Democrats: The Russian Revolutionary Movement under Alexander III*. Cambridge, Mass., 1983.

Naviazhskii, G. D. "V ozhidanii kholery." *Vrachebnaia gazeta*, no. 38 (1908).

Nedava, Joseph. *Trotsky and the Jews*. Philadelphia, 1972.

Nesterenko, A. A. *Ocherki istorii promyshlennosti i polozheniia proletariata Ukrainy v kontse XIX i nachale XX v*. Moscow, 1954.

Neuberger, Joan. "Crime and Culture: Hooliganism in St. Petersburg, 1900–1914." Ph.D. diss., Stanford University, 1985.

———. "Stories of the Street: Hooliganism in the St. Petersburg Popular Press, 1900–1905." *Slavic Review* 48, no. 2 (1989).

Nevskii, V. I. "Ianvarskie dni 1905 goda v Ekaterinoslave i Donetskom basseine." *Letopis' revoliutsii*, no. 10 (1925).

———. *Rabochee dvizhenie v ianvarskie dni 1905 goda*. Moscow, 1930.

———. "Sovety v 1905 godu." In *1905: Istoriia revoliutsionnogo dvizheniia v otdel'nykh ocherkakh*, edited by M. N. Pokrovskii, vol. 3, pt. 1. Moscow-Leningrad, 1927.

Nikolaenko, I. "Revoliutsionnaia rabota v luganskikh zh.-d. masterskikh (iz vospominanii)." *Letopis' revoliutsii*, no. 5 (1926).

———. *Revoliutsionnoe dvizhenie v Luganske*. Khar'kov, 1926.

Novopolin, G. "Iz istorii ekaterinoslavskogo 'Soiuz soiuzov'." *Puti revoliutsii*, no. 4 (1926).

———. "Iz istorii rabochego dvizheniia (1800–1903)." *Letopis' revoliutsii*, no. 2 (1923).

———. "Pervye 'bezporiadki' gornorabochikh (1887)." *Letopis' revoliutsii*, no. 2 (1923).

———. "Zubatovshchina v Ekaterinoslave." *Istoriia proletariata SSSR*, no. 2 (1930).

Otchet komissii po ustroistvu narodnykh chtenii v g. Ekaterinoslave za 1899 god. Ekaterinoslav, 1900.

Pal'chinskii, P. I. "Zhilishcha dlia rabochikh na rudnikakh Donetskogo basseina." *Gornyi zhurnal*, no. 9 (September 1906).

Pankratova, A. M. "Dekabr'skie dni v Donbasse v 1905 g." *Krasnyi arkhiv*, no. 73 (1935).

———. "Rabochii klass i rabochee dvizhenie nakanune revoliutsii 1905 g." In *1905: Istoriia revoliutsionnogo dvizheniia v otdel'nykh ocherkakh*, edited by M. N. Pokrovskii, vol. 1. Moscow-Leningrad, 1925.

———, ed. *Pervaia russkaia revoliutsiia, 1905–1907 gg*. Moscow, 1955.

Parasun'ko, O. A. *Polozhenie i bor'ba rabochego klassa Ukrainy, 1860–90-e gody XIX v.* Kiev, 1963.

Patkin, A. L. *The Origins of the Russian-Jewish Labour Movement*. Melbourne, 1947.

Paustovsky, Konstantin. *The Story of a Life*. Translated by Joseph Barnes. New York, 1982.

Peled, Yoav. *Class and Ethnicity in the Pale: The Political Economy of Jewish Workers' Nationalism in Late Imperial Russia*. New York, 1989.

"Perepiska ekaterinoslavskoi i luganskoi organizatsii s N. Leninym i N. K. Krupskoi." *Proletarskaia revoliutsiia*, no. 51 (1926).

Perrie, Maureen. *The Agrarian Policy of the Russian Socialist-Revolutionary Party, from Its Origins through the Revolution of 1905–1907*. Cambridge, England, 1976.

Petrovskii, G. "Vospominaniia o rabote na Brianskom zavode v devianostykh godakh." *Letopis' revoliutsii*, no. 2 (1923).

Pipes, Richard. *Social Democracy and the St. Petersburg Labor Movement, 1885–1897*. Cambridge, Mass., 1963.

Pokrovskii, M. N. *A Brief History of Russia*. Translated by D. S. Mirsky. Vol. 2. New York, 1933.

———, ed. *1905: Istoriia revoliutsionnogo dvizheniia v otdel'nykh ocherkakh*. 3 vols. Moscow-Leningrad, 1925–27.

Pokrovskii, P. "Kak zhivet donetskii shakhter." *Russkoe bogatstvo*, no. 12 (1913).

Polevoi, Iu. Z. *Zarozhdenie marksizma v Rossii, 1883–1894*. Moscow, 1959.

Popov, M. R. *Zapiski zemlevol'tsa*. Moscow, 1933.

Potolov, S. I. *Rabochie Donbassa v XIX veke*. Moscow-Leningrad, 1963.

Priimenko, A. I. *Legal'nye organizatsii rabochikh Iuga Rossii v period imperializma (1895 g.–fevral' 1917 g.)*. Kiev-Donetsk, 1977.

Ragozin, E. I. *Zhelezo i ugol' na Iuge Rossii*. St. Petersburg, 1895.

Rapoport, D. "1905 god na st. Dolgintsevo i Krivom Roge." *Puti revoliutsii*, no. 3 (1925).

Rashin, A. G. *Formirovanie rabochego klassa Rossii*. Moscow, 1958.

———. *Naselenie Rossii za 100 let, 1811–1913 gg*. Moscow, 1956.

Reichman, Henry. *Railwaymen and Revolution: Russia, 1905*. Berkeley, 1987.

———. "The Rostov General Strike of 1902." *Russian History* 9, pt. 1 (1982).

Resolutions and Decisions of the Communist Party of the Soviet Union. Vol. 1, *The Russian Social Democratic Labour Party*. Edited by Ralph Carter Elwood. Toronto, 1974.

Rice, Christopher. *Russian Workers and the Socialist-Revolutionary Party through the Revolution of 1905–1907*. Basingstoke, England, 1988.

Rieber, Alfred J. *Merchants and Entrepreneurs in Imperial Russia*. Chapel Hill, N.C., 1982.

Rimlinger, Gaston V. "The Management of Labor Protest in Tsarist Russia, 1870–1905." *International Review of Social History*, 5 (1960).

Robbins, Richard G. *The Tsar's Viceroys: Russian Provincial Governors in the Last Years of the Empire*. Ithaca, N.Y., 1987.

Rogger, Hans. *Jewish Policies and Right-Wing Politics in Imperial Russia*. Berkeley, 1986.

Rossiiskaia sotsial'demokraticheskaia rabochaia partiia. *Sud nad brianskimi rabochimi*. Geneva, 1901.

"Rotozei, ekskursiia znatnogo inostrantsa v malovazhnyi russkii tsentr." In *Ekaterinoslavskii kalendar'—al'manakh na 1898 god*. Ekaterinoslav, 1897.

Rozental', I. S. "Dukhovnye zaprosy rabochikh Rossii posle revoliutsii 1905–1907 gg." *Istoricheskie zapiski* 10 (1982).

Rubin, V. N. "Rabochii vopros na s"ezdakh gornopromyshlennikov Iuga Rossii." In *Nekotorye problemy klassovoi bor'by v periode kapitalizma*. Moscow, 1966.

Sanders, Joseph L. *The Moscow Uprising of 1905: A Background Study*. New York, 1987.

Schapiro, Leonard. "The Role of the Jews in the Russian Revolutionary Movement." *Slavonic and East European Review* 40, no. 94 (December 1961).

———. *Russian Studies*. Edited by Ellen Dahrendorf. New York, 1987.

Schneiderman, Jeremiah. *Sergei Zubatov and Revolutionary Marxism: The Struggle for the Working Class in Tsarist Russia*. Ithaca, N.Y., 1970.

Semenov, M. S. "Rostov-na-Donu i vostochnaia chast' Novorossii." In *Rossiia: Polnoe geograficheskoe opisanie nashego otechestva*, edited by V. P. Semenov-Tian-Shanskii, vol. 14. St. Petersburg, 1910.

Senchakova, L. T. *Boevaia rat' revoliutsii: Ocherk o boevykh organizatsiiakh RSDRP i rabochikh druzhinakh, 1905–1907 gg*. Moscow, 1975.

Seryi, Iu. I. *Rabochie Iuga Rossii v period imperializma, 1900–1913*. Rostov-on-Don, 1971.

S"ezd gornopromyshlennikov Iuga Rossi. *Kamennougol'naia promyshlennost' Iuzhnoi Rossii v 1901 godu*. Khar'kov, 1902.

———. *Trudy XVIII s"ezda gornopromyshlennikov Iuga Rossii, byvshego v g. Khar'kove s 1 po 14 dekabria 1893 goda*. Part 1. Khar'kov, 1894.

Shabel'nikov. "Dekabr' 1905 goda v Aleksandrovske (Zaporozh'i) (Iz vospominanii uchastnika vosstaniia)." *Puti revoliutsii*, no. 3 (1925).

Shanin, Teodor. *Russia as a 'Developing Society'*. Vol. 1. *The Roots of Otherness: Russia's Turn of Century*. Houndmills, Basingstoke, Hampshire, 1985.

Shatz, Marshall S. "The Makhaevists and the Russian Revolutionary Movement." *International Review of Social History* 15 (1970).

Shestakov, A. "Na zare rabochego dvizheniia v Donbasse." *Proletarskaia revoliutsiia*, no. 1 (1921).

———. "Vseobshchaia oktiabr'skaia stachka 1905 goda." In *1905: Istoriia revoliutsionnogo dvizheniia v otdel'nykh ocherkakh*, edited by M. N. Pokrovskii, vol. 2. Moscow-Leningrad, 1925.

Shklovskii, L. "Vospominaniia o 1905 gode." *Proletarskaia revoliutsiia*, no. 48 (1926).

Shmorgun, P. M. "Sovety rabochikh deputatov na Ukraine v 1905 godu." *Istoricheskie zapiski*, 49 (1954).

Shmyrov, I. "Iz istorii revoliutsionnogo dvizheniia v Luganske." *Letopis' revoliutsii*, no. 3 (1924).

Smidovich, A. L. "Ob organizatsii nochlezhno-prodovol'stvennykh punktov dlia gornorabochikh." *Vrachebno-sanitarnaia khronika Ekaterinoslavskoi gubernii*, no. 11–12 (November–December 1910).

Smidovich, P. "Rabochie massy v 90-x godakh." *Proletarskaia revoliutsiia*, no. 36 (1925).

Smirnov, A. "Vospominanie o pervom kruzhke sots.-dem. rabochei partii g. Ekaterinoslava v 1894 godu." *Letopis' revoliutsii*, no. 2 (1923).

Smith, R. E. F., and David Christian. *Bread and Salt: A Social and Economic History of Food and Drink in Russia*. Cambridge, England, 1984.

Soiuz russkikh sotsial'demokratov. *Rabochee dvizhenie v Ekaterinoslave*. Geneva, 1900.

Stanislavskii, V. M. "K voprosu o sanitarnykh usloviiakh zhilishch gornorabochikh Donetskogo raiona." *Vrachebno-sanitarnaia khronika Ekaterinoslavskoi gubernii*, no. 10 (October 1909).

Suny, Ronald Grigor. *The Baku Commune, 1917–1918: Class and Nationality in the Russian Revolution*. Princeton, 1972.

Surh, Gerald Dennis. *1905 in St. Petersburg: Labor, Society and Revolution*. Stanford, 1989.

———. "Petersburg's First Mass Labor Organization: The Assembly of Russian Workers and Father Gapon." Parts 1, 2. *Russian Review* 40, nos. 3, 4 (1981).

Szajkowski, Zosa. "The Impact of the Russian Revolution of 1905 on American Jewish Life." *YIVO Annual of Jewish Social Science* 7 (1978).

Taskin, E. *K voprosu o privlechenii i uderzhanii rabochikh na kamennougol'nykh kopiakh Donetskogo basseina*. Khar'kov, 1899.

Tatarskii, M. "Otchet ob epidemii kholery v Iuzovke i prilegaiushchikh shakhtakh i zavode Novorossiiskogo obshchestva Bakhmutskogo uezda Ekaterinoslavskoi gubernii v 1910 godu." *Vrachebno-sanitarnaia khronika Ekaterinoslavskoi gubernii*, no. 2–3 (February–March 1911).

Thompson, E. P. *The Making of the English Working Class*. New York, 1963.

Tobias, Henry J. *The Jewish Bund in Russia: From Its Origins to 1905*. Stanford, 1972.

Trebilcock, Clive. *The Industrialization of the Continental Powers, 1780–1914*. London, 1981.

Tretii s"ezd RSDRP: Protokoly. April–May 1905. Moscow, 1959.

Vanag, N. "Promyshlennost'." In *1905: Istoriia revoliutsionnogo dvizheniia v otdel'nykh ocherkakh*, edited by M. N. Pokrovskii, vol. 1. Moscow-Leningrad, 1925.

Vartminskii, A. E. "K voprosu o zhilishchnykh usloviiakh gornorabochikh Donetskogo raiona." *Vrachebno-sanitarnaia khronika Ekaterinoslavskoi gubernii*, no. 7–9 (July–September 1910).

———. "Ob epidemii sypnogo i vozvratnogo tifov v g. Mariupole." *Vrachebno-sanitarnaia khronika Ekaterinoslavskoi gubernii*, no. 9 (September 1909).

Venturi, Franco. *Roots of Revolution: A History of the Populist and Socialist Movements in Nineteenth Century Russia*. Translated by Francis Haskell. New York, 1960.

Ves' Ekaterinoslav. Ekaterinoslav, 1912.

Villari, Luigi. *Russia under the Great Shadow*. London, 1905.

Vinokurov, A. N. "Vospominaniia o partiinoi rabote v Ekaterinoslave." *Proletarskaia revoliutsiia*, no. 1 (1921).

Voroshilov, K. E. *Rasskazy o zhizni (Vospominaniia)*. Moscow, 1971.

Vtoroi s"ezd RSDRP: Protokoly. July–August 1903. Moscow, 1959.

Weinberg, Robert. "Social Democracy and Workers in Odessa: Ethnic and Political Considerations." *Carl Beck Papers in Russian and East European Studies*, no. 504 (1986).

———. "Worker Organizations and Politics in the Revolution of 1905 in Odessa." Ph.D. diss., University of California, Berkeley, 1985.

———. "Workers, Pogroms, and the 1905 Revolution in Odessa." *Russian Review* 46, no. 1 (1987).

Wildman, Allan K. *The Making of a Workers' Revolution: Russian Social Democracy, 1891–1903*. Chicago, 1967.

Wistrich, Robert S. *Socialism and the Jews: The Dilemmas of Assimilation in Germany and Austria-Hungary*. New Brunswick, N.J., 1982.

Woytinsky, W. S. *Stormy Passage: A Personal History through Two Russian Revolutions to Democracy and Freedom, 1905–1960*. New York, 1961.

Wynn, Charters Stephen. "Russian Labor in Revolution and Reaction: The Donbass Working Class, 1870–1905." Ph.D. diss., Stanford University, 1987.

Zaitsev, F. "Bol'sheviki Iuzovki do 1918 g." *Literaturnyi Donbass*, no. 10–12 (1933).

Zaks, A. B. "Trud i byt rabochikh Donbassa." In *Istoriko-bytovye ekspeditsii, 1951–1953*, edited by A. M. Pankratova. Moscow, 1955.

Zapiski Ekaterinoslavskogo otdeleniia Imperatorskogo russkogo tekhnicheskogo obshchestva. Ekaterinoslav, 1906, no. 6–8.

Zeikman, M. "Ekaterinoslavskii Soiuz bor'by za osvobozhdenie rabochego klassa, 1895–98 gg." *Letopis' revoliutsii*, no. 6 (1924).

Zelnik, Reginald E., ed. and trans. *A Radical Worker in Tsarist Russia: The Autobiography of Semen Ivanovich Kanatchikov*. Stanford, 1986.

Zipperstein, Steven J. "Old Ghosts: Pogroms in the Jewish Mind," *Tikhun* 6, no. 3 (1991).

Newspapers

Biulleten Ekaterinoslavskogo boevogo stachechnogo komiteta. Ekaterinoslav, 1905.
Burevestnik. Paris, 1906–10. Anarchist-Communist.
Donetskoe slovo. Lugansk, 1906.
Ekaterinoslavskii listok. Ekaterinoslav, 1885–1905. Daily.
Gorno-zavodskii listok. Khar'kov, 1889–1909. Association of Southern Coal and Steel Producers.
Iskra. Geneva, 1900–1905. Social Democrat.
Iuzhnaia zaria. Ekaterinoslav, 1906–15. Daily.
Iuzhnyi krai. Khar'kov, 1880–1916. Daily.
Iuzhnyi rabochii. Russia, 1900–1903. Social Democrat.
Jewish Chronicle. London, 1841–.
Khleb i volia. London, 1903–5. Anarchist.
Krasnoe znamia. Geneva, 1902–3. Social Democrat.
Listki Khleb i volia. London, 1906–7. Communist-Anarchist.
Listok rabotnika. Geneva, 1896–98. Social Democrat.
Nachalo. St. Petersburg, 1905. Legal Menshevik.
Novaia zhizn'. St. Petersburg, 1905. Legal Bolshevik.
Posledniia izvestiia. London-Geneva, 1901–6. Bund.
Pravo. St. Petersburg, 1898–1916. Liberal weekly.
Pridneprovskii krai. Ekaterinoslav, 1898–1916. Daily.
Proletarii. Geneva, 1905. Bolshevik.
Rabochee delo. Geneva, 1899–1902. Social Democrat.
Revoliutsionnaia Rossiia. Geneva, 1900–1905. Socialist Revolutionary.
Sotsial'demokrat. Geneva, 1904–5. Social Democrat.
Syn otechestva. St. Petersburg, 1890–1913. Legal Socialist Revolutionary weekly.
Vestnik Iuga. Ekaterinoslav, 1902–5. Daily.

Index